ion and Society 29

RAL EDITORS
Martin, *University of Vermont*
s Waardenburg, *University of Lausanne*

ON DE GRUYTER   BERLIN · NEW YORK

Reli

GENI
Luthe
Jacqu

MOU

Cargo Cults and Millenarian Movements

Transoceanic Comparisons of
New Religious Movements

Edited by
G. W. Trompf

MOUTON DE GRUYTER   BERLIN · NEW YORK   1990

Mouton de Gruyter (formerly Mouton, The Hague)
is a Division of Walter de Gruyter & Co., Berlin.

> The vignet on the cover of this book represents the symbol of the *Agathos Daimon,* the snake of the Good Spirit, known from Greek astrological and magical texts. As its Town God, the *Agathos Daimon* was believed to protect Alexandria, which was famous world-wide for its library with precious manuscripts and books.

Library of Congress Cataloging in Publication Data

Cargo cults and millenarian movements : transoceanic comparisons of new religious movements / edited by G. W. Trompf.
    p.   cm. — (Religion and society ; 29)
Includes bibliographical references.
    1. Cargo movement — Comparative studies. 2. Millennia-
lism — Comparative studies. 3. Adventists — Comparative
studies. I. Trompf, G. W. II. Series: Religion and society (Hague,
Netherlands) ; 29.
    BL2620.M4C37   1990
    291′.046 — dc20   89-28140
    ISBN 0-89925-601-5 (alk. paper)

Deutsche Bibliothek Cataloging in Publication Data

Cargo cults and millenarian movements : transoceanic compari-
sons of new religious movements / edited by G. W. Trompf. —
Berlin ; New York : Mouton de Gruyter, 1990
    (Religion and society ; 29)
    ISBN 3-11-012166-2
NE: Trompf, Garry W. [Hrsg.]; GT

♾ Printed on acid-free paper.

Data processing: Adam Tedja, Wysiwyg Design, Sydney, Australia. —
Printing: Ratzlow-Druck, Berlin. — Binding: Dieter Mikolai, Berlin. — Printed in Germany.

ACKNOWLEDGEMENTS

My thanks as editor are due to those who have helped inspire the final outcome of this book. I name before all geographer Dr Bryant Allen, of the Australian National University, who initially hoped to co-edit it with me and whose fine scholarship has naturally been utilized in chapters on Melanesia. Dr Harold Turner, always a friendly patron, has graciously commended the whole enterprise with his very perceptive foreword - almost an article in itself! - and was so helpful with proofreading. To Professor Jacques Waardenburg, my former colleague at the Rijksuniversiteit Utrecht, must go my thanks for the encouragement to continue the task and for still further proofing. The many references in this book to the Dutch contribution to European millennial history, let alone to Dutch and German colonial administrations in Indonesia, Melanesia and South West Africa, very much lend themselves to publication by Mouton de Gruyter in this series. I salute two trusty Research Assistants, Deborah Christian, Raymond Maxent and Ruth Lewin-Broit, for their labours, as also Margaret Gilet, who painstakingly and accurately committed the manuscripts to the computer. The James Macartney Hill Bequest, for which I hereby register my deepest appreciation, funded their wonderful work. The interest and patience of my wife and family, especially in the closing stages of the editing process, were much more than some of my hermit-like habits deserved. Lastly, I wish to express gratitude to all the contributors themselves, some of whom have waited much longer than others, some of whom rushed last minute additions to the computer, but all of whom have been paragons of cooperativeness and tolerance, even under the occasional excision and transplant of the editor's instruments.

The University of Sydney   Garry Trompf
St Neot's Day 1989

TABLE OF CONTENTS

List of Plates

List of Figures

List of Maps

FOREWORD

The interest and implications of this collection range much more widely than the language of the title or the known provenance of the editor might suggest. This width stems partly from the fact, which ought to be noted immediately, that the two terms in the title are by no means coterminous, despite the popular image of millenarian 'cargo cults' associated with Melanesia. Here we have accounts of movements that are millenarian with few or no signs of cargoist hopes, and of others where the emphasis is reversed. The editor's introduction spells out the distinctive and very comprehensive meanings of these two concepts, and will repay a second reading after the specific studies have been digested.

It is clear in the introduction that millennium, as a basic "structure of the human imagination" is "capable of capturing any psyche". This means that we are dealing with a basic human hope, authentically expressed in particular movements; no matter how bizarre some of these expressions are, the hope itself is neither eccentric nor a pathological aberration. It takes something more than the merely weird or irrational to sustain people like the Rastafarians through over half a century of opposition or the Jon Frum movement in Vanuatu through the vicissitudes of nearly fifty years.

It is this 'something more' that the reader should look for in these essays, and this discovery will help explain why millennial movements do not simply disappear before the advance of modernization. As the editor suggests, there are two very widespread factors at work to maintain these forms. In the Third World there is disillusionment through the failure of the great development hopes of the 'sixties and 'seventies; in the Western world there is the mounting sense of economic, social and ecological crises that are beyond human management. Can we say that these attitudes are unrealistic or that to turn to some millenarian solution is merely escapist? After all, the classic Christian hope climaxes in the Second Coming rather than in the gradual achievement of the Kingdom.

Likewise the cargo idea has to it a 'something more' than the merely material bounty that this unfortunate term most commonly suggests. Both the shiploads of modern goods from the ancestors in undeveloped Melanesia and the dollar prosperity promised to the poor in some of the grosser American cults should be

seen in their different degrees as the instruments of a longed-for human fulfilment. It was the monk Thomas Merton who back in the 'sixties saw something
of the underlying unity between aspects of the modern American scene and the
cargo cults of Melanesia. One of the interesting asides in this symposium is the
suggestion that it might well be the enclaves of Third World peoples within predominantly Western societies, bridging as they do both tribal and modern cultures, who can best show us how cargoism operates across the world. The essays
here on the Black Muslims and the Rastafarians would question this bridging
capacity, but the idea deserves further testing. What is becoming clear is that the
ethos of cargoism is widespread, takes many forms, and represents a particular
version of the desire for blessings that marks most religions. And again it is the
Christian faith, founded on an incarnation, promising the "resurrection of the
body" and therefore called the "most materialistic of all religions", that can least
afford to dismiss the cargo notion as crude and unspiritual.

Seen from these properly religious and widely human perspectives, both millennialism and cargoism show the power of ideas in human affairs and especially
in religions. Neither can be reduced to social epiphenomena despite the obvious
social conditioning of their particular historical manifestations. Nor can they be
regarded as mindless or irrational, as aspects of human pathology, when they
themselves can be seen as attempts to answer the basic pathology of the human
condition - its distorted existence and frustrated destiny. To that extent they are
realistic both in their sense of the human situation and in their determination not
to accept such an absurdity. They represent convictions about and commitments
to reality that operate at deeper levels than much of the naive optimism and self-
confidence of those in modern societies who so easily dismiss the movements
sampled in this volume.

While we can identify the deeper human and religious roots of such movements, we must at the same time recognize their own distinctive forms and maintain fairly specific meanings for each of these terms. This has to be done despite
the fact that they indicate a certain continuity with other forms by shading off
into phenomena that we would not want to call millenarian or cargoist. At several points in these pages the term "fringes of millenarianism" appears, where,
under the hard glare of social and historical facts, movements fade away into diffused hopes for a better future through hard work, a new use of the existing sys-

tems, or co-operation with other faiths towards shared goals. These processes may be identified in the Timor Spirit movement, in the Namibian movements, in the later Black Muslims and in some of the Rastafarians.

This indicates the problem of terminology and of the boundaries of particular terms, a problem demonstrated rather than solved in these essays. Suffice it to say that when any expectation of a new future becomes 'millennial', when any problems or tensions are elevated to the status of 'crises' so that all cults become 'crisis cults', and when any strongly-held secular convictions become 'religions', then the distinctions necessary to thought become eroded, and words lose meaning. This consideration must be placed against our tracing of the ways in which cargo and the millennium integrate into the most basic human concerns.

This point may be demonstrated by examination of the last three essays gathered under the rubric "Black America and Africa". Here the last item, the only one on Africa itself, uses the term millennial for its two movements, but has great difficulty in documenting this aspect. While indigenous Namibian movements are somewhat atypical with respect to most movements in Black Africa, in this regard they are quite representative. True millennialism and messianism are very rare, despite the common generic use of these terms for this continent, and cargoism in its specific meaning is properly applicable in only a few cases. The blessings sought are more in the realm of healing, family welfare, success in business or examinations, and guidance for immediate affairs through revelation. And the blessings are sought here and now rather than in some hoped for future. To such an extent is this true that when I discussed the Namibian situation with a colleague long experienced in Lesotho, he reported how it was almost impossible to find a point of contact between Biblical eschatology and its promises and the local culture.

It is not surprising therefore that the other two essays in this group reveal that both the Rastafarians and the Black Muslims largely fail in their attempts to find spiritual and cultural roots in Africa. The latter turn out to be Americans after all and now seek their better future in the American way. The Rastafari have never achieved more than a small token settlement that has survived over thirty years in Ethiopia, despite the centrality of the millennial hope of a return to their pristine existence before encountering the Europeans. 'Africa' is now transposed into a distinct cultural identity wherever they may be domiciled. When they spread, surprisingly enough, as far afield as New Zealand Maoris, the Africa motif has become absorbed into a local search for identity and a satisfying Maori way of life, and the millennial concern has virtually vanished. And yet in the Caribbean Rastafari the millennium remains, identified now with the fall of 'Babylon' rather than the return of the African diaspora to their heartland.

It is worth dwelling briefly on the relation of the Rastafari to new African religious movements. The differences are conspicuous indeed. Instead of organized movements with a centralized and hierarchical structure, with buildings for lively forms of worship, rituals such as baptism, emphasis on healing and exorcism, a prominent place for women, with public processions and missionary expansion, we find in the Rastafari a diffused and diverse amorphous movement that lacks all of the above characteristics. Perhaps a common reference to the Christian scriptures is the chief shared feature. It may be noted that Rastafari also show sharp contrasts with the other movements in this volume, especially those in the group of "White America and the Western World". There is a kind of primal innocence, a naive but moving spirituality, a moral authenticity coupled with a practical commonsense (despite the impractical Back to Africa theme) in the Rastafarian communities. Compared with the peaceful atmosphere of these gentle people, the life of many of the movements among the whites seems over-heated, strained, unstable and contrived.

A theme of special interest that appears in one of the Melanesian essays is that of the dangerous or eventful journey to far places, originally in the myths of the culture heroes, and recently in the historical travels of the founder or leader of a new cult. This journey undergirds religious or cultural innovation by providing a charter for the new ways. The journey brings authority from the Beyond and thus resembles the function of dreams as agents of innovation that has been described by Michele Stephen in the journal *Oceania*. This is an original contribution to the study of these movements and might well be pursued further in two directions. Firstly, is there anything equivalent to the journey in new movements less openly related to the local culture, such as the new independent churches? And secondly, how does this journey relate to the functions of the religious pilgrimages that are made in many of the older religions to actual historical shrines and sacred cities?

A more fundamental issue arises in connection with another of the

Melanesian essays, that on the Mt. Hurun movement in the Sepik area, and in one way or another it also concerns most of the movements in the volume. The fascinating Sepik analysis shows the local world view persisting through all the Western or modern forms of organization and activity, and governing their interpretation. It is clear that development agencies and many missions and churches have not taken this fact sufficiently seriously, for it is widespread in the developing world where so many of these new movements occur. This account could be an eye-opener for many who are puzzled at the problems they encounter either in development or in conversion, or simply in understanding what is going on.

Implicit within the minds of many readers will be the idea that there is a fundamental conflict between such persistent and very resilient traditional religious world views and the modern scientific view that supports the processes of development and coheres with much in the alternative Christian religious outlook. The author also implies something of this response. He strongly contrasts the religiously integrated world view in the Sepik, and indeed all religious views, with the ways of modern science, and therefore recognizes what he calls the ambiguous position of the missionary who wants to "defend the scientific culture to which he belongs, at the same time as he fights the rearguard action of a battle between science and religion". This would seem to be a fair description of the local situation, and corresponds with the nature of the Western culture that has invaded Melanesia through all the agencies of modernization, including the churches, which, as the author puts it, understand themselves in ambiguous relation to their own culture. This ambiguity appears in other ways in the essays on those more sophisticated movements in White America and the West that seek to use modern science and its technologies, and much pseudo-science, in the service of highly unrealistic, unhistorical and often bizarre religious systems that are quite unscientific at heart. It might be said that the Melanesian movements are more consistent in not attempting this impossible conjunction.

If, however, the conjunction cannot be made in some other more realistic and satisfactory way, what is the future both for the Melanesian and similar movements, and for the Christian churches in their ambiguous positions? Is it to abandon religious world views in order to share intelligently and consistently in the benefits of a scientific understanding of reality? This is the kind of question that presses upon us when we have finished the historical and phenomenological descriptions and analyses of these essays.

The answer lies in the contemporary critique of Western culture that is revealing the deep dichotomy between 'facts' and 'values', between the apparently public world of 'science' and the now conventionally private worlds of religion and morality. This cultural split is rooted in a false epistemology that goes back at least as far as Descartes and that assumed its most powerful forms in the Enlightenment and in Kant. This is the Western world view that lies behind the impasse described in the Sepik, and behind all religions that are in trouble with Western, i.e., modern, internationally diffused culture.

The contemporary position, however, with respect to the nature of science and of its relations to religion has changed dramatically even if this change has not yet penetrated most of Western society, either in its heartlands or in its furthest outreaches as in the valleys of the Melanesian mountains. In place of the dichotomy that has distorted Western culture, there emerges a new convergence of "the road of science and the ways to God", to use the title of the Gifford Lectures of Stanley Jaki, the foremost contemporary historian of science. This marks, on the one hand, the revolution in physics in the post-Einsteinian era, and the subsequent revolution in the epistemology of science represented by the work of Michael Polanyi. On the other hand there has been the revolutionary theological escape from the subjective liberalism of the Enlightenment and its aftermath, represented most distinctively by Karl Barth. And now there is the on-going exploration of the compatibility, indeed the close similarity, of the ways in which theoretical science opens up our knowledge of nature and in which theology articulates our knowledge of God. To choose two names from many there is the work of scientist-theologian John Polkinghorne, and of T.F. Torrance, the author of a major work under the title of *Theological Science* and of many other 'bridging' studies.

The reader who is restless at this stage is asked to think again of the plight both of the Melanesians in the Sepik and of their opposite numbers in other millennial or cargoist movements. Should we not respect the Mt Hurun movement members for refusing to abandon their integrated and religious world view by adopting the broken, divided culture of the West? Or are Westerners satisfied to export their own cultural confusions and mounting problems, along with the contributions of modern technology and authentic scientific knowledge and of their own major religious faith, and then to wonder why it does not work? Fortunately, as we have attempted to indicate above, another way is becoming available. For many Westerners the most useful contribution to these movements for the future is to work at the healing of the rift in their own culture. Only in this way can the innovative potential of millennial and similar movements lead to the transference from one world view to another that possesses both wholeness and a closer relation to reality, to how things really are as between nature, man and God.

This volume, therefore, is much more than a work for specialists, concerned with what might appear to be marginal phenomena in the broad spectrum of religions. In a vividly human and even dramatic way these movements expose some of the quite basic issues in our modern inter-cultural world, and while they possess their own distinctive and at times esoteric messages for their members they also speak unwittingly at other levels to us all.

Centre for New Religious Movements,   Harold W. Turner
Selly Oak Colleges, Birmingham

INTRODUCTION

G.W. Trompf

The Millennium

The term millennium has been typologized in modern social scientific scholarship to denote any perfected, blissful and trouble-free order of life in the future. In the Vulgate version of the Apocalypse, the Latin *millennium* has translated the Greek χιλιάς from the New Testament, both words referring to the one thousand year rule of Christ on Earth, or to the period when the Devil is held in bondage and the final End of the present cosmos approaches (Rev. 20:2, 5 ch. 21:1ff.) Modern usage acknowledges, however, that hopes comparable to those expressed in Biblical eschatologies have been aroused throughout human history, even before the birth of the Hebrew apocalyptic genre. As for millenarism, or other cognate abstractions (such as millenarianism, millennialism, chiliasm, etc.), they cover the collective espousal of belief in some dramatic, unsurpassable Set of Events in the world's future, while the phrase millenarian movement(s) has more specific application to groups of people very much on 'the tips of their toes' in expectation of such an occurrence. The Israeli sociologist Yonina Talmon has perhaps most ably put it of millenarian movements that they are those "religious movements" which "expect imminent, total, ultimate, this-worldly collective salvation".[1] Preliminary distinctions need drawing, therefore, between 1) the general idea of a millennium, 2) the elaboration of that idea into a cosmological or ideological frame of reference, and 3) such an intensification of hope in the impending actualization of millennial conditions that group preparations and related actions result. In this volume authors focus upon religious movements which can bear the appellation 'millenarian', or perhaps nearly so, but they are no less interested in the appeal of the millennial idea as such, and in the various constructions and degrees of embellishment brought to bear on it.

The social scientific classification and comparison of millenarisms really only begins in the late 1950s. Certainly the coinage millenarism itself is as old as the seventeenth century (as, too, are 'millenarian', 'millennial', 'chiliasm'), and certain satellite concepts, such as eschatology, messianism, apocalyptist and their European cognates, had been aired in theological literature before the end of the last century.[2] Various individual case studies of 'outbreaks' later to be described as 'millenarian movements' were made early on, furthermore, with James Mooney's account of the Amerindian Ghost Dance (1893) being notable among them. But the first systematic characterizations of millenarism as a recurrent and cross-cultural phenomenon waited until the decade after the Second World War.[3] And since the 1950s, following upon pioneering work by Norman Cohn and Henri Desroches, British and Continental authors have been dominant in the production of theoretical and synoptic monographs on the subject, given their readier access to reports about the reactions of indigenous peoples to colonialism.[4]

The theoretical study of millenarism, which bears a synergetic relationship to the rampant growth of casework studies of individual religious movements over the last thirty years, has brought with it both clarification and confusion. There has been enough clarity in the typologized application of 'millennium', 'millenarism', etc. to make them stick as useful categorizations, because there are indeed ideologies and groups for which the projection of a future Transformation is positively central, and of no little fascination is the expression of comparable futurological orientations across diverse cultures. In the following pages contributors to this collection make use of the millenarist typology in perfectly defensible fashion, even though it is referred to cultural phenomena as far apart as Californian communes, Melanesian cargo cults and African proto-nationalism. That is because the general idea of the millennium - the approaching realization of a "perfect age or a perfect land"[5] - is eminently capable of being filled out with a variety of imagined prospects in an enormous variety of contexts.

On the other hand, confusion and obfuscation have arisen because both the ongoing quest for satisfactory sociological classifications and the industry to document social movements have brought with them apparently competing categories. Those very same movements described by some scholars as 'millenarian' have also been placed under other rubrics, some very broad (such as 'revitalization movements', 'new religions', 'new' or 'independent religious movements', 'messianisms', 'en- or acculturative movements', 'adjustment movements', etc.),[6] others somewhat narrower ('sects', 'cults' or 'cult movements', 'nativisms', 'salvation movements', 'utopian projects', etc.).[7] The trouble is that no up-to-date systematic effort has been made to decide whether any of these epithets render any others redundant, or whether any given category should best be seen as a sub-category of another, or even whether social science is served better by a multiformity of categories which are cross-cutting rather than hierarchically arranged in terms of compass, structure, rationality, effect, etc.

These are only preliminary queries. Other questions have already arisen in reviews of synoptic studies of millenarism, because generalists have been inevitably prone to labour one general type or paradigm in an attempt to domesticate an extraordinary complex array of data. Thus Bryan Wilson, for one, has been criticized for trying to apply Western sect-types, with which he is highly familiar, to "religious movements of protest among tribal and Third World peoples", and foisting categorizations on them which are uncontextual and too constrictive.[8] Neo-Marxist Peter Worsley, for another, has rather too often tended to interpret Melanesian 'cargo cult' millenarisms in terms of their proto-nationalist implications rather than for any intrinsically religious qualities; and along with others he has been charged with too simplistic an equation of so-called 'cargo cults' with 'millenarianism', when others had been so wary of placing the region's diverse local eruptions under this one umbrella category.[9] Mention of Worsley's political interests, moreover, reminds one that political scientists have been wont to prefer quite another cluster of designations - such as 'protest movements', 'micro- nationalisms', 'political associations', even 'rebellions', etc. - also competing to cover the same phenomena of so-called millenarisms.[10] Depending on the concerns of different disciplines, too, and the weight given in them to possible reference-points in any one style of investigation, scholars may be asking of putative millenarian movements whether they are 'active' or 'activist' rather than 'passive' (more a socio-political interest), 'charismatic' or 'pentecostal' rather than otherwise (more an issue for missiologists, ecclesiologists, or psychologists of religion), whether 'pathogenic' or 'hysteroid' as against more 'realistic' or 'rational' (more a medical or general psychological matter), or more 'tightly structured' and 'cohesive' than 'nebulous' and 'loose-knit', or again 'institutionalizing' in contrast to 'ephemeral' (as sociologists especially like to learn).[11]   And so on the known uses of 'colligatory' language could go, undoubtedly valuable for being richly textured, yet highly confusing to the novice and susceptible to academics' games of jargonism and slick generality.

While theory has not kept pace with new data, however, and complexities forestalled law-like generalizations, a basic datum remains: the imaging of a wondrous future set of conditions free of present troubles, or perhaps even the affirmation that the actualization of such conditions is already occurring in a particular place, have become increasingly common the world over during the last one hundred years. Despite the considerable variety of contexts, the articles in this collection continue to confirm what earlier theorists, including members of the 1960 International Seminar in Chicago, have contended all along,[12] that the presaging and announcements of a 'millennium' are frequently the *foci fascinantes* around which collective activities, let alone certain impressive social movements, have been formed. This volume, what is more, is not only a special testimony to the prevalence of the millennial archetype in various regional contexts but also to the influence of millenarist thinking across oceans and continents, and to the way it has provided many and scattered groups with common universalized goals in a culturally and politically pluriform world. As I predicted in 1979, "there will be more frequent instances of millenarianism" during the next half century,[13] and this is because the very 'exportability' or 'cultural transferability' of the millennial idea manifests itself *pari passu* with the growing global (and mass-media-produced) awareness that all peoples share or are involved in common predicaments. The year 2,000 may be one latently significant focal point here, but not to be exaggerated;[14] more important is the shadow of the nuclear holocaust and the overtaxing of the Earth's resources, especially in First World consciousness, and the failure of political independence movements in the Third World to produce the panaceas which matched millenarist dreaming at the local or village level. Old yearnings for 'heavens on earth' have not only lingered, then, but they have been given more cogent reasons for lingering.

The 'classic' expressions of millenarism, as most readers will doubtless assume, are those in which the *neue Zeit* is thought to be clinched by superhuman Intervention. Not unnaturally, a prior reckoning of Christian Adventist or Doomsdaying movements in the West has provided the typical *entreé* into the subject for most scholars, before they have dealt with 'other cultures'. Western

Christian millenarist lines of thought, though there are interesting variations to it, have recurrently emphasized the visible Second Coming of Christ and the establishment of Christ's rule or the 'Kingdom of God' (usually on this Earth), which entail the general Resurrection of the Dead, the Last Judgement, and foreshadow an entirely 'new Heaven and new Earth'.[15] In this visualization, God is the all-powerful Being who sews up known history at its *Eschaton*, being as wonderfully capable of cosmic action as He was at the Creation. Most of these expectations, admittedly, have not been exclusive to Christianity, yet never have the Apocalyptic images of Biblical literature been more 'realistically' and fastidiously (dare I also say garishly?) decoded than in Western European expositions, and of late in a great (and largely Protestant) spate of pamphleteering (cf. ch.1).[16] Looking further afield, however, as this very volume will enable readers to do, we find rather different projections. Where tradition is resilient among colonized peoples, for example, as in various Melanesian cargo cults (chs. 1, 5-6) or in certain African protest (and incipiently nationalistic) movements (ch.10), the anticipated Transformation can involve the intervention of the Ancestors, or the reclamation of Power by the gods and spirits of tradition as a whole, rather than the materialization of those apocalyptic hopes aired by the whites. In other cases, the influence of Judaeo-Christian millennial discourse may be readily detectable, but with the deepest longings being more specifically irredentist - concerned with a group's return to a sacred homeland - than a welcoming of a more general divine 'Self-Disclosure' (ch.8). And again, outside the West (even though we must note their recent effects within it, ch.9), there are Islamic varieties of millenarianism to be considered.[17]

Differences in the cosmic scenarios foreshadowed, however, ought not blind one to the crucial parallels which lie in the typical human experience of 'eager anticipation'. No human is unfamiliar with this condition, because so much in everyday affairs - awaiting the harvest, the pay cheque, the rearrival of a long absent member of the family, and so forth - acquaints all of us with it. Anticipations of cosmic Transformation, on the other hand, obviously constitute special instances of it, because it is capable of developing into an all-consuming intensity (Norman Cohn would say fanaticism)[18] which colonizes the time and preoccupations of individuals or groups. The mere fact of intense expectation, of course, though degrees of intensification may make the difference between sim-

ply holding a hope and joining a coterie of folk who do their waiting and preparations in company, is not sufficient in itself as an explanation for millenarism.
Particularly when cross-cultural analysis and comparison are involved, knowledge of the psychology of different situations in which millenarisms or millennial activities become more visible (or more enthusiastically embraced) will be
much more fundamental hermeneutically. We have long had among us theories
of frustration, for example, or relative deprivation, or of social pathologies consequent upon prolonged repression, etc.,[19] and what is interesting is whether any
outburst of millenarist fervour is a reaction - indeed one among a number of possible reaction-types - to perceived invidious circumstances. Again, the experience of *crisis* - of facing some momentous problem - is a common experience of
humanity, and the manifold forms of group action in response to adversity - particularly religious responses - have already led one theorist to cut across other
appellations for new religious movements and write of so-called 'crisis cults'.[20]

This volume is replete with accounts of responses to recognizable hardship or
pressure, whether physical or psychological. The relativities are such, mind you,
that certain differences in 'form and content' naturally tend to result from situational disparities. In the modern First World, for instance, millenarists are usually much better off materially, yet still sense the world has 'gone off the rails',
while Third World protesters are frequently locked into positions in which total
despair can only be alleviated by blind(-looking) hope. Indigenous Third World
millenarian movements are almost inevitably more defined politically, as restate-
ments of cultural identity which are there to resist colonial oppression, whereas
recognizable political engagement by most First World 'classic' millenarisms,
even if they are commonly subscribed to in well-defined sectarian groups, has
been much less predictable (current connections between right-wing American
politics and 'Armaggedonists' notwithstanding). As one might have foretold,
moreover, the 'universalization' of the Millennium is more pronounced in First
World contexts; there is also more studied, 'conventional' talk (about the ecological crisis or the looming Third World War as the Biblically prophesied 'Time of
Troubles', for instance), or more chance of *avant-garde* or esoteric accounts of
the New Time (as the Age of Aquarius, mystical Dawn, etc.) (cf. chs. 1,3). The
content of articulated hopes in 'the Religions of the (colonially or economically)
Oppressed', by contrast, has an immediacy and intellectual angularity discharged

from the overwhelming experiences of wretchedness, worthlessness, identity loss and powerlessness themselves.

The 'situational psychology' of millenarisms, however, and especially of distinct movements propelled by a millennial prospect, is probably no better analyzed, and by no better means takes on comparative significance, than by locating the *objects of negativity* among the participants and dreamers. It is an unpalatable but necessarily ingested truth that millenarian movements (as with many varieties of protest) very rarely lack their butts of condemnation. In a condition of powerlessness, indeed, retribution is commonly projected by millenarists into a Future from which powerful, suprahuman acts of requital and reversal will be enacted - against the insuperable forces of opposition in the immediate present. In that light millenarism could be viewed as a vehicle for non-violent protest, since the final blows against evil are to be dealt by higher-than-mortal agencies. But that will depend. It will depend, for a start, on whether the visionaries in any pertinent group imagine that the expectant 'faithful' will be *cooperating* with God or Spirit agencies in some kind of battle at the End Time; and if so, whether they will wait until the ultimate theophany (as if, like the ancient Qumranites, they should only have their weaponry issued by angelic hosts before they would lift a finger against an imperialist), or will engage in a physical struggle in advance of any divine involvement (like the Thuringian peasants behind preacher Thomas Müntzer in 1530).[21] That option will also depend on whether there are any resources to fight, or enough faith to try military measures without adequate resources, or on whether, perhaps from the theological perspective, 'forcing the hand' of God is acceptable or not.

The whole question of choosing between violence and non-violence, moreover, will depend on any given group's identification of the 'enemy' (or the sources of invidiousness which have prompted millenarist agitation as a response). In the modern West, for example, targets for condemnation are often diffuse and so monstrous in proportion that nothing short of a stupendous Intervention by God, or a Third World War which will be guided to the right outcome by divine Providence, will meet the need for justice. Among church conservatives and sectaries, for instance, the relevant rhetoric is likely to evoke 'the rampant wickedness in the world', 'the total breakdown of Christian values', 'the perils of godless Communism', etc., but it is also possible that Biblically-oriented yet politically radical thinkers might appeal to eschatology as the only foreseeable solution to the world's worsening problems. There are lingerings of Reformation apocalypticism to be found, however, and thus a singling out of the reigning Pope, let us say, as Antichrist, and there are normally enough outspoken opponents accusing millenarists of being misguided, or enough defectors from 'the cause', for people to be singled out as deserving of supernatural wrath. Third World millenarian protestations, in contrast, generally have more specific objects of reprisal pinpointed from the start - the colonial (or neo-colonial) overlords and their lackies, usually with identifiable groupings (e.g. white officials and settlers rather than missionaries, or some but not all 'foreign' elements) being those destined to be swept aside by cataclysmic fiat - along, naturally enough, with ridiculers and defectors.[22]

What - or whoever is the point of negative 'payback', the minimum condition any millenarism will have to have for it to become an identifiable movement, and thus to be more than a collectively held set of beliefs, is the challenge of an altercation.[23] Almost without fail, millenarists will draw notice to themselves. This can be done, of course, by withdrawal. In modern Western history, the commune, or the creation of new settlements and newly ordained sacred space, or of an occult body, are well known enough, and examples of them are given detailed research in the first three chapters of this book. In such cases accusation, rejection, even persecution usually follow upon the 'difference' the millenarists create for themselves, so that they in turn come to be more specific than they were initially about 'the evil ones'. There is a spectrum of possibilities to be mapped, though, as I have suggested elsewhere,[24] between the clear absence of physical violence on the part of millenarists to their countenancing of violent conflict against antagonists. In the Third World (as in pre-modern Europe, both east and west), the contentious refusal of millennial groups to cooperate with the overlords has not only led to the setting up of an alternative way of life, which appears as a threat to public order (or orthodoxy, as in old Europe), but also to incipient revolutionism, or at least varying degrees of preparedness to remove the unwanted adversaries by force, as one kind of drastic action in favour of a presaged Perfection.[25] Despite variations as to the kinds of altercations created, however, or the lengths taken to achieve goals or retrieve losses, the common feature to be found in millenarian movements of some projected or intended 'counter-stroke' against a cosmic evil, threat or opposition, is undeniable, thus legitimating the category sociologically and providing a key tool for comparative analysis.

Another important and integrally related ingredient pressing for attention, and almost as valuable in comparative analysis, is the content and meaning put upon the expected Perfection, or Millennium, as a mythic or macro-historical displosion. By implication, for a start, Yonina Talmon suggested one possible means of distinguishing millenarism as ideology and a millenarian movement as social outgrowth when she concluded of the latter that its members looked to a "*this-worldly* salvation". Some millenarisms conceive the coming Perfection to be on the heavenly plane; those that foresee it to be on Earth are more likely to take concerted action to realize it.[26] The more material the content of the Millennium, in fact, the greater the likelihood of a quest for some technology or ritual to bring about its actuality (chs. 1, 5-6). The appeal of a millenarism, further, or its capacity to engender greater cohesive activity, will be often enhanced by more definite, if simplistic picturing of what is to be soon forthcoming, whether verbally or iconically.[27] The announced content of a Millennium will have all the more attractiveness, moreover, if it taps unconscious sources of energy, which is one facility of myth. Expressed myth, though, loses power if it is not relevant to the cultural *milieu* to which it is applied. Thus in primal societies, for instance, the heralding of an *Endzeit* which is supposed to emerge *de novo* - with angelic hosts, Jesus on the clouds of glory, or the arrival of the Mahdi, etc. - is not likely to have much staying power as the inspiration of a movement, not much, that is, in comparison to an envisaged future involving the *return* of culturally recognizable characters from a primordial *Urzeit*.[28] Among tribal peoples subjected to colonialism, the myths of exploits by the (more-than-human) culture heroes and (post-mortal) ancestors were critical in cultural *identity* - in conveying why a people had become what it is, and had managed what it had considering its primordial background. An appeal to the reappropriation of the Power of the 'Dream-Time' - the power which made culture possible in the first place - can obviously provide a vital motivation for Third World millenarian movements to recover the loss of pre-colonial autonomy and worthwhileness (ch. 4).

Many more observations may be made about millenarism. Long discussions may be had about cognitive problems arising for fervent believers when their dreams do not come true at the times nominated by 'prophets' or 'guiding stars' who lead them on. A leader's proffered rationalizations to cope with such dissonance, indeed, will be crucial in the saving or destroying of a movement. The process of 'institutionalization' will begin if the explanations for initial disappointments are satisfying to enough of the very first participants, who stay on to carry the movement to another phase.[29] The intensity of effervescence of those moments in which the movement first issued its challenges and hopes can then be reflected upon - in the early build up of a tradition - as the turning-point in a new and preferable direction, and the point making possible a new *communitas*.[30] The members may then still look to the Millennium, but avoid the mistake of proposing a time-table. Perhaps we should add here, 'at least for the time being', because the recurrent or spasmodic reenlivening of millennial yearnings will have to be accounted for. But for the most part 'expectant ones' cannot constantly consume themselves with their expectations without wearing themselves out. It is one of the paradoxes of millenarism, for instance, that its espousers, though once frenetic-looking, can later get on with the business of well-organized day-to-day activity, and in the modern West that has included the pursuit of high status and the attainment of noticeable material security.[31] (But other special points one might wish to pursue here should be left to the authors who follow.)

The Cargo

A propos material security, what of Cargo? What is meant by it, and where does it sit in relation to millenarian issues? Cargo capitalized (as it will commonly be found in subsequent chapters) denotes more than the items packed on vehicles, ships, aeroplanes or caravans. In this book it has also been typologized, because already in highly significant contexts it has come to connote more than goods in transit, or more than European-style or internationally marketed commodities which have made cargo such a distinctive device of global political economy today. In so-called 'cargo cults', for instance, which have been mainly but not exclusively a phenomenon from Melanesia,[32] the concept Cargo (in pidgin *Kago*) implies a totality of material, organizational and spiritual welfare, collectively desired as a replacement for current inadequacy, and projected into the imminent future as a coming 'salvation'.[33] *Kago* in cargo cult, then, is susceptible to being turned into the manifestations of a Millennium (again, typologically conceived). It can in this sense include what it cannot in ordinary English (or comparable) parlance: money (which both expresses and procures *Kago*) and also a *total* security (because what the 'whitemen' or foreigners possess in contrast to the lowly villager is so extraordinary that it already implies for him some miracle of transcendence).

Rashly, I have already defined cargo cults as those "activities arising from the expectation of abundant, supernaturally generated, Western-style cargo".[34] This suffices so long as one remembers that there are relative degrees of abundance anticipated (from unlimited to much smaller quantities); that applied to primal religions the 'supernatural' can be somewhat of a misnomer, since, among the projected bearers of the Cargo the ancestors have been most common, and they have been thought to be still part of the whole community; and that, to reiterate, the cargo of the foreigners symbolizes a virtual redemption from preexisting, to be specific Stone Age, conditions. The Melanesian cargo cult provides it with a *locus classicus*, then, in which collective hopes have been pinned on the outpouring of patently material blessings which are expressive of non-empirical forces. When these hopes are such that the arrival of Western-style goods is to be one component of a new order, in tandem with the return of Jesus let us say, or of the ancestors, or the paradisean order, or some other recognizably millennial motif, the identification of a cargo cult with a millenarian movement is admissible.[35] Still more is this a respectable equivalence if the term or idea *Kago* is used to epitomize a total Transformation to come.[36] On the other hand, Cargo and cargo cultism can also cover other than millenarist phenomena, and thus we must see them as intersecting, yet not coterminous.[37] In this very book, after all, are to be found millenarisms without hope of Cargo (cf. chs. 7, 8, 10).

If there is usefulness in distinguishing cargo from Cargo, moreover, the same applies with cargoism and cargo cultism, a distinction doubly helpful for showing why neither share quite the same boundaries as millenarism. Cargoism, or "cargo [or cargoist(ic)] thinking", as Peter Lawrence prefers,[38] is an espousal of belief in the 'religious' or 'deeper' significance of the whole range of internationally marketable commodities that has come with the Second Industrial Revolution and mass production. In their *Manifesto of the Communist Party* (1848), Karl Marx and Friedrich Engels rightly perceived the immense potential for capitalism to undermine every traditional social order.[39] Perhaps more slowly than they expected, yet by means far more astounding technologically than either of them foresaw, a thousand and one concrete statements of consumerism have come to be made in the furthest reaches of the Earth. Television has become available to virtually every Indian village (since 1975); transistor radios and cassette recorders sit in some of the most out-of-the-way villages of highlands New Guinea; Eskimos come into the trade stores to purchase cola and Amazonian Indians to buy tinned meat; and so on. There is a new world of more and more remarkable things, and the greatest, if often overlooked revolution of the last hundred years is that now millions upon millions of homes in richer parts of the world have more millions upon millions of gadgets, household appliances, time-saving devices, electrical outlets to go with them, etc., while still more millions upon millions of people in other, less privileged parts of the world would like to share in this extraordinary abundance, indeed in the veritable 'miracle' of it all.[40]

Both lack of access and want of knowledge as to how many of the new items of cargo work, in fact, endow them with a more than mundane significance for most peoples of the Third World. In the preliminary stages of adjustment, wholly new items may take on a highly numinous quality and what is valueless elsewhere will be treasure. Thus New Guinea highland warriors circumperambulated humble cotton shirts as they were disgorged from airplanes in the 1940s, making peace with the potentially dangerous forces they suggested, while select highland women died of blood poisoning for wearing empty tins as precious arm bands.[41] Further on in each local *Erklärungsprozess*, the coincidence of missionization and the appearance of new goods can be so linked that access to the latter is assumed to be dependent on embracing the newly introduced religious message. Keep going to church, in other words, and the Cargo will eventually come.[42] While this connection is natural for those peoples who have never seen factories and the like, and whose religions have been thought to provide tangible fertility and thus total security, and while the promise of material betterment is rarely absent from missionary preaching in any case, overly high hopes are usually not matched in the Third World by the (real) events of some bonanza, and thus altercations will eventually occur.

As with millenarian movements, it is most helpful for explaining the crystallization of a cargo cult, and for the comparative analysis of cargo cultism, to pinpoint the grievances which motivate collective action and make altercation inevitable. At this point we will perceive how cargoism denotes sets of ideas, beliefs and hopes rather than any discrete social phenomena, while the term 'cult' (though it can be salvaged for certain contexts) might as well be called 'movement' (or 'cult movement'), particularly since it has so often been attached to 'cargo' for mere alliterative reasons.[43] As Third World movements, cargo cults arise when groups mobilize themselves to prepare for entirely new goods which they consider ought to be theirs, and from which they ought not to be deprived. Thus Christianity can be all the more embraced, to take one option, but with idiosyncracies as various Pacific and African examples testify, and with the accusation that the missionaries have not told the whole story (about the secret of acquiring the Cargo). Or else disillusionment with Christianity (or at least one brand of it) can set in, because it did not 'produce the goods', and an alternative source of hope explored (e.g. tradition, synthetism, another denomination, etc.).[44]

When or while collective expectations approximate to an "imminent, ultimate, this-worldly" salvation of Cargo, then we will allow that cargo(ist) and millenarian movements have coincided both as category and phenomena.[45] Independent of the fervour of these expectations, by comparison, or with a marked lessening of 'manic' preparations, cargo cultism can manifest on its own right as a routine activity, the recurrent performance of certain practises being understood to create the conditions which will bring more money and more accessibility to the new goods, but with any grand, outpouring Cornucopia being left to an (at least temporarily) unpredicted future. A money cult, then, and these were not uncommon in Melanesia when it was realized that money was one key to the Cargo, is still a cargo cult. But the focus is on the periodic or alchemical ritual (of trying to multiply money in a spirit house, let us say), thereby perhaps rehabilitating our usage of 'cult' and any week-by-week gatherings for mutual support would reflect the institutionalization of millenarist enthusiasm already mentioned, the great Cargo Millennium, if it is retained, being set in an indefinite future, and thus no longer providing the pretext for any *exceptional* activity (to welcome any highly exceptional, because final set of events).[46]

Once this principle of differentiating the relevant categories is applied, it opens the possibility of a comparative, cross-cultural investigation of non-millenarian cargo cultism as well as of its more distinctively millenarian varieties. Thus rituals which are performed on a periodic basis to secure consumer items, no matter what the cultural context, and whether we are dealing with Hindu prayers to the new goddess Santoshi Mata for a badly needed refrigerator, or the repetition of a mantra for a television by a less affluent member of the Japanese sect Namu-Myoho-Renge-Kyo, are quite legitimately - certainly not unhelpfully - dubbed cargo cultist.[47] Analysts of Western culture will be tempted to place various expressions of habitual gambling in this class, and why blame them? When Lady Luck is portrayed as a guardian Angel in newspaper advertisements, along with "a true story" as to her rôle in upholding a "family's lottery-winning tradition", the presumed link between the recurrent ('ritual') act of buying a lottery ticket and the religious quest for total security is being appealed to.[48] My own work on the success of lottery organizations in Melanesia, and on the popularity of gambling games there, only goes to confirm the value of testing cargo cultism's trans-cultural applications.[49] Hitherto scholars have been reluctant to explore these applications, and uses of the term cargo cult outside Third World contexts have been more rhetorical than serious; but then this volume contains the first systematic attempts at a wider comparative analysis of cargo cultism, with newer Western religions especially in view (cf. chs. 1-2, 6).

In being prepared to take this cue, cargoism will automatically deserve reevaluation as an *ethos,* for its potency as a catalyst in motivating social change will be missed if it is limited to a set of beliefs and ideas (about access to or arrival of new goods, or about who deserves and will receive them). A cargoistic ethos is one in which new commodities, and the extraordinary achievements of modern technology as manifest in new things and facilities (including money), become the paramount goal of visible human acquisitions, and take on increasing power to be the very surrogates of that biocosmic vitality or fecundity so crucial for traditional societies. The ethos, however, provides the ground in which *both* high hopes and frustrations are fertilized. In the Third World the great disparity between those who enjoy and those who lack the goods has been the pretext for protest activity from the turn of the century. In the so-called 'developed World', because so many already have the access to the Cargo, the pressure is constantly on the members of society to consume and acquire in amounts sufficiently to maintain their self-esteem. In this more affluent situation frustration and thus recourse to a range of possible solutions arise from a perceived sense of deficiency (often conceived as a cosmic deficiency in waiting for a total salvation), but the needs and deprivations are more quantitatively than qualitatively different from the oppressed masses of the world's poor, and in no sense undermine the cross-cultural significance of the cargoist ethos as the hallmark of our age.[50] Important in comparative analysis here, naturally, will be studies of 'enclaves of the Third World' in developed countries, and thus of attitudes to wealth and power among the remnants of decimated indigenes, or the descendants of displaced black slaves and migrant labourers (cf. chs. 8-9).

I do not wish to give the impression that so-called cargo cultism is the major and most typically selected solution made by the frustrated in the present ethos. There are, after all, other albeit related options. One of them, intriguingly, is theft. If the Cargo cannot be procured by employment (because none is available) or by ritual (because it does not work), then theft is not merely one obvious recourse - and its common avail now a central problem for virtually all nation states - it is also one which can be ideologically justified, whether as act of necessity, equalization, or of retribution against the selfish.[51] Violent protest and revolutionary action are, of course, other possibilities just as capable of legitimation when the perceived or actual divisiveness between 'possessors' of the Cargo and those 'dis-possessed' of it has been accentuated. We are not to forget, though, the cargoist ethos in its broadest sense, and thus the latent, partly unconscious yearnings to participate fully and live authentically in a social life overpowered by materiality, and often without the more stable guideposts of old traditions. This synoptic apprehension of cargoism as an ethos is just as important for understanding millenarism, for the *Grundlage* of distinctively millennial ideas and actions is that endemic human longing for complete security and the absence of problems and sufferings -

> for some safe place where everything would be ordered and good and indestructable. a place where we could trust the trees not to fall down and crush us, the birds not to peck us to death, the earth not to split open under our feet.[52]

But we must move on.

On Comparing Cultures

Social scientific categorization, bringing with it such abstractions as millenarism and cargoism, is all too susceptible to the peril of reification. There are no better means of avoiding this danger than through experiencing the weight and resilience of cultural difference, and the particularity of local or regional histories in which alleged millenarisms, cargo cultism and their like have been manifest. This volume provides a variety of case studies, and although both America and Melanesia draw proportionately more attention, there is a reasonable variety of cultural contexts considered as well. Before briefly introducing these studies and their authors in turn, however, a little space should be devoted to the general problem of cross-cultural investigation, and the application of sociological categories to a wide dispersal of human activity.

'Culture', as is by now well known, has a number of different meanings, some of which have been better defined than others. Aside from the debate we must leave undiscussed about the relationship between culture and religion (on the ways in which culture is a product of religion or vice versa, for instance, on whether culture incarnates religion, or whether religion is a 'cultural system', etc.),[53] one of the more difficult questions raised by parts of this book concerns the viability of comparing and paralleling phenomena from contexts as far apart sociologically as 'primitive' New Guinea to 'ultra-sophisticated' California. Have certain cultures ontogenetic differences such that explorations into their comparability are *a priori* inadmissable? or preferably left to dare-devil synthesizers (like Lévi-Strauss)?[54] And are apparently comparable sets of ideas and new religious movements from societies highly dissimilar in organization, structure and complexity merely *analogous*, or parallel in some attenuated sense, rather than genuine instantiations of the same class of phenomena? Or in other words, can any given social scientific category only remain truly viable when not universalized but referred to some 'medium range' of cultural situations (such as 'tribal societies', or 'feudal societies', or 'fully modernized societies', etc.)?

The answers to such questions do not come easily, but articles in this volume provide comparative analyses and points of orientation which help answer them. At least it has already been made clear in this introduction, moreover, that both millenarism and cargoism have bearing on the human condition in general. As for the matter of comparing primitive and modern, and the applicability of 'colli-gatory' terms to the most diverse contexts, purists who prevaricate here should be reminded of the relativities in time, space and human valorization which suggest surprising comparability in the first place, and which also justify the very *effort* at comparative analysis as itself an exercise in common human (or inter-cultural) understanding. After all, the term 'primitive' (if it should be retained at all) *is* quite relative. Was it not a famous traveller who reserved the most pointed use of this term to the white 'Holy Rollers' of Kentucky and Tennessee, not to the Sioux or the Navaho?[55] And if, for reasons of psychology as much as for avowed purism, some of us might baulk at accepting any religious content to Cargo outside 'primitive' (and 'non-European') contexts, we ought to remember how some of its earliest known usages in English were suggestive of divine blessing - in the thoughts, for instance, of none other than Defoe's Robinson Crusoe.[56] Beliefs and articulated hopes, moreover, are quite capable of being borne in travel - across vast oceans as the sub-title of this book reminds one - and thus there is no reason why these notions will or cannot be incorporated and acted upon in any conceivable human culture. The idea and anticipation of a Millennium is really one of the world's most obvious cases in point. Although in the Western tradition this idea may immediately bespeak the notion of directional history towards a Final Event, or of great macro-periods (such as the return of the Golden Age), and although one should hardly expect snap reproductions of these additional, culture-specific conceptions in societies whose concepts of time and periodicity are quite dissimilar, the Millennium *qua* elementary idea, or basic 'structure of the imagination', remains capable of capturing *any* psyche.[57]

There has also been some interest, of course, and some controversy, over whether such categories as millenarism or cargoism, and satellite concepts from the sociology of religion like messianism, sectarianism, etc., are useful in characterizing *secular* developments, including those in the so-called Second World. Already in the 1950s strong links were being drawn by Cohn between Western 'fanatical' millenarism and secular totalitarianism, and the two Talmons, as a husband and wife team, were fascinated by the same connections.[58] The reality stands that structures of religion continue to accrue to virtually all ostensibly post- or non-religious human activities. The problem is how to achieve more than a suggestive and rhetorical comparative study of the relevant pieces of evidence, noting how Soviet communism, for example, has its Bible, Messiah, its sect-type church of the narrowly committed, and its futurist orientation toward a Millennium-like classless society (the originally unrealistic expectations of which were rationalized into bureaucratic institutionalism), or exploring how the modern money system does indeed have the structure of religion, as Norman O. Brown ably argues, and how extravagantly high expectations in the economy or government or science by the average citizen in the West might be more incisively and helpfully described as cargoist than not.[59] A few of the following papers provide materials for a more precise analysis of these matters (cf. chs. esp. 1, 6, 9).

The chapters of this book, all being case studies of one sort or another, enrich theoretical study and curb its over-simplification by a telling concentration on historical detail. In the first chapter I have been rather more ambitious than other writers in embracing a whole region, but mine is essentially an in-depth comparative study of a great Californian commune and new religious movements in Melanesia, undertaken to confirm that *both* millenarism and cargo cultism are viable cross-cultural categories. The 'comparative method', however, long respected as a basic means of establishing similarity and difference in social phenomena,[60] has not been employed formalistically, distrustful as I always have been of listing features in common or otherwise in point form. I have deliberately taken care to characterize the ethos in which respective developments have arisen, not wishing to create the illusion that movements as fascinatingly parallel as the Brotherhood of the Sun (or Sunburst commune) on the United States west coast and select Melanesian cargo cults derive from anything like the same milieux. I also concentrated on manageable themes: the fundamental importance of myth, or more accurately mythic macro-history, in the new religious movements under scrutiny, the logic of retribution, and the psychology of leading and being led in such movements.

John Bracht, who has been researching Mormon beliefs for twenty-five years and is currently engaged in doctoral studies at the Department of Religious Studies, the University of Sydney, and Gregory Tillett, who has received his doctorate through the same department and institution for a biography of the Theosophist Charles Leadbeater,[61] are the next contributors. Each concentrate on aspects of the Western millenarian trajectory. Bracht's work is very important in the elucidation of the concretization of divinity in Mormonism, and the materiality of the Mormon Millennium. His study chimes with E.L. Tuveson's thesis that distinctly American millennialism has to do with building the Kingdom of God on the face of the Earth,[62] but Bracht goes further to identify certain cargoist features in Mormon thought and practice. Tillett, for his part, and in keeping with his remarkable expertise in matters occult,[63] explores all too neglected areas of esoteric Adventism, or disclosures of 'hidden Messiahs' in late nineteenth and earlier twentieth century movements initiated by Europeans. The two articles on Western themes develop various implications I have left unexplored in my interpretation of a very complex Californian ideology, and all three of these articles pay attention to the 'whiteman's myths' (important for a better understanding of the subsquent articles on southwest Pacific developments), and also to the mobility of beliefs and ideas across great distances of the globe.

In the next section of the symposium, four contributors take on specific aspects of culturo-religious change in the southwest Pacific region (including Timor where one finds an intriguing melting-pot of 'South-east Asian', 'Australian Aboriginal' and 'Melanesian' human groupings). Ethnohistorian Roderic Lacey, co-editor of *Oral Tradition in Melanesia* and author of a work on the oral history of the Enga people in the New Guinea highlands,[64] treats the journey motif in the pre-contact and colonial history of Papua New Guinea. Described in myth, certain ancient and primordial journeys of transformation are undertaken in a time or space for which supernatural occurrences are likely, indeed expected to happen, the extraordinary secrets learnt and events transpired being taken as absolutely crucial for the peoples who hear the accounts. Proceeding through Lacey's reconstructions, we find that indigenous travellers in colonial times, and especially those journeys associated with cargo cult 'prophet' figures, seem to reopen the possibility of mythic time. The *neue Zeit* of the 'whiteman' and his goods, tackled most strikingly by cargo cult heroes, brings dreams of momentous change which are as extravagant as they are because the present transformations and conditions appear as great and miracle-filled as the traditional, mythic world of gods and spirits had always been made out to be.

Patrick Gesch, currently co-Editor of the anthropology journal *Anthropos*, and the author of the most detailed monograph study of a cargo movement ever written,[65] concentrates on the stages and forms of which that movement has taken on over two decades. His is a lesson in indigenous 'experiments with civilization' to uncover the undisclosed secret of the white's superior power and technology. Both Gesch and fellow anthropologist Lamont Lindstrom, whose article follows, are concerned to map the different presuppositions about bases of power and effectuation in 'primal' and 'modern-scientific' *Weltanschauungen*. Lindstrom, editor of a collection on drug usage in traditional Oceanic cultures,[66] brings theoretical insights to bear from Michel Foucault's work to compare regimes of discourse reflected in Melanesian cargo cultist and white American rhetoric, and their implications for a comparative understanding of knowledge and power.[67] Lindstrom's article links back to my own in its more ambitious attempt to compare materials from widely different contexts from opposite sides of the Pacific. While Lindstrom centres his attention on the meaning of Cargo and the question of knowledge, Graham Brookes, a missiologist, documents what he calls 'spirit movements'. This usage, which has already influenced the interpretation of recent Melanesian movements and derives from his Masters Dissertation,[68] covers both revivalist-looking activities within church life, as well as collective *rites de passage* incorporating previous outsiders into church involvement, that are marked by acclaimed manifestations of the Holy Spirit. These movements, sometimes pentecostal, sometimes involving other altered states, and oftimes associated with the outpouring of *charismata* (or divine gifts of healing, glossolalia, psychic perceptions of hidden wrongs, etc.),[69] also bear millenarian features, and Brookes' study conducts us to an interesting, newly emergent subject of enquiry into the fringes of millenarism.

The last section takes readers into another realm of black cultures, that of the Africans rather than the Melanesians. Part of the excitement of the symposium lies in the production of case studies which enable religions of the black oppressed to be more adequately compared. The various influences behind black millenarian and cargoist movements are given rich treatment as the pages unfold: the Bible, missionary Christianity, Garveyism, Islam, nationalism, consumerism - all of them so transplantable across seas and continents. And we are taught by all the papers on Melanesian, African and Afro-American situations, that new religious movements are not always so monolithic as the old sect-type paradigm suggests, and certainly not static. Fieldwork by the sociologist Karlene Faith throws new light on the hitherto poorly documented side to the Jamaican Rastafarians, that is, on its decentralized and rather diasporic manifestations in rural areas, and especially on the noticeable divergence of belief (and especially millennial and irredentist hope) among its followers. Despite differences and lack of coordination, this movement continues to grow rapidly throughout the Caribbean, and the impact of its music, and of the sentiments expressed in soulfull Reggae songs, have been immense internationally, especially on youth.[70]

Historians Dennis Walker and Zedekiah Ngavirue have plotted significant shifts in the history of African protest activities, each in their own way. Learned in Arabic and in the rise of Arab nationalisms,[71] Walker is able to exegete the ideological interaction between orthodox Islam and the less or unorthodox Black Muslims, and to follow the shift from the Black Muslims' more retributive, politicized millenarism under Elijah Muhammad to positions more or less accepting of political realities and the consumer society. Ngavirue, the one black writer in the collections, turns us away from America and Oceania, which are the two major geographical zones of attention in this book, and leads us back to Africa. It is not to the Ethiopia longed for by the Rastafarians, however, but to a region scantily documented in English and from which Ngavirue has emerged as the finest indigenous historiographer. In his analysis we are once again at one of those intriguing fringes of millenarism, at the points at which its protests spill over into proto-nationalism and the independent church experiment (so prevalent throughout black and equatorial Africa today).[72] The pieces by Walker and Ngavirue are interesting, when taken together, for illustrating the processes by which millenarist energies are institutionalized and channelled in the pursuit of more specific social goals. These processes, however, have hardly yielded parallel results: in South West Africa intensification of opposition to the ruling order increased in the period under Ngavirue's consideration (and also beyond), while the Black Muslims have recently become more accommodating to capitalism and white hegemony than was previously the case.

All the following contributions, it should be noted, impinge on millenarism, yet a few hardly broach the subject of cargo cultism. This is because the collection is not intended simply to elucidate relationships between millenarist and cargoist expectations but also to enrich and refine already existing analyses of millenarism as the better known and apparently broader area of study. The articles by Walker and Ngavirue, for example, raise questions about the place of millennial dreams in political protest and rebellions. In two entirely different settings, one finds the Black Muslims vociferating via a long-utilized eschatological and political rhetoric, while with indigenous Namibian reactions to colonial domination the millenarist hopes are more 'underlying' and ideologically attenuated, and encapsulated more in the yearning to recover lost homelands and tribal autonomy. The article by Brookes, too, focusses on forms of 'realized eschatology', and intense religious experiences which are relatively sufficient unto themselves (without being always thought of as the keys to material blessing). The greater body of the writings, however, has attention directed on both the Cargo and the Millennium as modes for comparative and integrative interpretation. It is perhaps the central aim of this volume to confirm that cargo cultism and cargoism are as useful in cross-cultural enquiry as millenarism has already proved to be, and my own detailed comparative research in the opening chapter is designed to establish first credentials in this respect. With the rapid, world wide advances in technology, it is certainly high time to endow the cultic and religious focus on the promise of new goods (or money) with an integrity of its own (at least when hermeneutically necessary), instead of constantly assimilating it back into millenarism or obscuring it under some other category.[73]

Most of the scholars in this book are Australian, or, as in the case of Scotsman John Bracht, have come to live in Australia. Among the Australians, only Patrick Gesch lives elsewhere, at Sankt Augustin, West Germany. Two North American scholars, Lamont Lindstrom from the United States, and Karlene Faith, Canada, join Zedekiah Ngavirue, Namibian, as welcome interlopers from afar in what is otherwise a significantly Australian scholarly enterprise. All of the scholars, however, herewith present research which they have undertaken overseas. Three of them I have very much appreciated as colleagues in Melanesian tertiary institutions, Roderic Lacey and Zedekiah Ngavirue in the History Department at the University of Papua New Guinea, and Patrick Gesch at the Holy Spirit Catholic Seminary, Bomana, Papua New Guinea. Gregory Tillett and Karlene Faith have also been highly valued colleagues of mine at one time or another, at the University of Sydney and the University of California, Santa Cruz, respectively. Three writers - Gesch, Tillett and Bracht - have been my doctoral students at different stages of my career at the Department of Religious Studies, the University of Sydney. I can thank modern travel facilities and the conference circuit for bringing me in contact with Lamont Lindstrom,

Graham Brookes and Michael Walker, a knowledge of whose researches came as a pleasant cluster of surprises.

On reflection, a rich variety of disciplines are represented here: myself as historian of ideas and religions, Bracht as historical theologian, Tillett as occultist, Lacey as ethnohistorian, Gesch as missionary anthropologist, Lindstrom as a more 'classic' anthropologist, Brookes as missiologist, Faith as sociologist (now criminologist), and both Walker and Ngavirue as historians, with the former having more specialist interests in literature and political science. Three of the authors are ordained churchmen, Bracht as a Presbyterian, Gesch as Catholic priest in the Divine Word Order, and Brookes within the Uniting Church of Australia. A fourth, Lacey, currently teaches in a Catholic college, and joins three others - myself, Lindstrom and Faith - as academics currently teaching in tertiary institutions. The fact that only a minority of the contributors are practising academics reflects, first, that researchers in religion can take on other tasks - to work on a government Anti-Discrimination Board (Tillett) (although he has recently returned to academia), to edit an international journal (Gesch), direct a church Mission Board (Brookes), or to live out a highly precarious but influential existence in one's conflict-ridden homeland (Ngavirue) - and second, that such scholars as Bracht and Walker still remain engaged in their postgraduate research (while they are also elsewhere employed). There are thus healthy elements of experience and wider-than-narrow-academic concerns in this volume, which has grown up over the last decade more out of a shared interest in the human condition than the desperation to publish about 'pet topics' (or else perish).

Notes

1. Y. Talmon, "Millenarian Movements", in *Archives Européennes de Sociologie*, 7 (1966), p.159, cf. also her "pursuit of the Millennium: the relation between religions and social change", in *ibid.*, 3 (1962), pp.125ff.
2. J. Murray *et al., Oxford English Dictionary*, vol.2, p.344, vol.6, p.447, cf. vol.1, p.386, vol.3, p.284, vol.6, p.375, etc. *Millénarisme* was known in French by the eighteenth century, P. Robert, *Dictionnaire alphabétique et analogique de la langue française*, vol.4, p.418, but *chiliasme* only this century, cf. *Dictionnaire de la langue Française*, (1899), vol.1, p.604. For the German story, we await the completion of the *Deutsches Fremdwörterbuch* by A. Kirkness. On theological usages, F.M. Schiele and L. Escharnack (ed.), *Religion in Geschichte und Gegenwart*, Tübingen 1910 edn., vol.1, pp. 519ff., vol. 2, pp. 544-5. Cf. also W.D. Wallis, *Messiahs. Christian and Pagan*, Boston, 1918, E. Troeltsch, *The Social Teaching of the Christian Churches* (trans. O. Wyon), London, 1931, pp. 712-4. For further background, G.W. Trompf, "Missiology, Methodology and the Study of New Religious Movements", in *Religious Traditions*, 10 (1987), pp. 95-8, 104.
3. Cf. J. Mooney, *The Ghost-Dance Religion and the Sioux Outbreak of 1890 (Fourteenth Annual Report of the Bureau of Ethnology to the Secretary of the Smithsonian Institution, 1892-93)*, Washington, 1896. On early theory, see especially the pages of the *Archives de Sociologie des Religions*, V (1958), with articles by G.R.S., Norman Cohn, Norman Birnbaum, P. Kovalevsky, etc. Cf., in anticipation, H. Desroche, "Dissidences religeuses et Socialisme utopiques", in *Année Sociologique*, and note also L. Festinger *et al., When Prophecy Fails*, Ser. 3, 1955, pp. 393-439, Minneapolis, 1956, ch.1, for an early American survey.
4. Cohn's *magnum opus* was *In Pursuit of the Millennium*, London, 1957, and Desroche compiled his *Dieux d'hommes. Dictionnaire des messianismes et millénarismes*, Paris, by 1969. For other theoretical monographs, e.g. P. Worsley, *The Trumpet Shall Sound*, London, 1957 (70); W.E. Mühlmann, *Chiliasmus und Nativismus (Studien zur Soziologie der Revolution*, vol.1), Berlin, 1961; H.J. Margull, *Aufbruch zur Zukunft*, Gütersloh, 1962; F. Sierksma, *Een nieuwe hemel en een nieuwe aarde*, The Hague, 1961; S.L.

Thrupp (ed.), *Millennial Dreams in Action (Comparative Studies in Society and History, Supp. 2)*, The Hague, 1962, esp. Introd. and ch. 3; K.O.L. Burridge, *New Heaven New Earth*, Oxford, 1969, B.R. Wilson, *Magic and the Millennium*, New York and London, 1973. Cf. the more recent overview by an American, Barkun, *Disaster and the Millennium*, New Haven and London, 1974.

5. Thus Thrupp, "Millennial Dreams in Action", in Thrupp (ed.), *op.cit.*, p.11.
6. Cf., e.g., A.F.C. Wallace, "Revitalization Movements: some theoretical considerations for their comparative study", in *American Anthropologist*, 58 (1956), pp. 264 ff.; "New Religions among the Delaware Indians, 1600-1900", in *Southwestern Journal of Anthropology*, 12/1 (1956), pp. 1ff.; cf. H. Biezais, "Zur Problematik der neuen Religionen", in Biezais (ed.), *New Religions (Scripta Instituti Donneriani Aboensis 7)*, Stockholm, 1975, pp.7ff.; L.C. Mair, "Independent Religious Movements in Three Continents", in *Comparative Studies in Society and History*, 1 (1958), pp. 113ff.; V. Lanternari, "Messianism: its historical origin and morphology", in *History of Religions*, 1 (1961), esp. pp. 55ff.; J. van Baal, "Erring Acculturation", in *American Anthropologist*, 62 (1960), pp. 108ff.; K. Murphy and T. Ahrens (eds.), *The Church and Adjustment Movements (Point, No.1, 1974)*.
7. Wilson, *op.cit.*, pp. 11ff. ('Of Sect and Church'); E.W.P. Chinnery, "Five Religious Cults in British New Guinea", in *The Hibbert Journal*, 15/3 (1917), pp. 448ff.; R. Linton, "Nativistic Movements", in *American Anthropologist*, 45 (1943), pp. 230ff.; J.W. Schoorl, "Salvation Movements among the Muyu of Irian Jaya", in *Irian*, 7/1 (1978), pp. 3ff., cf. Trompf, "Utopia", in M. Eliade (ed.), *The Encyclopedia of Religion*, New York, 1987, vol. 15, p. 160.
8. For a review of Wilson's work (cf.n.4), T.O. Ranger, in *African Religious Research*, 3/2 (1973), pp. 32-33.
9. Worsley, *op.cit.*, esp. pp. 262-4, cf. T. Bodrogi, "Colonization and Religious Movements in Melanesia", in *Acta Ethnographica*, 2 (1951), pp. 259ff. For the scholar least inclined to generalize about so-called cargo cults, J. Inglis, "Cargo Cults: the problem of explanation", in *Oceania*, 27/4 (1957), pp. 249ff. See also Trompf, "Mircea Eliade and the Interpretation of Cargo Cults", in *Religious Traditions*, 11 (1987) (forthcoming), and also n.45 below.
10. Cf. E. Hobsbaum, *Primitive Rebels*, Manchester, 1959; R.I. Rotberg and A.A.

Mazrui (eds.), *Protest and Power in Black Africa*, New York, 1970; M. Adas, *Prophets of Rebellion: millenarian protest movements against the European Colonial Order, (Studies in Comparative World History)*, Cambridge, 1979; R. May (ed.), *Micronationalist Movements in Papua New Guinea (Political and Social Change Monograph 1)*, Canberra, 1982; P. Hempenstall, *Protest or Experiment? Theories of 'Cargo Cults' (Research Centre for Southwest Pacific Studies Occasional Paper 2)*, Melbourne, 1981; H.V.E.T. van Velzen and W. van Wetering, "Affluence, Deprivation and the Flowering of Bush Negro Religious Movements", in *Bijdragen voor Land-Taal- en Volkenkunde*, 139/1 (1983), pp. 99ff. Cf. also R. Bastide, "Messianism and Social and Economic Development", in I. Wallerstein (ed.), *Social Change: the colonial situation*, New York, London and Sydney, 1966, pp. 467ff.

11. Cf., e.g. Worsley, *op.cit.*, pp. 40-1, 239-44, etc.; W.J. Hollenweger, *The Pentecostals*, London, 1972, cf. 14, etc.; B.G. Burton-Bradley, "Transcultural Psychiatry", in P. Solomon and V.D. Patch (eds.), *Handbook of Psychiatry*, Los Angeles, 1974, pp. 659-660; R. Robertson, *The Sociological Interpretation of Religion*, Oxford, 1972, ch.5.

12. Cf. S. Thrupp (ed.), *op.cit.*

13. Trompf, "The Future of Macro-Historical Ideas", in *Soundings*, 62/1 (1979), p.80.

14. Considering the little that eventuated (by way of 'social spasms') in the year AD 1,000. Cf. esp. E. Pognon (ed. and trans.), *L'An Mille*, Paris, 1947.

15. Cf. esp. Cohn, *op.cit.*, T. Olson, *Millennialism, Utopianism, and Progress*, Toronto and London, 1982.

16. Cf. e.g., S.G.F. Brandon, *The Judgment of the Dead*, London, 1967, chs. 3, 5-6, and on a listing of Christian pamphlets, see below, ch.1, n.82.

17. I think here especially of Mahdism, cf. e.g. L.C. Brown, "The Sudanese Mahdiya", in Rotberg and Mazrui (eds.), *op.cit.*, pp. 145ff.

18. And behind him, note R. Zinssen's much earlier *Rats, Lice and History*, London, 1937, pp. 80-84.

19. For background, esp. J. Dollard, N.E. Miller *et al., Frustration and Aggression*, New Haven, 1939, esp. chs. 7-8 (frustration); A. Adler, *Menschenkenntnis*, Leipzig, 1947 edn., pp. 21-2 (relative deprivation and adjustment), S. Freud, *Civilization and its Discontents* (trans. J. Strachey),

New York, 1961; C.G. Jung *et al.*, *Man and his Symbols*, London, 1964, esp. pp. 72-82 (repression).

20. W. la Barre, "Material for a History of Studies of Crisis Cult: a bibliographic essay", in *Current Anthropology*, 12 (1971), pp. 3ff., cf. also Burton-Bradley, *loc. cit.*

21. For the details, *War Scroll*, (IQM), vii-viii, T. Müntzer, *Politische Schriften* (ed. C. Hinrichs), Halle, 1950, pp. 5ff.

22. Esp. Trompf, *Payback: the logic of retribution in Melanesian religion* for *(Studia Instituti Anthropos)*, St. Augustin (forthcoming), ch.1, pt.A. More generally, esp. on millenarist needs for power manifestation, rescue and control, see I.D. Suttie, *The Origins of Love and Hate*, Harmondsworth, 1960, pp. 115-6.

23. I derive this point from Desroche, *The Sociology of Hope*, (trans. C. Martin-Sperry), London and Boston, 1979, pp. 118-9, etc.

24. Trompf, *Payback, op.cit.*, ch.2, pt. A, 2, iii.

25. For background, cf. G. Lewy, *Religion and Revolution*, New York, 1974, pt.1.

26. 'New Church' adherents, for instance, in following Emmanuel Swedenborg, claim the events of the Millennium have already happened in the spiritual realm (back in the eighteenth century). For background, e.g., W. van Dusen, *The Presence of Other Realms*, London, 1975, ch.4.

27. The literature of the Jehovah's Witnesses is an obvious case in point. See, e.g., *You Can Live Forever in Paradise on Earth* (Watchtower Bible and Tract Society), New York, 1981 edn. Yet cf. ch.1 below.

28. Sierksma, *op.cit.*, p.250, etc. cf. R.J.Z. Werblowsky, "A New Heaven and a New Earth: considering primitive messianisms", in *History of Religions*, 5/1 (1965), p.170.

29. For background, L. Festinger, *The Theory of Cognitive Dissonance*, Evanston, 1957.

30. For an important example, F.E. Williams, "The Vailala Madness in Retrospect", in his *"The Vailala Madness" and Other Essays* (ed. E. Schwimmer), Brisbane, 1976, pp. 385ff.

31. On this last point, see esp. G. Schwartz, *Sect, Ideology, and Social Status*, Chicago and London, 1970.

32. For other contexts, cf. R. Firth, *Elements of Social Organization*, Boston,

1951, esp. pp. 111ff.; G. Shepperson, "Nyasaland and the Millennium", in Thrupp, *op.cit.*, p.157; Trompf, *Religion and Money; some aspects (Charles Strong Young Australian Scholar Lecture Series 1)*, Adelaide, 1980, pp. 4, 10-13.

33. On Cargo as redemption or salvation, esp. Burridge, *op.cit.*, esp. pp. 4-8; J. Strelan, *Search for Salvation; Studies in the History and Theology of cargo cults*, Adelaide, 1977; B.H. Schwarz, 'The Symbolic Significance of Cargo in Melanesian Cargo Cults' (Masters dissert., University of Aberdeen), Aberdeen, 1976.

34. Trompf, "Introduction", to Trompf (ed.), *Prophets of Melanesia*, Port Moresby, 1981 edn., p.8.

35. Some scholars using the term millenarism (or its cognates) for cargo cultism at least have been cautious. E.g. P. Christiansen, *The Melanesian Cargo Cult: millenarianism as a factor in cultural change*, Copenhagen, 1969, esp. pp. 7-48. Others have been rather unquestioning in their usage, e.g. I.C. Jarvie, *The Revolution in Anthropology*, Chicago, 1964, p.50, etc. (because he is concerned with different, more philosophical issues), Worsley, *op.cit.*; and N. Sharp, *Millenarian Movements: their meaning in Melanesia (LaTrobe Sociology Papers 25)*, Melbourne, 1976 (because of a neo-Marxist Tendency to accept 'millenarian movements' as a wide-embracing category for one species of anti-colonial protest in the Third World). See also n.45 below.

36. Trompf, *Payback, op.cit.*, ch.2. We await the work by M. Reay on *Transformation Movements*.

37. Cf. my arguments in "Mircea Eliade, etc.", *loc. cit.*

38. Lawrence, "Cargo Thinking as a Future Political Force in Papua and New Guinea", in *Journal of the Papua and New Guinea Society,* 1/1 (1966-7), pp. 20ff.

39. See Marx-Engels, *Selected Works* (For. Lang. Pub. Hse. trans.), Moscow, 1951, vol.1, pp. 35-40.

40. For background, Trompf, "God as the Source of Wealth", in *Melanesian Journal of Theology*, 3/1 (1987), pp. 74ff.

41. R.M. Berndt, "A Cargo Movement in the Eastern Central Highlands of New Guinea", in *Oceania*, 23 (1953), p.51; Cf. Trompf, "Doesn't Colonialism Make You Mad?" in S. Latukefu (ed.), *Papua New Guinea: a century of*

colonial impact, 1884 to 1984, Port Moresby, 1989 (forthcoming).

42. Note esp. Lawrence, *Road belong Cargo*, Melbourne, 1964, pp. 73ff.

43. Cf. M.W. Smith, "Towards a Classification of Cult Movements", in *Man*, 59 (1959), pp. 8ff., 25ff., Trompf, "Mircea Eliade, etc.", *loc.cit.* For a curious attempt to differentiate 'cargo cult' from 'cargo movement', note B.M. Knauft, "Cargo Cults and Relational Separation", in *Behavior Science Research*, 13/2 (1978), pp. 185, 202.

44. Trompf, *Payback, op.cit.*, ch.2, pt.A; "Independent Churches in Melanesia", in *Oceania*, 54/1 (1983), pp. 51ff; H.W. Turner, 'The Hidden Power of the Whites: the Secret Religion Withheld from Primal Peoples' (unpublished typescript, used with kind permission), Aberdeen, 1976. In other places I have discussed the development of myth-histories spun out as alternatives to the historical visioning of the ruling group(s). On Melanesian experiments with history, for example, see Trompf, "Macrohistory and Acculturation", in *Comparative Studies in Society and History*, 31/4 (1989), pp. 619ff. (see also ch.1). For an example fundamental to the founding of the Black Muslim movement, see the opening section of ch.9, cf. Malcolm X, *Autobiography*, New York, 1966 edn., pp. 164ff.

45. See n. 35. Cf. F. Steinbauer, 'Die Cargo Kulte als religionsgeschicht- liches und missionstheologisches Problem' ('Doctoral dissert., University of Erlangen-Nürnberg), Nürnberg, 1971, esp. rear chart; C.E. Loeliger and Trompf (eds.), *New Religious Movements in Melanesia*, Suva and Port Moresby, 1986, introd.

46. Trompf, "Mircea Eliade, etc.", *loc.cit.*

47. On Santoshi Mata, Trompf, *Religion and Money, op.cit.*, p.13, n. 24, cf. A.J. Quisar, *The Indian Response to European Technology and Culture, 1498-1707*, London, 1982, for longer term background. On Namu Myoho Renge Kyo, I rely on fieldwork, San Francisco and Santa Cruz, California, 1975, cf. H. Thomsen, *The New Religions of Japan*, Rutland and Tokyo, 1963, pp. 111ff. Note also the Thai cargo cult centred on Queen Victoria, J. Harger, "Is the Goddess Amused?", in *The Sunday Times* (United Kingdom), 24 Dec., 1972, Spectrum suppl., p. 9.

48. Thus *The Sun* (Sydney), 28 May, 1987, p.12.

49. Trompf, "Gambling and Religion: some aspects", in M. Walker (ed.), *The*

Faces of Gambling, Sydney, 1988 edn., pp. 225-8 (forthcoming).

50. Trompf, "Salvation in Primal Religion", in D. Dockrill and G. Tanner (eds.), *The Idea of Salvation* (*Prudentia* Spec. Issue) 1989, pp. 223-4, cf. R.N. Bellah, "Religious Evolution", in *American Sociological Review*, 29 (1964), pp. 358ff.; J. Baudrillard, *Le système des objets: la consommation des signes*, [Paris], 1968, esp. pp. 232-9.

51. Trompf, *Payback, op.cit*, ch.3, pt.A, 3, iii.

52. From Penelope Mortimer's *The Pumpkin Eater*, Harmondsworth, 1964, p.156. Cf. also I. Progroff, *The Dynamics of Hope*, New York, 1985, and on the capitalist ethos, esp. E. Fromm, *The Sane Society*, New York, 1955, ch. 5, C.

53. For famous discussions in point, T.S. Eliot, *Notes towards the Definition of Culture*, London, 1948, pp.28-29, 33; C. Geertz, "Religion as a Cultural System". in his *The Interpretation of Cultures; selected essays*, London, 1975, pp. 87ff.

54. Cf. esp. Lévi-Strauss's *Totemism* (trans. R. Needham), Boston, 1962, ch.5; K. Goldstein, "Concerning the Concept of 'Primitivity'", in S. Diamond (ed.), *Culture in History* (Paul Radin Festschrift), New York, 1960, chs. 99ff.

55. J. Morris, *Coast to Coast*, London, 1962, p.72, cf. chs. 17-18.

56. Daniel Defoe, *The Life and Strange Surprising Adventures of Robinson Crusoe of York, Mariner* (1719), Dent edn., London, 1906 (56), pp. 49, 94, 290, 299, etc., cf. G. Overton, *Cargoes for Crusoes*, New York, 1924, p.ii.

57. Cf. my comments in "Mircea Eliade, etc." *loc.cit.*, on Eliade's approach in *The Two and the One* (trans. J.M. Cohen), New York, 1962, pp. 126ff., and those of other scholars.

58. Cohn, *op.cit.*, pp. 281ff., etc.; J.L. Talmon, *The Origins of Totalitarian Democracy*, London, 1952; *Political Messianism*, London, 1960; Y. Talmon, "Millennarian Movements", *loc.cit.*, pp. 198-200; R.P. Feynman, "Cargo Cult Science", in *Engineering and Science*, (Calif. Inst. of Tech.), 37/7 (1974), pp.10ff.

59. Cf. J. Taubes, *Abendländische Eschatologie; Beiträge zur Soziologie und Sozialphilosophie*, Bern, 1947; D.L. Macrae, "The Bolshevik Ideology", in his *Ideology and Society*, New York, 1962, pp. 181-98; N.O. Brown, *Life Against Death; the psychoanalytic meaning of history*, New York, 1959, p.240.

60. For background, esp. M. Ginsberg, *Evolution and Progress (Essays in Sociology and Social Philosophy,* vol.3), London, 1961, ch.6; E.J. Sharpe, *Comparative Religion; a history,* London, 1987 edn.

61. Some of Bracht's work has been proposed for publication as *Mormonism: Magnificant Illusion;* Tillett's *The Elder Brother: a biography of Charles Webster Leadbeater* was published in London, 1982.

62. Cf. Tuveson, *Redeemer Nation: the idea of America's millennial role,* Chicago and London, 1968; esp. chs. 2-3, cf. pp. 175-86.

63. See Tillett and N. Drury, *The Occult Sourcebook,* London, 1978; *Other Temples, Other Gods,* Sydney, 1980.

64. Lacey's fellow editor was D. Denoon (Port Moresby, 1981), cf. Lacey, *Oral Traditions as History: an exploration of oral sources among the Enga of New Guinea* ([Doctoral] dissert. microf.), Madison, 1975. See also Lacey's *"To Limlimbur,* the 'wanderers'. Reflections on journeys and transformations in Papua New Guinea", in *Pacific Studies,* 9/1 (1985), pp. 83ff.

65. Gesch, *Initiative and Initiation; a cargo cult type movement in the Sepik (Studia Instituti Anthropos 33),* St. Augustin, 1985.

66. Lindstrom (ed.), *Drugs in Western Pacific Societies (Association of Social Anthropology in Melanesia 11),* New York, 1987.

67. Cf. M. Foucault, *The Archaeology of Knowledge* (trans. A.M.S. Smith), London, 1972.

68. Brookes, 'Spirit Movements in Timor - a Survey' (Masters Qualifying dissert., Melbourne College of Divinity), Melbourne, 1977; 'The Influences of Some Primal Religious Experiences on the Belief and Practices of Atoni Christians, etc.' (Masters dissert., Melb. Coll. Div.), Melbourne, 1980.

69. See esp. J. Barr, "Spiritistic Tendencies in Melanesia", in W. Flannery (ed.), *Religious Movements in Melanesia Today, 2 (Point Series 3),* Goroka, 1983, pp. 1ff.; "A Survey of Ecstatic Phenomena and 'Holy Spirit Movements' in Melanesia", in *Oceania* 54/2 (1983), pp. 109ff.

70. R. James, 'The Absence of Caribbean-Wide Nationalism', in Trompf (ed.), *Island and Small-scale Nationalisms,* Sydney (forthcoming); A. Boot and V. Goldman, *Bob Marley: Soul rebel - natural mystic,* New York, 1982.]

71. Cf., e.g. Walker, *Development of Pan-Arab and Isolationist Egyptian National Ideas in Twentieth Century Egypt (Jabatan Sejarah Universiti*

Malaya: Kertas Seminar Jabatan 6), Kuala Lumpur [1978].

72. On Independent Churches in Africa, esp. B.G. Sundkler, *Bantu Prophets in South Africa*, London, 1961 edn., D.B. Barrett, *Schism and Renewal in Africa*, Oxford, 1968.

73. Yet cf. M. Kilani, *Les cultes du cargo mélanésiens: mythe et rationalité en anthropologie*, Lausanne, 1983, pp. 171-9.

The Pacific Circle

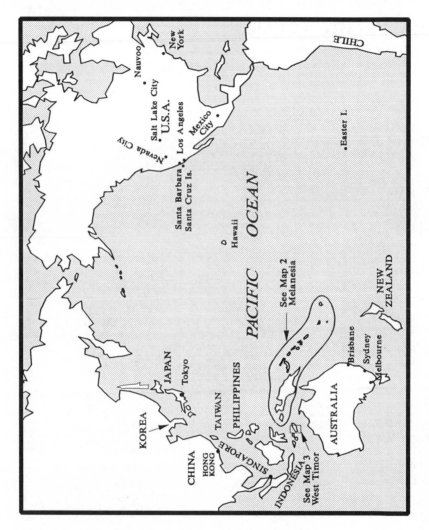

Map 1. The Pacific and its Rim

Chapter One

The Cargo and the Millennium on both sides of the Pacific

Garry Trompf

The Brotherhood of the Sun

On the eastern rim of the Pacific Ocean lies Santa Barbara, one of the world's richest 'small cities' (pop. *ca.* 300,000). A little less than 100 km from Hollywood and Los Angeles in the United States of America, it enjoys the mellow sunshine of southern California, with the exclusive wares of its *boutiquiers* shaded beneath stuccoed Spanish-style colonnades along its main thoroughfares. On my first visit in February 1975, the traffic lights along the twelve principal blocks of State Street appeared deliberately unsynchronized; drivers of the typically large limousines who plied along its course seemed trapped into surveying the merchandise at every available opportunity. If on subsequent visits such a license for fuel wastage had been abandoned, Santa Barbara has still continued to bask in sumptuousness. Rather symbolically, there lies to the southeast the plutocrats' suburban dreamland, leafy and sprawling Monticeto, and to the northwest, out beyond the fringes of a somewhat less salubrious Goleta, stands the home ranch of Ronald Reagan himself, the President of the 'eighties, protected by high-wire, hounds and a profusion of security guards.[1]

It was to Santa Barbara that one of its own sons, Norman Paulsen, returned in November, 1951. Paulsen (1929-   ), whose enthusiasm for a visionary quest to tap the secrets of the universe more than matched the impressive size and height of his own body, had been a young monk at the Self-Realization Fellowship hermitage, Encinitas (Los Angeles), over the five preceding years. His Master had been none other than Paramahansa Yogananda (1893-1952), acclaimed for his

Autobiography of a Yogi and for the first longer-term introduction of Yogic and Indian spirituality to America (from 1920).[2] Considering a relative uneventful-ness in the continuing life of the Encinitas Ashram itself, we may say that there have been two better known special claimants to the successorship of Yogananda's mission. One is the creator of the Ananda Community, the capti-vating "New Age Religious Community" at Nevada City, far to the north of Santa Barbara in central California. This is Donald Walters, otherwise named Swami Kriyananda (1926-), whose own *Autobiography of a Western Yogi* is enough to reveal his intentions as 'the Christlike Master's' continuator.[3]

The other is Norman Paulsen. Among different tokens of 'divine inheritance' he allegedly exerienced two post-mortem encounters with Yogananda during 1952-3, subsequently taking it upon himself to initiate others into *kriya yoga* (and what he then took to be the continuation of Yogananda's 'Brotherhood') at a Californian desert retreat "in the summer of 1955".[4]

Paulsen, however, eventually founded a community on a multitude of princi-ples additional to those expounded by his former *guru*. Two of its previous inmates have described it as "the most provocative communal group in America today",[5] yet perhaps at this stage it is enough to place it among various notable communes in the United States which sprang out of the 'counter-cultural' shift of consciousness in the 1960s, and to make plain that both Ananda and Sunburst may be examined within the wider context of burgeoning Californian preoccupa-tions with 'alternative life-styles'.[6] From the several studies of these experimen-tal communalisms we learn that most are recognizably 'utopianist' - re-enliven-ing a long tradition of American utopian communities, in fact - and not a few project visions of the future which are patently or virtually millenarist. Alongside or coupled with the traditional hope of the Second Coming and literal-ist projections of Christ's millennium-long rule over the Earth, stand intimations of a cosmic hinge between this blackening Age and a blessed one to come, or "the Dawning of the Age of Aquarius", and other variants.[7]

The commune founded by Paulsen is quite justifiably ranked under the mil-lennial umbrella, since, notwithstanding distinctly Eastern influences from the Self-Realization Fellowship, its ideological orientation has been significantly informed by Christian eschatological ideas. There are many things waiting to be said about its peculiarities as a 'millenarian movement', however, because of its religious platform's very complexity. It is preferable to begin with a general characterization of the Sunburst experiment and its career, after which we can proceed to an in-depth analysis of its millenarist - and cargoistic features.

The Brotherhood advertizes the essential unity of humanity's spiritual quests. Yogananda certainly conceived Yoga to provide a basis for a "Church of all Religions", yet his efforts at integrating different spiritualities focussed on 'the Indian' and 'the Christian".[8] Paulsen, for his part, drew together as many strands of the world's religions as he found valuable, welding them into what is now perhaps the most complex 'synthetism' of modern times. The coterie of young men and women surrounding him, at the time his new system was crystallizing in 1968, took the twin appellations of the Brotherhood of the Son or Sun (these two words being interchangeable) and Sunburst - the latter name acquiring fame in the commercial arena as the trademark of the Brotherhood's products. The organization's 'farm community' which grew steadily during the early seventies, in fact, took California's as yet unexploited organic food market by storm, and Sunburst natural foods (fruit juices, packaged dried fruits, etc.) were widely distributed throughout the United States, with the Sunburst *Cookbook* on shop shelves in the internationally burgeoning world of health food stores.[9] Yogananda had enjoined his followers "to encourage 'plain living and high thinking'", yet his famous soft brown eyes would have shown not a little surprise in finding the Brotherhood's expanded chain of supermarkets and warehouses in the Santa Barbara area by the later seventies, along with the diversity and complexity of Paulsen's teaching and communitarian interests.

By 1976 the Brotherhood possessed enough capital for a down-payment on an attractive 4,000 acre farm called 'Tajiguas', west of Goleta. Symbolically, it bordered on the (mere 500 acre!) property of Ronald Reagan himself; symbolically again, the swank Spanish-style ranch-house at its centre was unaffordable, to be purchased instead by film-star (and Scientologist!) John Travolta, who shared rights with the Brotherhood to their long-winding, security-fitted driveway. At this time 'prophet' Paulsen was at work on his autobiography (to be published in 1980), a fascinating entanglement of self-explanation and visionary rapportage partly designed to overcome the effects of a serious rift within the commune which had developed in the late seventies, and to relieve the Brotherhood of a bad press. A number of events had borne with them both division and opprobrium. With the revelation that over $10,000 worth of rifles and ammunition had been stockpiled at their farm in the Los Padres National Forest during 1975, local newsprint maligned the Brotherhood adherents as a millennial cult fortifying militarily for Armaggedon; and by 1980, with Charles Manson's notorious trial eleven years behind it, Paulsen's organization was actually rated among sects as "the most dangerous in the world".[10] Changes in space and time, including a variety of published reflections and comments up to the present, only go on to confirm how puzzling and different has been this new social creation, and how intriguing and intricate the web of ideas lying behind its manifestations. Millennial expectations were indeed critical for its emergence and continuance as well as for its image, but these expectations have been projected and character-ized with different emphases through time, and they have been intertwined with other, sometimes modifying, sometimes complementary, themes. Among these latter we may isolate what we may call special 'cargoistic' features.

A fuller treatment of this "great Californian commune" awaits another space.[11] It is my intention in this paper to explain first the attraction and ratio-nale of this particular movement in terms of millennial and cargoist thinking, though in such a way as to elucidate comparable ideological trajectories in the Western American *milieu*, and to open a still wider comparative investigation of related Pacific phenomena. It so happens that the shared religious views and interests of the Brotherhood of the Sun have become increasingly centred on the Pacific - both as ocean and vast region. Investigation of this movement is appo-site, in fact, if only for the kinds of symbolic qualities and cross-cultural implica-tions which beckon us to survey and draw comparisons with 'kindred phenome-na' within the compass of "the Pacific circle".[12] Not that the movement is sim-ply evocative in this respect or handy for the image-building so often required for such a *tour d'horizon* as this, for it also affords the opportunity for hard-nosed comparative study of some of the more impressive 'cult outbursts' on the Pacific rim, and an attempt to plot certain historical trends over the last one hun-dred years or so which help explain these eruptions.

Demanding our attention first, then, are the Sunburst movement's millenarian and cargoist characteristics as such, and in particular their intriguing ideological integration, before broader perspectives will be developed. As elucidated in my introduction, so-called cargoism and millennialism come to overlap as types of collective expectation when the imminent coming of an utterly transformed Cosmic Order is linked with the arrival of a radically different range of material goods. These goods are understood to issue from a 'supernatural' or quite supra-normal source - out of the world of spiritual beings.

The *locus classicus* of this interconnection, of course, lies in the Melanesian cargo cult, across the other side of the Pacific from California, yet since we have argued that religious projections of a Millennium or Cargo - when analyzed typo-logically by the investigator - have not been limited geographically, so we have already been bound to acknowledge that the association of the two sets of expec-tations is a cross-cultural phenomenon (see Introd.). The Melanesian cargo cult simply expresses the linkage most paradigmatically - those not ready for it might say 'most crudely or naively' - because products of Western technology have burst in on Stone-Age cultures as virtual miracles (more especially since the sec-ond half of the nineteenth century and thus since Europe's Industrial Revolution). Where this dramatic cultural contrast is lacking, though, oneiric visions which couple such impending events as the Second Coming of Christ or God's final intervention in world affairs with the dawn of an untold 'high-tech' Prosperity have still made their striking appearances.

In the introduction it was conceded that some collective dreams of a millenni-um reject the prospect of supernatural technology in favour of a superabundant yet 'natural' Paradisal Garden or some such archetype, all suggestions of tiresome work, factory production and hardware being driven out of the 'Heaven-on-Earth'. When millenarism and cargoism are wed, however, at least the images of modern technology and scientific achievement will be retained, so that the prophesied new Order can even be articulated as the very apex of Modernity rather than (exclusively) that of a Great spiritual Return, and at times it can bear a strong ring of Science Fiction (or some 'science mythology') about it. That, we shall show, is true of the Brotherhood of the Sun, and it is our object to account for this development in its context, and to use it as an instrument of trans-Pacific investigation, with the phenomena of Melanesian cargo cultism especially in mind.

Of great interest are the grounds on which integrations of millennial and car-goist expectations are based. In Melanesia, as in other so-called Third World contexts, cargo cultism is one by now famous response to European colonialism.

The expectations have arisen, then, not only out of native peoples' encounter with strange new goods *tout simple*, but also from within the broader context of these peoples being taken over, from the time of the earliest startling intrusions of outsiders (mainly by Europeans) to those stages when colonial impositions undermined group tradition, autonomy and identity. Within the complex interaction between ruler and ruled, moreover, there has flowed a variety of ideas, from both indigenous and introduced sources, which have been used by Melanesians to explain why the circumstances they face have arisen and by what manner of event they will be altered (cf. chs. 5-6). Cargo cult futurology, as one might have guessed, typically grants the Cargo (i.e. European-style goods and all that they symbolize), to the local blacks, the goods being thought to arrive supranormally at the cosmic hinge between the removal of white (or even neo-colonial) over-lordship and the breaking in of the Spirit Order (the return of the Ancestors, or the Second Coming of Jesus as proclaimed by the missionaries, etc.).[13]

The *Grundlagen* for comparable integrations of millenarism and cargoism, even if in remarkably different contexts, such as those of the West, also call for recognition and analysis. In the Brotherhood of the Sun, our present case in point, there is a conscious rejection of the prevailing (so-called First World) ethos, and one is bound to ask why this and other Western social experiments follow from dissatisfaction with the predominating patterns of society. Thus an important enquiry as any in the study of Western new religious movements - especially those of a millenarian ilk - concerns how or why shared paradigms about the past and present of 'this (unacceptable) world' provide the bases for most of these groups' cosmic anticipations, since their eschatological visions usually presage a replacement rather than offer glorification of existing conditions. As with the Melanesian phenomena, we are encouraged to look at broad contexts in which this visioning sharpens, and to explore the complexity of ideas in circulation through which expectant groups - as new religious outgrowths - give shape to their futures. In the modern West, with its societies so extensively industrialized and its high per capita expectations as to living standards, we would hardly be surprised when we find religious consciousness revolting against crass materialism in the name of other-worldliness, as it has since the Old Testament prophets and Plato.[14] Once we discover, however, that various groups hold out this-worldly millennial prospects which include and celebrate high-level technology, or the Cargo, then the business of analyzing the context, attitudes to it, and the interplay of ideas within it, become still more demanding and of fascination for comparative study.

Returning to the Brotherhood of the Sun, we are now bound to probe the senses and manner in which it presents both millenarist and cargoist *personae*. And there is no better means of doing this than through a straightforward elucidation of the movement's mature ideology or 'systematization of ideas', which owes its formulation almost exclusively to 'prophet-figure' Norman Paulsen. I use the term 'mature' advisedly, because the lineaments of the Brotherhood's 'belief-system' were evolving into greater coherence up until the mid-'seventies. It must needs be a small part of our task, admittedly, to touch on the stages in this evolution, and to trace dissected avenues of influence back to their earlier presence in other intellectual and spiritual milieux. On the other hand it is preferable to start with an account of Paulsen's fully-fledged theory, because, a remarkably complex syncretism as I have already intimated it is, its dual projection of the Millennium and the Cargo has only crystallized in time, bringing with it linkages between many ideas to explain past, present and future into the 1980s.[15]

The central core of Brotherhood belief is as much cosmically spatial as it is temporal. It has come to focus on the mythic (but to the members historically verifiable) continent of Mu, two major land masses of which were mysteriously obliterated from the central Pacific around 12,000 BC, leaving only Australia and New Guinea (each on the same continental shelf) as the only remains.[16] The lost Mu- or "Mother"(land) - is the sacred location on which the events most fundamental for the destiny of humanity are imagined to occur. The best clues to Mu's original inhabitants, for Paulsen, are in fact the Australian Aborigines and the New Guinea natives, yet like the black Africans and South American Indians, they were undergoing throughout prehistory the most painfully slow biological evolution on this continent toward the status of *homo sapiens*. Only by genetic interference could this process thus be expedited - to produce the modern human type known today. Many readers will be familiar with aspects of Paulsen's reconstruction: the "ancient foundation race" of modern humanity derives, not from some other terrestrial zone, but from outer space visitations.[17]

One million years ago, fleeing from a 'Star Wars' scenario in another part of our galaxy, physical beings - now to be identified with "the Gods of Heaven and

Earth" in various religions - descended to earth. These were the so-called Builders, who landed over 500 thousand years ago and created their first city in eastern Mu (800 miles west of present day Easter Island), who decided to speed up the genetic evolution of Earth's primitives (more than 400,000 years ago), who were discovered and had to fight with their enemies (from about 350,000 years ago), and who were still on their continent to create the conditions for *homo sapiens* in their laboratories around 200,000 B.P. From this last act, the four created races - bearing the colours of Red, Blue, Yellow and White as their Builders' "image" (cf. Gen. 1:26) - spread across the face of the globe, having had revealed to them the Tree of Life (or "knowledge of the central nervous system and its forces and powers") (cf. Gen. 2:9). Because of the continuing conflict between the Builders and their enemies (the Nephilim, cf. Gen. 6:4), however, these races were scattered apart from each other. The Nephilim, further, tried their own hands at producing comparable creatures. Far from being God's special creation, in fact, Adam and his descendants turn out to be none other than rebellious products of these cosmic perpetuators of evil, and the former only escape enslavement through the whisperings of a wise serpent (Gen. 3:1-7). As for the Builders themselves, in the course of time their peaceful Naacals, or the priests of Mu, who are their descendants, left the motherland. Some 30,000 years ago they trekked via Burma and India to Egypt, arriving well in advance of great wars and cataclysms. Then comes the Earth's collision with a huge asteroid which destroyed the continent of Atlantis (in the Atlantic) - an event causing the Great Flood - as well as Mu's substantial disappearance beneath the Pacific ocean around 12,000 BC. These upheavals further sealed the separation of the true 'foundation races'.[18]

Apart from the capacity of this "mythological macro-history"[19] to solve the imagined riddles of humankind's origins - special Creation being made to square with Darwinian evolutionism, the presumption that intelligent life exists on other planets melding with traditional geocentrism, and a kind of 'polytheism' being admitted in without denial of a God who lies behind all - Paulsen's teachings about Mu are also meant to disclose immense significance for present human experience and the world's presaged destiny. The Builders are none other than God's angels and their Mu has not been limited to the Earth. References to *Mus* as divine 'space vehicles' in ancient Mesopotamian records have persuaded

Paulsen that the Builders persistently contributed to human civilization through making contact from space, and that the 'flying saucer' sightings of recent times are of the Builders' spaceships in constant operation. Indeed the liveliest and most content-filled of Paulsen's personal visionary experiences, disclosures from the other side by which he has maintained his 'charismatic authority'[20] over the Brotherhood and added more and more pieces to his syncretistic Story-Myth over three decades, are those to do with contacting the Builders, even flying in their crafts. If Paulsen had early applied *kriya yoga* techniques for 'astral travelling' or bliss experiences of the Universe as a whole, what he made of strange lights in the Californian desert between 1950 and 1961 afforded many more specific details - later related to Paulsen's reading - for filling out the cosmic drama. In the very pyramidal shape of the space Mu, indeed, he apparently found the embodiment of macrohistoric continuity, reflecting the ancient technological achievements on continental Mu and the Builders' contribution to the birth of civilizations (with Sumerian ziggurats, Egyptian and Meso-American pyramids, etc.), as well as the key to the world's future (cf. Plate 2).[21]

The future turns out to be a Return of the divine presence(s). It is structurally analagous to the reactualization of Paradise once Lost as the famous (largely Augustinian) Christian paradigm has it.[22] It is also parallel, if we can here herald our subsequent discussion, to the return of the ancestors, or to those culture heroes from mythic primordiality we find awaited in much Melanesian cargo cult consciousness. The millennium above all entails "The Return of the Ancients", the angelic Builders, who must win in the final struggle over their evil enemies, yet whose victory for good happens to be possible only with the collapse and virtual destruction of modern society as we know it. The thin thread of the Builders' influence on the earth at the time of crisis - the current time - is understood to be vested in Paulsen's mind, which they have specially "programmed" to hold the mysterious truth until the world situation is ripe for radical change to the better.[23] The Cargo in this Millennium, we note, cannot therefore simply be some superabundance of the technics and commodities already prevalent in the West, and associated with "greed for wealth and power", "prestige (and) ... the treadmill of competition" that are "destroying any concept of brotherhood".[24] It is rather a superior technology, an access to materials currently unknown to humanity and an extraordinary harnessing of the universe's as yet unexploited powers, particularly those of the Sun, so that men and women can truly "follow the simple laws of God and nature".[25] The paradisal image of the perfect Garden, a traditional idealization meant to be sought in the creation of the commune,[26] is integrated with the dream of scientific miracle. Even the space *Mus* are revealed to contain lush internal gardens under the astounding constructions of their domes, made by those with the "ability to create any new environment" they want. And Paulsen has received the materialization of mysterious objects betokening that "The Motherland" is "now returning again", which is by clear implication the restoration of Eden.[27]

Much more could be added to this part of the exposition, but it seems hardly advisable to press on without first tracking down some of the sources of this cosmic visioning, as much to elucidate the western American and Pacific rim ethos in which it has arisen as to show further how the totality of Paulsen's thought was pieced together, and what relation his teachings bear to more prevailing thought patterns in western America. The task of locating sources is not easy, mind you, if only because of Paulsen's proclivity to interlace many and varied speculative threads, and because his writings - without footnotes and intended to reinforce his own authority as a commune's "prophet" - rarely indicate literary bases of inspiration. Here, however, we can at least cover the most obvious well-springs.

If we are (for methodological reasons) to set aside Paulsen's own revelations, the 'sacred geography' of Mu was apparently mediated to Paulsen through two sets of written sources, first those of mythic (or fictitious) archaeology, especially that found in the works of Col. James Churchward (1880?-1930?) on "the Lost Continent of Mu" (published in the early 'thirties), and secondly those of occultist Age theory propagated in the not unrelated literature of the Rosicrucian and Theosophical type in California.[28] Churchward is notorious for the kind of claim frequently made in the neo-Gnostic "Ancient Wisdom Family" of small religions, namely that of access to the true source of spiritual enlightenment - in his case Mu's archives, long stored in India. He was allegedly able to decipher the lost civilization's hieroglyphs simply by letting their meaning well up from his inner consciousness.[29]

Paulsen acknowledges Churchward as a key authority. The former's location

Plate 1. Norman Paulsen and his friends

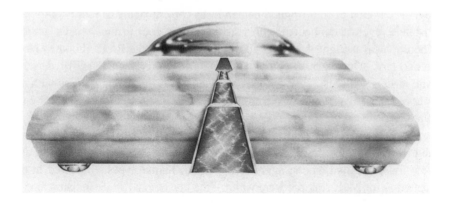

Plate 2. A Space *Mu* as experienced in Paulsen's Visions

of the first 'true' human beings on Motherland Mu, his reference to migrating Naacals (or Mu priests), and his acceptance that the megaliths of Oceania and pre-Christian America are the remnants of this lost 'original' civilization, are all Churchwardian features.[30] But the themes pursued about this lost continent are also from more mainstream occult quarters. Rosicrucians and Theosophists used the name Lemuria much more than Mu, Theosophy's founder Helena Blavatsky contending that Lemuria was peopled by humanity's 'Third Root Race', of which nothing survived but "Australia, ... a few surviving islands ... on the face of the Pacific and a large bit of California".[31] The Brotherhood of the Sun have acknowledged this identification by naming their Los Padres ranch 'Lemuria', and making much of the fact that one of the smaller Santa Cruz or Channel Islands off the Santa Barbara coastline was called 'Limu' by the local (Chumesh) Indians (see below).[32] Rosicrucian W.S. Carré was an important contemporary of Churchward's who was first to give something of a cosmic significance to Santa Barbara and the climatically pleasant West Coast, declaring it "unquestionably the only now-existing location of the earliest races of men who have reached a civilized state of development".[33]

Over and above these influences, and although remaining set within the framework of a once flourishing, then fated Pacific Eden (Churchward) and of an unfolding but secret Divine Plan (the Wisdom Family tradition), other bits and pieces of Paulsen's myth-history have special derivations, a few well worth noting. The notion of four original human races corresponding to four colours, for instance, even if connected with teaching about four primary races in sub-Theosophical thought, has been above all related by the Brotherhood to Hopi Indian lore. Quoted most commonly in this regard is White Bear Fredericks, who made a significant visit to the commune in 1972 (marrying Paulsen with his fourth wife, Mary!), and who told how the four distinct colours of Hopi corn types represented the four primary skin colours of humanity.

On Paulsen's understanding, again partly inspired by Churchward, the peaceable Hopi were red descendants of Mu fortunate to escape the cataclysm and now living isolated among aggressive, inferior human types. Involved in the scattering for Mu's collapse were whites - the mysterious 'white Indians' reported by early European explorers to inhabit the Santa Cruz islands,[35] so that between these islands and Hopiland, or between two areas sacred to the memory

of the Motherland, all the projects and expansions of Sunburst have been enacted. A broad wedge of territory running from Santa Barbara toward the Hopis'
Mesa Verde (or Four Corners) was considered through most of the 1970s to be
the land (actually the 'Empire of the Sun') destined for the Brotherhood, a piece
of sacred geography expressive of the community's critical role in a hinge-point
of world history.[36]

The motif of conflict between cosmic powers sitting behind and alongside
Paulsen's version of the Mu saga draws, once again, on more than one source.
Intriguingly, certain Amerindian - specifically Californian Indian - myths evoke
such a struggle.[37] The specific idea of the Nephilim as Forces of Darkness (=
cosmic deviants or Fallen Angels), goes back to the ancient work of I Enoch
(esp. 86:1-6), a scripture known to Paulsen. The idea also smacks of Seventh
Day Adventist theology about the great battle (or "Controversy") between Christ
and Satan in the heavens while events on earth are played out below. Ellen G.
White's form of Adventism, after all, has been an influential Californian phenomenon, and a millenarism entailing a pioneering concern for cooperative
health food marketing.[38] As for other neo-Gnostic strands, Paulsen's own bibliography fails to acknowledge his reading into Alice Bailey, literature of the 'I
Am' movement, and a mystical book by George van Tassal about flying saucer
visitations. With these and further works, Paulsen webbed his account of
Creation and the Builders. God emerges as the primordial "Spirit Mother and
Father", their divine offspring Light as "The Great Central Sun-Son (or 'Sun of
God'), and after Him come the Angel Men and Women[39] who created the four
(coloured) races of the True Humans in Heaven - who are the Builders (and by
implication the supreme Brotherhood) before they arrive at Mu. With the denigration of Adam, further, and his rather neo-Ophite favouritism toward the
Serpent, Paulsen's neo-Gnosticism is all the more blatant.[40]

If all these aeonic developments are redolent with West coast tracts of occult
Wisdom and 'cosmic consciousness', however, the ideas of 'astronautical' genetic interference with Earth's backward primitives, of horrendous 'Star Wars' and
their massive consequences before known civilizations, and of space-visitor's
contributions to these later technological achievements, hail before all from
Erich von Däniken, whose writings were enthusiastically discussed within the
Brotherhood in the early seventies.[41] And the datum which enables Paulsen to

identify continental Mu with the spaceships of divine or angelic astronauts was provided by a rather more serious exercise in occult or speculative archaeology - Zecharia Sitchin's *The Twelfth Planet* - which accepts the translation of the Sumerian word *mu* as rocket-ship. Sitchin's genealogy of the ancient Sumerian gods provided Paulsen with names he could grace upon those figures allegedly involved in the great conflict between Builders and Nephilim, and thus introduced him to famous works on Mesopotamian archaeology and religion by which he could enshroud his reconstruction in a veiled garb of scholarship.[42]

We are hardly to forget the Bible in all this. It has been one of Paulsen's fundamental interests to make more sense of the Bible than he thought was managed by conventional Christianity, and to help others "find Christ outside organised Christianity" in his "Judeo-Christian Brotherhood".[43] What the Californian has striven for in his teaching is to amalgamate much in the more traditional, if not literal approach to 'salvation history' with both Gnosticizing and Eastern spiritualizations of this conventional framework. Yogananda, of course, had treated Christ as but one of a series of *avatars* or else "Great Prophets" - with Krishna, Rama, the Buddha, etc. - even if at the same time quoting very freely from the New Testament to suit the Western context. This made it easier for him to speak of "the Christ" issuing primordially from God, and of the Second Advent as a coming again to the receptive "souls of men anywhere".[44] Paulsen has taken a step further to secure 'the best of both worlds' by characterizing Christ as the supreme Builder.

In his pre-existence Christ is the Angel Man who enters into the sphere of, or becomes one with, the "Great Central Sun-Son", somewhat like Origen's ancient paradigm of the one perfect soul among all the pre-existent (human) ones - that of Jesus - being forged like an iron in the fire with the Divine. Paulsen would have drawn Origen's anathema, mind you, for distinguishing two types of humans, one of earth and one like fallen angels, the old Gnostic teaching about this second category having its parallel in Paulsen's reference to space beings.[45] But for Paulsen Christ is deliberately allowed to retain his cosmic centrality. He is the key Agent behind Creation, the monitoring of the cosmic conflict, and the achievement of the final victory of his fellow Builders. Something of the Logos doctrine is maintained, then, and there are shades of the old patristic doctrine of the visible appearances of Christ before his Incarnation. We are left with the clear impression, however, of the heavenly corporeality of Christ and of other 'divinities', something strongly smacking of Mormon teaching. Paulsen picks for his Biblical examples, not the stranger who visits Abraham by the oaks of Mamre or wrestles with Jacob until the break of day, but the mysterious "Melchisedec" [*sic*], a figure central to the Mormon (and before that Masonic) priesthood.[46]

Melchisedec (-Christ), perforce of Paulsen's macro-historical framework, was vital for the achievements on Mu long before Abraham (see below). Christ as Jesus of Nazareth turns out to be Melchisedec in disguise, with the supreme Builder filling up the natural man Jesus "like an empty bottle" at the time of the Baptism - an old tack of 'Adoptionist' Christology mediated during the present century in Theosophical and related circles.[47] Melchisedec-Christ thus dips in and out of history - even issuing Paulsen's very first spiritual call as a lad by handing him "Christ's New Testament", and later healing him of appendicitis - and he has also disclosed himself to Paulsen as the crucial behind-the-scenes operator on the Builders' space vessels.[48] The freedom of movement assumed, and the association of Christ with astounding technological potential, enables Paulsen to explain to his own satisfaction why it is the Sun is such a predominating symbol in the world's religions - especially among the great pyramid builders as far apart as Egypt and the southern Americas.[49] Although he has apparently spent time on their theories, Paulsen has no need of the diffusionists (from Perry Smith to Thor Heyerdahl),[50] because he refers similarities back to the activities of the Builders (more von Däniken's style). Legends of the 'White God' of Meso-America, for example, indicate ante-diluvian visits by the Builders, whose names are remembered and who supervised the temple building even before the Biblical Flood.[51]

The resulting eschatology possesses the dual advantage of allowing for both a mystical Christ lying behind significant, recurrent physical appearances and a world in which the Son can express himself in something as modern and fabulously technological as a space capsule and a Star Wars-type struggle. In one mystical sense the Second Coming is an ever-present, inner possibility, yet in the concretely futurological sense events will occur which betoken the intensification and resolution of a final combat, followed by the genuine "Return of the Ancients".[52] There were a few years (1973-4), it seems, in which Paulsen supposed that these momentous events would unfold in the Holy Land. At that stage he and the Brotherhood were the proud possessors of one of the largest schooners off the American West Coast, and Paulsen, who derived his Christian name from Northman and made something of the supposition that his Viking ancestors had once attempted to re-link the scattered races of Mu, contemplated the possibility of sailing his disciples to Israel to see the action.[53] By 1975, however, it was clear to him that the projected 'Empire of the Sun' in California itself was the key focal-point of the world's impending transformation. If trying to eschew talk of a literal return of Christ for all to see "on the clouds of Heaven" (Dan. 7:13) and on American soil - a visioning which, along with his talk about pre-existent souls, a lost continent, wandering tribes and divine visits to the American Indians, would have put his position close to that of Mormonism (cf. ch. 2 and see below) - he was nonetheless amply specific about the forthcoming Armageddon-type eruption. "We see our world today", he wrote in 1975(?), "sitting on the brink of destruction".

> Now come the famines across the faith of the earth, just as he [= Jesus Christ] said they would, right on schedule. We have about 2-1/2 years left - no more ... All government agencies will begin to collapse. Money will be worth nothing; they'll burn it in the streets, as well as the cities. It's going to be a most difficult situation. I hate to look at it. But you all, ...who love God, must survive and go on ... I feel, in this Brotherhood, that I am surrounded by God's angels.[54]

I suspect this way of putting things was highly informed by the publication of Yogananda's 'World Prophecies' by Kriyananda at Nevada City (in 1973). Paulsen, however much his syncretistic tendency had taken him away from the teachings (and especially Indianizing thrust) of the Spiritual Realization Fellowship, never retracted his self-understanding as Yogananda's successor. The meditative approach to the Brotherhood's worship, in any case, which still mainly consists of silent contemplation in the lotus position and entails techniques of *kriya yoga*, derives directly from Paulsen's days at Encinitas and from his first attempts in 1955 to pass on to a group of friends what he had learnt at the hermitage. That remains true even though Paulsen has now come to teach that the Builders taught the same yogic techniques on Mu in distant Antiquity, and that a tradition of true worship and community can be traced back through such groups as the Hopi and the Essenes (among whom lived Jesus the Christ).[55] It should not be surprising, then, that Paulsen should snatch from Yogananda's edited predictions, images of a world racked by "a terrible depression ... far worse than the last", and by upheavals in which

> millions will starve to death, or be killed in global wars as nations strive to exploit the available food supplies.[56]

The book of Yogananda's prophecies and Paulsen's projections from the mid-seventies, further, also have in common the notion that there will be survivors of the coming Crisis, and for both Yogananda, and Kriyananda as a closer follower, those survivors would be members of tight-knit, food-storing "cooperative communities".[57] On the other hand, Yogananda linked the problems ahead to Indian Age-Theory, to the conclusion of the worst macro-cycle called the *kali yuga* which would eventually give way to "A New World" of the *krita yuga*.[58] For Paulsen the images used about the future have a more complex lineage. What is set out in realistic detail in Yogananda's World Prophecies as the political economy to come is also related to Biblical projections of false prophets, the second coming of Elijah, of Christ, the four horses of the Apocalypse, Armageddon and that final cosmic battle between the forces of light and darkness which the Builders are destined to win. After their victory the Builders will return in large numbers, bearing with them their wisdom. Their supreme technology - the 'Gold of the Gods' if you like - will be humanity's. Thus will dawn none other than "the Age of Aquarius, or the Age of the Brotherhood", the phrases Paulsen preferred to describe the Millennium, the era being ushered in which will take "one thousand years ... (to) be loosed".[59]

Paulsen's own self-understanding as the "signpost" to the new Age is fundamental to the whole story, if kept somewhat veiled by the Brotherhood's literature. Born an Aquarian (3rd February), Paulsen holds that the Age of Aquarius broke in with a major solar eclipse on his 33rd birthday in 1962. At night on the same date he was arrested for drunken driving, irreparably damaged his foot with a fall in gaol and subsequently saw a vision of Lucifer's incursions on the Earth.[60] But he also claims that "the Second Coming of Christ began" on New Year's day just over twelve months earlier (1961), when he heard angels' songs announcing it, encountered space *Mus* in the Californian desert, and was allegedly designated by Christ in one of them as "a member of the eternal and immortal priesthood created by ... Divine Parents".[61] From those early days until the mid-'seventies, Paulsen evidently identified himself with the Elijah, "the prophet before the great and terrible day of the Lord" (Mal. 5:5) who was also John the Baptist (cf. Mk. 9:13) and conceived as a charioteer returning from outer space (II Kgs. 2:11, cf. Rev. 6:1-8).[62] Paulsen's role in connection with Aquarius was taken to be 'universalized' when he was invited as the leader of the Brotherhood to speak to the Aquarius Conference in February 1972, at which meeting he declared "the full energy" of the Aquarian Age to have begun on January 1, 1971, the year "the bunch of Aquarians" at the natural food centre called "The House of Aquarius" in Santa Barbara got themselves fully established in the mountains.[63] After Paulsen's marriage ceremony with Mary 'Mu' in 1972, furthermore, on the very same birthday they each shared, the unexpected officiant White Bear was reported to have designated the Brotherhood's founder *Pahana*. This is "the long lost white brother" expected by the Hopi to return certain missing pieces of their tablets and to "work out with them a new and universal brotherhood of man" (after the eventual conclusion of an oppressive rule).[64] Even descendants of Mu, then, had singled out Paulsen as cosmically crucial, and interviews among Brotherhood members revealed that the events of the marriage were by far the most influential in legitimating Paulsen's 'charismatic authority'.

By 1977, however, it was palpable to members that their leader was taking on a role equivalent to Christ. Along with twelve elders surrounding him (with some of them taking apostles' names), others were dubbed Elijah and John the Baptist, and the prophet became increasingly aloof from his communards, implying for himself the highest status of all while at the same time engendering the distrust of a weighty minority bent on asking critical questions. The re-titling of his autobiography from *Sunburst* to *Christ Consciousness* is indicative of the shift.[65] On one reading of the phenomenological approach, we perhaps ought to be content with leaving matters at this - by noticing, as with all religions, how certain happenings and persons acquire more and more significance over time. When we realize that new meanings were constantly being fed into the Brotherhood's 'ideological pool' by Paulsen himself, on the other hand, we are bound to ask probing queries about his motives and manipulations.

Reflecting on Paulsen's autobiography, and remaining attentive to millenarian and cargoistic features, one may fairly conclude it to be richer than any for the psychoanalytical study of a religious leader in the contemporary world. Six hundred pages from a bricklayer untrained in the literary arts is staggering enough; yet it is the very *naiveté* of the work - the ingenuousness with which the most extraordinary visions and 'encounters of the third kind' are related, the shifts between grand elation and utter despair, his sad trailing through broken marriages, and the open references to his alcoholic problems and a stint in a psychiatric hospital - which all reveal a pathology of self-acclamation and self-deception. The motivation for writing the massive tome itself is clearly shown to have most to do with the rising number of defections between April and July 1979.[66] The phenomenologist of religion may tend to shy away from psychoanalytic interpretations for fear of letting religious claims speak for themselves, but the recognition of self-aggrandisement for what it is - *als Solches* to use Edmund Husserl's phrase[67] - will be essential in this case for understanding the very pragmatics, or day-to-day decision making, consequent upon Paulsen's millenarist and cargoist *mentalités*.

Late in 1974 Paulsen charged his followers to prepare for Armageddon. He ordered the building of a concrete fortress, the half-built ruins of which remain at Lemuria ranch. The fort, significantly, bore gun-slits in its walls. The Brotherhood was expected to have to defend itself against the rise of "the ruthless", who would be bent on destroying "the innocent" in the Last Days. At 'Lemuria' the innocent who fled from Santa Barbara to the desert would find refuge; over 30 tons of soya beans were sealed and packed in the fort's storage space and each commune member was "required to have a backpack with clothing and first aid supplies ready to go", when the great 'Trouble' erupted. Whatever antipathy Paulsen and the members detected among the Santa Barbara populace, and any occasional insults and shotgun outbursts they experienced in the mountains (on Gibraltar Road), were taken as symptoms of approaching conflict.[68]

Most important, however, is the 'engineered pretext' which was used to justify Paulsen's purchase of an arsenal. The leader ordered the Secretary, then David Eddy, to shoot five rounds from a rifle into the façade of the Sunburst office on Cota Street very early in 1975. Reporting the pretended attack, the

Plate 3. Paulsen leading the Brotherhood's Worship at Sunburst Farm

Plate 4. 'Tajiguas' Ranch surrounding the Weaver family

local Sheriff's office advised Paulsen to take measures for the community's defence. He did just that. It was in this general context that Paulsen pulled a revolver from his car glovebox and held one Lauro Ortiz at gunpoint, when he thought he had spotted some drug smuggling in front of a chemist shop; a presumptive act for which he was arraigned and later fined in court (Jan.-July, 1975). It was in this context, much more significantly, that "a secret army was prepared with a high stockpile of sophisticated automatic weapons" and "thousands of rounds of ammunition", concentrated at the fortress. The revelation of the details in the press took many Brotherhood members by surprise and led to the first wave of defections from the movement.[69]

After this exposé only half of the weapons were returned, so that, three years later, when Paulsen was arrested for a drunk-driving charge and beaten up by police for resisting arrest, he was able to give a compulsive order for two 10-wheeled army trucks from 'Tajiguas' to be driven through the County Sheriff's office walls in reprisal. Brotherhood members were ordered by a telephone message to man the trucks with automatic rifles and open fire on making entrance, but fortunately select elders persuaded Paulsen to countermand his own orders, and he later preached about the episode as a 'test'.[70] That episode belongs to a later situation in which the very possession of the great 'Tajiguas' ranch itself became the focus of eschatological and cargoistic lines of thought. Sunburst had become a multi-million dollar enterprise and Paulsen's order reflects the mixture of his heightened sense of power at the time and the growing opposition to his personal style both within and without the Brotherhood.

His concluding autobiographical reflections of 1980 on 'Tajiguas' encapsulate much of what we have been arguing about the oneiric expectations of the movement and its 'prophet', as well as the 'megalomaniacal-looking' tendencies emerging in Paulsen's leadership style. The ranch and the whole Sunburst enterprise are characterized as "a base station for the Builders", symbolic of the near-to-be realized return of Eden, the communism of Mu, and of the once-lost order of technology in which "young men and women could become space pilots or scientists, or pursue whatever trade they felt drawn to". His statement of this 'neo-cargoist' dream sits side by side with the stated principle that "the by-product of living a life of harmony with the Spirit is to have physical abundance".[71] And on the second last page of his enormous work, Paulsen blatantly lays bare his extraordinary and cosmically-central rôle at history's turning-point. He is and has always been a Builder, and a militant one at that.

> I volunteered to be a warrior over one million years ago. I remember it all vividly and only make this claim to verify my position in all this. I was, at one time, one of the ancient rulers of Mu and her people. I have been the captain of many divine celestial Mus in the past. The 'Star Pilot' [the schooner] is a reflection of my own star-ship out in space, lost forever in the war. I have been space ship-wrecked many times and marooned on planets waiting to be picked up. I volunteered for this mission and I will see it through to the end.[72]

The student of religion has at this point a difficult choice to make between what we might call 'purist phenomenology' and 'critical realism', between an unprejudiced, relatively sympathetic account of an individual's magnetizing leadership and an open recognition of Paulsen's utter self-aggrandisement. In more psychological terms it is the choice between a more accepting avoidance of literalism - treating Paulsen's self-account as "secrets of the vast Profound within us", to use Dicken's phrases[73] - and the isolation of some socio- or psycho-pathic syndrome. In terms of the study of altered states and of the psychology of religion in particular it is the choice between a less suspicious acknowledgement of 'bliss experiences' and a stress on the fictive, fabricating, dare I say over-imaginative factor.[74] Whatever should be the right and proper methodological assessment for the case, though, there is no gainsaying that the continuing systematization of the Brotherhood's ideology relates directly to the ongoing business of Paulsen's own self-estimations, and that the further heightening of claims about himself in the late 'seventies were commensurate with crises borne by his organization.

Communards were leaving - 62 between April and July of 1979 - and mainly for the avowed reason that Paulsen was not what they thought he had been or what he now pretended to be. If these members had stayed loyal through the years of public criticism about the cache of weapons at 'Lemuria', this was because they did not have problems over the necessity of violence in the Last Days. But when it came to disillusionment about their leader - when it appeared that allegations of his alcoholism, drug-taking, manipulations, pediastry and promiscuity could be substantiated - they left, caught, and most definitely feeling very burnt, in a 'cosmic vacuum' (such store having been set on the

Brotherhood's and its prophet's role in world history).

During my interviewing not a single member disavowed drug-taking before entrance into the commune, stating that it was precisely the prohibition against "tobacco, alcohol, drugs of any kind or eating of flesh" that attracted them and met their basic needs at the time most.[75] In the first half of the 1970s, moreover, celibacy was the prevailing rule (even if no one, admittedly, easily or usually kept to it), and although marriage and child-bearing were accepted later in the decade, teaching about the rediverting of sexual energies to higher things was consistently voiced.[76] During 1975, intriguingly, Paulsen began supplementing Yogananda's practice of *kriya yoga* with teachings from the Taoist text *The Secret of the Golden Flower* (which in its 1975 re-introduction by Charles San makes more of sexual sublimation), as well as from Essenic monastic regulations.[77] For Paulsen to betray his own prescriptions, therefore, as well as to dominate the commune's finances to purchase a $10,000 Jeep, hire Lincoln limousines for official visits, earmark over $150,000 for personal expenditure each year, take off to Palm Springs for extended holidays (with his wife whom he later spurned), and to arrogate such authority to himself that he was as Jesus and could condemn defectors to Hell, was too much to accept from those convinced that allegations of hypocrisy were right.[78]

Troubles tumbled one upon another by 1981. An attempt to replace Paulsen by former Yogananda disciple Rev. C. Bernard had failed; defectors had tried (unsuccessfully) to get back their personal investments in court; competing big business enterprises went into the 'organic foods market' and began undercutting Sunburst's prices; Paulsen and the organization found themselves less able to pay bills and mortgage payments; Santa Barbaran officialdom (with the Inland Revenue Service included) questioned the legal propriety of Sunburst's doings both on land and sea; and the dream of escape to Katherine, in the desert far north of that one last great slab of Mu, came up against both hard logistical odds and the opposition of Australia's Minister for Immigration.[79] By September 1982 the remaining Brotherhood members had packed their bags, and, with the hope that proximity to Mormon territory and ideology would be more conducive to their goals, they resettled on a half-million acre ranch in Wells, northeastern Nevada, turning their backs on California forever.[80]

The Millennium and the Cargo: From Western America to Eastern Australia

As the Introduction already hints, many of the elements of the Brotherhood's career have shown up in the millenarisms and dreams of prosperity through international 'contemporary history'. As earlier suggested, also, sectors of the Pacific rim contain a wealth of material ideal for comparative analysis and the tracing of influence. To begin with 'classic Western' millenarisms, we find them abounding in the United States western states, where religious pluralism is currently rampant. The West has harvested years of westward movements by disaffected families and groups, who have typically deemed the order they left behind to deserve a Last Judgement and have looked upon their new home as a land of total, golden Opportunity.[81] Sectarianism has reached its extremes with the so-called 'garage churches' of California, churches virtually 'privatized' for extended families or tiny coteries, who hear husband and wife preacher/singer combinations over a microphone in confined sheds. Pamphlet upon pamphlet, book upon book which herald Jesus' Return, Armageddon (or a Third World War), the Apocalypse, the Last Judgement, and the General Resurrection, probably have their largest readership in western America; and along the coastline, the more conventional Christian expectation that it will not be long before God 'sews up history', sits alongside and is often compounded with 'disaster consciousness' - the threat of a nuclear holocaust and World War 3, or the more immediate possibility of an earthquake comparable to that brought by the San Andreas fault-line in 1906.[82] Small wonder, then, that the theme of survival we uncovered in connection with Sunburst makes its appearance in literature which is most popular along the seaboard, in science fiction as well as Christian eschatological and more esoteric catastrophe-oriented writing. From Roger Corman's *The Day the World Ended* (1955), moreover, to the television series *Alien* and such films as Spielberg's *Close Encounters of the Third Kind* (1977) and Coppola's *Apocalypse Now* (1979), Hollywood has done much to capitalize upon these prominent *mentalités*, injecting into the bargain the notion that non-earthlings and their arrival are bound up with the destiny of Earth and with the saving of a worthy remnant.[83]

We are not to forget the 'New Age' and 'Aquarian' themes of the 1960s, with their attendant 'Hippies' and 'Flower Children', nowhere more in the lime-light than at Haight-Ashbury and Berkeley, on the other side of San Francisco Bay. The many connections between millenarism and this new age conscious-ness still await detailed explorations. A few scholars have noted the visioning of God seated in great Judgement and other apocalyptic motifs from among those youths reporting so-called 'Acid [or LSD] trips'; perhaps the most famed of the groups who were introducing electric music at the time took the portentous name of "The Grateful Dead", and were among those announcing that the psychedelic revolution was the end of the known world; while the 'Jesus freaks', concentrat-ed most heavily in Los Angeles, spoke as much about the downfall of the stale established order as about living Christianity in faith and with a simple commu-nal and alternative life-style.[84] Communes themselves, most prolific in the American west, were symptoms of both new age and millenarian orientations (see above). As one young communand and "earth-lover" put it

There's a lot of people who want the Apocalypse. Instead of looking at it as the death force, there's the possibility of the emergence of something new, a re-shuffling of the deck.[85]

The potential intertwining of all these developments and themes are gathered up most evocatively in a short poem by one Grady Stark, alias 'Osmoses', volumes and volumes of whose verse emerge out of the haze of marijuana and from the sense of an impending doom for all but what he calls a "Ghost Dance Remnant Faithful". "Chaos", the poem from Santa Cruz begins,"god/ order/ darkness, light/ earth, air, fire, water/ life/ plant, animal/ man/ division/ man, woman/ tools/ division/ work, play/ division/ day, night/ black, white/ one/ two, three, four/ five/ culture/ six/ technology/ seven/ nations/ eight/ armies/ nine/ holocaust/ one. zero/chaos."[86]

One of the paradoxes of millenarism, however, is the frequency with which its protagonists are to be found getting on with the business of this life when one might have logically expected them to give up on what this world could offer. To account for the conundrum by asserting that any initially intense attention to the prospect (and perhaps proposed dates) of a millennium could not possibly be kept up is a useful first thought. That in itself, however, will not explain why some millenarists - members of Sunburst, for instance - turn out to prosper materially, and why heightened expectation of an *Endzeit* either generates so many new institutions or infuses old ones with new energy. A more adequate explication, in any case, will take note of that fact that what in general terms in this book we refer to as millenarism and cargoism are similar and related enough panaceas. If one hopes for a radically better cosmos in the future it is not illogical to be found trying to create the best one can out of the present one; if one dreams that the future holds eventual (and thus including material, this-worldly) blessing, then taking steps practically expressive of one's dreams' realization can be seen as premonitorily (perhaps 'technologically') appropriate.[87]

To comprehend the American situation, though, one would have to probe so much further, and with caution over the complexities. Ernest Lee Tuveson provides a good beginning with his thesis that, in general, distinctively American millennialism has been about the creation of the Kingdom of God on American soil.[88] But here it is time to add some reference to "the American Gospel of Success", or to "the American Dream" of personal and collective prosperity, a cultural leitmotiv which has not escaped the notice of social historians.[89] If we were in search of the cargoistic thread in the entanglements of American consciousness this is where we are sure to find it, in the hope - shouted out in television advertisements and the media, preached upon crudely from the black Rev. Eikerenkotter's New York cinema church across to the white Rev. Schuller's Crystal Cathedral in the west, and symbolized at the very social pinnacle by a grand 'White House' - of secure and ever-increasing access to money, of possessing a dwelling together with the cargo it must needs contain, and of running one decent vehicle, at the least.[90] Desires about such tangibilities are highly relative, admittedly, depending as they do on knowledge of the possibilities, station, 'class', and the degree of deprivation, as well as on imagination and proneness to 'pipe dream'.[91] And they do not always sit easily either with 'the religious sensibility' in general or classic millenarism in particular. On the other hand, no one could give an adequate account of *mentalités* in the American west without acknowledging the human drift toward its myth-laden *opportunities*, from Gold Rush days in the 1850s to Hollywood's 'Golden Years', and beyond. In what has allegedly become the most highly advanced society in the world technologically the coming of the Cargo has become a natural expectation - everyday and periodic - but bearing with it something of the sense of magic that archaic peoples attached to the rich harvest.

Prima facie, the Eastern spiritual insights gaining favour from the 'sixties do not sit well with this burden of materialism, in fact their world-denigrating aspects have been appealed to as part of the counter-cultural, New Age critique of the American Way. It is surprising, though, how quickly gurus and meditative techniques have become marketable;[92] and how readily incorporated into that cultic or quasi-religious mishmash through which Americans are constantly offered health, wealth and happiness.[93] It is also interesting that Eastern teachings with an *apocalyptic* message have been by far the most popular when it comes to serious commitment. We have already referred to Yogananda's 'World Prophecies'. For him, significantly, the USA was at present a desperately sick society, yet it would nonetheless emerge as the sole victor in a fourth World War, with its spiritual communes a key to a better future.[94] In the mid-'seventies, the Ananda Marga gave the world only 40 years before it would fall under the necessary rule of *sadvipras*, 'philosopher-kings' ruling behind the scenes; while from the mini-city of *sannyasins* on the 64,000 acre ranch in Oregon, Rajneesh declared that "two thirds of humanity would be wiped out by the year 2000" - through AIDS.[95] As with classic millenarism, it was the elect who counted cosmically, who would be saved, and who would reap a future prosperity.

All the tendencies in western America we have just surveyed with a 'bird's eye view' have manifested themselves elsewhere in the Pacific or are at least paralleled. In eastern Australia, it was to be expected, there has developed from the 'sixties a process locally dubbed 'Americanization', both welcomed for its comforts and excitement yet hated for its threat to cultural integrity. It has meant a succumbing to heightened consumerism with all the neon-lit street-sides and 'magical' media advertising in its train, and a sun-basking in the relative affluence of "the Lucky Country", made possible by foreign investment and the exploitation of raw materials.[96] Founded as a penal colony and constantly subject to the vagaries of the environment, white Australia has spawned various romantic visions about its own spaciousness and pattern of 'mateship' but has rarely figured as a Paradise Regained or the setting for a this-worldly Millennium.[97] On the other hand, the 'tradition' of waiting for the arrival of goods which were not manufactured in the country, with a dependence on Europe that was lessened steadily by degrees during the nineteenth century but died hard as a fixture in settler consciousness, is an important (if sadly neglected) datum in Australian culture. Moving on to the present, and as one outcome of this 'tradition', we find unimpeded, relatively equitable and quick access to the Cargo - car, house and yard (with their appliances), office equipment, etc. - now have as obvious a fulfilling, pleasurable, exciting and 'spirit-building' role in steadily secularizing Australian life as community activities (including distinctly religious ones) have had in the past. There is thus an 'Australian Dream' to be documented. While one of Eugene O'Neill's tragic heroines may have fantasized her daughter's future living in a grand mansion, dressed in silks and satins, and riding in a carriage with coachman and footman,there is the archetypal farmer to be found in Australia, dreaming of "keeping sheep and making money", as Patrick White has it, and there are the spacious brick villas lined up in the outer suburbs for first home-buyers by the developers, as well as Lady Luck of the highly popular lotteries and a business world which, proportionately speaking, holds out "more prizes, advertizes more possible worldly paradises and projects higher standards of family affluence than any other society on earth".[98] The difference between the United States and Australia in all this regard, however, is that in the former the Cargo is recurrently blessed and legitimated by religion, which remains robust if often garish, while in Australia the accumulation of European-style (or internationally marketable) goods has become a 'surrogate religious' comfort, more sufficient unto itself.[99]

That is not to say, of course, that the cargoistic-looking trajectory in modern Australian life has developed independently of white Australian religion. On the contrary, it appears from the counter-cultural reactions of the late 'sixties and early 'seventies, and from the more recent rejections of the past expressed in the charismatic movement and the new fundamentalism, that there was during the first post-War decades too close a nexus between middle class comforts and 'the Christian way' to be convincing. And that 'Christian way', incidentally, was in the main as defused of a millennial thrust as any Christianity could be, so imbued was it with 'homeliness' (or 'hearth culture' as Hugh Stretton has called it) and so relatively untouched by trauma had Australia been during its history.[100] In the 'seventies came the communes (especially in tropical Queensland) and the sects, both Christian and Eastern.[101] They were statements against affluence, and very often their critiques took the form of doomsdaying. "Bye bye Miss American

Pie" was a favourite song on the lips of the Australian Children of God, strongest in King's Cross, Sydney, where they could announce that the Australian and not just American "levy was dry".[102] By and large, admittedly, apart from Ananda Marga (who had divided up Australia and the Pacific into a grid of waiting mission fields), the eastern groups appealed more as condemners of materialism than creators of a new Age.[103]

By the end of the 'seventies, however, traditional Christian millenarian themes were being heard in charismatic and conservative quarters, and, following the drift of overseas publications (including the Texan Hal Lindsey's book *The Late Great Planet Earth*), 'the signs of the times' were being read from international crises - from the OPEC challenge, the arms race, etc.[104] Rather than being a challenge to materialism as such, mind you, or the high level of access to the Cargo enjoyed by the average Australian, these movements reflect more a breaking of the nexus between middle class existence and spirituality, as if the former had deadened the latter and the latter should possess an unencumbered vitality of its own. Others, of course, have preferred a religious style which takes this nexus for what it is. As a visitor to Sydney in March 1987, for example, Robert Schuller asked for $45 a seat to attend his special service, anticipating that some of 33,000-odd Australians who watch his Sunday morning 'Hour of Power' would be more than willing to pay.[105]

There would doubtless be value in encompassing related data and tendencies in a whole range of Pacific contexts. The phenomenon of Sun Moon's Church beckons, for instance, with its presence in South Korea, west coast America and eastern Australia, with its projection of a necessary Third World War and beyond that a scientifically subdued "natural world" and "extremely pleasant social environment on earth."[106] In South Korea it will startle as to how many other millenarian-oriented indigenous churches abound; in Japan much of relevance will surprise, from eschatological (and 'sectarian') Buddhism to the syncretic Mahikari's group's teaching about the lost Pacific continent of Mu; and in today's China we are hearing more about the infiltration of millenarian Christian sects and the enticements of consumerized cargo. Back on the west coast of Latin America, furthermore, neglected as it is in comparative study, the competition between North American Protestant missionaries and long-established Catholic clericalism is sharpening (the former preaching in a characteristically eschatological vein), while in Hispanic America the United States is almost ubiquitously associated with the most highly prized life styles and commodities.[107] But it is above all in changing Melanesia where there have erupted many and varied new religious movements which offer the most fruitful and fascinating points of comparison with the western American developments we have been documenting (or indeed with Western and European expressions of millenarianism and cargoism on both sides of the Pacific).

Melanesian Cargo Cults

What makes the Melanesian movements invaluable for comparative study is that, with the so-called 'cargo cults' in particular, a naive yet arrestingly honest identification is made of the expected coming of Cargo with a 'Millennium' of some sort or other, thus rendering explicit an interrelationship which is more usually implicit in similar-looking movements of the West. At the same time, while the settings and cultural contexts vary so markedly from one side of the Pacific to the other, the new religious movements of Melanesia reflect many of the themes - the synthetisms, for instance, or the creative myth-making - and many of the organizational problems - such as the self-aggrandisement and special indulgences of prophet leaders, the mismanagement of funds, etc. - that we have isolated in western American cults and communes.

As with our study of the Brotherhood of the Sun, it is consistent with our purposes and concern to illustrate apposite comparisons and connections that we concentrate on select ideological patterns in Melanesian cargo cults and then discover what bearing these might have on the leadership and organization of these new religious movements. It should also be confessed that, as with the Western materials, the religious phenomena of adjusting and 'modernizing' Melanesia presents too vast and complex an array of experiments to summarize in a small compass.[108] The themes discussed will necessarily be conditioned and narrowed by our prior more detailed treatment of the Sunburst movement, while we leave other related articles about Melanesian and American issues in this book to help fill out the comparative picture and connective tissues more completely (see chs. 2, 5-6).

Since the myth-historical account of Mu provided so crucial a set of clues to the futurology of the Brotherhood, it should come as some interest that the most crucial item on the agenda of cargo cult studies is the role of myth. It is as perceptible as day itself that cargo cults have been about group expectation, yet depending on geographical context, or on the degree and length of interaction between 'intruders' and 'newly contacted', the content, even galvanizing effects, of the expectations can vary widely.[109] Behind the variations in hope, situation and results, however, there almost invariably lies some *stori* (pidgin: story, myth-narrative, etc.).

Let me illustrate these basic points. In a well-known movement called the *Kivung*, for example, in the Mengen culture area of the Pomio district in eastern New Britain island, oneiric features were directly related to what was reported by Mengen labourers after they worked in 'Tolailand', or in the neighbouring region to the northeast, where there lie Melanesians with one of the longest histories of interaction with colonizing outsiders (especially at Rabaul under the German and Australian administrations), and with the greatest access to the material fruits of the modern technology. 'Relatively deprived' and on the very fringes of modernity, members of the Mengen *Kivung* have made regular and nocturnal money offerings since the mid-'seventies to encourage the return of their ancestors (pidgin: *tumbuna*), who, upon re-appearance, are assumed to be able to bring into being by a mere wish anything their fellow villagers desired - houses of permanent building materials, automobiles, refrigerators, radios and so forth. It is for this reason not very surprising that those Mengen who are better informed of the wider world have projected that a city the size of New York will rise up on the shores of Jacquinot Bay.[110] In other places and settings, however, anticipations have been different. Out to sea on isolated Iwa Island, for instance, it was sufficient for the returning dead to bring a shipload of tinned bully beef (1950); in the newly contacted central New Guinea highlands they were to bear *limited* quantities of newly introduced valuables - steel axes, cloth, new sorts of animals, as many pieces of shell money as were available to white explorers, occasionally guns - to appear out of sacred lakes, or at specially prepared cult houses and sites (especially between 1940 and 1955).[111]

In many other cases we find that the departed are not anticipated to return alone; their coming coincides with the Return of Jesus as taught by the mission-

aries or garbled by indigenous message-bearers who have heard them.[112] Here
'classic' cargoism as found in Melanesia sometimes merges with 'classical
Christian' millennial expectations, and in certain quarters, most significantly
with the Seventh Day Adventist missionary enterprise (which has produced in
Melanesia a proportionately higher percentage of Adventists than anywhere
else), we discover Western Christian dreams of the Millennium satisfying or substituting for an almost endemic cargoism.[113] Christianity can be taken on, moreover, for its potentiality to unlock the door to the whites' cargo. In the Madang
area between the Wars, for instance, it was widely conceived to be the whiteman's ritual for procuring the whiteman's goods, analogous to the blacks' magical repertoire for ensuring fertility in the gardens. All through Madang's colonial
history, further, the mission message to "seek first the Kingdom of Heaven and
then all these things will be added unto you" (Matt. 6:33), was interpreted with
the emphasis on the *things* to follow the acceptance - the *kaikai* (= food, or material results) of one's beliefs.[114]

As for the galvanizing effects of cargo cultist expectations, these differ in
degree in accordance with the social pressures which exist for generating or dis-
sipating any energies for confrontation against the colonial (or neo-colonial)
order. Thus some would-be attempts at cargo cultism are 'fly-by-night', many
coming to nothing because the leadership is unconvincing or too narrowly based
socially, or because the first promised predictions of a transformation did not
eventuate, or because colonial authorities and local consensus opposed them.
Others, by contrast, can flourish despite initial instances of 'failed prophecy',
even despite evidences of tricksterism and duplicity in the leadership, and especially in spite of opposition from Government and/or Mission. Thus the
researcher is left with a spectrum between highly transient eruptions and those
impressive movements which, although commencing with a certain manic intensity (with preparing wharves or aerodromes for projected boats and airplanes, for
example), eventually became respectable competitors in the game of independent
churches or church denominations, or of political parties and lobby-groups.[115]

These and other variables thus recognized, however, we note that no known
cargoist experiment has arisen without some reflective or partly theoretical ratio-
nale, and it is undoubtedly the highest-priority of research into cargo cultism that
one identifies that complex of reasons, worked out by the leadership and impart-

ed or filtered down to the membership, by which a new social development makes its case for existence and envisages the near future of the cosmos. It is here that myth is of critical importance because it is interpretation of and commentary upon shared myth that point to and disclose the sacral significance of expected events, as well as generate and legitimate those collective actions made in response to the expectancies. Cargo cult myths range from crucial traditional myths revalorized for new contexts to innovative and creative forms of *bricolage*, often through re-telling Bible stories in the light of indigenous beliefs or in wedding Biblical accounts and traditional narrative materials into new 'mythic histories'.

Some of the recurrent redeployment of traditional myths are well known enough to Melanesianists. A veritable *locus classicus* is surely to be found in the Biak-Numfor region of northwest Irian Jaya (formerly Dutch New Guinea), where the myth of Manamarkeri ('the scabious fellow') portrays a rejected old man as the one who has had revealed to him *Koreri* (the place of eternal life and wealth), and who, in being chased from his homeland, emerged as culture hero to found primary settlements and to be first in demarcating the boundaries of the Geelfinck Bay cultures. Small wonder that, upon the impact of the German and Dutch missionaries, Manamarkeri becomes the alternative to Christ in protest cults (at least from the 1880s onwards) - as the despised sufferer yet the bearer of salvation (which in Melanesia is a total of physical and spiritual well-being).[116] In my own researches I have documented the life of a Fuyughe prophet-figure who sought to protect his people from white intrusion by an appeal to a neighbouring culture's impelling aetiological myth about cosmic catastrophe. Ona Asi, alias 'Bilalaf' the prophet, at one stage warned that if his people so much as looked upon a white the great earthquake which had once brought the present rivers and valleys into existence, as this myth conveyed, would be repeated. A useful strategy for non-cooperation! used at the same time he was prophesying the arrival of wealth for the Fuyughe from some undisclosed spirit source (in 1942).[117]

In some instances many pointers that some myth is being appealed by cultists will be there, yet with its content being kept secret. In the Madang area after the War, for example, and following a good six years of Catholic and Lutheran mission activity, the great Yali (of the Ngaing village of Sor in the Rai coast hinterland) organized the most effective cargo cult organization ever, with his *lo-bos*

('law bosses') from as far west as Manam Island to as far east as the Huon peninsula.[118] It is intriguing how, unbeknown to the most thorough of Western
researchers, Yali and his close confederates kept hidden the guiding myth of
their activities. Rejecting both Mission and Administration in disillusionment,
and returning to *pasin bilong tumbuna* (the ancestral way) as the only sure road
to the Cargo, Yali resorted to traditional Ngaing myth (*parembik*) as the true
explanation of his people's dilemma in the face of colonialism. In the crucial
myth, a great (cosmic) tree, which contained all wealth (including animals) in its
branches, was felled by people in primordial time. Its enormous trunk and
branches fell away from Ngaing territory, only its stump remaining, and it was
therefore necessary to find the means by which free access to wealth could be
restored.[119]

Of much more interest for our present purposes, however, are myth-histories,
or what I have referred to elsewhere as the "mythological macro-histories" of
Melanesia.[120] With the arrival and continuing intervention of the outsiders, significantly, we may affirm history had to begin in the more-than-parochial sense.
For a start, untold centuries of the primal, Stone-Age round of existence were
brought to an end by immensely dramatic events already 'eschatological' in their
character.[121] The institutions, especially the schools, sponsored by the coloniz-
ers, and the geographical corridors they created for people to see beyond their
confined, often land-locked *cosmoi*, linked each ancestral way - each local cluster of myths, genealogies, migration - and exploit-stories - to other sets of traditions, discussed and subjected to rough comparison by a hundred-to-one patrol
carriers, indentured labourers on plantations, native constables, and the like.[122]
Given the accompanying spread of mission talk, though, the group of narratives
and *stori* most to provide small-scale societies' traditions some special place in
'world history' were those found in the Bible. It was not secular Western history
which was of any great import in this acculturation process, for 'wider cosmiza-
tion' almost inevitably required the whites' sacred history, since its beginnings
with Adam and Eve, Noah and the Flood, the migrations and genealogies of
Genesis, and the vicissitudes of Israel, were natural analogues to local pre-liter-
ary cultural repertoires.[123]

Out of such conational inter-mingling, various synthetistic narratives or
freshly inspired myths have emerged with ideological significance for new reli-

gious movements. A crucial leitmotiv is the true location of the sources of Power,[124] which is typically placed at a far distant point - a Mu-like geo-mythic positioning, if one likes - to which only the ancestors, or the culture heroes, Christ or God, have immediate access. From this point will issue the Cargo, or in other words the Melanesian Millennium, which, even when only limited amounts of goods might be expected, clinches the end of the old order - both the pre-contact lack of access to the Cargo *and* the unwanted colonial situation (in which the 'native' always loses out) - and marks the radical Transformation into *eine neue Zeit*, with no (expected) turning back.[125] Not only do narratives or mythic schemae presage the coming of some Cargo-carrier from such a true source, but the cosmographic referencing serves the purpose of explaining why local peoples have hitherto not experienced the great 'Breakthrough'. Even in new religious movements which have been deliberately divested of cargoist associations by their leaders, or which have ostensibly arisen for other purposes, this leitmotiv is almost invariably discernable, if sometimes only in the simplest, undeveloped linkage between a local Melanesian cosmos with some (putatively universal) events of the Bible.[126]

From Madang Peter Lawrence documented the historical development of these cognitive adjustments to the 1970s. Traditional to various seaboard peoples in the area was the Manup-Kilibob myth cycle, and depending on the version, one or other of two culture heroes, the brothers Manup and Kilibob, bestowed different gifts and skills *in illo tempore*, when they fashioned out features of the Madang cosmos. Even into the post-contact situation, the basic myths of this cycle conveyed the impression that the Power to re-enliven the creative forces of such heroes, or to reappropriate items for material and total well-being, was near at hand and accessible through the right rituals and actions. There were assurances, moreover, that although the two culture heroes had quarrelled, they had either been reconciled after their exploits, or would be so in the future, their relationship having an obvious bearing on the Madang peoples.[127] Once there developed a wider conception of the world, through 'mission talk', and once the relative inaccessibility to the Cargo was palpable, because of the inevitable inequities of colonial arrangements, the Source and availability to it looked much more difficult. The determinative Biblical events - the 'Fall', the stupidity of Ham in witnessing his father's nakedness (and thus being sent to populate New Guinea without the Cargo as early cultist talk had it)[128] - were all placed well away from Madang itself, 'thousands of miles' away if the missionaries were to be believed.

The impetus to accept this distancing, however, not only came from the new authorities - the white teachers - but from the very need to account for what was simply not known before, that there were other types of people, such as the whites (and of the course the Asians who had filtered in). Here stood a conundrum of a kind analogous to the one met by the Europeans upon the discovery of the Americas, and which has generated mythic accounts of Israelite and other wanderings, from Sigüenza y Góngora's *Phoenix of the West* in the 1680s up until the Mormon revisioning of history (cf. ch.2), and beyond to the speculations of Paulsen, just to name a few *stori bilong waitman*.[129] Thus it was to be expected among Melanesians adjusting to fresh information and puzzles that they would posit Mu-like regions through which mysterious peoples and goods could be explained, and be doing this in terms of their own cosmographic frameworks and cultural expectations. Among the Asmat in 1952, just to illustrate this last point from the southern coast of Irian Jaya (then Dutch New Guinea), some *bricolage* gained currency that it had been two Asmat women who brought on the Flood and who promptly went off to the land of the whites in an aeroplane they had made with their own hands. These two, the narrative tells, took the names Marie and Wirerimina (Queen Wilhelmina), and from them descended Jesus and the Mission on the one hand and the Dutch government on the other, both lines therefore originating back with the Asmats themselves.[130]

Back among the Madangs we find that, on the eve of the Japanese invasion in 1941, the old culture heroes Manup and Kilibob were being identified with Jesus, or God, or Satan. According to the visionary Tagarab, a large man who was as acclaimed for the strength of his hands as for his predictions about the destruction of Madang, the local god Kilibob was the one who had given the Ten Commandments, commissioned Jesus to the task of guarding the spirits of the dead, and later sent the missionaries. He had previously become angry with the Madangs for rejecting the Cargo he offered and for choosing inferior items - bows and arrows instead of guns, canoes instead of dinghies, etc. - but after residing in Sydney and Jerusalem for a long time, he "decided to become the God of the Europeans". Since the missionaries he sent "failed to tell the truth", however, his "attitude was changing" toward his people, who had been left in bondage to his brother, Manup-Satan. So very soon, Tagarab taught, Kilibob was returning in person in a ship full of European-style goods and munitions, to drive out the whites, "missionaries included". Such an event, what is more, had its apocalyptic dimensions. The ancestors would all come back - "in the guise of Japanese servicemen", in fact - and all "would be heralded by the occurrence of storms and earthquakes of unprecedented severity and number".[131]

As precisely as anywhere, we find the connection forged in Tagarab's myth between reconstructing what is (mythically) true about the nature of the cosmos in time and space and taking the right course of action (which in Tagarab's case meant turning against the whites and siding with the new victors).[132] In a colonial and volatile situation, this 'cosmic construction of reality'[133] assures one of possessing the truth *instead of* others' falsities. In Millenarian and cargoistic orientations, taking the right course means making appropriate sorts of preparations for what the true account of the universe implies one should expect, and when. We are thus discussing rational strategies here, not illogicalities and a total absence of any scientific outlook. Knowing the outcome by hindsight ought not to evoke our prejudgement. For it simply remains true that different interpretations of the world become the premises on which highly varying, and sometimes remarkably surprising, anticipations can be built. Thus the very type of connection we were exploring in 'a cult group' within what is technologically the most advanced society of all on one side of the Pacific, also manifests itself in paradoxes and adjustments among the so-called 'primitives' of changing Melanesia on the other.

The narrative creations emerging from the new religious movements of Melanesia, of course, do not invariably fall into the same straightforward patterns, even if the principles just enunciated and the concern to tap the true source of Power do almost always apply. In some latter-day *stori,* for instance, it has been envisaged that the sacred (macro-) histories of the whites and blacks ran in parallel sequence but in complete separation, such that blacks have no need to pay any attention to the whites' *Heilsgeschichte* because of its irrelevance to indigenous conditions, and because the blacks have their own equivalents to Jesus.[134] Of great interest, though, and more comparable to the creations discussed earlier, are myths and accompanying expectations related to America, and its role as cosmographic centre and source of redemption in select Melanesian cult or separatist movements. Because of the United States' outstanding military presence in the southwest Pacific during the Second World War - in particular because of the massive amount of Cargo they brought to the war theatre, and the noticeability of black (Afro-American) soldiers fighting alongside whites, and a measure of fraternization between servicemen and indigenes during mop-up operations - hopes for the future among small-scale societies were significantly affected.

In the 'Long Story of God', for example, a narrative theology propounded in the Admiralty Islands by Paliau Maloat, the founder of Melanesia's first independent (or 'native'-originated) church in 1946, *Amerika* is held in honour for "wanting to show us the road that would make us all right" (*oraitim yumi*). Powers which dominated the Admiralties (or Manus) are denigrated in turn - the Germans, the Australians, the Japanese - but God "sent them back". Only America "did not forget the talk of Jesus", and although the Australians thus far succeeded in blocking them, "another country ... will come" (and by strong implication it is America) and "will get rid of them all".[135] As is well known, the representation of America as Saviour hardly stops here among Pacific protest movements. Make-shift armies have been formed capitalizing on America's supposed invulnerability (cf. ch. 6); when various Manus saw a photograph of Paliau under the Statue of Liberty after his United Nations-sponsored visit in 1962, they thought he had visited God; the Tungaks in a cult on New Hanover collected money to "buy President L. Johnson" as their own head of state; the leaders of a marginalized Tolai group called *Kivung Lavurua* were twice imprisoned for spreading rumours that America would bomb the (unwanted) town of Rabaul; and so on. In each case the hopes and provocative activities relate back to stories which contain the meaning of this cosmos, and disclose the secrets of power, *in nuce*.[136]

America even has its place as a stepping stone in the Mormon-like migration story of Prince Beldigao (or Levi Moses Solomon), acclaimed an ancient hero by the separatist Remnant Church in the Solomons. An Israelite who found his way to Malaita in the eighth century BC, bringing news of the True God long before the missionaries, Beldigao made a covenant on his way that whatever government was established in America, the same ... would also be established in the land in which Beldigao finally settled.[137] With such inside knowledge (which incidentally owes something to Seventh Day Adventism), and in attempting to establish a theocracy (like America is supposed to have achieved!) before "the personal return of the Lord Jesus Christ" (and not the coming of the Cargo), the Remnantists have reason to feel and be special.[138]

All these ideological (or in the main neo-mythological) developments are innovative cultural constituents providing the most illumination of Melanesian millenanian and cargoist activities. The implications we have seen in the myth-history of the Sunburst organization for the career of the Brotherhood and its leadership as a whole can be just as effectively applied to most independent religious movements of Melanesia. In almost all of the latter the leaders have claimed the experience of visions or of privileged access to 'the other side';[139] they have typically assumed autocratic control over funds collected in advance of the future transformation, and thus produced disaffection among adherents expecting more rewarding tangibilities than actually inspire,[140] and they often take special license - sexually and in personal wealth - apparently out of keeping with the ideals they propound.[141]

The few movements without 'charismatically authoritative' leadership aside, it has been the "guiding star" of each experiment who has magnetized the elements of a new *communitas*, naturally using the pre-existing model of the village. Even by Melanesian political standards, the deferring to this innovative authoritarianism is remarkable. Membership is subscribed to by fees, reciprocal relations are more or less limited to adherents, new regulations or *lo* are adopted, orders are obeyed implicitly to undertake the most ambitious projects (such as the building of huge meeting houses or churches, suburban-looking villages, airstrips, wharves, etc.), and novel patterns of group behaviour are adopted (such as collective morning ablutions, drilling, exercising, etc.).[142] For all their appearances as non-violent strategies, moreover, or as alternative styles to the order imposed by Government or encouraged by Mission, Melanesian cargoist and millenarian protests have quite commonly generated physical confrontation - in the form of riots, for example, the occasional push to eliminate individual expatriates by force, even the mustering of 'armed forces' for something like a 'final conflict'.[143]

It is plainer than daylight, as I have also shown of the Brotherhood of the Sun and comparable Western phenomena, that group involvement in all these experiments is the result of ideas. A sufficient number of captivated persons imbibe them; myths, regulations and single directives from a 'prophet-leader' become charters for action.[144] The garbling and relative comprehension of the group's ideological platform apart, and the role of social pressure in mobilizing membership also granted, the intellectualist analysis of social forces definitely holds its own when it comes to the initiation of new movements and 'causes'. "Humans make their own history", as Marx averred, even if "they do not make it under conditions they choose". Thus, although the myths they spin and the thoughts they formulate reflect their conditions, these cannot be said to be the direct product of those conditions.[145] The sculpture cannot be said to have been determined by the stone, even if a strong grain on what is already there is likely to condition the sculptor's response to the material. Thus we are quite at liberty, and in as methodologically secure a position as any, to use story (let alone systematically arranged sets of ideas) as the index to social forms. That is hardly the only analytical tack one can or should adopt; but it is one legitimate method, especially when analyzing religion.

Our approach here is one expression of what has loosely been called 'legitimation theory'.[146] What we have suggested of communal activities is that at least small-scale 'counter-cultural' experiments depend on the crystallization of convincing, and archetypally-impelling ideas for their motivation. They can certainly not be passed off as relatively mindless responses to adverse circumstances or relative deprivation. Perhaps there is reason to suspect - especially in comparing Melanesian with Western myth-historical materials, or more traditional Melanesian *stori* with visibly acculturated ones - that some shared accounts of the truth about the cosmos are much more reflections of the unconscious mind (through dreams, visions, etc.) when contrasted with more intellectual and syncretic 'compositions' (as in the Sunburst or Malaitan cases, let us say). Yet even then it is not how the mythology or ideology came into existence but that it has had its effects, and has gained acceptance, which counts. No one is in a position to deny, either, that the creative *bricolage* or systematization of notions may take time to reach a more polished or elaborate form. After all, the movements we have been discussing are definitely in response to social situations and psychological needs. But the movements are only movements because someone has allegedly been able to make sense of what is going on in the world, and thus provided a rationale - a "purposive cause"[147] - for the actions of those concurring with the particular 'construction of reality'. As I have argued elsewhere, just the feeling of disaffection with the known order or just the longing for a perfect replacement to imperfection is not enough to engender more than *ennui* and sporadic rage. It is reflective activity - in terms of reprisal, the working out of a logic of retribution which can even be built into myth-history - that mobilizes, for people want to be 'on the right side'.[148] They not only want to be 'winners' or 'victors' (taken in the broadest and most inclusive sense), but they want to know the 'true nature of their situation' (at the very least reassurance as knowledge) and their meaningful place or destiny in the cosmos. In this sense religion does not only take you "to the heart of people" but to the core issue in social scientific methodology.[149] "The beginning of criticism is the criticism of religion", if I may extrapolate from Marx,[150] yet it seems that the more we play down the role of ideas (most of which, in containing a religious dimension, do not make sense to the secularist), the more likely our methodologies will falter, and we will eventually have to return to the criticism of religion as the last and major duty rather than the first hurdle.

Despite the many variations and patently different contexts, then, it is neither unrewarding or premature to compare millenarism and cargo cultism on both sides of the Pacific. Fascinating in themselves are the images which peoples on one side have of those on the other, especially the idealizing projections that it is in the far reaches of the Pacific Zone that solutions to the human predicament are found. Remarkable, too, are the many parallels which can be drawn between new religious movements in diverse cultural quarters of this region, and the special connections which exist in terms of the impact of Western missionization on the islands and of island mysteries on the American imagination. Most important, however, is the datum of social experimentation and the magnetic quality of mental creativity in the social phenomena under scrutiny, leading us to question afresh our interpretative tools and to ask yet again what it is to be human.[151]

Notes

My thanks are due to the Regents of the University of California, the Fulbright Hays Foundation, the Research Grant and Special Duty Overseas schemes of the University of Sydney, and the Research Committee of the University of Papua New Guinea, for funding the research behind this paper.

1. For long-term historical background to the city, esp. W.A. Hawley, *Early Days of Santa Barbara*, Santa Barbara, 1987. For basic information on the modern city, e.g., P.J. Thompson, *Santa Barbara; Discover America's Eden*, Santa Barbara, 1984, cf. *Encyclopedia Americana*, vol.24, p.236.

2. *Autobiography*, Los Angeles, 1972, esp. chs. 37-38, 47-49. On earlier developments, e.g., M. Comans, 'Swami Vivekananda and the Formation of the Rama Krishna Movement' (Masters dissert., University of Sydney), Sydney, 1980.

3. I allude to the subtitle of Kriyananda's *The Path*, Nevada City, 1977 (cf. esp. pt.2), and also to T.A. Nordquist, *Ananda Co-operative Village; A Study in the Beliefs, Values, and Attitudes of a New Age Religious Community (Skrifter utgivna av Religionshistorika Institutionen i Uppsala 16)*, Uppsala, 1978 (cf. esp. pp.66, 78, however, where we learn that the Self-Realization Fellowship do not recognize Walter's successorship).

4. Paulsen, *Sunburst; Return of the Ancients; an Autobiography of Norman Paulsen*, Goleta, 1980, pp. 247-51, 291, 302 (quotation), and later, pp. 480, 485, 538. Hereafter I have preferred to refer most frequently to this first edition of Paulsen's autobiography, rather than to the one adjusted and published outside California, entitled *Christ Consciousness*, Salt Lake City, 1986. On background to *kriya* (activity) in yoga, e.g. M. Eliade, *Yoga; immortality and freedom* (trans. W.R. Trask), (*Bollingen Series 66*), Princeton, 1969 edn., pp. 39, 260, 395. On brotherhood in the Aims and Ideas of the Self-Realization Fellowship and in Yogananda's thought, *Autobiography of a Yogi, op.cit.*, esp. p.573, cf. pp. 339-40, 512, 551; yet cf. *infra* on the 'Holy Brothers' as a later development in Paulsen's concept of Brotherhood.

5. D. and W. Weaver, *Sunburst: a people, a path, a purpose*, San Diego, 1982, s.v. sub-title, and note pp.161-76 for references to comparable communes.

6. For important background, see T. Roszak, *The Making of a Counter Culture*, New York, 1969. Cf. also T. Robbins and T. Anthony (eds.), *In Gods We Trust: new patterns of religious pluralism in America*, New Brunswick, N.J., 1981; S.M. Tipton, *Getting Sacred from the Sixties; moral meaning in conversion and culture change*, Berkeley, 1982, and the literature cited below in ns. 82-4.

7. The literature on contemporary American communes is too extensive to list here in full. For what I take to be the most significant monographs (in chronological order), G.R. Fitzgerald, *Communes; their goals, hopes, problems*, New York, 1971; R.E. Roberts, *The New Communes*, Englewood-Cliffs, 1971; R.M. Hanter, *Commitment and Community; communes and utopias in sociological perspective*, Lincoln, 1972; K. Melville, *Communities in the Counter Culture*, New York, 1972; R.S. Ellwood, *Religious and Spiritual Groups in Modern America*, Englewood Cliffs, 1973; L. Veysey, *Communal Experience*, New York, 1973; J. Jerome, *Families of Eden; communes and the new anarchism*, London, 1974; H. Gardner, *The Children of Prosperity*, New York, 1978; J. R. Hall, The Ways Out: utopian communal groups in an age of Babylon (International Library of Sociology), London, 1978; J. Case and R.C.R. Taylor (eds.), *Co-ops, Communes, and Collectives*, New York, 1979. For background to the history of north American utopianism, esp. J.H. Noyes, *History of American Socialisms*, Philadelphia, 1870 (reprint. as *Strange Cults and Utopias of 19th Century America*, New York, 1966); C. Nordhoff, *The Communistic Societies of the United States*, New York, 1875 (1966); R.V. Hines, *Californian Utopian Colonies*, London. 1953; M. Holloway, *Heavens on Earth; utopian communities in America 1680-1880*, New York, 1966; L. Foster, *Religion and Sexuality; three American communal experi- ments of the Nineteenth Century*, New York, 1981; Trompf, "Utopia", in M. Eliade (ed.), *The Encyclopedia of Religion*, New York, 1987, vol.15, p.161.

8. See esp. his *The Science of Religion*, Los Angeles, 1974, cf. Kriyananda, *op.cit.*, p.310 (quotation, and Jnanavatar Swami Sri Yukteswar Giri, *Kaivalya Darsanam the Holy Science*, Los Angeles, 1972 edn., p.111 (longer term background). For an example of something broader, note Yogananda, *The Master Said*, Los Angeles, 1957, p.105.

9. Paulsen, *op.cit.*, esp. pp. 480, 485, 552ff. Cf., *Los Angeles Times*, 3 Feb.,1974, p.2; *The Californian Certified Organic Farmers' Newspaper*, Spring, 1974, p.74; S. Duquetta, *Sunburst Farm Family Cookbook*, Santa Barbara, 1976 (1st edn.), 1978 (2nd edn.).

10. *Sunday Telegraph* (Australia), 30 Feb., 1980, p.3; 22 June 1980, p.11 (quotation); and on the first reporting of the arms cache, *Santa Barbara News and Review*, 4/9, 7 March, 1975; pp. 1, 6-8; *San Francisco Chronicle*, 10 March, 1975, p.3; *The New York Times*, April 6,1975, p.1. On the more recent developments at Goleta, Oral Test- imony (hereafter OT): esp. Joe Belton, 21 Aug., 1980 at "Tajigues", cf. Weaver, *op.cit.*, pp. 72-3, etc. On Manson, esp. V. Bugliosi and C. Gentry, *Helter Skelter; the true story of the Manson murders*, New York, 1975.

11. Trompf, *The Rise and Fall of a Great Californian Commune* (in preparation).

12. For this concept, N. Harper (ed.), *Pacific Circle 1-2*, Brisbane, 196-72.

13. For much more extensive exploration, Trompf, *Payback: the logic of retribution in Melanesian Religions (Studia Instituti Anthropos)*, St. Augustin (forthcoming), ch.2, pt.3.

14. (North) America itself is colonized on the basis of this revolt, which is also later articulated upon the emergence of cities, e.g. in Thomas Jefferson's 1801 Inaugural Address. Cf. esp. C.L. Sandford, *The Quest for Paradise*, Urbana, 1961, pp. 126-7.

15. I have been satisfied to take Paulsen's first edition of his autobiography as pivotal (1980), cf. above n.4, since adaptations in the second edition relate to the community's post-Californian phase (see below).

16. Paulsen, *op.cit.*, pp. 324, 355, 375, 425.

17. *Ibid.*, esp. pp. 334, 355 (quotation), 360-1 (on Mu etymology), 383. For sources, see below.

18. *Ibid.*, pp. 327 (first quotation, 335, 354 (with second quotation) 374-5, 394, cf. 354 (image), 397-402. Cf. p.381 for some complexities. The term Builder has a long history in esoteric circles. On Freemasonry, for example, J.F. Newton, *The Builders; a story and study of Masonry*, London, 1918.

19. For background to the term, esp. Trompf, "The Future of Macro-Historical Ideas", in *Soundings*, 62 (1979), p.73.

20. For background to the usage of this concept in the study of leadership in new

religious movements, see Introd., 1, where work by Max Weber and Peter Worsley has been kept in mind. Here I take *charisma* to be the gift of making contact with the Other World, which at least at *depth* was taken in the Brotherhood to be the exclusive 'property' of Paulsen as "prophet" (see below).

21. Paulsen, *op.cit.*, pp. 175-85, 205-9, 261-96, 321-6, 409-45, etc. Cf. also plates on pp. 106, 270, opp. p. 338, opp. p.354, pp. 351, 363, 406, 445, 462, and for bibliog. New Edn., pp. 484-6. Cf. also 'Sunday Communion 2 June 1974, Our Eternity' (mimeograph, Santa Barbara, 1974), pp.3-5; *Lord of the Spirits* (pamphlet), Santa Barbara, n.d. (I suspect 1975), pp.5-6, etc.

22. Trompf, *The Idea of Historical Recurrence in Western Thought*, Berkeley, Los Angeles and London, 1979, vol.1, pp. 205ff. (Augustine), cf. vol.2 (forthcoming), ch.1 (Milton).

23. Paulsen, *op.cit.*, pp. 409 [and book's subtitle] (Return), 426 (programming), 436-9, 458; "God and his Angels", Dec. 15, 1974 (mimeograph, Santa Barbara, 1974), p.3.

24. *Sunburst*, pp. 206-7.

25. Duquette, *op.cit.*, p.5, cf. Paulsen, *op.cit.*, pp.353-5, etc. For precedents to such ideas about a mysterious and vastly superior space ship technology, e.g., P. Boudreau, *An Astral Journey*, New York, 1967, pp. 26, 32 (a Californian author). In various accounts of the lost continents of Lemuria or Mu (and of the 'Akashic' records left by them), superior technology is emphasized (see n.28 below), as it is also of Atlantis; cf. J.D. Rea, *Patterns of the Whole*, Boulder, 1986, vol.1, pp. 50-1.

26. Esp. [Paulsen], *Brotherhood of the Sun* (pamphlet), Santa Barbara, n.d. [1970s], [pp. 6-8, 11-13]; *Sunburst Communities*, Santa Barbara, 1979; *Sunburst Communities; What is Sunburst?* Santa Barbara, 1980 (both newspaper format), Weaver, *op.cit.*, esp. chs. 3-4.

27. Paulsen, *op.cit.*, pp. 440-1 (first quotation), pp. 303-6, cf.p.305 (second quotation), chs. 35, 45, etc., cf. 'Communion with the Lord in the House of David' [heading uncapitalized, cf. below], (mimeograph, Santa Barbara, n.d. [1970s]), p.4 (Mu=Eden). The notion of space gardens is not so far-fetched when one considers the 1986 proposals to create such by NASA ([U.S.] National Aeronautical and Space Administration).

28. Churchward, *The Lost Continent of Mu* (1931); *The Children of Mu* (1931); *The Sacred Symbols of Mu* (1933); *The Cosmic Forces of Mu* (1934); *The Second Book of the Cosmic Forces of Mu* (1935) [the last two verging toward classic occultism] (all reprod. in the Paperback Library, New York, 1968), cf. H.S. Santesson, *Understanding Mu*, New York, 1970 (esp. p.13 on Churchward-Blavatsky 'complimentarity'). For the occult writers mentioning Mu (otherwise referred to as the lost Pacific continent of Lemuria), note esp. W.S. Cervé, *Lemuria; the lost continent in the Pacific*, San Jose, 1931 (34), esp. pp. 30-91, cf. p. 104 for Mu-Lemuria identification (Rosicrucian, and Churchward's source?)' H.P. Blavatsky, *The Secret Doctrine* (1888), Pasadena, 1963 reprint, vol.2, pp. 6-7, 171, 316-20; *Isis Unveiled*, New York, 1893, vol.1, p.594n [where we learn of L. Jacolliot's, *Histoire des vierges; les peuples et les continent disparu* (Paris, 1874), probably the earliest speculative book about a Lost Pacific continent (Theosophical); Alice Bailey, *Esoteric Astrology*, New York and London, 1976 edn., e.g. vol.3, pp. 159-60 (Alice Bailey Movement separating from the Theosophy); Elizabeth Clare Prophet, *The Great White Brotherhood in the Culture and History of America*, Colarado Springs, 1976, pp.166-7, 243-5 [cf. also Paulsen, *op.cit.*, pp. 184-5] (The 'I Am' Movement), cf. also R. Norman and Unarius students, *Lemuria Rising*, El Cajon, 1976-7, 4 vols. The usage of Mu (or near equivalent) evidently goes back to Augustus le Plongeon's *Queen Moo and the Egyptian Sphinx*, New York, 1900.

29. See P. Kolosimo, *Timeless Earth*, London, 1973, pp. 53-8; and on the 'Ancient Wisdom Family', J.G. Melton, *The Encyclopedia of American Religions*, Detroit, 1986 edn., esp. p.121, cf., on Theosophy in California, E.A. Greenwalt, *California Utopia: Point Loma: 1897-1942* (ed., W.E. Small and H.Todd), San Diego, 1978 edn.

30. Paulsen, *op.cit.*, p.20n., 324, 599 (2nd edn., p.484); cf. Churchward, *Lost Continent*, esp. p.43, and chs. 4, 9-12, *Children*, ch.2, etc.

31. *Secret Doctrine, op.cit.*, vol. 2, p.328, cf. G.A. Barborka, *The Divine Plan*, Madras, 1964, p.292. The Lemuria conception owes itself to zoologists Philip Schater and Ernst Jaeckel (England and Germany respectively), in pursuit of a lost continent (in the Indian ocean) to explain the distribution of lemurs. See R. Wauchope, *Lost Tribes and Sunken Continents*, Chicago and

London, 1962, p.38, yet cf. C. Gallenkamp, *Maya*, Harmondsworth, 1981 edn., p.58.

32. Cf. C.F. Holder, *The Channel Islands of California*, Chicago, 1910, p.25 on Limu Island (and another island traditionally named Liqui*muymu*, and a village on Limu called Ninu*mu*). Also note T. Hudson, 'The Chumash Indians' (unpublished lecture, Santa Barbara Museum of Natural History, 13 March, 1982) on the name as Limur, and cf. H.L. Bancroft, *The Works*, San Francisco, 1886, vol.1, p.402 on the name as Liniooh!

33. Cervé, *op.cit.*, pp. 24 (quotation), 30, 217-9, etc. For background, cf. also M. Heindel, *The Rosicrucian Cosmo-Conception; or mystic Christianity*, Ocean Park, 1911 edn.

34. Paulsen, *Sunburst*, pp. 355, 381, 495ff., cf. F. Waters (with F. White Bear Fredericks), *The Book of the Hopi*, New York, 1963, pp. 3-28, 39, fig.4, pp. 164-7 (but differing from the Brotherhood's version on races); Churchward, *Lost Continent*, pp. 178-9, cf. Paulsen, *op.cit.*, ch. 50. On the four (-five) colours in sub-Theosophical (e.g. Anthroposophical) sources, R. Steiner [notes by others of his lectures], *The Mission of the Folk Souls* (trans. A.H. Parker), London, 1970, Lect. 6, pp. 100-110 (but Steiner has black not blue, and yellow-brown as well as yellow to cover the Malays), cf. *Cosmic Memory* (trans. C.E. Zimmer, 1959), New York, 1981 edn., pp. 48-49; *An Outline of Occult Science* (trans. M. and H. Monges), Spring Valley, 1961 (72), pp. 216-222 (access to this literature through courtesy of Neil Anderson); and see on Mahikari, below. For longer term background, note the reference of the four colours to the four mountains (and quarters) surrounding Mount Meru in Mahayana Buddhist cosmography. For background, R.F. Gombrich, "Ancient Indian Cosmology", in C. Blacker and M. Loewe (eds.), *Ancient Cosmologies*, London, 1975, pp. 118ff.

35. Paulsen, *op.cit.*, p. 381; OT: Fredd Dunham, 10 July, 1982 (in Santa Barbara). The literature relating to the white Indians is complex. Cf. esp. Fr. Z. Salmerón, *Relaciones (Documentos Históricos de Méjico Pt. III, vol.4)*, Mexico City, 1904, p.118; Bancroft, *op.cit.*, vol.1, p.402 (citing various sources); [Anon. trans., "Father Antonio de la Ascension's Account of the Voyage of Sebastian Vizcaino, in *Quarterly of the California Historical Society*, 7/4 (1928), esp. p.351; H.R. Wagner, *Juan Rodriguez Cabrillo; dis-*

coverer of the coast of California, San Francisco, 1941, p.41; cf. C.F.
Holden, *The Channel Islands, op.cit.*, which contains a translation of a pertinent passage of Cabrillo's log, on p.21. Of side relevance to the Brotherhood
is the story of the lone woman on San Nicolas Island. See M. Geiger,
O.F.M., *Juana Maria; the lone woman on San Nicolas Island*, Santa Barbara,
n.d. [1970s]; S. O'Dell, *Island of the Blue Dolphins*, New York, 1960 (fiction). I thank the Librarian at the Santa Barbara Mission for access to most of
the documents referred to above.

36. Trompf and E. Oliver, Fieldnotes, 1975. Cf. also Paulsen, 'God and His
Angels Dec. 15 1974' (mimeograph), p.3; Oliver, 'An Outline for the Study
of the Brotherhood of the Sun' (unpublished typescript, University of
California, Santa Cruz), Santa Cruz, 1975, p.3, where the trajectories of
spread are imagined to run not only from "the Channel Islands to Mesa
Verde" but also "from Mt. Shasta to Mexico City". Mt. Shasta is in northern
California, and was important earlier when Paulsen's feelings about links
with Mother Mary and the 'I Am' Movement were stronger (see also below),
since Paulsen may well have learnt first about Lemuria from her (*Sunburst,*
pp.184-5). After the purchase of Tajiguas Ranch, however, there was more
talk of the cosmically significant triangular and wedge relationship between
the Ranch, the Santa Barbara holdings as the inland sites of significance (OT:
Roger Powell, 17 Feb., 1987).

37. Cf., e.g. W. Gleeson, *History of the Catholic Church of California*, San
Francisco, 1871, vol.1, p.135.

38. E.G. White, e.g. *Testimonies for the Church*, Mountain View, 1948, vol.3, pp.
114-5, cf. *The Great Controversy*, Mountain View, 1971 edn., *Counsels on
Diet and Foods*, Takoma Park, 1938. On Enoch in Paulsen, *op.cit.*, (2nd
edn.), p.485 (s.v. Horne, C.R.).

39. Paulsen, *Sunburst*, p.345, but first an angel Man and Woman as singulars, a
neo-Gnostic motif of the Heavenly Adam. Cf., e.g. H. Jonas, *The Gnostic
Religion*, Boston, 1963 edn., pp. 202-3.

40. See esp. Paulsen, *op.cit.*, pp. 337-355. For literary background to all the
above, esp. A. Bailey, *The Reappearance of Christ*, New York and
London,1970 edn.; G.R. King, *The Unveiled Mysteries*, Chicago, 1935 (9)
(cf. also Melton, *op.cit.*, p.127, col.2); G. van Tassel, *The Council of Seven*

Lights, Los Angeles, 1958, esp. ch.3 (with thanks to Roger Powell), cf. also Blavatsky, *Isis Unveiled,* vol.1, pp. 593 ff., and note *Secret Doc.,* vol.2, p.528 (Eden-Serpent far from being Satan); Jonas, *op.cit.,* p.93 (Ophites). Note that Paulsen lived with van Tassel and married his daughter in 1954 (Paulsen, *op.cit., chs.* 32-33).

41. Esp. von Däniken's *Chariots of the Gods?* (trans. M. Heron), New York, 1969 (71); *Gods from Outer Space* (trans. M. Heron), New York, 1972; *The Gold of the Gods* (trans. M. Heron), New York, 1974; *In Search of Ancient Gods* (trans. M. Heron), London, 1974. Cf. Paulsen, *op.cit.,* (2nd edn.), p.486, s.v. von Däniken; and also A. and S. Landsburg, *In Search of Ancient Mysteries,* London, 1974; *The Search of Lost Civilizations,* New York, 1976 (also listed in Paulsen's later bibliog.).

42. Z. Sitchin, *The Twelfth Planet,* New York, 1976, pp. 132-141, 156-7, cf. also p.121 for the genealogy. Respectable works by Charles Woolley, Samuel Kramer, Anton Moortgat, James Pritchard, etc. are listed in Paulsen's bibliography; *op.cit.,* pp. 599-600, 2nd edn., p.485.

43. Paulsen, 'Jesus and Melchisedec' (mimeograph [the early makings of an autobiography?]), Santa Barbara, n.d. [1970s] (first quotation); Constitution [or Doc. of Incorporation] (mimeograph), Heading, p.1 (second quotation).

44. Yogananda, *Autobiography,* pp. 321, 346-7, etc. (*avatar,* Prophet), chs. 26, 33, 35 etc. (Christ), cf. Kriyananda, *op.cit.,* pp. 448-9 (Second Coming).

45. Paulsen, *Sunburst,* pp. 339-347, cf. Origen, *De Principiis* II, vi, 3, etc. (union of Christ's soul), II, viii, (via) (anathema).

46. Cf. H. Chadwick, *Early Christian Thought and the Classical Tradition,* Oxford, 1966, p.16 etc. For the Biblical allusions, Gen. 14:18-20, 18:1-16, 32:24-30. On Mormonism, J. Bracht, 'Mormonism: the search for a personal God' (Masters dissert., University of Sydney), Sydney, 1988.

47. Paulsen, 'Our Eternity: Sunday Communion June 2 174' (mimeograph), p.14. Cf. for long term background, J.N.D. Kelly, *Early Christian Doctrines,* London, 1960 edn., pp. 115-9 on Adoptionism.

48. Paulsen, *Sunburst,* pp. 30-34, 293-4, 413, 439.

49. Note Paulsen's references to P. Tomkin's works, *Secrets of the Great Pyramid,* New York, 1971, and *Mysteries of the Mexican Pyramids,* New York, 1976, in his bibliog. (*Sunburst,* p.600). Cf. also W.T. Olcott, *Myths of*

the Sun, New York, 1914; W.J. Perry, *Children of the Sun*, London, 1923; A. Caso, *Aztecs; people of the sun (Civilization of the American Indian Ser. 50)*, Oklahoma, 1958; J. Hawkes, *Man and the Sun*, London, 1963; G.H. Gossen, "Temporal and Spatial Equivalents in Chamula Ritual Symbolism", in W.A. Lessa and E.Z. Vogt (eds.), *Reader in Comparative Religion; an anthropological approach*, New York, London, etc., 1979, p.119, etc.

50. Cf. esp. W.F. Perry, *op.cit.*, G.E. Smith, *Human History*, London, 1930 (cf. e.g., figs. 48, 60); T. Heyerdahl, *American Indians in the Pacific*, London, 1952; and for a Mormon view, P.R. and M.F. Cheesman, *Early America and the Polynesians*, Provo, 1975.

51. Paulsen, *Sunburst*, esp. pp. 373-381. Cf. for background, L.T. Hansen, *He Walked the Americas*, London, 1963.

52. The balance is best expressed in the offset pamphlet *The Brotherhood of the Sun,* Santa Barbara, n.d. (mid 1970s), p.3. We may detect the influence of Alice Bailey, who expressed Theosophy eschatologically, with an emphasis on the coming of a divine hierarchy (cf. Melton, *op.cit.*, p.126, col.2).

53. OT: Albert _____ 22 Feb., 1975.

54. Paulsen, *Lord of the Spirits*, p.11.

55. Paulsen, *Sunburst*, esp. ch.50; *et idem* [ed.], *The Brotherhood, op.cit.*, (mimeog.) p.1 (on Essenic community). 'The Life of the Essenes' (mimeograph, extract from C.D. Ginsburg's *The Essenes* (1864), London, 1955, for use by the Brotherhood), esp. [Paulsen], 'Jesus the Essene'(mimeograph, n.d.). pp.9-10; Note E.B. Szekely's *The Essene Gospel of Peace*, San Diego, 1974 (and Paulsen's eventual acknowledgement of it in *Op.cit.* [2nd edn.], p.486), *The Essene Jesus*, San Diego, 1974.

56. Yogananda, *The Road Ahead* (ed. Kriyananda), Nevada City, 1973, pp. 8, 36.

57. *Ibid.*, ch.11.

58. Yogananda, *Autobiography*, pp. 193-4.

59. Paulsen, 'God and His Angels', p.7, cf. also p.3.

60. *Sunburst*, pp. 452-6, cf. also [Paulsen], 'Our Purpose' (mimeograph, n.d.), p.1 (on signpost).

61. Paulsen, 'Communion with the Lord in the House of David', v.s., 'The House of David which I shall raise up in those Last Days' (mimeog., n.d.),

p.3 (first quotation); *Sunburst*, chs. 44-5, esp. p. 439 (second quotation).

62. 'Communion', s.v. 'House of David', p.8 (Elijah); cf. the mural in the State Street store, as in the pamphlet, *The Brotherhood of the Sun*, p. [21], cf. also Paulsen, 'First Book of the Communion' s.v., 'O Living Ones ...' (mimeograph, n.d.), pp. 3-4.

63. 'Aquarian Conference Feb.4, 1972', esp. p.4; *Sunburst*, p.483 and ff.

64. OT: esp. John Slater, Rick Yule, Andrew ____, Chris ____, Grady Stark, July, 1975. See Waters and White Bear, *op.cit.*, p.38, cf.p.37, yet cf. Waters, *Pumpkin Seed Point; being within the Hopi*, Chicago, 1969, ch.13; F.J. Dockstader, *The Kachina and the White Man*, Alberquerque, 1985, pp. 10-11.

65. Trompf, Fieldnotes among Defectors, esp. Feb., 1987. For background, Mary Every, "Evolving into - and out of - Sunburst Community", in *Santa Barbara News-Press*, 7 Feb., 1982, p.2; Weaver, *op.cit.*, esp. chs. 9-11; P. Meyer, 'Santa Barbara's Historical Communes' (unpublished typescript, Santa Barbara, 1983?) (by kind permission); N. Welsh, "Ashes to Ashes ...", *Santa Barbara News and Review*, 9 Feb., 1984, p.9.

66. See *Sunburst*, esp. chs. 26-27, 30, 35, 43-7 (on visions, marriage problems, etc.), and esp. p.523 (against defectors), cf. also p.468 (exposing his first wife's blackmail).

67. See esp. D. Carr, "History, Phenomenology and Reflection", in D. Ihde and R.M. Zaner (eds.), *Dialogues in Phenomenology*, The Hague, 1975, pp.156-75.

68. OT: esp. Rick Yule, David Eddy, Chris ___, Roger Powell, 1975-86, cf. Meyer, *op.cit.*, p.7 (quotation).

69. Trompf, Fieldwork, 1975, 1986, cf. *Santa Barbara News-Press*, 21 and 31, Jan. 1975, 23 March 1975, 31 July 1975. *Santa Barbara News and Review*, March 1975, pp.6-8; Meyer, *op.cit.*, p.7 (quotations).

70. I date the order to Dec., 1977 (deliberately decline to identify the persons who were given it). Cf. *Santa Barbara News-Press* 29 March, 1978; 24 April, 1978.

71. *Sunburst*, pp. 522 (two), 520 for respective quotations.

72. *Ibid.*, pp. 522-3.

73. Prologue to 'The Frozen Deep', in *Complete Plays and Selected Poems of*

Charles Dickens, Plymouth, 1970, p.243.

74. Thus, on the one side, an approach found recently in N. Coxhead (ed.), *The Relevance of Bliss*, London, 1985, and on the other G.J. Tillett, *The Elder Brother; a biography of Charles Webster Leadbeater,* London, 1982.

75. Trompf, Oliver and Stark Fieldnotes, 1975, cf. Const. s.v. 'Objectives 2E' for the quotation.

76. Trompf *et al.*, 1975, and esp. OT: Albert _____, Feb., 1975 (early 1970s); Weavers, *op.cit.*, chs. 1, 7, 10; and esp. Joe Belton, Aug. 1980 (later 1970s).

77. OT: Roger Powell, Feb., 1987, cf. C. San's Introduction to the Causeway edn. of *The Secret etc.* (trans. R. Wilhelm, comm. C.J. Jung), New York, 1975, p.xii, cf. pp. 69-70.

78. It is impossible to name all the persons voicing these allegations because they prefer not to risk the possibility of litigation. For one relevant statement, P. Hardy, "Founder of Sunburst Faces an Embattled Future", in *Santa Barbara News-Press*, 24 June, 1979, p.B.3, col.1.

79. Thus OT: esp. Mark Beauparliant, Feb., 1987 (on Bernard); *Santa Barbara News-Press*, 18 June 1981 (defector's suit); OT: esp. Joe Belton, Aug., 1980 (business competition); *Santa Barbara News-Press*, 28 Aug., 1977, 1 Feb., 1979., 28 Aug., 1979, 25 Sept., 1979, 21 Aug., 1981, etc. (legal and IRS problems); OT: esp. Joe Belton, Aug., 1980; *Sunday Telegraph* (Sydney) 3 Feb., 1980, p.3; 22 June, 1980, p.11 (Australia).

80. *Santa Barbara News-Press*, 21 Aug., 7,18, 17 Sept., 1982; cf. Paulsen, *Christ Consciousness, op.cit.*, cf. 47 (on 'Big Springs Ranch').

81. For background, O. Handlin, *The Uprooted*, New York, 1951; G.R. Taylor (ed.), *The Turner Thesis concerning the Role of the Frontier in American History (Problems in American Civilization Ser.)*, Boston, 1956 edn.

82. The relevant pamphlet and small monograph literature is massive and I can only begin to list the relevant literature. For general background, see P.W. Williams, *Popular Religion in America*, Englewood-Cliffs, 1980, esp. pp. 119ff., 216ff.; G. Halsell, *Prophecy and Politics,* Westport, 1986 (I thank W. Jobling for drawing my attention to this work and Walvoord's below); for a sample, e.g., J.F Walvoord, *Israel in Prophecy* Grand Rapids, 1962; H.W. Armstrong, *The United States and Britain in Prophecy,* [Pasadena], 1967(80); R.W. de Haan, *Israel and the Nations in Prophecy,* Grand Rapids,

1968; C. Smith, *End Times*, Costa Mesa, 1978; W. Malgo, *In the Beginning Was the End*, West Columbia, 1983 (small booklet), *The Kingdom Herald* (British- Israelite), July-Aug., 1980; *The Watchtower* (Jehovah's Witnesses), e.g. Oct. 1, 1986, (periodicals); S.J. Schwantes, *The Final Battle: Armageddon!* Nashville,[1970s]; [American Christian Missionary Church (non- Sectarian)], *Soon-Coming World-Shaking Events! as foretold by God Almighty!* La Verne, 1975(?) (pamphlets); S. Kirban, *Guide to Survival; how the world will end*, Wheaton, 1968; W. McKee, *The Return*, Wheaton, 1972; V. Kulvinskas, *Survival into the Twenty-first Century*, n.p., 1981, E. Whisenant, *88 Reasons why the Rapture will be in 1988*, Grand Rapids, 1987, cf. R. Iacopi, *Earthquake Country*, Menlo Park, 1971 edn., D. Lessing, *Memoirs of a Survivor*, London, 1974, etc. On relating apocalyptic to cosmic conspiracy theory, e.g., K. Hoyt *et al.*, *The New Age Rage*, Old Tappan, 1987, ch. 9; for longer term and literary background, D. Robinson, *American Apocalypses; images of the end of the world in American litera-ture*, Baltimore and London, 1983; F. A. Kreuziger, *Apocalypse ands Science Fiction; a dialectic of religious and secular soteriologies (American Academy of Religion Ser. 40)*, Chico, 1982; and on religious 'privatization', esp. T. Luckmann, *The Invisible Religion*, New York, 1967, pp. 28, 69, etc.

83. For relevant literature on UFOs and new religious activity, e.g., L. Festinger, *When Prophecy Fails*, Minneapolis, 1956; D.L. Leslie and G. Adamski, *Flying Saucers Have Landed*, London, 1956; T. Bethurum, *Facing Reality*, Prescott, 1959; A. Michel, *The Truth about Flying Saucers*, New York, 1967 edn.; B.H. Downing, *The Bible and Flying Saucers*, London, 1968; *SCP Journal* 1/2 (1977), *passim;* R. Kirby, *The Mission of Mysticism*, London, 1979, esp. pp. 108-111, L. Mundo, *The Mundo Report*, New York and Los Angeles, 1982, cf. C.F. Hunter and R. Buck, *Angels on Assignment*, Kingwood, Texas, 1979. For a recent case in newsprint, *The Observer*, 12 Oct., 1975, p.6; *San Francisco Sunday Examiner and Chronicler*, 19 Oct., 1975, p.5. For recent reflections on the development of popular interest in flying saucers, esp. J. A. Keel, "The Man who invented Flying Saucers", in *Whole Earth Review*, 52 (1986), pp. 54-6; D. Curren, "In Advance of the Landing. Folk Concepts of Outer Space", in *ibid.*, pp. 62-9. On more esoter-ic catastrophe theory, e.g., A. Vaughan, *Patterns of Prophecy*, Santa Fe,

1985, chs. 9,12, esp. pp. 165-6 (where Mu is also mentioned). Cf. also, on the non-written media in purveying millennial ideas, R. Frankl, *Televangelism; the marketing of popular religion,* Carbondale, 1987.

84. Esp. P.G. Stafford and B.H. Golightly, *LSD: the problem-solving psychedelic,* New York and London, 1967, ch.6 (visioning); T. Wolfe, *The Electric Kool-Aid Acid Test,* New York, 1968; H. Harrison, *The Dead Book,* London, 1973; J. Hobbs and M. Frederick, 'The Grateful Dead as a Millenarian Movement' (unpublished typescript, University of California, Santa Cruz), Santa Cruz, 1975 (Grateful Dead); R.C. Palms, *The Jesus Kids,* Valley Forge, 1971; D. Pederson, *Jesus People,* Pasadena, 1971; M. Jacob, *Pop goes Jesus,* London and Oxford, 1972 ('Jesus freaks').

85. J. Baldwin, L. Kahn *et al.,* "Alloy", in *The Last Whole Earth Catalogue,* Harmondsworth, 1971, p.117.

86. Stark, [Works], vol. 1, p.43 (= Notebooks submitted to N.O. Brown 1970-1, p.11) (poem), vol.6, p.1803 (first quotation) (both typescripts).

87. For background, esp. E. Troeltsch, *The Social Teaching of the Christian Churches* (trans. O. Wyon), New York, 1931, pt. 4; G. Schwartz, *Sect, Ideology and Social Status,* Chicago and London, 1970.

88. Tuveson, *Redeemer Nation; the Idea of America's Millennial Role,* Chicago, 1968, cf. *Millennium and Utopia,* Berkeley and Los Angeles, 1949.

89. Cf., e.g., M. Rischin (ed.), *The American Gospel of Success,* Chicago, 1968; J.J. Clark and R.H. Woodward (eds), *Success in America,* Belmont, 1968; L. Chenoweth, *The American Dream of Success,* North Scituate, 1974.

90. Cf. Trompf, *Religion and Money; some aspects (The Young Australian Scholar Lecture Series 1),* Adelaide, 1980, pp. 10-12.

91. The last allusion is to Eugene O'Neill's *The Iceman Cometh,* London, 1947, p.77, etc.

92. Cf., e.g., G. Mehta, *Karma Cola,* London, 1979.

93. For important books in this connection, H. James, *The Varieties of Religious Experience (Gifford Lectures, 1901-2),* London and Glasgow, 1960 edn., lects. 4-5; cf. F.S.Shinn, *The Game of Life: how to play it,* Marina del Rey, 1925; *The Secret Door to Success,* Marina del Rey 1940; C.F. Stocking and W.W. Totheroh, *The Business Man in Syria,* Chicago, 1933; N. Hill and W.C. Stone, *Success through a Positive Mental Attitude,* New York, 1960 (note

also Hill's *Think and Grow Rich*, Greenwich, Conn., 1963); K. Copeland, *The Laws of Prosperity*, Fort Worth, 1974; O. Mandino, *The Greatest Success in the World*, New York, 1981, cf. A. Murray, *The Prosperity Tapes* (Mentronic Systems [UK]), Suffolk, 1986, etc.

94. Yogananda, *World Prophecies, op.cit.*, ch.6, cf. pp.116-27.

95. See E.J. Sharpe and Trompf, "The New Sects", in *Current Affairs Bulletin*, 58/4 (1981), p.19 (Ananga Marga); S.J. Palmer, "Commitment and Community in the Rajneesh Foundation", in *Update*, 10/4 (1986), pp.8-9.

96. Cf. esp. D. Horne, *The Lucky Country*, Harmondsworth, 1964 (71); *Money Made Us*, Harmondsworth, 1976; P. Sheehan, *Crisis in Abundance*, Harmondsworth, 1980.

97. Note esp. C. Lansbury, *Arcady in Australia*, Melbourne, 1970; R. Ward, *The Australian Legend*, Melbourne, 1958; G. Serle, *From Deserts the Prophets Come*, Melbourne, 1973; E. Willmot, *Australia: the Last Experiment* (1986 Boyer Lectures), Sydney, 1987, p.35.

98. E. O'Neill, *A Touch of the Poet*, New Haven, 1957, p. 63, cf. pp. 146, 173; P. White, *The Aunt's Story*, Harmondsworth, 1963, p.80; Cf. also M. Jones, "The Promoters Move in on the Great Australian Dream", in *Sydney Morning Herald*, 16 August, 1986, p.161; Trompf, "Gambling and Religion; some Aspects", in M. Walker (ed.), *The Faces of Gambling*, Sydney, 1988 edn., p. 227.

99. Trompf, *Religion and Money, op.cit.*, pp.1-6, cf. also J. Grover, *Struggle for Cargo: what cargo cultists are doing in Australia*, Adelaide, 1983, esp. p.15.

100. Stretton, unpublished seminar presentation on Australian culture, to the History Department, The Research School of the Social Sciences, Australian National University, May, 1971. I owe to Kenneth Boulding, pers. comm., 1981 the comment on Australia without trauma. The longer-term history of Australian millenarism, however, is not to be discounted, and awaits attention. Cf., e.g., H. Mayer, *Marx, Engels and Australia (Sydney Studies in Politics 5)*, Melbourne, 1964, p. 39. Odd revolutionist cases, including the stock-piling of arms for Armageddon, have been known; cf. of late, *The Sun* (Melbourne), 7 Jan., 1989, pp.1-2. In this paper I have no opportunity to consider millenarism and cargoism in the black Australian experience; yet for the awakening of an interest in these, e.g., B. Glowczewski,

"Manifestations symbolique d'une transition économique: le 'Juluru', culte intertribal du Cargo", in *L'Homme,* 23/3 (1984), pp. 7ff.; H. Petri and G. Petri-Odermann, "A Nativistic and Millenarian Movement in North West Australia", in T. Swain and D.B. Rose (eds., *Aboriginal Australians and Christian Missions,* Adelaide, 1988, pp. 391ff.

101. Cf. esp. J. Lindblad, "Alternative Australia; Where the Drop-Outs Are", in *The Bulletin,* 27 March, 1976, pp. 32ff; P. Cock, *Alternative Australia,* Melbourne, 1979.

102. Fieldwork (Australia and Papua New Guinea), 1975-6, cf. Sharpe and Trompf, *Sects, op.cit.,* pp. 8-11.

103. *Ibid.,* p.19.

104. Lindsey, with C.C. Carlson, Melbourne edn., 1970. Over and above the sort of American literature referred to in n.82 *supra,* one also has to account for the impact of local (and English) millenarian traits, e.g., J.M. Hunting, *Israel My Son,* Melbourne, 1970; J. Strong, *The Dooms- day Globe,* Sydney, 1977 edn.; B. Smith, *Warning,* Brisbane, 1980 (with *Second* and *Third Warning,* 1985 and 1989); Anon., *What does the Future Hold?* (pamphlet), Sydney, 1987; and for relatively more restrained works, e.g., C. Chapman, *Whose Promised Land?* Sydney, 1983. For newspapers, e.g. *Eastern Herald* (Sydney) 18 March, p. 36.

105. *The Sun* (New South Wales), 27 Feb., 1987, p.15.

106. Sun Moon, *The Divine Principle,* New York, 1977 edn., p.102 cf. pp. 104, 424, 530. See also Trompf, "God as the Source of Wealth", in *Melanesian Journal of Theology,* 3/1 (1987), p. 80.

107. H. Thomsen, *The New Religions of Japan,* Rutland and Tokyo, 1963, pp. 215-6, etc.; W. Davis, *Dojo; magic and exorcism in Modern Japan,* Stanford, 1980, ch.5; S.J. Palmer, *Korea and Christianity,* Seoul, 1967; P. de Beer, "Religious Sects Worry China", in *Le Monde* (Eng. trans. in *Guardian Weekly,* 135/16, 19 Oct., 1986, p.13); M. Taussig, *The Devil and Commodity Fetishism in South America,* Chapel Hill, 1983; Trompf, Fieldnotes in Latin America, 1965, 1982-3, 1987.

108. For general works, esp. P. Worsley. *The Trumpet Shall Sound,* London, 1970 edn., P. Christiansen, *The Melanesian Cargo Cult,* Copenhagen, 1969, J. Strelan, *Search for Salvation,* Adelaide, 1977; F. Steinbauer, *Melanesian*

Cargo Cults (trans. M. Wohlwill), Brisbane, 1979.

109. See esp. Trompf, *Payback, op. cit.,* ch. 2.

110. Trompf, "Keeping the *Lo* under a Melanesian Messiah", in J. Barker (ed.), *Christianity in Oceania; ethnographic perspectives (American Society for Anthropology in Oceania Monograph 12)*, Manham, 1989 (forthcoming).

111. For the relevant information, A. Kaniku, 'Milne Bay Cargo Movements' (unpublished handwritten MS., UPNG), Port Moresby, 1977, pp.1-3 (Iwa Is.); R.F. Salisbury, "An 'Indigenous' New Guinea Cult" in *Kroeber Anthropological Papers,* 18 (1958), pp. 67ff.; R.M. Berndt, "A Cargo Movement in the Eastern Central Highlands of New Guinea", in *Oceania,* 23/1 (1952), pp. 40ff.; Trompf, "Doesn't Colonialism Make You Mad?" in S. Latukefu (ed.), *Colonial Administrations and Development in Papua New Guinea,* Port Moresby, 1987 (forthcoming) (all New Guinea highlands cases).

112. Thus, e.g. the cases cited by Worsley, *op.cit.,* pp. 120, 164, 209-10, 221-3, cf. Steinbauer 'Die Cargo-Kulte als religionsgeschichtliches und missions theologisches Problem' (Doctoral dissert., University of Erlangen-Nürnberg), Nürnberg, 1971, rear chart.

113. R. Dixon, "The Seventh Day Adventists", in S. Latukefu (ed.), *The Christian Missions in Papua New Guinea and the Solomon Islands and their Contribution to Development,* Port Moresby (forthcoming).

114. Cf. esp. D. Huerter, "The Battle for the Abundant Life", in *Point,* 1 (1974), pp. 123 ff.; G. Fugmann, pers. comm. Nov., 1976 ('results').

115. Cf. esp. Trompf, *Payback, op.cit.,* ch.2, sects. A, 2, ivff.

116. Esp. F. Kamma, *Koreri; messianic movements in the Biak-Numfor Culture Area,* The Hague, 1972, pp. 125ff. Cf. esp. K. Burridge, *New Heaven, New Earth,* Oxford, 1969, pp. 51-2, 63-9; F. Steinbauer; *Melanesische Kargo-Kulte,* Munich, 1971, p.156; Strelan, *op.cit.,* pp. 59-64, on the importance of mythology in the interpretation of cargo cults.

117. Trompf, "'Bilalaf'" in Trompf (ed.), *Prophets of Melanesia,* Port Moresby, 1987 edn., pp. 49-50.

118. P. Lawrence, *Road belong Cargo,* Manchester, 1964, pp. 150ff., 200ff.; T. Ahrens, "'Lo-Bos' and Christian Congregations in Astralabe Bay", in *Point,* 1 (1974), pp. 29ff.; A. Maburau, "Irakau of Manam", in C.E. Loeliger and

Trompf (eds.), *New Religious Movements in Melanesia,* Port Moresby and Suva, 1985, pp. 14-5, etc.

119. P. Silate, "Yali's Cargo Cult; comments on Old Secrets and New Developments", in Trompf (ed.), *Essays on Melanesian Religion,* Suva (forthcoming).

120. Trompf, "Macrohistory and Acculturation", in *Comparative Studies in Society and History* (forthcoming).

121. Trompf, "Interpreting the Melanesian World View; Man Facing Death and After-Life in Melanesia", in N. Habel (ed.), *Powers, Plumes and Piglets,* Adelaide, 1979, p.135. On the notion of 'realized eschatology' as background, cf. C.H. Dodd, *The Apostolic Preaching and its Developments,* London, 1944 edn., pp. 79ff.

122. For background, J. Hides, *Savages in Serge,* Sydney, 1938; B. Allen, 'Information Flow and Innovation Diffusion in the East Sepik District, Papua New Guinea' (doctoral dissert., ANU), Canberra, 1976; R. Lacey, ch. 4 *infra.*

123. Cf. Trompf, "Secularization for Melanesia?" in *Point* (Spec. Issue), 1977, pp. 215-6.

124. Ahrens, "Concepts of Power in a Melanesian and Biblical Perspective", in *ibid.,* pp. 61ff. (and also in German, in H. Bürckle (ed.), *Theologische Beiträge aus Papua Neuguinea,* Erlangen, 1978, pp. 13ff.); *Unterwegs nach der verlorenen Heimat,* Erlangen, 1986, esp. pp. 71ff.

125. Cf. F. Tomasetti, *Traditionen und Christentum im Chimbu-Gebiet Neuguineas (Arbeiten aus dem Seminar für Volkerkunde der F.W. Goethe Universität* 6), Wiesbaden, 1976, pt.D.

126. Cf. Steinbauer, 'Die Cargo-Kulte, etc.', *op.cit.,* rear chart.

127. Lawrence, *op.cit.,* pp. 21-24, 71. Cf., on mythic time, M. Eliade, *The Sacred and the Profane* (trans. W.R. Trask), New York, 1959, ch.2.

128. Lawrence, *op.cit.,* pp. 76-7.

129. The work under that title has been lost. Cf. I.A. Leonard, *Don Carlos de Siguenza y Góngora,* Berkeley and Los Angeles, 1929, pp. 92-6; B. Keen, *The Aztec Image,* New Brunswick, 1971, p.192.

130. Following H. Nevermann, E.A. Worms and H. Petri, *Die Religionen der Südsee und Australiens,* Stuttgart, 1968, p.108. Wilhelmina was Queen of Holland, 1890-1948.

131. Lawrence, *op.cit.*, pp. 100-102, with P.102 for quotations.

132. Tagarab sided with the Japanese, only to be killed by them when he protested against their harsh behaviour towards the Madangs (during the time the Allies were regaining New Guinea, 1944). *Ibid.*, p.110.

133. Here I modify the verbiage of P. Berger and T. Luckmann, *The Social_8*, New York, 1967.

134. See Trompf, "The Theology of Beig Wen, the Would-Be Successor to Yali", in *Catalyst*, 6/3 (1976), pp. 168-71; cf. "Independent Churches in Melanesia", in *Oceania* 54/1 (1983), pp. 56, 67-8.

135. In T. Schwartz, *The Paliau Movement in the Admiralty Islands 1946-1954 (Anthropological Papers of the American Museum of Natural History 49)*, New York, 1968, pp. 256-7, cf. Trompf, "Macrohistory, etc.", *loc. cit.*

136. Trompf, *Payback, op.cit.*, ch.2, sect. A2iva (Paliau); D.K. Billings, "The Johnson Cult on New Hanover", in *Oceania*, 40/1 (1969), pp. 13ff., W. Longgar, "The Johnson Cult of New Hanover", in Trompf (ed.), *Melanesia and Judaeo-Christian Religious Traditions*, Port Moresby, 1975, Bk. 4 opt. 3, pp. 25ff.; N. Miskaram, "Cargo Cultism on New Hanover", in Loeliger and Trompf (eds.), *op.cit.*, pp. 75 (p. 80 for quotation) (Johnson Cult); C. Tirpaia, "The *Kivung Lavurua* Movement among Sections of the Tolai Community of East New Britain Province", in Trompf, *Essays, op.cit.*, (forthcoming), cf. also A.T. Boyce, 'Cargo Cult Theories and Cargo Cult among the Tolai' (unpublished typescript UPNG), Port Moresby, 1973, pp. 42ff.

137. M. Maetoloa, "The Remnant Church" (Study B), in Loeliger and Trompf (eds.), *op.cit.*, p.139, cf. pp. 137-44 as a whole.

138. *Ibid.* (Study A), p.128, cf. Trompf, "Independent Churches, etc.", *loc. cit.*, p.62 on the Millennium not being *klos tu mas* (imminent).

139. In general, Worsley, *op.cit.*, e.g., pp. 69-70, 111-2, 219-28; Trompf (ed.), *Prophets, op.cit.*, pp. 92-8, 133-41, etc. M. Stephen, "Dreams of Change: the Innovative Role of Altered States of Consciousness in Traditional Melanesian Religion", in *Oceania* 50/1 (1979), pp. 3ff., etc. For particulars in the material being dealt with here, note e.g., Schwartz, *op.cit.*, p.257 on Paliau.

140. Trompf, *Payback, op.cit.*, ch.2, sects. A,2,iv,a; B,l.

141. Important examples include Paliau, so *ibid.*, ch.2, sect. A, 2, iii, Teosin, so M. Rimoldi, 'The Hahalis Welfare Society of Buka' (Doctoral dissert., ANU), Canberra, 1971, ch.5; Yali, so L. Morauta, *Beyond the Village Monographs on Social Anthropology)*, London and Canberra, 1974, p.42, etc. For the classic cases of leadership license in Pacificcoast cults of America, J. Sparks, *The Mind Benders*, Nashville, 1979 edn., pp. 257ff. (Jones and the People's Temple); H. Milne, *Bagwan; the god that failed*, Santa Fe, 1987; F. Fitzgerald, *Cities on a Hill*, New York, 1987 edn., pp. 247ff. (Rajneesh); cf. also T.W. Adorno, *The Authoritarian Personality*, New York, 1983 edn., for useful background.

142. Trompf, *op.cit.*, ch.2, sect. A, 3, ch.1; Hogbin, *Experiments in Civilization*, New York, 1970.

143. Cf., e.g., Kamma, *op.cit.*, pp. 168ff.; Lawrence, *op.cit.*, pp. 110-5 (on 'armies', rebellions); D. Fergie, "Prophecy and Leadership; Philo and the Inawai'a Movement", in Trompf (ed.), *Prophets, op.cit.*, p.94; M. Roberts, "The Kiriaka 'Cargo Cult'" in Loeliger and Trompf (eds.), *op.cit.*, p.43 (on isolated acts of violence).

144. For myth as charter, esp. B. Malinowski, "Myth in Primitive Psychology", in his *Magic, Science and Religion*, Garden City, 1954, p.32, n.4, p.54, n.10, pp. 97-101.

145. I allude to Karl Marx, "The Eighteenth Brumaire of Louis Bonaparte", in Marx-Engels, *Selected Works* (Eng. Trans., For. Lang. Pub. Hse.), Moscow, 1951, vol.1, p.225.

146. For background, esp. E. Gellner, *Legitimation of Belief*, Cambridge, 1974.

147. Thus R.G. Collingwood, *Metaphysics*, Oxford, 1940, pp. 285ff.

148. Trompf, *Payback, op.cit.*, ch.2, sect. C,1-2.

149. Thus Huston Smith, *The Religions of Man*, New York, 1965, p.10.

150. Marx, *Zur Kritik der Hegelschen Rechtphilosophie: Einleitung*, in Marx/Engels, *Werke (MEGA)*, Frankfurt, 1927, Pt.1, vol.1/1, pp.607-8.

151. For a *tour d'horizon* of further comparative religious study between California and Melanesia, E. Carpenter, *Oh, What a Blow that Phantom Gave Me!*, London, 1976, esp. pp. 11, 77-83,87-90, 105-111.

White America and the Western World

Chapter Two

The Americanization of Adam

John Bracht

No other religious movement has done more to sacralize America than Mormonism. For them, the United States is, in a sense unparalleled in popular thinking, 'the promised land'. Its scriptures make this an article of faith. The Book of Mormon first published in the early 19th Century has a Sixth-century B.C. prophet fleeing from Jerusalem called Nephi, receiving a revelation from the Lord: "...inasmuch as ye shall keep my commandments, ye shall prosper, and shall be led to a land of promise; yea, even a land which I have prepared for you; yea, a land which is *choice above all other lands*."[1]

America in the Book of Mormon

Some 900 years before Columbus stepped ashore on an island in the Gulf of Mexico, baptizing it San Salvador and claiming it for the King and Queen of Spain, Nephi and his family "did arrive at the promised land; and ... went forth upon the land, and did pitch our tents."[2] While Columbus to his dying day remained ignorant of the true identity of his discovery, extant charts and log books confirm the reality of that discovery. He had opened up the way to the New World. On the other hand, no evidence archaeological or otherwise, exists to confirm the Semitic civilization which descended from Nephi,[3] though this particular claim for America remains a cardinal tenet of the Mormon faith.

Prior to the coming of the Nephites was another migratory group of Hebrews (?) fleeing from the Middle East between 3,000 - 2,000 B.C. This group, the Jaredites, were one of the peoples who were scattered at the time when the Lord confounded language at the Tower of Babel. Their history fills fifteen chapters of only one book of the Book of Mormon, the book of Ether. Jared speaking with his brother, muses about a new home for the people, "And who knoweth but the Lord will carry us forth into a land which is choice above all the earth."[4] Again the land of promise is America. Here they are promised they will become a great nation, "and there shall be none greater than the nation which I will raise up unto me of thy seed, upon all the face of the earth."[5]

The implications of this account are obvious. Centuries before the Lord told Abram to leave his country, and promised to make him "into a great nation" and gave him "this land to take possession of it",[6] Jared is offered the land of America. This means that America takes precedence over Israel in Mormon sacred history. It also helps us to understand how Mormonism can make such extraordinary claims for America's future.

In a revelation given through Joseph Smith the Prophet on July 20th, 1831, the Lord proclaimed that "the land of Missouri is the land which I have appointed and consecrated for the gathering of the saints. Wherefore this is the land of promise, and the place for the city of Zion."[7] It is a long haul from Babel to 19th Century frontier America, but the claim remains the same, the only change being the delineation of a particular part of America. Previously in New York, less than a year after the Mormon Church had been founded, the Lord told Joseph that he sought to give him greater riches "even a land of promise, a land flowing with milk and honey." The Lord covenants with the prophet in Abrahamic terms promising the land "for the inheritance of your children forever, while the earth shall stand." As if to outdo Abraham's inheritance "the great I AM" adds, "and ye shall possess it again in eternity, no more to pass away."[8]

Unlike many 19th Century millenarians who speculated about the time of the Second Advent and the inauguration of the new age, Joseph Smith appointed a place instead. It has always been a fundamental principle of Mormonism - the Church of Jesus Christ of *latter-day* Saints - that it exists to establish the cause of Zion. This means, in the prophet's words, that a people must be "perfected and prepared to meet the Lord Jesus Christ when he shall appear in great glory."[9] The prophet's own scriptures, the Book of Mormon, and the writings of Enoch in the Book of Moses, speak of the "momentous obligation and responsibility of building the New Jerusalem in the Dispensation of the Fulness of Times."[10] To accomplish this Herculean task Joseph Smith did two things. First he presented to the world an American-based history of Antiquity, in the Book of Mormon. Secondly, through him Zion was to be established in the last days for the salvation of humanity. It was to be the beginning of the end of God's dealings with the race, the climax of salvation history. Supremely confident in the destiny that awaited his people, the prophet issued his challenge to the 19th Century:

> I calculate to be one of the instruments for setting up the kingdom of Daniel by the word of the Lord, and I intend to lay a foundation that will revolutionize the world. It will not be by sword or gun that this kingdom will roll on: the power of truth is such that all nations will be under the necessity of obeying the Gospel.[11]

The Kingdom of Daniel was to commence in the Republic of Washington. Columbia, "the gem of the Ocean", had been foreseen in the Book of Mormon. In 1 Nephi chapter 13, the young son of Lehi receives a vision in which he sees the nations of the gentiles. He sees a man inspired by the Spirit of God "to go forth upon the many waters" (Columbus), "unto the seed of my brethren, who were in the promised land" (Nephi's expatriate Jews who had migrated to the Americas in the 6th Century B.C.). Nephi, peering into a future over twenty centuries removed from his own, sees "other Gentiles" who "went forth out of captivity, upon the many waters" (pilgrim fathers and other early settlers in America). He foretells the wars between the whites and the Indians, as well as the American War of Independence - "And I beheld their mother Gentiles (the British) were gathered together upon the waters, and upon the land also, to battle against them." Neither British mismanagement of the war nor American battle tactics were responsible for the American victory, "the power of God was with them (the Americans) and ... the wrath of God was upon all those that were gathered together against them to battle" (the British).[12] America's destiny under divine protection is that she is to be the land upon which the Kingdom will be established. God's power will lift her up "above all other nations" for God has covenanted with Nephi's father that his seed (the Jews who landed in America in 600 B.C.) "should have (America) for the land of their inheritance."[13]

The Book of Mormon gives America a wondrous antiquity in which Jaredites, Nephites and Lamanites rather than Olmecs, Mayans, Aztecs or Incas emerge as the really significant civilizations. The setting and history of the Book of Mormon are as equally impressive as the Bible, and America itself effectively becomes the "Old" World. Peter Meinhold sees in the Book of Mormon the "expression of an American quest for a usable past which represents a native American historical consciousness unrivalled to this degree and intensity in the entire range of American historical thought."[14] When one considers the scope of the Book of Mormon's historical content and the races involved in its accounts, it becomes obvious that Meinhold's assessment is a most perceptive one. Again it must be stressed that no understanding of Mormonism's future expectations for America is possible without appreciating what it made of America's past. If wondrous things are yet to occur on the American continent it is only because the Lord has already wrought mighty miracles through the ancient inhabitants of that land.

The Book of Mormon claims to be the equivalent of the Old and New Testaments. It covers a period of twenty-five centuries though the bulk of the book is dated from 600 B.C. to 421 A.D. The history's location is presumed to be central and south America. The record contains fifteen books written by ancient Hebrew-American prophets and kings. In the current edition (1982) the contents run to 531 pages. The original records were engraved on metal plates fashioned from a gold-copper alloy and discovered buried in a hill in New York State in 1824. The unknown language of the plates is described in the record itself as "reformed Egyptian".[15] When the book was first published in 1830, it gave its advocates the nickname "Mormon" since he was one of the chief figures who wrote the original.

Reference has already been made to the major migratory groups who came to America from the Middle East as early as 2,000 B.C. The first group, those that fled from the confusion of the Tower of Babel were the Jaredites. They took with them animals, birds, fresh-water fish and seeds for all types of domestic crops. After four years of preparations in the wilderness of the "valley of Nimrod" (?) they built eight barges to carry them on their epic voyage half way around the world.

The Jaredite migration was successful and a great civilization was established in Ancient America. It lasted for almost two millennia, destroying itself through internal conflict and brutal warfare *ca.* 600 B.C. The Lord had promised that the

Jaredite civilization would be greater than any other, and is alleged to have been contemporaneous with those of Babylon, China, Egypt and Assyria (even though there is no evidence of its existence outside the Book of Ether). To understand how Zion will incorporate more than just the inhabitants of the American continent we need to consider the second migratory group who succeeded the Jaredites.

This group journeyed to the Americas in the 6th Century B.C. during the first year of the reign of Zedekiah, King of Judah. Judah was facing conquest by the Babylonians. Jeremiah was preaching that captivity by Babylonia was inevitable and unavoidable (Jeremiah 21:3-10), and that no alliance would save Zedekiah from his fate. The Bible speaks of those events as a time of God's judgement. God was using Nebuchadnezzar as his instrument of judgment on an unfaithful people. Two options were given the inhabitants of Judah. They could stay in Jerusalem and die by the sword, famine or plague, or they could go out and surrender to the Babylonians and escape with their lives. No third option is mentioned. Despite the gloom, Jeremiah prophesied that a remnant would be saved and would later return from captivity to rebuild the shattered kingdom. In this way the promises of God would be fulfilled., and despite the unfaithfulness of his people he would "bring them back to this land: (Jer. 24:6). It is precisely at this point that the Book of Mormon account diverges.

A prophet named Lehi, father of Nephi, said to be a contemporary of Jeremiah, is told that there is a third option. The righteous within Jerusalem are to escape captivity and death altogether, journey into the wilderness, build a boat, and be led across the waters to America! God will be their "light in the wilderness", lead them towards "the promised land", "deliver you from destruction."[16] In what sense America is the promised land for the children of Abraham is never explained. While God says to Jeremiah that the Babylonian scourge is his inescapable judgement on his people, he says to Lehi and Nephi that they are to be delivered from that same judgement. The Bible speaks of only one promised land - that promised to Abraham. The Book of Mormon changes this promise and has God leading a righteous remnant to another promised land Abraham never conceived of - America.

This group of Hebrews consisting of Lehi, his wife Sariah and their sons Laman, Lemuel, Sam and Nephi, as well as the families of Zoram and Ishmael, fled Jerusalem into the Sinai wilderness.

On the shores of the Arabian Sea, the little colony built and provisioned a boat and set sail across the waters. Mormons believe their voyage carried them eastwards over the Indian Ocean, then right over the Pacific to the western coast of America, where they landed about 590 B.C. In this land of promise they quickly established themselves and in the course of a few generations their numerous posterity had taken possession of the land. Before Lehi died, he made a prophecy in which he identified a choice prophet and seer whom the Lord would raise up in the last days. He would be a descendant of Lehi, who was of the tribe of Manasseh, and would be great like Moses. His mission would be to bring forth God's word to future generations. The future prophet and deliverer is to be named Joseph, and this, according to Mormons, is a wonderful prophecy about the Prophet Joseph Smith. Following Lehi's death a division occurred among the Nephite people. Some followed Nephi, and others Laman, Lehi's eldest son. These divided peoples became known as the Nephites and Lamanites. The two groups increasingly opposed one another, and the more wicked Lamanite faction was cursed by God. The mark of the curse was a darker skin to distinguish them from their brethren and discourage intermarriage. Thousands of people who were before "exceedingly fair and delightsome" became dark and loathsome, their skin of "blackness" designed to make them less "enticing unto my people".[17]

Of all the peoples mentioned in the Book of Mormon, only the descendants of the Lamanites allegedly exist today.

> The Lamanites while increasing in numbers, fell under the curse of divine displeasure; they became dark in skin and benighted in spirit, forgot the God of their fathers, lived a wild nomadic life, and degenerated into the fallen state in which the American Indians - their lineal descendants - were found by those who rediscovered the western continent in later times.[18]

In the course of the Book of Mormon's history we discover that the few Lamanites who united with the Nephites were numbered among the Nephites, and "their curse was taken from them, and their skin became white like unto the Nephites."[19] Such incidents merely preview an even greater and more universal blessing of the Lamanites which the Book of Mormon predicts will occur in the last days. It envisaged a time when the Gospel (Mormon) would be preached to their descendants "and their scales of darkness shall begin to fall from their eyes; and many generations shall not pass away among them, save they shall be a white and delightsome people."[20] From the very beginning of its history, the Mormon Church has always had a special burden for the American Indian. It approached them with the announcement that they were the remnant of a once mighty people who had once inhabited the Americas and that God meant to make them great again. The Church informed them that the history of their real forefathers was to be found in the Book of Mormon.

The Mormons are the only group in the United States who have a theological view of the Indians, i.e., they are not merely interested in their conversion but in their contribution to the sacred history of America. In January 1833 Joseph Smith said the Book of Mormon identified "our western tribes of Indians" as ... "descendants from that Joseph which was sold into Egypt." His words spoken over a skeleton unearthed in Illinois in 1834 indicate that the final great battles of the Book of Mormon history took place in that region of the United States. John Taylor, one of Joseph Smith's successors spoke of missionary work of the Indians being an urgent task "if we desire to retain the approval of God." Perhaps the greatest advocate of Indian missions and Indian rights was the late President Spencer W. Kimball (1895-1985), 12th President Prophet of the Mormon Church.[21] The Book of Mormon speaks of a day when the curse on the Lamanite will be lifted and they will realize again, their heritage and destiny - their true identity as children of Israel. This eschatological event is called "the Day of the Lamanite" and President Kimball believed it had begun in his lifetime, "the day of the Lamanite is surely here and we are God's instrument in helping to bring to pass the prophecies" of the Book of Mormon.[22] We shall consider later what those prophecies entail. The Lamanite is Mormonism's only tangible link with its sacred American past. In the absence of any archaeological evidence they are a living relic, one which motivates hope for future events which are yet to transpire on the American continent.

Mormon scholars have for years been down-playing exaggerated claims for Book of Mormon archaeological 'evidences'. Mormon apologist Blake Ostler recently attempted a defence of the Book of Mormon by suggesting that it may be an expansion of an ancient work. Joseph Smith, he suggests "built on the work of earlier prophets to answer the nagging problems of his day". Ostler believes that the Prophet provided "unrestricted and authoritative commentary, interpretation, explanation and clarifications based on insights from the ancient Book of Mormon text and the King James Bible. The result is a modern world view and theological understanding superimposed on the Book of Mormon text". Later he cites John L. Sorenson, leading Mormon archaeologist and scholar as admitting that "despite vigorous debate no concrete evidence exists establishing a Book of Mormon archaeology". Ostler believes, like most Mormons that something akin to the Ebla discovery may yet turn up. For the moment then, Mormons can still go on believing that the Book is a factual account of America's past, and therefore a true indicator of its future, while living in the hope that their faith will be verified at some later date.[23]

The most significant event to occur in the Book of Mormon is the appearance of Christ in the Western hemisphere following his resurrection in Judaea. He allegedly appeared to the Nephites, preached the gospel, established his church - which survived for about two hundred years - and promised to return one day to that continent. Mormons find in legendary sources of the Incas and Mayas support for their belief that a great white bearded God visited ancient America. Whether the legends speak of Quetzalcoatl of the Nahua, Virakocha of the Peruvians or Kukulcan, the Mormons believe the true identity of the fabled figures is Jesus Christ. "The short ministry of Christ in America had such lasting effects that 1900 years later his visit can be recognized by the legends and other knowledge available."[24] Although a major problem arises that such legendary culture-heroes are not at all contemporary with the historical periods in the Book of Mormon - the Toltec god Quetzalcoatl (the Plumed Serpent), for instance, emerging too late in time to be considered a candidate for Jesus Christ[25] - nevertheless as a further means of sanctifying America, the Book of Mormon's account of Christ's visit is significant.

Some years after the Book of Mormon was published as a record of God's dealings with the ancient inhabitants of the Americas[26] Joseph Smith came into possession of some ancient Egyptian papyri which he claimed to translate by the inspiration and power of God.[27] The translation took the form of two books of sacred scripture, one being the Book of Abraham and the other, the Book of

Moses. It is the latter, containing the original and expanded text of Genesis which bestows upon America the ultimate glorification. Mormon hopes for the future are partly based on the revelations about the American past which this text contains. In the Book of Genesis we are told that Enoch, the seventh from Adam, "walked with God; then he was no more, because God took him away" (Gen. 5:24). Whatever became of Enoch we do not know, other than that "God took him." Where the Old Testament is silent, the Book of Moses has much to say. It offers two descriptive chapters on the life of Enoch (chapters 6 and 7 of the Book of Moses). Through "modern revelation" Joseph Smith announced that the entire pre-diluvian civilization of Genesis had actually been sited in ancient America. The modern revelation became the basis of Mormon hopes for the latter-day establishment of Zion on the American continent, but that hope itself was firmly based on America's amplified and epic past.

Enoch in Joseph's Book of Moses received a superior revelation of the Earth's history, including the coming of Christ and his redemption. Enoch preached the gospel to many nations and called the people to repentance. When the enemies of God came against him and his people, Enoch "spake the word of the Lord, and the earth trembled and the mountains fled ... and the rivers of water were turned out of their course ... so powerful was the word of Enoch."[28] Despite this display and the subsequent rising out of the sea of a new land, the wicked did not repent. Enoch then built a city called "The City of Holiness, even Zion" where all the righteous seed of Adam took up residence. In time the entire populace became so righteous that God decided to bless the people in a special way. Bettering the Genesis account, where it is recorded that Enoch alone was taken away by God, the Book of Moses has the whole city of Enoch taken away!

> And Enoch and all his people walked with God, and he dwelt in the midst of Zion; and it came to pass that Zion was not, for God received it up into his own bosom; and from thence went forth the saying, Zion is fled.[29]

The whole city, including houses, farms, fields, cattle and people, was "translated" and removed from the surface of the planet earth. In a Mormon commentary on the subject we read the following:

In 2,948 B.C. when Enoch was 430 years old, he and the population of
the entire city of Zion were translated and removed from the earth to
another planet. This quickening process was a remarkable physical meta-
morphosis whereby the seeds of death were neutralized within them and
their bodies became subject to a higher system of physical laws ... As
President Brigham Young commented: 'He (Enoch) obtained power to
translate himself and his people with the region they inhabited.[30]

Smith once explained that the power of translation is a power which belongs to
the priesthood, but that it has "been kept hid from before the foundation of the
world ... to be revealed in the last times."[31] By exercising this very priesthood
power Enoch was able to transform himself, his people and their city so that it
could withstand the shattering experience of being lifted from the surface of the
earth, and whisked through interplanetary space. This extraordinary event in the
Earth's history is said to have occurred about the time when the Sumerian civilization was rising to greatness in the lower Tigris-Euphrates Valley, and during
the period of the first two dynasties (3,200 - 2,700 B.C.) of ancient Egypt.
Enoch and his people became messengers of God or ministering angels to populations of other planets - "Terrestrial Bodies".[32]

At the last day or near the end of the present age, the "translated" portion of
earth, with Enoch's people on it, will come through inter-stellar space again,
enter Earth's orbit, and descend to where it was before. (Some popular Mormon
speculations identify the locale for the Enochian civilization as having been in
the Gulf of Mexico, which will be filled up again at the End). The lost Ten
Tribes of Israel, too, will again return from their hidden place in the "northern
regions" to join with the city of Zion. Mormon eschatology, of which we will
say more in the next section of this study, clearly identifies the events which will
precede Christ's second coming. The return of these two ancient groups is an
essential and integral part of the establishment of Zion and the building of the
New Jerusalem. It is an expression of what we shall suggest is the Mormon
'Cargo Cult', and Mormon eschatology is very descriptive of the preparations
which must be made before that Cargo can be received.

Mormons suggest that the tribes are still on Earth, but scattered throughout
various regions. They believe that when Joseph Smith spoke about the tribes

coming forth at the last day from the "north countries" that he meant northern Europe or Asia. The church still holds to the view that the location of the lost tribes is still the Lord's secret, and that anyone claiming to identify their location is speaking without authority. Only the North Polar regions theory, that they are secluded behind or under the icebergs of the polar regions, is thought to be supported by Mormon scriptures which suggest that before the tribes can come forth in the last days, they must "smite the rocks, and the ice shall flow down at their presence."[33]

Further on the subject of the whereabouts of the tribes, James E. Talmage, a past Mormon apostle and theologian has written:

> From the scriptural passages already considered, it is plain that, while many of those belonging to the Ten Tribes were diffused among the nations, a sufficient number to justify the retention of the original name were led away as a body and are now in existence in some place where the Lord has hidden them ... their return constitutes a very important part of the gathering, characteristic of the dispensation of the fulness of times.[34]

Previously we noted that Smith saw his primary task as preparing and perfecting a people who would be fit to meet the Lord when he shall return and reign from his American Zion. We noted that he went about this challenge by first presenting the world with a radically new version of American antiquity. This version gave validity and sanctity to the American continent as a promised land. The validity is based on the sacred nature of latter-day scriptures sich as the Book of Mormon and the Book of Moses. It is now time to consider the Prophet's other means of furthering his epochal mission.

Joseph Smith taught that the Book of Mormon "was the most correct book on earth, and the keystone of our religion".[35] In the light of what the book did for America's past, this statement is readily understood. Everything that Mormons yet hope for in America is based on the 'reality' of what God has already accomplished on that continent. In this respect Mormonism links up with Judaism and Christianity as a religion whose basic premises are fundamentally established on the foundation of historic, saving events. In this, Mormonism is probably more akin to the Jewish concept of the Holy Commonwealth than to the Christian concept of the apocalyptic kingdom. That is, Mormonism equates the New Age with a realized eschatology which focuses on a particular continent and a chosen people living under prophetic circumstances. The Old Testament elements are all there - the land, the people, the holy city and the temple. The major distinction, of course, is that the Mormon Zion is even more universalist than the Jewish. The American New Jerusalem embraces a chosen people who include Gentiles, American Indians and Polynesians. It is also not exclusivist in the sense that it views world rule in the Messianic age as radiating from two capitals - the Jewish Jerusalem and the Missouri Zion. In contrast to more typical Christian millenarism, it is more distinctly political and materialistic as a 'Zionism'.

The Mormon blueprint for America's future is supplemented by the Prophet's personal revelations. Most of these are bound within the covers of the Doctrine and Covenants, while others are recorded in diaries, journals and histories of the church. Smith's own articles of faith - thirteen in number - express the Mormon view of revelation. "We believe all that God has revealed, all that he does now reveal, and we believe that he will reveal many great and important things pertaining to the Kingdom of God." This explanation of the dynamic nature of Mormon truth, renders inspired all the utterances of the founding Prophet and his successors. The Tenth Article of Faith utters a basic truth and hope to which all those successors have subscribed:

> We believe in the literal gathering of Israel and in the restoration of the Ten Tribes; that Zion (the New Jerusalem) will be built upon the American continent; that Christ will reign personally upon the earth; and, that the earth will be renewed and receive its paradisiacal glory.[36]

How was this hope of the "gathering" expressed in early Mormon history and what does it entail?

Early Zionism and the Church of Jesus Christ of Latter Day Saints

The Mormons were not alone in their views of the "gathering" and the eschatology of the latter days. Nor were they alone in their views of America. What makes these views seem so peculiar today, is that they are no longer common-place on both sides of the Atlantic.[37] There was a time, however, when they were, and thus when Mormon views would have appeared far less radical or eccentric. Transferring Hebrew concepts to new worlds and seeking to build the Biblical Kingdom of God on earth, are hardly pursuits original to Mormons. Protestants, especially Puritan Protestants, had given expression to such ambitions long before Mormonism made its unique contribution. The Puritan ascendency resulted in a movement among the English for the return of the Jews to Palestine. This was considered a necessary prelude to the establishment of the millennial kingdom and the reign of Christ. This partial Judaization of Protestant England went hand in hand with a concern for the gathering of Israel. It was Puritan concern that would eventually lead to the re-admission of Jews to England. They had to be allowed to go farther before they could go nearer - to their ancestral home. The Diaspora needed to be made complete before the ingathering could commence (Deut. 28:64).

Most interesting for the Mormon concept of gathering is the work of Manasseh ben Israel, the learned Rabbi of Amsterdam, who felt called to hasten the coming of the Messiah . His 1650 publication of *Hoc est, Spes Israelis (The Hope of Israel)* elaborated on this idea of the completion of the diaspora as a prelude to the prophetic gathering. His expectations were greatly encouraged by the writings of a Jewish traveller, Antonio de Montezinos who told a tale of Indian tribes in the West Indies who practised rituals of Judaism and appeared to be Hebrews. Montezinos considered them to be of the tribe of Reuben, one of the ten lost tribes of Israel. Spanish missionaries in South America had already propounded the theory that the American Indians were the lost Ten Tribes. Viscount Kingsborough (1795-1837) propounded this theory in his massive nine-volume work *The Antiquities of Mexico* (1831-48). Kingsborough was convinced that the Aztecs and Mayas of Mexico and Central America were descendants of the ten tribes of Israel. The theory had been canvassed up to three hundred years prior to the *Antiquities* but no one had set it forth in such monumental detail as Kingsborough.[38] Mormon scholars and Book of Mormon apologists are fond of quoting from this source, especially since the Viscount equated Quetzalcoatl with Jesus of Nazareth.[39] Ever since the Puritans landed in New England, however, the idea of American Indians having a Hebraic origin has remained popular up to and including the 19th century.

Within three decades before the publication of the Book of Mormon, at least six books or papers were distributed in the United States. Bearing on this hypothesis was an essay written by Charles Crawford of Philadelphia in 1799, written to prove that many of the Indians were descended from the lost tribes. *A Star in the West* (1816) by Elias Boudinot of Trenton New Jersey, founder and first president of the American Bible Society; *The Wonders of Nature and Providence Displayed* by Josiah Priest, published in Albany (1825); and a *View of the Hebrews* published by Ethan Smith, written in Vermont (1823); as well as the writings of Increase Mather and Jonathan Edwards "The Book of Mormon (therefore) offered as reasonable an explanation as any for the time".[40] All helped spread this theory. Only the Book of Mormon today, however, perpetuates this myth of the Hebrew-Americans, although we should note that the Book of Mormon nowhere claims that the peoples it describes are related to the lost tribes, but rather that they are descended from Jews living in Jerusalem in the 6th Century B.C.

Montezino's alleged discoveries were enthusiastically adopted by Manasseh ben Israel as evidence that the dispersion of Israel had actually been accomplished. If children of Abraham had been found in the newest of the worlds discovered, then surely Israel had been scattered among all the nations. He saw the existence of American Hebrews as a sign that the time for the reunion of all the tribes of Israel under the Messiah was fast approaching. In the year before his *Spes Israelis* appeared, significantly, John Owen was found preaching before the House of Commons about the "bringing home of his ancient people to be one fold with the fulness of the Gentiles... in answer to millions of prayers put up to the throne of grace." (1849)[41] So it can be readily seen that this aspect of Mormon eschatology, i.e., that the gathering of the Jews precede the establishment of Christ's millennial kingdom, was a concept borrowed naturally from prevailing Christian thinking in 17th, 18th and 19th Century England and America. The Church of Scotland in the 19th Century was particularly burdened with a sense of mission to the Jews. It expressed the conviction that Israel's future was bound up with the final evangelization of the whole earth. In 1839 a deputation of four Church of Scotland ministers visited Palestine to inquire about the state of the Jews. One result of this mission was the establishment of a work among the Jews at Budapest. The Irish General Assembly established a work among the Jews in Syria in 1844. Whatever the General Assembly of the Church in Scotland or Ireland felt it was inspired to do, only the newly-established Church of Jesus Christ of Latter-day Saints actually claimed to have received a divine commission to direct the special work of the gathering of Israel. Just as Joseph Smith had sanctified America's past through the contents of the Book of Mormon, so he sanctified his own church's right to direct the affairs of the future through modern revelations.

In a vision which he claimed to have received, along with Oliver Cowdery, at Kirtland Ohio, April 3rd, 1836, the Prophet received information and authority which eclipsed that of all his contemporaries. The vision occurred within the walls of the Kirtland Temple and involved the appearance of heavenly beings including Christ, Moses, Elias, and Elijah.[42] Moses made his appearance to transfer to Joseph Smith "the keys of the gathering of Israel from the four parts of the earth, and the leading of the ten tribes from the land of the north." Elias offered the keys of his dispensation, and Elijah likewise.[43] As a result of this vision the Prophet appointed two of his apostles - Orson Hyde and John E. Page - to travel to Palestine and actually dedicate that land for the gathering of the Jews.

Orson Hyde, though deserted by his companion in New York, went on to visit with leaders of Jewish communities in London, Amsterdam, Constantinople and Jerusalem. He passed through nations engaged in war and endured many hardships at sea. On Sunday morning, October 24th, 1841, he climbed alone to the top of the Mount of Olives in Jerusalem and solemnly dedicated that land for the return of the Jewish people.[44]

Hyde built stone altars on both the Mount of Olives and Mount Moriah as memorials of his prayer. In all, Hyde travelled more than 20,000 miles on this mission. The scope of the Prophet's vision was quite astonishing, for here is an instance of his determination to establish Zion in the last days. At that time there were no Mormons in the Utah territory. The Church had established its temporary gathering place in Nauvoo, Illinois and would not move from there until five years after Hyde's historic mission to the Holy Land. Yet from Nauvoo, the Prophet sent his missionaries and apostles to Britain and the Continent and arranged for the transportation of thousands of European converts to the

American Zion. At the same time as this work was being supervised he was also concerned with the gathering of the Jews and the reclamation of the ancient Lamanites among the Indian tribes of North America.[45]

Christian writers and evangelists had already pronounced their own benedictions on the land "choice above all other lands." Cotton Mather, in his *Magnalia Christi Americana*, went to great lengths to document "Christ's Great Deeds in America." Jonathan Edwards, pondering the Great Awakening in 1740, considered himself to be witnessing the prelude of a glorious work which would eventually renew the world of mankind, "and there are many things that make it probable that this work will begin in America."[46] The Mormon saga presented itself as the catalyst for this "glorious work" emerging in the eastern states as part of the primitivist gospel movement. Mormonism was the most successful heir and exponent of the primitive gospel movement or "restorationism."

For so many seekers on the frontier Smith alone was supreme in creating a new, visible religious society. His eschatology was familiar to them but with one obvious difference. For the Prophet, eschatology was no mere theological speculation, it was a blueprint for present action. "In form the Mormons remained firmly premillennialist, but in substance the optimistic post-millennialism of the 'redeemer nation' took over. The good life, spiritual and temporal, was to be built by men under the guidance of God."[47] Smith announced the voice from heaven that Roger Williams had wanted to hear. He created the New Testament Church most Campbellites had sought. But where others only prayed for the age of paradisiacal glory, the Mormon Prophet actually laid the foundations for it. He announced the principles of the "gathering" and looked to the west for the building of the New Jerusalem. He told his followers that Christ would not return to the earth until the saints had established moral, social and political conditions fitting for the rule of Christ on earth. Jedediah Grant, later to become a counsellor to President Brigham Young (1847-1877), expressed it well when he said, "If you want a heaven, go and make it."[48] Other movements would make mistakes setting dates for the coming of he Lord and the end of the present world order. Smith's genius lay in that he concentrated more on building the new order rather than anticipating it. He chose a place - America - rather than a time.

As Klaus Hansen has put it,

> Not until the Jews had returned to their ancient homeland, and not until a
> modern Israel in North America had created a viable nation from which
> the law could "go forth", would the eyes of the faithful behold the glory
> of the coming of the Lord... to Joseph Smith the utopian society would be
> realized, not by miracles, but by means... Mormonism also claimed to be
> a world religion, applicable to all mankind, but its mission was to be ful-
> filled through a peculiar identification with American nationalism.[49]

Converts in the British Isles, Scandinavia and Western Europe were greatly
attracted to such a vision. They accepted the invitation to plan for a millennium
which would be built by human hands. The gathered saints were to wait for the
new age, "but in great comfort and with full human freedom and dignity".
Others had emphasized the trials of the suffering remnant, but the American
saints were invited to embrace the "triumphs of a prospering remnant."[50] The
young Mormon Church in New York State had no reservations about its destiny.
It considered itself to be the prophetic stone of Daniel that was to roll forth and
fill the whole earth. Mormons saw themselves as the chosen people, the royal
blood of Israel's scattered remnants. As the Book of Mormon had transformed
Indians and Polynesians into Hebrews, as well as the continent into the promised
land, so the Mormon Gospel revealed to its disciples, their true identity. One of
the offices of the Mormon priesthood was that of Patriarch. The patriarchs give
blessings to individual Mormons, telling them through inspiration what God has
planned for their lives. The blessing also serves to identify the lineal descent of
the person. In every case Mormons are told that they are of the house of Israel,
and specifically, descendants of Ephraim or Manasseh. In this way they become
literal descendants of Abraham, heir to the blessings of his children, rightful
inheritors of the earth promised to Abraham. Unlike the Christian relationship to
Abraham which is based on individual faith, the Mormon relationship is based
on an alleged blood line, a corporate identity. They really believe themselves to
have the blood of Israel in their veins.[51] All non-Mormons are branded as
"Gentiles" and that includes Jews. The restoration of the true church means that
the day of salvation is at hand, Zion is lifting up her ensign to the nations, and
men must rally to that standard or be visited with the judgements of God.

In pursuing this dream of an American Zion, the Mormons have attempted again and again to establish their own city-state. During the 19th Century most of the attempts failed - Kirtland Ohio, Independence Missouri, and Nauvoo, Illinois. Salt Lake City, Utah, founded in the late 1840s, is the most successful attempt to date. All four cities bear the marks and monuments of the Mormon dream. The site for the New Jerusalem was well known to the early Mormons. As we saw at the very beginning of this study, the holy place, the "centre place" was to be located in Missouri, not Illinois or Utah.

In an 1831 revelation the Prophet elevated the American dream to unprecedented heights.

> Hearken, O ye elders of my church, saith the Lord your God, who have assembled yourselves together, according to my commandments, in this land, which is the land of Missouri, *which is the land which I have appointed and consecrated for the gathering of the saints. Wherefore this is the land of promise, and the place for the city of Zion.* And thus saith the Lord your God, if you will receive wisdom, here is wisdom. *Behold, the place which is now called Independence is the center place; and a spot for the temple is lying westward, upon a lot which is not far from the courthouse.* Wherefore it is wisdom that the land should be purchased by the saints, and also every tract lying westward, even unto the line running directly between Jew and Gentile; And also every tract bordering by the prairies, inasmuch as my disciples are enabled to buy lands. Behold, this is wisdom, *that they may obtain it for an everlasting inheritance.* [52]

Why Missouri? After the Church moved from its initial establishments in New York State to Kirtland, Ohio, the Prophet received a revelation telling him to prepare for the building of Zion. At that time no particular place was designated. Then in June 1831, as a result of difficulties some of the saints were experiencing in Ohio, the Prophet received divine instructions directing some of his people to "flee the land" and take their journey "into the regions westward, unto the land of Missouri, unto the borders of the Lamanites." [53] His reference to the "borders of the Lamanites" simply indicates that he was sending them to the extreme western frontiers of Missouri, and of the United States, the very limits of the young Republic. The July 20th revelation quoted above made it clear that the focus for the gathering was to be on the border between the wilderness and the United States. Independence was the last outpost before the Rocky Mountains or the desert regions of Santa Fe, the jumping-off place for wagon trains moving west to California and Oregon. The first Mormons to reach Missouri had gone there as missionaries to the Indians as early as 1830. When the Prophet was forced to leave Kirtland, Ohio in January 1836, he determined to join his far-flung settlements in Jackson County Missouri.

On May 18th, 1838 while touring Daviess County, Missouri, the prophet surveyed a fertile valley skirting the Grand River. As he gazed admiringly on the scene he received a revelation identifying the place as "Adam-ondi-Ahman." He announced that he had had a vision in which he had seen Adam gathered with all his children in the valley. After discovering a pile of stones which he identified as an altar upon which Adam had offered sacrifices, he elaborated on his vision:

> "Here is the real valley where Adam called his posterity together and blessed them." He also told them that Jackson County was *once the Garden of Eden from which Adam was driven* and after travelling northeast seventy miles, built the altar on which he stood, and offered sacrifice unto the Lord. One of the number later wrote: "I thought it a great privilege to be at that time with the Prophet, and to hear his words regarding the mound and pile of rocks laid up in so early a period of the world's history.[54]

With a glance over a Missouri landscape, Smith surveyed thousands of years of ancient and Biblical history and identified Adam as an American. Mormons ever since have understood the first seven chapters of the Book of Genesis to have taken place in the Americas. Noah's ark was built somewhere in what is now Mexico or the United States, and during the chaos of the flood it drifted over to the Middle East. Humanity had its origins in America, and America, as we noted previously, is the true, old world. This is an epic whose mystique still permeates Mormon thinking today. Following the revelation of the Prophet and the command of God to gather to the "Center Place", the Mormons laid out new towns in frontier Missouri, Adam-ondi-Ahman, Gallatin, Millport, Haun's Hill and De Witt. A steady stream of immigrants in covered wagons, cut deep ruts in the Missouri plains. By the summer of 1838, there were 15,000 Mormons in northern Missouri.

As early as August, 1831, the Prophet had assisted in the laying of the first log for a house as a foundation of Zion in Kaw Township, twelve miles west of

Independence. At the same time he consecrated and dedicated the land of Zion for the gathering of the saints. On the 3rd August, the spot for the Temple was dedicated, a little west of Independence. This temple was to be the greatest of all the temples built by the Latter-day Saints, the temple to which Christ would return before appearing to the world at the last day. It would be the glory of Zion, the sacred centre of the Centre Place. Yet the temple has never been built. It is now part of Mormon eschatology. The Missouri period in Mormon church history was one plagued with enormous difficulties and savage persecution. To understand the nature of that persecution we must quickly review what the Mormons attempted to do in Missouri in their pursuit of Zion.

Joseph Smith had created a plan for the City of Zion, and allegedly received information on the establishment of the law of its consecration or Order of Enoch. His vision of the City of Zion suggests not one immense city, but rather a succession of cities of moderate size scattered throughout the land. These cities were to contain populations of between 15,000 and 20,000 people. When one city had been laid down and equipped, "lay off another in the same way, and so fill up the world in these last days, and let every man live in the city, for this is the city of Zion."[55] The plans for the cities indicate they they were to be one mile square, divided up into ten acre plots. Public buildings were to be in the centre of the city on squares 15 acres in size. In imitation of the fabled Enoch, every Latter-day Saint was to consecrate his property to the Bishop, the Lord's Agent responsible for purchasing lands in Jackson County, Missouri. The Bishop would then decide what each family needed for its essential support and would make that family stewards over their own property. What was considered additional or excessive for any individual's needs was "kept in my storehouse, to administer to the poor and needy." It was to be a "covenant and a deed which cannot be broken."[56] The 'Order of Enoch', however, was no more successful in Jackson County than it had been in Kirtland, Ohio.

Given more favourable circumstances, some modified version of the Law of Consecration might have worked, but the Mormon experience in Missouri was one of the most difficult of its whole history. Obviously, any group attempting to establish a society within a society, a new order laying eternal claim to its God-given inheritance, was destined for trouble. No one county in Missouri - and there were about eighteen - could hold all the Mormons, and they were overflowing in the northern region. An anxious populace could foresee the day when the Mormons would dominate the entire state. Some Mormon historians like William Edwin Berrett admit that conflict between Mormons and non-Mormons was inevitable and that it "would have been strange indeed had it not occurred."[57]

Mormon talk of building Zion, a sanctified society that would one day fill the whole land, naturally made Missourians nervous. Though the Mormons had to purchase all the land they settled, they still spoke of it as a land given to them by God. Added to this was the fact that the Mormons had earlier established contact with Indian tribes in this region, declaring to them that they were part of God's chosen people and destined by God to share in Zion's inheritance. In a frontier state this teaching was easily misunderstood.

The economic and social success of the Mormons aroused the enmity of their neighbours. The industrious and cooperative spirit of the Mormons was a cause of real alarm. In some instances one to two thousand Mormons moved into particular areas or townships in less than two years. Log cabins went up in a few days. Mormon businesses thrived and traded mainly among themselves for goods and services. Wagon trains passing through Independence were more likely to do business with Mormon merchants. Few could compete with such highly organized and efficient competitors. The Mormons boasted that Zion would grow until it encompassed all of Missouri. This was highly probable and explains why the Governor of Missouri did little to interfere in the mobbings against the Mormons, which eventually drove them from the State.

In the most appalling conditions and in the midst of winter, the Mormons abandoned all their settlements in Missouri and headed east to seek refuge in Illinois and Iowa. They lived in tents and dug-outs, suffered sickness and disease and were destitute of almost all their possessions. Property estimated at $2,000,000 fell into the hands of their enemies. The cost of such conflict, in terms of disillusionment and cynicism on the part of many Mormons, was also great. Many drifted away from the church and some became the Prophet's bitter opponents.

In the winter of 1839-40, thousands of weary, defeated Mormons crossed the Mississipi, finding temporary refuge in Quincy, where the local "Gentiles" were sympathetic and outraged by their suffering. Travelling north to swampy Commerce, and hearing of Smith's determination to establish a new gathering place in Illinois, there must have been those who wondered whether the dream of Zion would ever be realized - especially because the Prophet was to blame his own people for the failures in Missouri. In an 1833 revelation directed to those "afflicted, and persecuted, and cast out from the land of their inheritance", the Lord informed the saints that such afflictions had come upon them "in consequence of their transgressions." They were told that they had to be chastened and tried like Abraham, that they were guilty of "jarrings, contentions, envyings, strifes, lustful and covetous desires", and that they had "polluted their inheritance." The revelation contained a note of reassurance. It stated that "they which have been scattered shall be gathered." The dream was to remain intact. "Zion shall not be moved out of place, notwithstanding her children are scattered. They that remain and are pure in heart, shall return, and come to their inheritances, they and their children... to build up the waste places of Zion."[58] A year after that, a new revelation placed Jackson County, Missouri, in the realms of an indeterminate future.

> Therefore,in consequence of the transgressions of my people, it is expedient in me that mine elders should wait for a little season for the redemption of Zion. That they themselves may be prepared... may be taught more perfectly... and know more perfectly concerning their duty, and the things which I require at their hands.[59]

Mormon resilience in the face of opposition and an unwavering determination to establish the Kingdom of God on earth, triumphed over all the misery and defections and cynicism. The shaping of such a disheartened band into the populace of a new and thriving city is surely one of the most extraordinary phenomena of the Mormon story. Between 1839 and 1846 the saints flourished in what proved to be the most successful attempt at Zionization to date. They transformed a tiny village on the banks of the Mississippi into the largest city in Illinois - Nauvoo. Converts from England and the Continent streamed into this remarkable frontier city bringing with them their devotion to the Prophet and fresh infusion of enthusiasm for Zion. A Nauvoo Legion was formed, which at its height numbered 5,000 men. The Prophet, astride a white horse paraded before the legion with the imposing rank of Lieutenant-General. In this city, the place of his greatest power and influence, he developed his church and doctrine, introduced controversial new doctrines and practices such as polygamy and poly-theism, and laid the foundations of a political kingdom of God, a vast theodemocracy.

In Nauvoo, a secret organization known as the Council of Fifty was formed to develop a world government in preparation for the Second Coming of Christ. Joseph Smith was crowned and anointed King over the immediate House of Israel, exercising a kind of ecclesiastical regency until Christ should come. This crucial Council was organized in March, 1844. It was not considered to be syn-onymous with the Government of the Church, significantly, but was designed for the ultimate government of the world. It was organized in secret for the purpose of providing a "benign rule for all people, without election."[60] It anticipated the imminent arrival of the Millennium and the ascendancy of Mormonism.

The prophet's ambition was boundless. In May of 1844 he presented himself as a candidate for the office of President of the United States. Whether or not he expected to win, he certainly intended it as an opportunity to bring the Mormon cause before the nation. As far as his political views were concerned, one con-temporary Mormon writer has said that they "display the vast scope of interests of the Prophet and something of his aggressive, fearless nature."[61] Less sympa-thetic of such political involvement are Mormon historians Arrington and Bitton. They admit that such political ambitions increased hatred against Smith, and are evidence of the fact that "the Mormons could not resist using the ballot box to protect their interests". They note that the basic assumption of Mormon political unity was not finally abandoned until the early 1890s when Mormons, in the interests of gaining Statehood for Utah and surviving as a corporate entity, sur-rendered their distinctive practice of polygamy and submitted to the secular authorities, dividing their votes between the national parties.[62]

Five years of Mormon residence in Illinois created the same tensions with Gentile neighbours as had existed in Missouri. Joseph Smith's secret practice of polygamy and his newly expanded doctrines of the Godhead (i.e., that God was once a man who evolved to deity and that men could become gods themselves), led to dissent within the church. A number of prominent men withdrew and sought a reformation of the Church. They wanted it to return to its doctrinally more simple days in New York and Ohio. This reformist party published a paper called the "Nauvoo Expositor" to expose secret and abominable teachings of the leaders of the church, and to call the prophet to repentance. The Prophet responded by having the press declared a public nuisance and ordered it destroyed. The action proved fatal for Joseph Smith and was the last excuse his enemies needed to form committees against him, draw up warrants for his arrest on charge of riot and request the Governor to mobilize the state Militia to establish law and order in Nauvoo. The rest is now history. On the evening of June 27th, 1844 an armed mob stormed the jail in Carthage Illinois where Joseph and his brother Hyrum had been imprisoned on charges of sedition and destroying a printing press. Following a brief assault, both Joseph and Hyrum lay dead. With his death the dream of laying the foundation that would revolutionize the world, the new Zionic equivalent wharf or landing strip for the imminent receipt of earthly and heavenly blessing, gifts and power, seemed to die too.

Two years later, Brigham Young, President of the Quorum of the Twelve Apostles led the main body of the Mormons west. Behind them, lay the city of Nauvoo, abandoned, invaded by their enemies and filled with the sounds of drunken riot. The magnificent Temple, centre-piece of the city fell prey to incendiaries. Within years the city crumbled to insignificance and decay.

The dream of establishing Zion in America, now came through Brigham Young. At Winter Quarters "of the Camp of Israel" Omaha Nation, West Bank of the Missouri River, near Council Bluffs, Iowa, Joseph Smith's successor received a revelation (Jan. 14 1847). The people were now to be organized into companies of hundreds, fifties and tens, covenanting to keep "the commandments and statutes of the Lord our God", so that "Zion shall be redeemed in mine own due time." Again the weary refugees are told that they must be tried in all things, "that they may be prepared to receive ... even the glory of Zion."[63] Inspiring words worthy of the epic then underway, sustained the Saints on their westward wanderings. "I am he who led the children of Israel out of the land of Egypt; and my arm is stretched out in the last days, to save my people Israel."[64]

Not all Mormons recognized this to be the word and will of the Lord. Many had already left the church in total disillusionment. Others had formed splinter groups in the period following the prophet's assassination when there was a scramble for positions of leadership. One particular group was hesitant to move from the region. In 1852 groups in Wisconsin and Illinois commenced the "Reorganization" of the Church and requested Joseph Smith III, son of the slain

Prophet, to lead them as President. He waited until 1860, and then formed what came to be known as the Reorganized Church of Jesus Christ of Latter Day Saints. Emma Smith, the widow of Joseph Smith, always remained with the Reorganized Church, recognizing her son, not Brigham Young, as the "martyr's" successor.

While Brigham Young was building a new Mormon empire in the western territories, the Reorganized Church continued to grow in Wisconsin, Illinois and Iowa. Its first headquarters was at Plano, Illinois in 1865 and then in Lamoni, Iowa in 1881. In the only contests over title to property held by the church before 1844, both were decided in favour of the Reorganized Church by courts in Ohio (1880) and Missouri (1894). The result was that the minority group of Reorganites gained possession of the Kirtland Temple and eventually established themselves again in Independence Missouri. That city is today the world headquarters of the Reorganized Church, whose Auditorium occupies a strategic portion of the site designated by Joseph Smith for the building of the final temple.[65]

Brigham Young (1801-1877) succeeded the Prophet Joseph Smith and led the Church for 30 years. He was the great pioneer prophet who first successfully settled the American western wilderness and found a permanent home for Mormonism. Faithful to the dreams of his church's founder, he sought to establish the Law of Consecration in Utah in the 1850s. He launched the cooperative movement in the late 1860s and the United Order in 1874. None of it survived into the twentieth century. Much of it was threatened and undermined by the lure of Californian gold, the Utah War over polygamy, the coming of the railroad in 1869 and the expansion of the American Republic which left no room for a new or independent economic order. The realization of the United Order was again deferred. "Men must first organize their own lives; then they might be united into a more perfect social and economic order. Faith was the instrument of change, not institutions".[66]

The Millennium and the Cargo in Mormonism

In all the materials so far considered, from Joseph Smith's visions of cosmic time and space to the expansion of Mormonism at the present time, one cannot but be struck by an intense commitment to America's divine destiny. Coupled with this is the grand theme of Zionism, for it is also through the restoration of Zion just as much as in the redemption of America - or in other words, through involvement in God's plan of fulfilment for two divinely ordained Jerusalems that the Church's mission is endowed with cosmic significance. The Church is the spiritual and temporal entity that is one day destined to dominate the earth. To be outside the society of the Church, would mean that a member would be deprived of his inheritance and his redemption.

There is a sense in which Mormonism feels a certain kinship with Judaism.[67] In the past century and a half it has experienced an entry into the promised land, periods of apostasy and persecution, conquest and exile, partial restoration and a present anticipation of a new Messianic Age. The exile occurred in Illinois and in Utah, the partial restoration can be seen in the reorganization of the Church in Independence Missouri. And for the Mormons, the coming of the Messiah must be preceded by the establishment of a material kingdom and a sanctified people, a "fit future dwelling place". Max Brod has argued that, although other religions may be able to do without materialization, ... it is of the very essence of Judaism that it cannot follow suit," with its need for "a small corner of the map, a local concern". Brod protests that his faith cannot exist as a mere pure idea; it must be expressed in a material and concrete way. This is Zionism, a concept "empowered by the this-worldly miracle" by which Judaism "can regain unlimited significance on a higher level."[68] In the same way, the Mormon Zionism is meaningless without its own corner of the map, its own local concerns in Missouri. If any such comparison may be made between Judaism and Mormonism with regards a sacred history and Zionist ideal, it must recognize that the Mormon version is greatly compressed, realizing itself in historical events which cover decades rather than centuries.

In what way have the previous rehearsals for Zion - Kirtland, Independence, Nauvoo, Salt Lake City - provided clues for the establishment of the New Jerusalem, the arrival of the new age with its expected 'Cargo'? Has the dream changed? Is it imminent? What preparations if any, are presently being made for its arrival?

Thomas Alexander speaks of Mormonism in 'transition' and stipulates the period between 1890 and 1930s.[69] Jan Shipps writes of the "Millennial Vision Transformed".[70] Gottlieb and Peter Wiley also postulate the "Transformation of the Kingdom of God" and speak of the "Great Accommodation" which commenced in 1890.[71] All are agreed that Mormonism has experienced a radical transformation of its structures and emphases and that present-day Mormons travelling back in time to 1880 would find the world of Mormondom "a very unfamiliar territory" with considerable change between pioneer Mormonism and 20th century Mormonism.[72] Gottlieb and Wiley as well as Shipp, see the closing decades of the 19th century - the period when the church was struggling to maintain its practice of polygamy against government pressure - as a critical turning point in Mormon history.

Shipps in particular views LDS President Wilford Woodruff's Manifesto, abolishing the practice of plural marriage as the "division between the past and the present".[73] The abandonment of this distinctive dogma as well as the disappearance of the political kingdom "involved a fundamental alteration in the manner of exercising political and economic power".[74] Shipps develops the idea that without 'boundaries' to set them apart, to give them a sense of separateness (as in the Zionic communities) and specialness, the identity of Zion's people is at stake. The abolition of a distinctive practice and the incorporation of Utah into the secular state, transformed Mormon identity and eschatology. Because personal identification with a city, a region of America, a particular holy commonwealth is no longer possible for all Mormons, other realities have come to be emphasized in an attempt to preserve the concept of a chosen people. She notes that Mormon identity before was more a corporate than an individual thing, whereas today, an individual character is preserved through attention to diet (not drinking coffee or tea or alcohol, or smoking), greater attendance at meetings of worship where mere residence in a Mormon community was identity enough before. Beyond the Manifesto of 1890, Shipps focuses on President Joseph F. Smith's Conference Address in 1916 as a critical evidence of transformation. By highlighting the spiritual rather than the temporal, "timeless theological and doctrinal matters" instead of contemporary concerns like the disappearance of a theocracy in an encraoching secular republic, Smith established a "basis for a metaphysical bonding between the nineteenth-century Mormon experience and its distinctly dissimilar twentieth-century counterpart".[75]

In this sense we may say that Smith's contribution to Mormonism was akin to Ezra's reading of the Law (Neh.8) which marked the beginning of what we call

Judaism as opposed to the traditional Old Testament Hebrew faith. Does this mean that Mormon millennial expectations had changed? Until the 1930s, Utah was synonymous with Zion. The Church did not encourage settlement outside Utah. Conversion elsewhere in the world, entailed emigration to Zion in preparation for the imminent arrival of the millennium. When the change of attitude did come it solved "a basic revision of Mormon millennial doctrine and the recognition of that revision in the world outside the Mormon community".[76] The internationalization of Mormonism proper did not occur until the 1960s.

Four years after Utah became a State of the Union, forever abandoning Brigham Young's theocratic cooperative commonwealth, President Lorenzo Snow expressed the conviction that the "time has come to commence to redeem the land of Zion". In November 1900 he declared: "There are many here now under the sound of my voice, probably a majority who will have to go back to Jackson County and assist in building the temple".[77] His successor Joseph F. Smith, 6th President of the Church, downplayed the imminence of the millennium, reinterpreting the doctrine of the Kingdom of God so that its earthly application, so Utah-centred before, was postponed to the millennium. James E. Talmage, Apostle, even went so far as to say that the Church was only the beginning of the Kingdom of God on earth and that no earthly individual or church could claim temporal rule on earth or establish the new era. That would be left until the "coming of the King".[78] This was a far cry from Jospeh Smith's original plan to revolutionize the world through the establishment of the Kingdom of God by human effort. Nevertheless the doctrine of the gathering as such remained intact, was never denied. Disappointment that the climax of history had not yet occurred, led Mormons to develop a greater sense of mission in the prolonged period of time that remained.

Joseph Smith had always taught that his people had to be living worthily in order to build the Holy City. If its foundations have not yet been laid, it is because the Mormon people themselves are not yet ready to live by those laws which will prevail in the new order. As the visions of the millennium grew dimmer, the Church shifted from its attempts to build a separate heavenly society and focused instead "on building an autonomous religious culture that would involve its members in a spiritual life on a daily basis and touch all aspects of their lives.[79] This meant living the life of a saint wherever they might be, developing the kind of character, ability and resources which could then be employed in service to the worldwide Church. It is a church whose membership, presently nearing seven million, is doubling every fifteen years.

That they have achieved this in terms of social building, material and economic success and strong personal identity as a people, is beyond question. Having failed to establish itself as a separate social, economic and political unit, Mormonism now thrives wherever it finds itself. It is the largest religious organization in the states of Utah and Idaho, the second largest in Arizona, California, Hawaii, Nevada, Oregon, Washington and Wyoming. As much as a third of its present membership is outside the USA.[80] It boasts considerable assets in real estate, property, farms, mines, clothing mills, radio and TV stations, insurance companies, newspapers, industries, schools, a university, welfare farms, investment portfolios, pineapple and sugar plantations, etc. The church owns 700 satellite receiver dish antennas for television, making it the largest private video network owner in the world. It is certainly the largest religious media owner in the world, as well as being the single largest ranching enterprise in the U.S.A. With business assets at $2.2 million, its assets in land, buildings, educational institutions, insurance companies, commercial, industrial and communication properties approach $8 million.

It is served by some of the world's best business and administrative talent, its own leading church authorities often being people who have proven their 'worthiness' for office, by their success in the business world. These have included and in some instances still do, figures like, Nathan Tanner, one-time minister of Lands and Mines (Alberta, Canada) and head of Trans-Canada Pipelines Company Ltd. Upon retirement he was called to become second counselor to the Prophet in 1963, becoming the guiding light in church finances.J. Willard Marriott, of Marriott Hotels; Lee Bickmore, Chairman of Nabisco; Nixon Treasury Secretary and Chicago Banker, David Kennedy; Victor L. Brown, top executive at United Airlines, later to become Presiding Bishop of the Church, Franklin D. Richards, lawyer, real estate investor and one-time commissioner of the Federal Housing Authority during the New Deal (later became an Apostle); F. William (Bill) Gay, top man in Howard Hughes organization; George Romney, past Gov. state of Michigan and President of American Motors; C. Jay Parkinson of Anaconda; Glenn Neilson of Husky Oil; Robert Kirkwood of F.W. Woolworth and Stanton Hale of Pacific Mutual Life insurance, to name a few! The present and 13th Prophet of the Church, Ezra Taft Benson was Secretary of Agriculture under Eisenhower. Sterling McMurrin served and T.E. Bell is serving, as U.S. Commissioner of Education and David Gardner is President of the University of California, L.A. Twelve Mormons sit in the U.S. Senate, and eight in the House of Representatives. Others are active in the CIA and FBI.[81]

Such individuals are part of a people which is dedicated to personal achievement and eternal progress "a people sufficiently selfless, dedicated and disciplined to take up the reins of world government in the wake of an expected collapse of earthly authority". The millennial dream is far from dead, and present Mormon achievements are pursued not only for personal satisfaction but in anticipation of a time "when the people of the earth shall come to them for instruction and leadership, and 'the law shall go forth from Zion'".[82]

The drawbacks of such achievements are revealed in reports which indicate serious problems caused by the pursuit of wealth and success. Officials of the Securities and Exchange Commission - the Wall Street Journal once referred to Salt Lake City as the "sewer of the securities industry", the "scam capital" of the U.S. where shady entrepreneurs "traded on Mormon loyalties, trust, and the growing desire to 'make a buck' as a sign of success".[83] From 1980 to 1983 the Utah U.S. Attorney estimated that about 10,000 investors, mostly Mormons, had been fleeced of about $200m. The Church has repeatedly warned its people against dishonest men and false "claims of endorsement or participation by church leaders".[84]

After quoting Mormon Church leader Hugh Pinnock as admitting that in 1981 Utah was third in the nation for business loan defaults, authors Gottlieb and Wiley conclude: "The problem ultimately, was not simply the Mormon disposition to trust and obey their leaders; it had to do, as the 'Church News' pointed out, with the celebration of money and wealth, the triumph of Mormon entrepreneurialism ... the belief expressed that the accumulation of wealth is some kind of sacred obligation".[85]

Despite such scandals, critics of the Church who judge it to be a money-making enterprise, forget the essential fact that all the wealth and power is dedicated to one end - building the Church and Kingdom of God. Its daily income of between $1-3,000,000 and easily one billion a year, is largely channelled into

building chapels and temples, financing missionary ventures, maintaining welfare and relief agencies, producing church literature, subsidizing education at the
United States' largest privately owned university - Brigham Young University,
etc. The impressive aspect of the church's income is that derived from the
tithing of its people - one tenth of each wage-earner's gross income, as one indication of devotion to the cause. Mormons may have failed to live by Joseph's
Order of Enoch or Law of Consecration in the 1830s where everything was consecrated to the church and then distributed on the basis of need; they may have
witnessed the demise of Brigham Young's cooperative movement in the Utah
Territory but they are still perhaps the most dedicated church group in terms of
giving of their time, energies and money for the upbuilding of the church. Such
sacrifice is observed not only in their tithing but in the ongoing success of the
Welfare Program begun in 1936 as a response to the Great Depression.

Church leaders are confident that their people will one day be ready to consecrate their all to the Lord and therefore usher in the New Age. Apostle Marion
Romney expressed such a confidence in 1973: "Until I can pay my tithing and
make liberal contributions of my money and labor to the Welfare Program,
including Fast offerings and so forth, I will not be prepared to go into the United
Order, which will require me to consecrate everything I have and thereafter give
all my surplus for the benefit of the kingdom. I think the United Order will be
the last principle of the Gospel we will learn to live and that doing so will bring
in the millennium".[86]

Arrington, Fox and May admit that the majority of Mormons are not preoccu-
pied with the possibility of an imminent call to move to Missouri to live the
United Order in preparation for the second coming, but asserts that such a teaching remains official doctrine. Mormon character and thinking is such, they
believe, that the "potential for a sudden renewal of communitarianism remains".
In the event of a world catastrophe the potential of Mormons to respond to the
call of their leaders and pool their resources to insure group survival, suggests
that "the response could be dramatic". They conclude "Fired by the assurance
that they were being granted the inestimable privilege of bringing Joseph Smith's
plan to fruition in preparation for ultimate cosmic events ... the force of such a
people could be staggering".[87]

All this to say that the transformation or accommodation of Mormonism as the result of frustrated millennial hopes, has not extinguished the dream. And unlike Christians who share similar millennial hopes, the Mormons in a unique way, continue to lay the foundations, amass the resources, raise the structures and place in position, the material and organizational elements which will be necessary for the transition to the new world. At this point it may seem that any association of Mormon expectations with so-called cargo cultism is misguided, for surely the sheer socio-economic productivity of the whole Mormon 'venture' sits in the starkest contrast to Melanesians destroying their traditional means of livelihood and then waiting around for the arrival of European goods, as the popular image of cargo cults has it. But then that, after all, is only a popular image, and there have been cargo cults in Melanesia which have coupled their extravagant hopes of future wealth with feverish enterpreneurial-looking activity. In the histories of most such cargo cults, moreover, the early oneiric excesses were followed by more realistic exercises in 'collective development' (cf. chap. 5). In non-Melanesian cargo cultism, too, as with the Brotherhood of the Sun (see chap. 1) has business activity and visions of unbounded treasure sit side by side.

Admittedly, however, there is value in distinguishing the aspects of Mormonism which are more akin to American 'prosperity religion' (or 'cargoism' in broad terms, as some might prefer) and those features clearly comparable to classic cargo cultism (cf. chap. 1, n.89). For the case is, all that the Mormons have been establishing is to be offered and shared with the returning people of Enoch and the lost ten tribes, who likewise will bring their knowledge and amazing skills and treasures to blend with those of the children of the Prophet. The projection of a presaged miraculous display of 'New Wealth' (or the structural equivalent of Cargo) is thus undoubtedly present. However long the time of its appearing may be, no other people so consciously and constantly prepare for it. What then, in conclusion, is on the agenda for the future?

The name of the Mormon Church - The Church of Jesus Christ of Latter-day Saints, reflects the Mormon conviction that the twentieth century constitutes part of the last days of Earth's history, the "dispensation of the fulness of times." This is of course, a conviction widespread in the Christian world, but apart from Dispensationalists who envisage a distinct Jewish eschatological achievement in the Middle East, only the Mormons involve America in a future of apocalyptic proportions expressed in Christian terms. Like Christians, Mormons believe that

Christ will return to the earth. Unlike Christians Mormons have inside information as to the exact location and circumstances of his return. Beyond that they claim that their preparations alone are necessary and critical for the Second Advent to occur. The special Cargo expected from supernatural sources is destined to descend upon the American continent and for that purpose an impressive 'landing strip' must be prepared - the New Jerusalem. When this event transpires, it will revolutionize the American continent, creating the vast theodemocracy the Prophet Smith planned for. It will flow out from the Missouri Zion to transform the whole earth, to restore it to the glory of Paradise. In general terms it will follow this sequence of events.

1. At a time yet future, the missionaries of the Mormon Church will be called home and the Church will cease its proselytizing activities throughout the world. The reason for this will be that God will have considered that humanity has had sufficient opportunity to accept the Mormon Gospel. God will withdraw his spirit, and terrible judgements will be unleashed on the earth. The Apostle, Orson Pratt once spoke of a time when the Lord would cry, "Come home, come out from the midst of these Gentile nations ... ",[88] a calling to mark the end of the period of general wickedness and preparatory wars and will begin the period of wars of devastation.

2. There will be wars of total destruction, natural catastrophes and supernatural plagues in terms of John's Apocalypse. All Mormons will gather to the Rocky Mountain region in and around Salt Lake City, seeking refuge from universal tribulation. Nations will collapse in a period of unprecedented international anarchy, violence and bloodshed. The United States Government will totter on the brink of ruin but will be saved by the Mormons. Liberty and justice will be preserved only in Zion among the Saints. Many people among the Gentiles will flee to Utah to escape the effects of the dissolution of western civilization.[89]

3. At an appointed time, all the Saints gathered in Utah will move eastwards to Missouri, to inherit the "waste-places of Zion." God will have swept that state clean of its inhabitants in preparation for their arrival. Once in Missouri, their holy city, the New Jerusalem, will be built. Nothing at all is said about how the

members of the Reorganized Church with their world headquarters in Missouri, fit into all of this. It is assumed that by that time, they will either have amalgamated with the Utah-Church or will be annihilated. Whatever, "there will not be left so much as a yellow dog to wag his tail."[90]

The city, New Jerusalem will grow rapidly and many people will be drawn to it. A great temple will be raised in Independence which will contain the throne for the expected Messiah. Such colossal enterprises will obviously cost a great deal in terms of wealth and energy. Orson Pratt declared last century that when the time came to build up Zion "wealth will be poured into the laps of the Latter-Day Saints till they will scarcely know what to do with it." He foresaw that they would be the richest people on the face of the earth and "having their millions ... they will purchase the land, build up cities ... build a great capital city."[91] According to the Book of Mormon, the Lamanites or remnant of Jacob, will assist the Mormons in building Zion, and others state that Brigham Young, Joseph Smith, and various early brethren will also be assisting and directing - as resurrected beings.[92] The ancestors, we may say, will be returning with the Cargo.

4. A secret meeting held at Adam-ondi-Ahman, in Missouri, will precede the second coming of Christ to the world. The meeting will be attended by hundreds of thousands of people, mortal and resurrected. Adam, the Presiding High Priest over the Earth, and all the great Patriarchs and Prophets will be in attendance. All those who have ever held the Priesthood and keys of authority (as Mormons allege the Old Testament figures did) will turn them over to Adam, who will then in turn, give them back to Christ. For Mormons, Adam is the Prince of this world whose "Fall" into mortality has made possible the coming of pre-existent spirits into this world. He opened up the way for human existence to be tested in preparation for progress towards perfection. He is, in Mormon theology, Michael the Archangel in his pre-existent form. Adam in a sense, will be coming home - to America, for "Adam-ondi- Ahman, the land of God, the dwelling place of Adam - surely it is a blessed and holy place!"[93]

5. The establishment of the New Jerusalem will be the signal for the lost Ten Tribes and the City of Enoch to return to the earth. In order to build this great

city, the Mormon people themselves will have become a wholly sanctified people, obedient to all the commandments, having overcome every unholy or impure practice, and becoming invincible among all nations.[94] Not only will theirs be the greatest most splendid city the world has ever known, it will be eternal.

> ...The sun shall no longer be necessary by day, nor the moon by night ... the glorious divine light that will lighten up the heights of Zion ... That true light which is of God, will be rendered visible to the eyes of all the inhabitants of that city.[95]

In October, 1838, the Prophet Smith commanded the rulers of the world to bring their wealth to Zion.[96] Upon his death the Twelve Apostles issued a comparable proclamation for the Gentiles to make their repentance putting "your silver and your gold, your ships and steam-vessels, your railroad trains and your horses, chariots, camels, mules and litters, into active use for the fulfillment of these (Zionic) purposes."[97]

Additional wealth and resources will arrive from a more extraordinary source already discussed earlier; for "they who are in the north countries coming forth" ... shall smite the rocks, and the ice shall flow down at their presence" (cf. n. 50). To enable these long lost Tribes of Israel to reach Zion in Missouri a "highway shall be cast up in the midst of the great deep." Unknown for centuries "they shall bring forth their rich treasures unto the children of Ephraim, my servants" (= Mormons in America), with even mountains trembling at their presence."[98]

Following the arrival of the Ten Tribes, a missionary force of 144,000 High Priests will be chosen to penetrate the world and bring back to Zion all who are of the House of Israel, to bring "as many as will come to the Church of the Firstborn" (cf. Rev. 7:1-8).[99] The picture presented is one of a sanctified and glorious centre in Independence, Missouri, pulsating with power, energy and the divine presence, and continually enlarging its boundaries. The Mormons will settle first by the millions, then millions of Lamanites - Indians of North, Central and South America and Polynesians. The Lord Jesus Christ will visit the city and appear in the Temple. At the same time the Jews will also be gathering at a greatly increased rate in Palestine. Back in Missouri, one further group will then make its appearance: the people of the city of Enoch. That ancient metropolis with its translated inhabitants now in their translated state, will descend from the heavens to join with the saints in Jackson County, Missouri. The Mormon Book of Moses speaks of this ecstatic reunion "when they shall fall upon our necks, and we will kiss each other; and there shall be mine abode, and it shall be Zion ... and for the space of 1,000 years the earth shall rest."[100]

6. Finally, Christ himself will appear before the whole world in terms of the New Testament return in glory. With Christ on earth again, a thousand years of peace and prosperity will commence, Zion will spread to cover the entire globe, and the nations shall be taught the way of salvation. Taking Isaiah 2:3 as evidence for two world capitals during the millennium, Mormons proclaim that "The law will go out from Zion (Independence, Missouri), the word of the Lord from Jerusalem (Palestine)." So Christ will have two thrones and preside from both capitals at different times throughout the Millennium.

These Zionic dreams and plans are still very much a part of contemporary Mormonism. Dr Alma Burton in his *Toward the New Jerusalem,* speaks of the wickedness rampant in the world today and writes: "Lest we fall prey to feelings of helplessness and doom as we view conditions around us, let us not forget that the Lord has promised the saints a place where none of these evils will exist, a city of Zion inhabited by a sanctified people. As we contemplate this city, the splendor and majesty of its buildings, temples and grounds, defy all description ... The people who reside there will be a happy, vital, prosperous people who love God, their neighbours and themselves".[101]

As for the other 'Mormon' church, we find that the Reorganized Church has recently added to its book of doctrine and covenants revelations which speak of a future temple. On April 1st, 1968, President W. Wallace Smith received a revelation in which the Lord declared that "the time has come for a start to be made toward building my temple in the Centre Place", and at that Church's World Conference in Independence Missouri, (3 April, 1984), came the instruction to "let the work of planning go forward". At the beginning of 1989, $18.9 million of a committed $52.6 million had been deposited in the Temple Fund (460 million being the sum needed).[102]

Interestingly, however, the site chosen by the Prophet Smith a century and a half ago is presently divided by three different Mormon groups. The Church of

Christ - Temple Lot, owns two and a half acres of the original 63-acre temple lot and the Utah-Mormon Church owns 25 acres, plus hundreds of acres in the Independence and Kansas City area.[103] The Reorganized Church presumably owns the remaining thirty-five and a half acres.

When the Mormons attended the dedication services for the Salt Lake Temple in 1893, they believed they were looking at a building destined to last through the Millennium. They built it of granite and intended it to last forever. All such structures throughout the world are considered previews of the city that will be built in Jackson County, a city similarly meant to last forever. Their works, in other words, will be immortalized. God will reward their mighty efforts. They have always believed in what they could see and feel and create with their own hands, always judged heavenly realities by earthly models; always thought that if they worked hard enough, perfection could be achieved. They are the children of the gods and imagine that "nothing they plan to do will be impossible for them" (thus Gen. 11:6).

The 12th President of the Mormon Church, Spencer W. Kimball (1895-1985), speaking of the redemption of Zion and the building of the New Jerusalem said: "this day will come; it is our destiny to help bring it about! Doesn't it motivate you to lengthen your stride and quicken your pace as you do your part in the great sanctifying work of the Kingdom? It does me. It causes me to rejoice over the many opportunities for service and sacrifice afforded me and my family as we seek to do our part in establishing Zion."[104]

In the very concreteness of their hopes, we find millennialism and cargoistic hopes are integral for them. That it is important, furthermore, in both their mythic imaging and active missionization, that peoples (indeed places!) are brought together from their separateness across the oceans, serves to clarify the special way Mormons have developed restorationist and irredentist themes prevalent in both the Christian and Jewish worlds, and also goes to confirm that their movement is just as readily compared to 'Zionisms' as to 'millenarisms'.

134   *John Bracht*

Notes

1. *The Book of Mormon*, 1 Nephi 2:20. (The Church of Jesus Christ of Latter-day Saints, Salt Lake City, Utah, 1982 edn.).
2. 1 Nephi, 18:23.
3. D.G. and R.T. Matheny, quoted in "Mormon Archaeology", *Salt Lake City Messenger*, Issue No. 55, January 1985, p.15.
4. *The Book of Mormon, op.cit.*, Ether 1:38.
5. Ether 1:43.
6. Genesis 12:1-2; 15:7, 17-20.
7. *Doctrine and Covenants*, Section 57:1-2, (The Church of Jesus Christ of Latter-day Saints, Salt Lake City, 1982 edn.). *The Doctrine and Covenants* (hereafter *D & C.*) is the volume of Mormon scripture containing the revelations of the Prophet Joseph Smith and his successors.
8. *D & C.*, 38:18-20.
9. *History of the Church of Jesus Christ of Latter-day Saints*, Volume 4 (Period 1. History of Joseph Smith the Prophet, by himself) (ed. 6 vols. B.H. Roberts), Salt Lake City, 1951, p.230.
10. Burton, *Toward the New Jerusalem*, Salt Lake City, p. 21.
11. Burton, *Discourses of the Prophet Joseph Smith*, Salt Lake City, 1965 edn (3rd, rev.), p. 130.
12. Nephi 13:12-19.
13. *Ibid.* v. 30.
14. P. Meinhold, "Die Anfänge des amerikanischen Geschichtsbewusstseins" *Saeculum*, 5 (1954), pp. 65-86, paraphrased in K.J. Hansen's *Quest For Empire*, Lincoln, 1974, p. 29.
15. The Book of Mormon several times refers to the "Reformed Egyptian" in which it was written. According to 1 Nephi 1:2, it is a record in the language of Nephi's father Lehi "which consists of the learning of the Jews and the language of the Egyptians." Mormon 9:32 attempts to explain why orthodox Hebrews would not have kept their record on the gold plates in Hebrew. The plates were apparently not sufficiently large to be inscribed in Hebrew and the Hebrew had already been altered by these exiled Jews in America! No example of "reformed Egyptian" exists to date.

16. 1 Nephi 17:13-14.

17. 2 Nephi 5:21.

18. J.E. Talmage, *A Study of the Articles of Faith: Being a Consideration of the Principal Doctrines of the Church of Jesus Christ of Latter-day Saints*, Salt Lake City, 1962 edn. (29th), p.260.

19. 3 Nephi 2:14-16.

20. 2 Nephi 30:5-6. This rendition "white and delightsome" appears in all editions of the Book of Mormon up to and including that of 1961. Interestingly, in the 1982 edition the wording has been changed so that it now appears as "pure and delightsome". The reason for this is not difficult to see. In 1978 the Mormon Church changed its historic position barring Negroes from holding the priesthood or office in the Church. Since that date it has naturally sought to avoid any reference to a previous "curse" on the black people. The Book of Mormon reference is one current example.

21. D.J. Whittaker, "Mormons and Native Americans: A Historical and Bibliographic Introduction", in *Dialogue: A Journal of Mormon Thought*, 18/4 (1985), pp.39-40.

22. *Ibid.*, pp. 44-45.

23. Blake T. Ostler, "The Book of Mormon as a Modern Expansion of an Ancient Source", in *Dialogue*, 20/1 (1987), pp.66, 101.

24. F.S. Harris, Jr., *The Book of Mormon - Message and Evidences*, Salt Lake City, 1961 edn, p.153. Cf. also ch. 1, p.50.

25. J Soustelle, *Daily Life of the Aztecs on the Eve of the Spanish Conquest* (trans. by P. O'Brien), Harmondsworth, 1968, p.15.

26. Introduction to the Book of Mormon.

27.. The papyri were discovered in 1967 in the New York Metropolitan Museum of Art by Dr. Aziz Atiya, and found to be the same authentic parchments which Joseph Smith purchased in the late 1830s. The "translation" allegedly made from them was first examined in 1912 when the Episcopal Bishop of Utah, Franklin S. Spaulding, sought the opinions of leading Egyptologists like W.M. Flinders Petrie and James H. Breasted. They claimed the translation was an "impudent fraud" and "pure fabrication". Their examination of the woodcuts reproduced in the Pearl of Great Price clearly indicated that the Egyptian engravings were not about Abraham and Moses. The discovery of the papyri in this century meant that a thorough translation could be made and compared with that of the Prophet. One Mormon scholar, Dee Jay Nelson, who has since left the Church, and other non-Mormon scholars, have confirmed that the translation of Joseph Smith is a fraud. The eleven papyrus fragments are a Book of the Dead - an ancient funerary text for a deceased woman by the name of Ta-Shere-Min. Also known as the Sen Sen Book of Breathings, it dates from the Ptolemaic period and certainly not from the time of Abraham.

28. Moses 7:13-14.
29. Moses 7:69.
30. W C. Skousen, *The First Two Thousand Years*, Salt Lake City, 1962, p.191.
31. Joseph Fielding Smith, *Teachings of the Prophet Joseph Smith*, Salt Lake City, 1949, p.170.
32. *D & C.*, 45:11-12.
33. *Ibid.*, 133:26.
34. J E. Talmage, *Articles of Faith, op.cit.*, p. 189.
35. *Teachings, op.cit.*, p. 189.
36. 10th Article of Faith of the Church of Jesus Christ of Latter-day Saints, found in the History of the Church, *op.cit.*, vol.4, pp. 535-541.
37. British Israelism still attracts some attention today, but is primarily confined in its expression to the Worldwide Church of God founded by Herbert W. Armstrong with Headquarters in Pasadena, California. It sees the British and American peoples as literal descendants of the lost ten tribes.
38. G Daniel, *The First Civilizations: The Archaeology of their Origins,* Harmondsworth, 1971, p. 141.
39. T.S. Ferguson, *One Fold and One Shepherd*, Salt Lake City, 1962, p.138. Ferguson, one-time President of the New World Archaeological Foundation, largely sponsored by the Brigham Young University for the purpose of discovering Book of Mormon evidences in Central America and Mexico, has since left the Mormon Church. After twenty years of searching for evidences he concluded that the case was hopeless.
40. R.L. Bushman, *Joseph Smith and the Beginnings of Mormonism*, Chicago, 1984, pp.134-135. Cf. G. H. Fraser, *Is Mormonism Christian?*, Chicago, 1977, p.131.

41. I.H. Murray, The Puritan Hope: A Study in Revival and the Interpretation of Prophecy, London, 1971, p.100.

42. In his 1836 vision Joseph Smith claimed to see two Old Testament figures, Elias and Elijah. This is a very obvious confusion and misrepresentation. Elias is merely the Greek New Testament name for Elijah. They are of course not two, but one. The Prophet would have been safer if he had designated Elisha and Elijah as the two who appeared to him.

43. *D & C.*, 110:11-14.

44. *History of the Church, op.cit.,* vol. 4, pp. 454-459.

45. *Ensign* (Monthly magazine of the Church of Jesus Christ of Latter-day Saints), October 1985, pp. 73-74.

46. Jonathan Edwards, 'Thoughts on the Revival in New England'; in *The Works of President Edwards,* New York, 1879, vol. 3, p.313, cf. Mircea Eliade's comments in his essay "Paradise and Utopia: Mythical Geography and Eschatology", in F.E. Manuel (ed.), *Utopias and Utopian Thought,* London, 1973, p. 264.

47. Oliver, *Prophets and Millennialists: Uses of Biblical Prophecy in England from the 1790s to the 1840s,* Wellington? 1979, p.228. Cf. Introd., n.61.

48. Grant, *Journal of Discourses,* vol. 3, p.67 (from 26 volumes of Latter-day Saints General Authorities Messages, Liverpool, 1854-1886).

49. Hansen, *Quest for Empire: The Political Kingdom of God and the Council of Fifty in Mormon History,* Lincoln, 1974, pp. 18-21.

50. Oliver, *op.cit.,* p.229.

51. Mormons explain the concept of "believing blood" in this way: "In general the Lord sends to the earth in the lineage of Jacob those spirits who in pre-existence developed an especial talent for spirituality and for recognizing truth. Those born in this lineage, having the blood of Israel in their veins and finding it easy to accept the Gospel, are said to have believing blood. Since much of Israel has been scattered among the Gentile nations, it follows that millions of people have mixed blood, blood that is part Israel and part Gentile. The more of the blood of Israel that an individual has, the easier it is for him to believe the message of salvation as taught by the authorized agents of the Lord." Mormons understand that the Holy Spirit creates a blood-type change in the individual being blessed. (B.R. McConkie,

Mormon Doctrine, Salt Lake City, 1966 edn., p.81).

52. *D & C.,* 57:1-5.

53. *Ibid.,* 54:7.

54. J. Barrett, *Joseph Smith and the Restoration,* Provo, 1967, pp. 300-301.

55. *History of the Church, op.cit.,* vol.3, pp. 282-283.

56. *D & C.,* 42:33-35.

57. *The Restored Church,* Salt Lake City, 1963, pp. 116ff.

58. *D & C.,* 101:1-6, 17, 18.

59. *Ibid.,* 105:2-10.

60. Williams in *Dialogue,* (1966), pp. 46-47, quoted by J. and S. Tanner, *Mormonism: shadow or reality?* Salt Lake City, 1982 edn., p.414.

61. Berrett, *op.cit.,* p.179.

62. L.J. Arrington and D.Bitton, *The Mormon Experience: a history of the Latter-Day Saints,* New York, 1980, pp.52-53.

63. *D & C.,* 136:1-4, 17, 18, 31.

64. *Ibid.,* verse 22.

65. A. Smith (Compil.), *The Church in Court* (Herald Publishing House Pamphlet No.1241), Independence, 1911, pp. 4-5.

66. Arrington, F.Y Fox and D.L. May, *Building the City of God: Community and Cooperation Among the Mormons,* Salt Lake City, 1976, p.9. On political issues, esp. Arrington and Bitton, op.cit., p.282, etc., cf. *Christianity Today,* (Jan.18, 1985), pp.61-3. E. Decker and D. Hunt in their sensationalist 'exposé' of Mormonism entitled *The God Makers* (Eugene, 1984) misrepresent Mormon political involvement in the U.S.A. They see Mormon organization and the "Zion kingdom" as something which must be viewed in the larger context of a Mormon takeover of the world. They are advocates of the conspiracy theories which envisage an occult-based, Satan-inspired, Anti-Christ masterminded plan for world domination.

67. For background, H.Wouk, *This is my God: The Jewish Way of Life,* New York, 1976, p.263.

68. Brod, *Paganism-Christianity-Judaism: A Confession of Faith,* (trans. W. Wolf), Montgomery, 1970, p. 263.

69. Alexander, *Mormonism in Transition: A History of the Latter-Day Saints 1890-1930,* Chicago, 1986, pp.237-238.

70. Jan Shipps, *Mormonism: The Story of a New Religious Tradition*, Chicago, 1985.
71. Gottlieb and P. Wiley, *America's Saints: The Rise of Mormon Power*, New York, 1984, p.13.
72. *Mormonism, op.cit.*, pp.109, 113.
73. *Ibid.*, p.114.
74. *Ibid.*, p.115.
75. *Ibid.*, p.125, 140, 141.
76. *Mormonism in Transition., op.cit.*, p.237.
77. *Ibid.*, pp. 288-289.
78. *Ibid.*, p.289.
79. *America's Saints, op.cit.*, p.52.
80. D.M. Quinn, "From Sacred Grove to Sacral Power Structure", in *Dialogue*, 17/2 (1984), p.9.
81. *Ibid.*, p.9, cf. America's Saints, *op.cit.*, pp. 109, 110-113, 117, 118-119; and on business matters, J. Heinerman and A. Shupe, *The Mormon Cooperate Empire*, Boston, pp. 55, 75, 119, 120, 125.
82. *Building the City of God, op.cit.*, p.361.
83. *America's Saints, op.cit.*, p.120.
84. *Ibid.*, p.121.
85. *Ibid.*, p.122.
86. *Building the City of God, op.cit.*, p.361.
87. *Ibid.*, p.361, 362, 364.
88. *Journal of Discourses, op.cit.*, vol.18, p.64.
89. *D & C.*, 97:23-26, cf. also 45:68-9, and *Journal of Discourses, op.cit.*, vol. 2, pp. 182, 317, vol.26, p.334.
90. *Ibid.*, vol.9, p. 270. The author once wrote to the Reorganized Church asking about this Utah-Mormon plan to return to Jackson County, Missouri. Major Smith replied: "We have no fear of the Mormons returning to Jackson County. Who is Brigham Young to say there wouldn't be as much as a yellow dog left in Missouri? We believe much more in the Lord and His work than we do in the words of Brigham Young." (Letter dated Jan. 30, 1970).
91. *Journal of Discourses, op.cit.*, vol. 21, p. 136, cf. vol.8, p.354. Some ana-

lysts have noted a change in Mormon investment portfolios - a new concern with investment liquidity. They believe that the church currently puts about half a billion dollars into short-term investments, and that in recent years "well over 80% of the church's stock and bonds investments have been adjusted to fit into the new liquidity strategy". Heinerman and Shupe argue that church leaders have developed a more sober, even apocalyptic attitude that influences the investment department. "They convey a sense of impending economic catastrophe on a national scale, an extension of the doomsday millennial expectations...despite the no-nonsense busdiness acumen usually brought to many corporate decisions, the church's theology and prophecies still shape investment policies" (*Op. cit.*, pp. 113-5).

92. Cf. 3 Nephi 21:20-24. See also Journal of Discourses, vol.15, pp. 362-363; vol.18, pp.355-6.

93. R. McConkie, *The Millennial Messiah: The Second Coming of the Son of Man,* Salt Lake City, 1982, p. 585.

94. See Moses 7:18, cf. *Journal of Discourses,* vol. 17, p. 112.

95. *Ibid.,* vol. 24, pp. 28-9.

96. D & C., 124:3-6, 11, cf. Rev. 21:24ff. for possible source of inspiration.

97. *LDS Millennial Star,* Liverpool, England, Oct. 22, 1845 ('Proclamation of the Twelve Apostles of the Church of Jesus Christ of Latter-day Saints').

98. *D & C.,* 133:21-32. Cf. also *LDS Messenger and Advocate, op.cit.,* 2/1 (Oct. 1835), p.194.

99. *D & C.,* 77:7-11.

100. Moses 7:62-64. Cf. also Gen. 9:22-3, Exod. 33:20, John 1:19, and 1 John 4:12 in Smith's "Inspired Version of the Bible".

101. See Burton, *op.cit.,* pp. 3, 5; Kimball, *apud Conference Reports* (Proceedings of the General Conferences of the Church of Jesus Christ of Latter-day Saints), April, 1978, p.121; McConkie, *Mormon Doctrine,* Salt Lake City, 1966 edn., pp. 855-6.

102. Cf. Alma Burton, *Toward the Reorganized Church's Book of Doctrine and Covenants,* Independence, 1978, Sects. 149, 150, 156 (quotation); R. Holmes, "We are Building a Temple", in *Saints Herald Australia,* 6/2 (1989), pp. 18-20, cf. Prophet Wallace B. Smith's account of his vision of the Temple, in *ibid.,* 6/1 (1989), p. 4.

103. Gilbert Scharffs, *The Truth about the God Makers,* Salt Lake City, 1986, pp. 125.

104. *Conference Reports,* Proceedings of General Conferences of the Church of Jesus Christ of Latter-Day Saints, April 1978, p.121.

Chapter 3

Esoteric Adventism; three esoteric Christian Adventist Movements of the first half of the Twentieth Century

Gregory Tillett

The end of the nineteenth century was almost an Age of Adventism, with the Second Coming and its imminence being developed as the themes for many popular religious movements. The majority of these movements proclaiming the Second Coming devoted themselves to enthusiastic activities to attract as much attention as possible, and to draw as many people as possible into the work.[1] Most of them looked to a fairly conservative, evangelical idea of the Second Coming of Christ, in which he would descend from on high to take his place as King of the world, and almost all were committed to a fundamentalist theology. They tended to reject priesthood, tradition, ritual, sacraments and mysticism.[2] They sought a return to "primitive Christianity", and saw the established Churches as examples of the distortion and perversion of this original faith. And, of course, most of the Adventist movements of the late nineteenth and early twentieth centuries proclaimed the facts of the anticipated Coming openly and loudly for all the world to hear.

But there were exceptions to these general rules. There were Adventist movements which kept their adventism carefully veiled in symbolism and imagery and secrecy, and took up almost all the themes rejected by the majority of Adventist movements, cultivating ritual, priesthood, mysticism and secrecy, and rejecting fundamentalist theology. This paper examines three of these atypical Adventist movements, and notes a number of themes common to all three. These may be summarized in the following way:

1. *Unorthodox process of the Advent:* the Second Coming was not expected to occur in the traditional manner.

2. *Unorthodox Christology:* the person of Christ was not understood in the traditional way.
3. *New Age:* the Advent was to herald the beginning of a new evolutionary era in the history of the human race, a New Age and a new civilization, with the emergence of a new race of mankind, and would certainly not be the "End of the World", or a final judgment.
4. *The War as Purification:* the World War (I in two cases, II in one) was a special purificatory process as preparation for the Coming.
5. *Secrecy:* the three movements maintained varying degrees of secrecy regarding either the fact, or the details of the Coming. They can be placed along a spectrum of wholly secret (esoteric) - wholly public (exoteric) thus:

*Esoteric*_____*Exoteric*
              (1)   (2)   (3)

Movement (1) was wholly secret, its members sworn to keeping even the fact of its existence and their membership in it from outsiders; it had virtually no public outlet, although in later years a small group, associated with the Anglican Church, was established to gently draw outsiders into one aspect of its work. Movement (2) had an inner group, the existence of which was public knowledge but the teachings and practices of which were kept secret; it also had an outer, public organization presenting a more orthodox and less Adventist philosophy. Organization (3) was overtly a public organization, the aims, teachings and activities of which were openly presented; however, it was controlled by a small, inner group, and the actual details of the anticipated Coming were kept secret from the majority of its members. All three groups had both public and private interpretations of the Coming; the more esoteric the teachings, the less orthodox they were in terms of traditional Christian theology. All three talked of "the Second Coming", and encouraged this phrase to be represented as meaning "the Second Coming of Jesus Christ as understood in the Christian Churches", while in fact their inner teachings presented quite a different interpretation.

6. *Church associations:* all three movements had associations with, and in two cases, direct links to Churches. Movement (1) attracted a significant number of Anglo-Catholics, including clergymen, and encouraged its members to attend Anglo-Catholic services. Movement (2) effectively took over a small, independent church with a basically Catholic ceremonial and theology, and Movement (3) was controlled by the same inner group as also controlled a small, independent Church which also presented a Catholic ceremonial, but with a rather unorthodox theology. All three sought to permeate Christianity with their message, but subtly, and without directing propaganda towards Church authorities.[3]

7. *Adventist Geography:* the three movements identified certain geographical locations - within Australasia - as being of special significance for the Coming, and for the emergence of the New Race which would appear as a result. All three sought to establish special spiritual centres in these geographical locations.

8. *Healing:* all three believed that the "restoration" of spiritual healing was an important part of their work, and engaged in ceremonial healing services.

9. *Ceremonial:* all three movements were strongly ceremonial, using ritual, vestments, and elaborate symbolism, deriving from the traditions of the Catholic Church.

10. *Magical:* all three movements emphasized the use of magic of various forms (e.g. magnetizing talismans, invoking angels and supernatural entities, emanating special vibrations), together with the importance of ceremonial purity (e.g. abstinence from flesh foods, alcohol, drugs and, under some circumstances, sex).

11. *Freemasonic influences:* there were elements of Masonic ritual and teaching in all the movements, and, in all cases, some Masonic rituals were directly translated into the Adventist ceremonial system.

12. *Communities:* there was an emphasis on the importance of establishing spiritual communities, monastic or semi-monastic, within which work for the Coming could be undertaken. Those living within the communities were seen to possess superior spiritual status to those outside, but, in general, the communities were largely dependent on the ordinary members

for their support.

13. *Visionary authority:* as with most Adventist movements, authority was based upon the charismatic and visionary authority of one or two individuals who claimed to have direct contact with spiritual beings and realms beyond physical or intellectual perception. Personal contact with the Person whose Coming was anticipated was also claimed, as was communication with various saints or masters on the "inner planes", from whom teachings and instructions were received.

14. *"Black Powers":* the movements believed that, as a result of their work for the Coming, they were the subject of attack by "Black Powers", evil forces in both the physical and spiritual worlds. In some instances, the use of these malevolent powers as explanations for failures within the movement or in the psychic experiences of members almost amounted to collective paranoia. In some cases the evil powers were identified with individuals within the world (i.e. Black Magicians) who were engaged in campaigns to destroy the Adventist group.

Each of the three movements will be described in some detail, and an account of the history and theology of each given. Comparisons and parallels can be made from these basic outlines, and need not be explained in detail. The chart summarizes the similarities between the three movements.

Stella Matutina and the Return of Christian Rosenkreutz

The legend of Christian Rosenkreutz, a mysterious and Christ-like figure, has haunted Western occultism, and it was in anticipation of his Second Coming that the Order Stella Matutina worked during the first quarter of this century. The Rosicrucian legend began with the appearance of four pamphlets in Germany bertween 1614 and 1616.[4] These recounted the legend of Christian Rosenkreutz (or, as he has tended to be called in occult circles, C.R.C.), and gave a history of the Order supposedly established by him. The son of a German nobleman, he was said to have travelled to the Middle-East in search of Wisdom, and was initiated into a secret order in Arabia. Returning to Germany he established an Order devoted to the pursuit of esoteric knowledge, and upon his death C.R.C. was buried in a vault. A hundred and twenty years later the body was discovered by some brethren of the Order. Following the publication of the pamphlets, the authorship of which has been the subject of continuing disputes, the idea of the Rosicrucians and their secret Order caught the popular occult imagination, and from the 17th century to the present day literally hundreds of esoteric groups have claimed Rosicrucian descent.[5] Innumerable occultists have searched for the "true Rosicrucians" and their secrets, and some have claimed to have found them. Various scholars have devoted themselves to analyses of the original pamphlets, and even to the search for the tomb of "Father C.R.C."[6]

During the magical and mystical revival in England during the last quarter of the nineteenth century, the quest for the Rosicrucians became, for some occultists, a positive obsession.[7] In London a group of eminent Freemasons founded the *Societas Rosicruciana in Anglia* to pursue the search for the lost knowledge of the Rosicrucians. This Order claimed its rituals had been discovered in old manuscripts found in the archives of Freemasons Hall in London, and traced its Rosicrucian "succession" from a group in Australia. It worked a series of nine degrees based on alchemical and Qabalistic symbolism, none of these people showing any signs of great literary skill or special knowledge of occult symbolism.[8]

Around 1887, several eminent Freemasons, who were also members of S.R.I.A. (as it was known), claimed to have discovered manuscripts referring to Rosicrucian ceremonies in Germany, and to have made contact with an officer of the Rosicrucian lodge concerned.[9] As a result of the correspondence that followed, the Hermetic Order of the Golden Dawn was established in London, and gradually expanded to include temples throughout England, and, eventually, in France and the U.S.A. A number of eminent literary figures (including W.B. Yeats) were active members of the Order, studying its extensive syllabus of occult, mystical and magical material, and working through its elaborate degrees. Notable members of the Order included Sir William Crookes, Florence Farr, Arthur Machen and A.E. Waite.[10]

In 1891 the correspondence said to have been carried on with the authority in Germany ceased, supposedly because of the death of the correspondent. Disputes arose over leadership and authority within the Order, and it began to fragment. Originally governed by a Triad, the Order came under the control of one man, S.L. MacGregor Mathers, after the death of one member of the Triad and the largely unexplained resignation of the other.[11] Mathers claimed to have made direct contact with the "Secret Chiefs" of the Order, super-human beings on the "inner planes", from whom instructions, rituals and teachings were received via trance mediumship or various forms of automatic writing.[12] Mathers' autocratic attitude alienated many members of the Order, including Yeats, and led to the establishment of two dissident groups in England; one was led by Dr R.W. Felkin, and the other by A.E. Waite. Further problems were caused by claims that the original documents, supposedly received from Germany, had been forged by one of the founding members of the Triad, that there was no mother temple in Germany, and accordingly had been no correspondence with an officer of it. By about 1900, three groups operated in England, each claiming to perpetuate the original Golden Dawn Rosicrucian tradition received from Germany. Two of these - *Alpha et Omega* under Mathers, and *Stella Matutina* under Felkin - claimed direct contact with the Secret Chiefs, and even, on occasion, with C.R.C. himself. The third, the Fellowship of the Rosy Cross, under A.E. Waite, amended its rituals and practices to become a fairly conservative Catholic form of Christian mysticism and ceremonial.[13]

The *Stella Matutina*, under Dr Felkin, became more and more concerned with the direct contact with hidden Masters, and gradually with an expectation of a Second Coming of C.R.C. Felkin was born in 1858, and had studied medicine at Edinburgh University. Before completing his qualifications he spent some time in Africa as a medical missionary, and after completing his studies he practised medicine in Edinburgh, where he married his first wife, Mary. Together they joined a Temple of the Order of the Golden Dawn in Edinburgh under the leadership of J.W. Brodie-Innes. Around 1895 they moved to London, and joined the largest Golden Dawn temple, which was under Mathers' leadership. Felkin also joined a small secret group within the Golden Dawn known as The Sphere, which was established about 1897, and devoted itself to work in the development of mediumship, automatic writing, clairvoyance and various psychic methods of contact with the Secret Chiefs, and out-of-the-body explorations of the inner planes.[14] Felkin enthusiastically participated in all these activities, and developed psychic powers.

Following the schisms in 1900, the Lodge to which the Felkins belonged continued in a confused state for some years, eventually taking the title, Mystic Rose, with Felkin as one of its governing triad of senior members. He was very anxious to make direct, personal contact with the Secret Chiefs, and from 1901 onwards spent some time each year travelling in Germany in search of these masters and the traditional Rosicrucians on the physical plane. By 1906, using the methods cultivated in The Sphere, he believed he had made direct psychic contact with the Secret Chiefs, and even occasionally with C.R.C. as well as with a group of "Sun Masters". Lengthy messages and instructions were received from these exalted personages, together with doctrinal, ritual and administrative directions for the Order, now known as *Stella Matutina*.

By 1907 Felkin was receiving messages from an entity taking the name Ara ben Shemesh, who said he came from the "Temple in the Desert" where he lived with the "Sons of Fire". This Temple was the place to which C.R.C. had gone for his occult training. Ara ben Shemesh intimated that C.R.C. was preparing to return to the world, and would do so by taking possession of an adult male body, through which he would teach his latter day disciples, and usher in a New Age. Twelve of his disciples would accompany him, likewise taking over adult bodies of members of Stella Matutina. Members of the Order were pledged to strict secrecy regarding these messages, and likewise to complete unquestioning acceptance of and obedience to them. Each member swore that he or she would accept and obey the instructions received through "the appointed medium" without delay, and would make no attempt to discover their origin.

In 1910 Felkin was again in Germany seeking physical contact with the successors of the original Rosicrucians, and searching also for the temple from which the original Golden Dawn derived its authority. He was introduced to Dr Rudolph Steiner, an eminent German scholar and occultist, who had risen to become the most influential member of the Theosophical Society in Germany.[15] Steiner's interest and occult approach were both Western and Christian, and he quickly found himself in conflict with the oriental and anti-Christian bias of the Theosophical Society. Eventually, in 1912, he broke with the Society over the question of the Second Coming (in the person of J. Krishnamurti - see section (3) below) and established the Anthroposophical Society.[16] By 1920, admittedly, Steiner was still actively involved in the Theosophical Society, and also in several other ceremonial and magical organizations, although in later years both he and his disciples played down, or completely denied, this involvement.

Steiner's occult career had developed from 1902 onwards and began with his membership in an occult Masonic rite and a group claiming Rosicrucian origins, and another claiming to derive from the original Illuminati. He had also been chartered to lead the German lodge of the *Ordo Templi Orientis* (Order of Oriental Templars); this Order is best known for the teaching of sexual magic, but Steiner did not reach the higher degrees within which the sexual teachings were communicated, and his own theories interpreted sexuality in terms of an energy which should be transmuted for spiritual purposes. Steiner was also a high ranking member of the Masonic Rites of Memphis and Mizzraim.[17]

Felkin was greatly impressed by Steiner and came to the conclusion that he was a link with the Secret Chiefs, if not one of the Secret Chiefs himself. He was admitted to some of Steiner's occult workings and received various ritual initiations from him in 1912. Thereafter Felkin introduced some additional ritual grades into his own *Stella Matutina,* basing them in part on *Ordo Templi Orientis* workings, and in part on Egyptian symbolism and mythology. Also in 1912 he travelled to New Zealand, partly in connection with work for the *S.R.I.A.,* of which he was a high official, and partly to establish *Stella Matutina* temples, which he did under the title of *Smaragdine Thalasses* (Emerald Seas). He was gradually drawing the conclusion that a New Age was beginning, that this would be initiated by the Second Coming of C.R.C., and that a special community should therefore be established to assist in its implementation. He saw New Zealand in particular, and the southern hemisphere in general, as having a special role to play in this scheme of things.

By 1914 he had returned to Europe and was again travelling in Germany seeking the Rosicrucians; the World War rather took him by surprise, not having been predicted in any of the numerous psychic revelations from the Secret Chiefs, with whom he was in communication on the Inner Planes, and he was obliged to flee Germany using his influence with high ranking Freemasons in that country to facilitate his escape. He returned to England with the distinct belief that the Coming was fixed for somewhere within the period 1926-1935, and claimed to have met certain of the Secret Chiefs face to face in Germany, receiving the announcement of C.R.C.'s imminent return directly from them. Twelve members of the *Stella Matutina* temples were to be selected as "vehicles" for the coming of the Twelve Disciples of C.R.C., and C.R.C. would himself manifest through a senior member of the Order. The implication was that this would be Felkin himself.

The *Stella Matutina* members were encouraged to maintain their contacts with Christian Churches, and many, if not most, of them were Anglo-Catholics. There was an overlap between *Stella Matutina* and another Order working what might best be described as ceremonial mysticism of an Anglo-Catholic variety, the Cromlech Temple.[18] This consisted almost entirely of Anglo-Catholics, with a large percentage of clergymen. Some members of *Stella Matutina* received psychic instructions or directions from the Secret Chiefs to join the Anglican Church, and to encourage the clergy to develop magical interests. They interpreted the symbolism of the Church, and their own psychical experiences during services, in terms of *Stella Matutina* teachings. In January, 1915, Ara ben Shemesh gave instructions that healing work was to be developed within the Order, and an Anglican clergyman, also a member of the Order, was appointed to initiate and lead this work. The healing activities eventually led to the development of a separate organization, rather removed from the magical-mystical work of the Order, and finally became the Guild of St Raphael, which still undertakes healing work within the Anglican Church.[19]

By the middle of 1916 Felkin had departed for New Zealand, where he settled permanently. He had been told, from the Inner Planes, that this country was virtually a laboratory for the development of a new species, free from the old symbols and associations of past civilizations, occultly "virgin soil". Whereas in the past London had been the geographical focus of *Stella Matutina* work, the Secret Chiefs now foreshadowed greater things in the Southern Hemisphere. "New life" would spring up "when the present disturbances have cleared the ground". The War was seen as "an inevitable means of destroying the old order of things". From 1917 onwards a positive flood of visions, revelations and messages poured forth from the Inner Planes, but from 1919 onwards *Stella Matutina* began to suffer from the same sorts of internal problems as had torn apart the original Golden Dawn. The distances between London and New Zealand made communication difficult. Several members, apparently overwhelmed by the flood of visions into their psyches, either withdrew and devoted themselves to strenuous opposition to any form of occultism, or simply went mad.[20]

By 1921 the Order was on the verge of collapse, and was obviously not going to endure until the anticipated Second Coming of C.R.C. between 1926-1935. In 1922 Dr Felkin died, and his widow and daughter continued the Order thereafter; but it was little more than a shell of its former self. The eminent members were withdrawing and activity was fading; W.B. Yeats resigned in about 1923. The fervent enthusiasm for the Second Coming and the New Age gave way to a re-emphasis on the traditions inherited from the Golden Dawn, and a fairly conservative magical-mystical approach replaced the former adventism.[21]

The Confraternity of the Kingdom of Christ and the Second Coming of Christ

The Confraternity of the Kingdom of Christ had its origins in the religious experience of John Sebastian Marlow Ward and his wife, Jessie. Ward, born in 1885, was the son of an Anglican clergyman, was educated at Trinity Hall, Cambridge, and served as the headmaster of a boys' school in Rangoon, before becoming the head of the Intelligence Department of the Federation of British Industry in 1918. Ward was also actively involved in Freemasonry, and the author of numerous works on that subject. He became known as one of the greatest living authorities on Masonry and occultism; many of his books are still in print.[22]

Late in 1928 Ward and his wife began to undergo a series of mystical experiences, the culmination of which was an instruction to prepare for the "end of the age" and the Second Coming of Christ. The Wards were ordered to establish the Confraternity of the Kingdom of Christ as a means of preparing for the Coming, and through a series of meetings in their London home they gathered together people interested in this work. A further series of mystical experiences culminated in the Wards being "led by the Angelic Guardian of the Work into the presence of Christ the King and by Him solemnly consecrated for the task and given the requisite authority to organize the work". This was in May, 1929, and by February, 1930, Ward had resigned from the Federation of British Industry and began to work full-time for the establishment of an Abbey for the Confraternity.[23]

On June 24, 1930, a mediaeval tithe-barn was purchased, and dedicated under the title "The Abbey of Christ the King". Seven members, including the Wards, constituted the founding members of the Confraternity, which was established within the Church of England, and with the approval of the Anglican Bishop of St Albans. It seems, however, that neither the Bishop nor any other Church of England authority was fully aware of the "inner purpose" and nature of the Confraternity, or of the mystical, visionary authority claimed by its founders. On February 14, 1931, the tithe-barn, re-erected on the property of Hadley Hall, in New Barnet, Hertfordshire, was consecrated as a chapel for the Confraternity by the Bishop of St Albans, Dr Michael Furse. In their preliminary work for the end of the age, the Wards had begun to collect antiques, believing these would serve as relics of the old order once the new order was established, and the Chapel was decorated and furnished with a collection of mediaeval furniture, fittings, stained-glass and paintings.[24]

In addition to the Chapel and living quarters for members of the Confraternity, a school was opened under the title of St Michael's College, and a museum and folk-park opened. The extensive collection of historical material served both as an attraction to the public to visit the Abbey, and also as the nucleus of a museum of humanity's past achievements, so that when the present world order collapsed "the Abbey may form both the spiritual and cultural centre from which may radiate the Civilization of the succeeding age".[25]

The Confraternity consisted of three Orders. The First Order involved a six month Postulate, a three year Novitiate and, following profession, life vows of Poverty, Obedience and Self-sacrifice. Celibacy was not included, and there was no objection to married couples joining the Confraternity, or to members marrying one another. Members of the First Order renounced the world completely, and lived and worked totally within the community under the authority of Mr and Mrs Ward (known as "Reverend Father" and "Reverend Mother"). The Second and Third Orders had less demanding requirements and were for those who could not completely renounce the world or live in community. All members of the First Order, once professed, were given Latin mottoes by which they were henceforth known within the Confraternity.[26] Ward was known as *Custos Custodiens*, Mrs Ward as *Altius Tendo*; other mottoes included *Filius Domini*, *Servus Dei*, *In Manibus Dei*, *Serva Matris* and *Via Crucis*.

The Confraternity eventually broke with the Anglican Church. The Bishop of St Albans refused to renew the licence of the chapel on the grounds that, without authority, Ward had opened it to the public. However, the actual reasons for the break were more complicated, and by the time that Ward wrote to Dr Furse formally separating the Confraternity from the Anglican Church on September 25, 1935, he had already been ordained to the Priesthood and Consecrated to the Episcopate by Frederick Charles Aloysius Harrington, who claimed to head the Orthodox Catholic Church in England. Harrington's actual situation was a complicated and confusing one, as was that of the Orthodox Catholic Church.[27] It is sufficient here to provide a brief outline of the history of the Orthodox Catholic Church without exploring in detail the complexities of its origins and history.[28]

A Frenchman, Joseph René Vilatte, had established a Mission to Belgian migrants at Green Bay in northern U.S.A. and was ordained to the Priesthood by the Old Catholic Bishop of Berne, Switzerland, on June 7, 1885. The Mission suffered considerably as a result of its difficult relationship with the Protestant Episcopal (i.e. Anglican) Church, and Vilatte subsequently sought to ensure his independence by uniting with one of the Orthodox jurisdictions. After a brief period under the Russian Orthodox Church, he became associated with the Independent Catholic Church of Ceylon, Goa and India, and was consecrated to the Episcopate on May 29, 1892, by Mar Julius I, Bishop of that Church, with the permission of the Patriarch of Antioch.[29] A subsequent Patriarch, under pressure from the Anglican Church, repudiated the Consecration, although its regularity at the time was unquestioned.[30] Vilatte continued working for his ideals of a non-Roman Catholicism and a Western Orthodoxy until his death in France on July 8, 1929.[31]

On December 19, 1915, Vilatte had consecrated Frederick Lloyd to the Episcopate in Chicago, U.S.A., to assist him in leading what was known as the American Catholic Church. Lloyd had formerly been a clergyman of the Protestant Episcopal Church, within which he had been elected to the Episcopate, but from which he had resigned.[32] On September 29, 1929, Lloyd consecrated John Churchill Sibley to the Episcopate to lead Church work in England, and it is from this date that the work of the Orthodox Catholic Church in England commenced. On March 8, 1935, Sibley consecrated Ebenezer Johnson Anderson (also known as Kwamin Ntsetse Bresi-Ando) to extend the work of the Church of Africa, but Anderson broke with his consecrator almost immediately, and consecrated Frederick Harrington to the Episcopate on September 1, 1935.[33]

It was from Harrington that Ward received his original Ordination and Consecration, but, being dissatisfied with his consecrator's inability to produce evidence of his own Consecration, he visited Sibley and was persuaded that Harrington's claims were invalid. Sibley offered to re-consecrate him, and did so on October 6, 1935, after previously re-ordaining him to the Priesthood. Various other members of the Confraternity were also ordained to Minor Orders, Mrs Ward was made a Deaconess, and a Priest was ordained. Following the death of Archbishop Sibley on December 15, 1938, Ward was elected as Archbishop-Metropolitan of the Orthodox Catholic Church in England.

Life at the Abbey at New Barnet was strictly regulated by timetable. The day began at 5:15am and ended at 10:00pm, and was divided between religious devotions and work, either in the school, the gardens or the house. At this time the Confraternity consisted of fourteen members, ten sisters and four Canons Regular. They were under the authority of the Father and Mother Superiors (i.e. Bishop and Mrs Ward) who had responsibility for the men and the women respectively.

In 1945 a series of events occurred which led to the Confraternity leaving England, and developed a growing sense of persecution mania among some of its members, especially Mrs Ward. A young girl, Dorothy Lough, had wanted to enter the Confraternity, and did so without her parents consent, taking the name of Sister Therese. Her parents subsequently took legal action to force the girl to return home, and when the case came up for hearing in April, 1945, a great deal of press attention focussed on the Abbey, the Wards, and their religious beliefs and practices. Mr Justice Cassels made many very unfavourable remarks about the Confraternity and granted an injunction to prevent the Wards harbouring the girl. The Wards, however, arranged for her to leave the Abbey and go into hiding in London; she never contacted her parents again.[34]

Ward was anxious to remove the girl from the jurisdiction of the British Courts, and arranged for a false passport and identity papers to be obtained for her, prior to taking her, and most of the members of the Confraternity, out of England on July 13, 1946. The precise reasons for the Wards' preoccupation with Sister Therese has never been fully explained; it has been suggested that they believed she was to be the mother of the coming Christ, whom they believed to be about to Incarnate again, by a Virgin Birth, through a girl within the Confraternity, but this was denied by officials of the community.[35] Her presence in the community once it left England was kept secret, and even the fact of her death, many years later in Australia, was made known to the remaining members in England only years after it occurred.[36]

The Wards and the Confraternity settled in Cyprus, initially on a farm given to them by Gerald Gardner, best known as the founder of modern witchcraft in England.[37] When this land proved unsuitable for farming, they moved to another estate and developed citrus farming; their relationship with the neighbouring people was good, but difficulties developed as the result of anti-British feelings connected with an independence movement. It was assumed within the Confraternity that the Second Coming would occur within the community, which would then serve as the spiritual centre for a new world order; it was also assumed that both Bishop and Mrs Ward would remain alive to see the Coming. When, on July 2, 1949, Bishop Ward died, the community was thrown into chaos, and his widow appears to have suffered a major psychiatric breakdown, from which she never recovered; this manifested in a persecution mania, an inflexible sense of her own divine inspiration and infallibility, and a refusal to accept advice in any matters. Under Mrs Ward's direction, the community suffered great privations and hardships as her "divinely inspired" methods of agriculture, medicine and administration failed to meet even the basic needs of the members. Money was almost totally absent, food became scarce, and malnutrition caused breakdowns in health. But the members, however they may have felt personally, remained obedient to her instructions. Although nominal authority within the Confraternity was in the hands of Colin Mackenzie Chamberlain (known as *Filius Domini* in religion), whom Ward had consecrated as his successor, Mrs Ward retained effective power over all the affairs of the community.

Shortly after Ward's death, as a result of the political situation on Cyprus, the Confraternity moved, initially settling in Ceylon for a brief period. Plans were made, as the result of revelations through Mrs Ward, to settle in India, but the climate and economic difficulties prevented this. In 1955 the Confraternity travelled to Sydney, New South Wales, and established itself at Blackheath in the

Blue Mountains. Plans were made for the purchase of a farming property at Caboolture in Queensland, and by 1964 some of the Confraternity had moved to this new centre. Mrs Ward died on February 4, 1965, and Chamberlain in March, 1964; she was succeeded as Mother Superior by Sister Regina, and he by Archbishop Peter Gilbert Strong.

Both Archbishop Strong and Sister Regina remained away from Caboolture, working in secular occupations to pay for the farm and to financially support the members living there. A Chapel was built in 1969, and a house completed for the members of the First Order. Members of the Second Order were permitted to build houses on the land. It was not long, however, before divisions appeared in the community. Members at Caboolture resented the authority of Strong and Sister Regina, since they were seen to be "in the world" and not in the community. The community developed the sense of its special mission beyond that originally seen by Ward; they concluded that the coming Christ was to be born within their community at Caboolture, his mother being a member of the Confraternity, and they would be the special chosen people in the New Age. Eventually, effective control of the Confraternity was taken by a new Reverend Mother, who installed Bishop Donald Ball as nominal head of the community. Continuing divine revelations support the new authority system, and in recent years the name of the Orthodox Catholic Church has been changed to The Orthodox Church of Christ the King. The community consists of about twenty members, most of them either descendants of the original Confraternity members in England, or their children.

Strong established an independent Orthodox Catholic Church in Brisbane, and consecrated several bishops, two of whom now lead other independent churches in Brisbane and Perth. Strong was eventually the subject of considerable press publicity as the result of certain sexual teachings he was promulgating, and left Brisbane to settle in Sydney, where he leads a small Orthodox Catholic group. None of the Australian groups have any links with the Orthodox Catholic Church in England, which represents the remnant left there when Ward moved to Cyprus. The Church in England has gradually returned to a more orthodox theology, with no emphasis on an imminent Second Coming in the sense understood by the Wards.

All the Australian groups continue, more or less, to promulgate the adventist esoteric theology of J.S.M. Ward. His theology was basically gnostic, emphasizing that the true teachings of Christianity have been kept from the majority of Christians, and been revealed only to a select few within the Churches. These secret teachings included the idea of reincarnation and *karma*, the belief that the Holy Spirit is feminine (i.e., God the Mother), and that the Son is the Third Person of the Trinity, begotten by the union of the First (the Father) and the Second (the Mother).[38] Ward compiled, and the Confraternity used, a number of secret rituals designed to symbolize and communicate these esoteric teachings and the progress of the soul they described; the rituals, which were performed by the Confraternity from its beginning, are based on Masonic rites, and show evidence of Ward's attempt to fuse Masonic and Catholic ceremonial.[39]

The Order of the Star in the East, and the Return of the Lord Maitreya

The two movements previously considered, *Stella Matutina* and the Confraternity of the Kingdom of Christ, have been esoteric adventist movements centring on one organization. Even in the case of the Confraternity, its association with the Orthodox Catholic Church was uncomplicated, the Church being seen in traditional Catholic terms as the ecclesiastical jurisdiction within which the religious Order existed. In dealing with the Order of the Star in the East and the esoteric adventism deriving from the Theosophical Society, complications and complexities abound. In fact, there was *one* theology and *one* leadership controlling *one* movement, but this movement worked through more than a dozen different organizations. The organizations inevitably insisted that they were independent and autonomous, perhaps sharing similar ideas and ideals, but otherwise unconnected; in fact they shared common membership, common leadership and common aims. They were governed by the same sources of visionary authority, and often met on the same premises. Claims to autonomy were little more than myths propagated to attract new members with special interests.[40]

The majority of Adventist movements in the West, esoteric or exoteric, have taken up Western themes, either deriving from Christian or Western esoteric tradition. The most notable exception to this general rule was the esoteric adventist movement centring on the person of Jiddhu Krishnamurti, and working through the Order of the Star in the East and various other organizations associated with the Theosophical Society between 1909 and 1929. The question of whether or not the Second Coming actually occurred in Krishnamurti or whether it did not, remains a debating point in Theosophical circles. There are some of Krishnamurti's modern disciples who declare that he is the World Teacher (Lord Maitreya or Christ) but that the majority of those who worked with him prior to his attainment of the status of World Teacher have failed to recognize him as such. Certainly, Krishnamurti attained an international position as a philosopher and religious teacher (although he would object to that latter description), and his influence remains widespread.[41]

The Theosophical Society was founded in New York in 1875 by a Russian woman, Helena Petrovna Blavatsky, and an American, Colonel Henry Steel Olcott.[42] Throughout its history it has been divided between two aspects: its outward and official status as an organization dedicated to brotherhood and the pursuit of knowledge, with no doctrines, dogmas or teachers, and its actual and practical position as an organization very much committed to specific teachings, dogmas and teachers. From 1875 onwards, throughout the lifetime of Madame Blavatsky and for some years afterwards, the Society devoted itself to the propagation of a syncretistic occult and religious philosophy, heavily oriental and, in parts, distinctly anti-Christian, which H.P.B. (as she was universally known) claimed to have received from the Masters of the Wisdom, superhuman beings resident in Tibet and isolated parts of the orient. Following her death in 1891, and the succession of Annie Besant to the effective leadership of the Society, the approach changed somewhat.

Mrs Besant, a woman of remarkable abilities and broad interests, came under the dominating influence of a member of the Society, a former Anglican curate in England, Charles Webster Leadbeater, who claimed great psychic powers, direct contact with the Masters and exalted status as an occultist.[43] Under Leadbeater's direction, through Mrs Besant, the Society developed what his critics denounced as "Neo-Theosophy", a new version of the old teachings, often in clear contradiction to the teachings of H.P.B. The Society was effectively split as a result of Leadbeater's influence, and several groups broke away to operate independently. Although Leadbeater had left the Anglican Church in 1884 to follow H.P.B. to

India, and had taken *pansil* as a Buddhist, he gradually recovered his enthusiasm for Christianity, and by 1909 was presenting interpretations of Christian doctrines in a Theosophical style in his writing and teaching.[44] He had been the subject of considerable scandal in 1905-6, and had been obliged to resign from the Society after allegations of sexual misconduct with boys committed to his charge, but by 1909 he had been reinstated and returned to the international headquarters of the Society at Adyar, in Madras, India.

It was in the early months of 1909 that Leadbeater "discovered" an Indian boy, Jiddhu Krishnamurti, on the beach near the T.S. Estate at Adyar. The boy, the son of an Indian official of the Society, was sickly, poorly educated, dirty and of unprepossessing appearance, but Leadbeater claimed an immediate spiritual affinity with him, declaring that the boy, despite appearances, would be a great spiritual teacher. As the result of Leadbeater's interest the boy was taken under the special care of officials of the T.S., and, together with his brother, Nityananda, was given special education, training and care. Leadbeater claimed to have psychically investigated the past lives of both boys, and declared that Krishnamurti was destined for great things in this lifetime.[45] Already, in December, 1908, Mrs Besant had intimated that a new World Teacher was to appear; in Theosophical doctrine, each of the world's great religions had been founded by a manifestation of the same official of the "inner government of the world", that is, one of the Masters. Generally it was taught that the Master responsible for religious teachings, known as the Bodhisattva, occupied the bodies of various religious figures, teaching through their physical bodies temporarily, and then returning to his own body at his residence in Tibet.[46] This was the case with Sri Krishna and Jesus. In the latter case it was taught that the man Jesus, a devout disciple, had been overshadowed by the Bodhisattva (known in Christianity as the Christ, and in Buddhism as the Maitreya) at the moment of his baptism, and that the Christ withdrew from the man Jesus shortly before the crucifixion.[47] From early in 1909 there was an anticipation in some Theosophical circles that the Maitreya would again take over the body of a disciple, and found a new religion for a New Age.

By the end of 1909, it was firmly established by Leadbeater and Mrs Besant, and a small group of their disciples, that the Maitreya would take over the body of the boy Krishnamurti, once he had been trained and prepared for that event.

He was thus subject to a rigorous training programme; he was kept apart from other boys, fed on a special diet, and trained to make contact with the Masters whilst "out of the body".[48] In January, 1911, an organization known as the Order of the Rising Sun was established at Benares by George Arundale, a leading Theosophist, to draw together all those in India who believed in the near Coming of the World Teacher. This idea was taken up by Mrs Besant, and an international organization, The Order of the Star in the East, was founded in July, 1911, to proclaim the imminence of the Coming. The Order avoided any detailed official explanations of how, who or when, and spoke only in general terms about belief in the imminence of *a* Coming. Within the Order, however, members, who were also members of the T.S., were kept informed of all such details. Branches were established throughout the world, shops opened to sell literature and religious objects, and magazines were inaugurated.

In 1912 the Society was further divided when Rudolph Steiner led the majority of members in Germany into a separate existence as The Anthroposophical Society. Steiner rejected the emphasis on Adventism which had come into the T.S., and the denigration of Christianity in favour of eastern religions. Various other groups within the T.S. also went into schism over the Advent question, but in general terms the membership of the Society rose dramatically, and membership of the Order of the Star also increased. Numerous subsidiary organizations were also founded, usually upon instructions received from the Masters, to promote various work in connection with the Coming. In 1912, James Ingall Wedgwood, a leading member of the T.S. in England, founded the Temple of the Rosy Cross, an Adventist ceremonial order, which acted out rituals designed to symbolize the Coming; he also spoke privately of an expectation that Christian Rosenkreutz would also return.[49]

Two other organizations were also established which worked for the Coming, and which have continued to the present day: the Co-Masonic order, and the Liberal Catholic Church. Co-Masonry had been established in France at the end of the 19th century as a Masonic reform movement admitting women to the Craft; Annie Besant had been a pioneer of its work in England.[50] In revising the rituals of Co-Masonry, Leadbeater introduced a number of specifically Adventist themes, and the ceremonial was regarded as preparatory work for the Coming. The majority of Co-Masons were also members of the T.S. and the O.S.E. The

Liberal Catholic Church, a theosophical independent church, was established in London in 1915-16 by James Wedgwood, and quickly came to be seen as a movement working for the Coming; messages were relayed to its bishops via Leadbeater and were said to come from Christ himself in which he spoke of the Church's role in his imminent Advent, and gave directions for its administration. He was to make use of the Church when he came to earth again, and it would be the nucleus of the "future religion of mankind".[51] James Wedgwood was the Liberal Catholic Church's first Presiding Bishop, and Leadbeater its second. All the early bishops, clergy and members were active Theosophists, and most were also actively involved in the Order of the Star and in Co-Masonry. Leadbeater, for example, was one of the senior officials of the Order of the Star, and head of Co-Masonry in Australia, and also occupied high positions in the multitude of subsidiary organizations which came into being. Many of these were virtually still-born, or lingered for a few years before fading away. Some, like the Guild of the Mysteries of God, emphasized the Christian relevance of the anticipated Coming; others, like the Order of the New Age, had a more secular appearance.

In general, all members of the O.S.E. were also members of the T.S., but there was a small percentage of non-Theosophists who accepted the Adventist ideas. The Order tried to make its appeal universal by emphasizing that the anticipated Teacher was the obvious fulfilment of the hopes of all the world's religions: the Messiah of the Jews, the return of Christ for the Christians, the Maitreya of the Buddhists, the Mahdi-Imam of the Moslems, the Jagat Guru of the Hindus, Saoshyant of the Zoroastrians, and so on. In so doing, they revealed considerable ignorance of what the world religions actually taught, and created simplistic versions to support their argument that all religions were basically one, with the same truths merely phrased in different languages. Insofar as the Order and the Coming had an appeal to any religious groups, it was to some Indian Hindus, and some western Christians; few members of other religions were attracted, and some religious officials positively denounced the claims.

Leadbeater's contact with the Masters brought forth a multitude of revelations regarding the Coming, and the role of all the associated organizations. Three World Movements were eventually designated as the major themes for the work of the World Teacher: the Theosophical Society, Co-Masonry and the Liberal Catholic Church.[52] By the middle of the 1920s, a scheme for the founding of a World Religion (which would be the religion of the World Teacher, drawing out the common themes in all the existing world religions), a World University (which would award degrees upon the authority of the World Teacher) and a movement for the work of the World Mother (the female aspect of the deity, in part to be identified with the Virgin Mary, but also with all the feminine aspects of all the world religions) had been formulated. It was anticipated that all these world organizations would unite all men in a common bond of brotherhood under the World Teacher, with the visible government of the world reflecting the invisible government of the inner planes.

Leadbeater also proclaimed the coming of a new race of men, linking it with Theosophical teachings that mankind passed through a series of Root Races, each focussing in a major civilization, and each composed of a number of Sub-Races. Of each Root Race, one Sub-Race emerged as the seed-bearer for the new Root Race, and Leadbeater proclaimed that the coming of the Sub-Race to initiate the next Root Race was then obvious in California and Australia. It was a part of preparations for the Coming. Leadbeater developed an elaborate, occult anthropology as the basis for predictions about the future development and civilization of the world; the New Age would be centred on the west coast of the U.S.A., Theosophical teachings would form the basic philosophy and religion of the people, and psychic powers and contact with the Masters would be commonplace. He explored the future with his psychic powers and described the technology of this New Age in terms reminiscent of science fiction.[53] He also identified "specimens" of the new Sub-Race amongst young Australian men and women who were different, not only psychically and spiritually, but also physically and intellectually. (We ought to note that 'myth-histories' referred to elsewhere in this volume have been influenced by or are parallel to such Theosophical reconstructions; see chs. 1-2).

Spiritual or occult centres were established in various parts of the world; the major ones were at Adyar (India); Huizen (Holland) and Sydney (Australia), and devout members of the T.S. visited these places, either to stay for intense periods of occult training, or by way of pilgrimage. Mrs Besant spent most of her time at Adyar, Leadbeater at Sydney and James Wedgwood at Huizen. Auxiliary centres, linked with one of the major centres, were set up in other countries; there was one at Camberley (England) and Ojai (U.S.A.).

A series of problems developed with the potential Vehicle for the Coming, Krishnamurti. Firstly, in 1912, his father, antagonized by the alienation of his son by the Theosophists, and encouraged and financed by enemies of Mrs Besant and Leadbeater, engaged in a long legal action to regain custody of the young man. Mrs Besant, after losing the case in India, eventually took the matter to the Privy Council in London, and won an appeal. However, the ensuing publicity led to a revival of all the old sexual charges against Leadbeater, and various allegations against eminent members of the Society and associated organizations. The second problem was more alarming: Krishnamurti had progressively shown himself to be annoyed by the extravagant claims made on his behalf, and was unenthusiastic about the rigid system of dogma which had developed to explain the Coming and his part in it. His relationship with Leadbeater, originally very close, gradually faded, and he began to teach in a way which brought into question everything proclaimed by Leadbeater and Theosophy. He openly criticized all ceremonial movements, all the subsidiary activities, all sources of spiritual authority, and many of the basic assumptions underlying Theosophy.

The death of his brother, Nityananda, in 1925, disillusioned him further; he had been told, upon the spiritual authority of Leadbeater and messages from the Masters, that Nitya would be present for and would play a major role in the Coming. After Leadbeater settled in Sydney in 1915, his direct contacts with Krishnamurti were minimal, and although he continued to publicly proclaim the young man's role in the scheme of things, and to give every outward appearance of respect and reverence, he was privately unhappy about his protégé's teachings and independence.[54]

The whole scheme centring on the Coming reached something of a climax in 1925. At a Star Camp (i.e. a convention organized by the Order of the Star) at Ommen in Holland, a series of startling "revelations" were given out by George Arundale and Wedgwood. Previously, Leadbeater had been the principal spokesman for the Masters, and had been cautious about making public any dramatic messages. But, far away from the modifying influence of Leadbeater, Arundale, Wedgwood and various lesser figures, issued pronouncements and directions allegedly from the Masters, which rocked the whole movement, and attracted international press publicity. It was announced that twelve "Apostles" had been appointed to work with the Lord Maitreya when he came, and that all twelve had attained the highest spiritual and occult status, being Arhats, beyond the need to reincarnate on earth and at the level of the Masters of the Wisdom. Only eight of the twelve were announced publicly: Leadbeater, Mrs Besant, Wedgwood, George Arundale and his Indian wife, Rukmini, Oscar Kollerstrom, and C. Jinarajadasa, a Singhalese pupil of Leadbeater.

Leadbeater disapproved of these revelations, and regarded them as dangerous and destructive to the whole movement. Krishnamurti likewise rejected them, and sent a messenger to Mrs Besant to state his disapproval. She was torn between her sincere commitment to him as a person, and her uncritical acceptance of the revelations and suffered what appears to have been a serious nervous breakdown, accompanied by a physical collapse, from which she never properly recovered. Neither Leadbeater nor Krishnamurti publicly denounced the messages, but the Vehicle made his rejection of occult claims, revelations, Masters, spiritual status and authority quite obvious in his addresses to the thousands who now regarded him as their teacher. This basic conflict between the words of the Vehicle and the teachings of his mentors caused widespread confusion and dissatisfaction in Theosophical circles. Who was speaking the truth? What was the truth? Was Krishnamurti speaking as the World Teacher (in which case he was virtually infallible) or merely as a man who would, one day, be overshadowed by the World Teacher? Although discussed at length in Theosophical journals, the issue was never really decided. Privately, Leadbeater regarded Krishnamurti's public utterances as ill-informed personal opinion; on those few occasions on which Krishnamurti made statements with which Leadbeater and his associates agreed, they declared he had been "inspired".

In the midst of all the controversy, the Lord Maitreya, the Christ, temporarily occupied the body of the Vehicle, Krishnamurti - or so it appeared to many of his followers. This event occurred at the Theosophical Society's Indian estate at Adyar in December, 1925. On the 28th, whilst addressing a large gathering of his followers, Krishnamurti began a statement in the third person (referring to Maitreya as "he") and suddenly changed into the first person ("I"). Thousands of those present were inspired and overwhelmed, Mrs Besant amongst them. But some were unmoved and declared that nothing miraculous had happened.[55]

Over the next four years Krishnamurti became more and more independent, and less and less interested in even showing a pretence of adhering to the

Theosophical line. His constant criticism of basic ideas - like the Masters, initiation, authority, psychic powers - proved very irritating indeed to Leadbeater, and extremely upsetting to Mrs Besant, who frequently expressed her desire to resign as President of the Society to follow Krishnamurti totally. She was prevented from doing so by instructions to remain at her post, received from the Masters via Leadbeater. Krishnamurti, although still nominally the Vehicle for the Coming, was rarely referred to personally by Leadbeater, even when speaking directly about the Coming. Leadbeater noted, and criticized, direct contradictions in Krishnamurti's teachings, claiming they represented the "path of the mystic", whereas his own teachings, as those of Theosophy, represented the (superior) "path of the occultist".

On August 3, 1929, before a large gathering of the Order of the Star in Holland, Krishnamurti dissolved the Order and effectively renounced his role as Vehicle for the Coming as understood by Theosophy. He had never denied or affirmed that he was, or is to be, the World Teacher. He rejected all the basic concepts behind the work for the Coming, organizations, leaders, personalities and teachings, declaring that his mission was to set men totally free, not simply to provide new decorations for their cages.[56] For the Theosophical Society and its associated movements his action was devastating; membership fell dramatically, individuals who had devoted their lives to work for both the Society and the Coming were totally disillusioned with one or the other, if not with both, and organizations officially committed to the Coming were seriously embarrassed. The Liberal Catholic Church, for example, had modified its official document on theology, *The Statement of Principles and Summary of Doctrine*, to include a direct reference to the impending Advent; it promptly modified this to refer to the symbolic advent of Christ in the heart of the true Christian.[57]

From all over the Theosophical world, as in the popular press which had closely monitored the whole movement, questions were asked: what had gone wrong? who was responsible for the failure of the Coming - the prophets or the Vehicle? These were questions never fully, or officially, answered. Mrs Besant suffered yet another severe breakdown in health, and declined both physically and psychologically until her death in 1933. She made no attempt to explain the Coming away, and remained totally devoted to Krishnamurti, but torn between this loyalty and her obedience to the commands of the Masters as communicated by Leadbeater. Leadbeater himself offered no public explanation for the failure; but in private he denounced Krishnamurti for having allowed his "ego" to get in the way, obstructing the Maitreya from occupying his body. In a public statement on the matter he merely said that Krishnamurti represented the "path of the mystic", which was but one approach and not the only approach; his teachings were to be seen as being directed at the ordinary, unenlightened man, and were therefore necessarily exaggerations and deliberately provocative.[58] Jinarajadasa, one of Leadbeater's pupils, who had never especially liked Krishnamurti, declared that the Coming had been but postponed to allow World War II to come and go. Wedgwood, who had never been enthusiastic about Leadbeater's interpretation of the Coming, simply declared that the whole thing had been a mistake.

Most of the movements associated with the Coming dissolved; the Theosophical Society, the Liberal Catholic Church and the Co-Masonic order have continued, with traces of Adventism in various formularies, but with no official definition of their meaning. The great world movements - Religion, University, Mother, Government - all vanished virtually without trace. Leadbeater continued his occult work in Sydney until the early 1930s, and then moved more or less permanently to Adyar after Mrs Besant had become, in the words of one critic, *non compos*. He was strongly antagonistic to Krishnamurti in private; publicly he refrained from comment. Returning to Australia at the beginning of 1934, Leadbeater suffered a heart attack and was taken off the ship at Perth, where he died on March 1st. His body was taken to Sydney for cremation, and Krishnamurti attended the service, although remaining outside the crematorium.

Krishnamurti himself has continued to the present day as an internationally known and respected philosopher; his claim that the past is of no relevance has provided justification for his refusal to discuss the events of his earlier and formative years, and until recently he claimed he was unable to remember any events prior to about 1930. Through several Krishnamurti Foundations in various parts of the world his teachings - although he rejects the view of himself as a teacher, or of his addresses as teachings - have been promulgated, and schools and study centres established. A wide range of his books, almost all transcripts of addresses, is in print, and numerous studies of his teachings have been written.

Although Madame Blavatsky had stated, in various of her writings, that the year 1975 would see the emergence of a new teacher to rekindle the fire of occult knowledge, and despite enthusiastic anticipation on the part of many Theosophists that that year would see a revival of the "ancient wisdom", it has passed without a Theosophical advent. However, 1981 saw the return of Krishnamurti to the Theosophical Society Estate at Adyar, from which he had more or less been expelled after Mrs Besant's death by George Arundale who succeeded her as President, and this return has been interpreted as of great occult significance and symbolic importance by some authorities with the Theosophical Society. He recently died, however, in 1987.

Of the three movements considered, none has claimed that the anticipated Coming has occurred, and only one looks forward to its imminence in the near future. Yet, in the height of their activity, each of the groups actively proclaimed the immediate proximity of the Second Coming, and encouraged its members to work fervently for it. None offered official explanations or apologies for the failure of the original prophecies, or has subsequently officially questioned the accuracy or the infallibility of the original prophets. Each of the movements appealed to what it saw as a continuous tradition of esoteric wisdom, passed down from the very beginning of time to the present day, of which it represented, in its time, the most perfect expression. This wisdom is underlying all the religions of the world, including Christianity, but has been hidden from the multitudes simply because they are not ready to receive it. This, in part, explains the absence of explanations or apologies; none of the movements felt a need to explain or justify to "outsiders", the unenlightened and uninitiated. In many ways all three movements contained elements of what might be called "spiritual fascism", arguing that the masses needed to be directed, manipulated and controlled by the enlightened few (of which they constituted the majority) who knew what was best for everyone else. The masses could not be expected to understand or appreciate what was being done (and to) them by the appointed representatives of the Powers behind the world.

From their original positions of influence, either through a few eminent members (as in *Stella Matutina*) or large numbers spread throughout the world (Order of the Star in the East), all three movements have deteriorated and declined in membership, often partly as the result of internal dissension and division.[59] They

Figure 1

TABLE OF CORRESPONDENCES BETWEEN THREE ESOTERIC ADVENTIST MOVEMENTS

Confraternity of the	Order Stella Matutina	Kingdom of Christ	Order of the Star
Exoteric-Esoteric	Wholly esoteric; no public group	Teachings esoteric but public group	Theoretically public, but effective control by esoteric group
Authority	"Secret Chiefs" *via* chosen messengers; nominal structural by charismatic leaders	Christ and Archangels *via* chosen messengers; nominal structural power in fact controlled by charismatic leaders	Christ and Masters *via* chosen messengers; nominal structural power in fact controlled by charismatic leaders
Theology	Christian symbolism; gnostic content	Christian symbolism; gnostic content	Some Christian symbolism; gnostic content
Ritual	Primarily ritualistic	Primarily ritualistic; some formal teaching	Primarily formal teaching; associated movements primarily ritualistic
Associated organizations	One	One	Numerous
Membership	Secret; not exclusive; little overlap with other similar organizations	Public; exclusive; little overlap with other similar organizations	Public; not exclusive; considerable overlap with other associated groups
Community	Special semi-monastic communities	Special monastic communities	Special semi-monastic communities
Missionary	No	Not actively	Actively
Method of Coming	Overshadowing	Virgin birth	Overshadowing
New Age	Yes; post-Coming	Yes; post-Coming	Yes; post-Coming

have, however, been replaced in the occult world, by more recently established esoteric adventist movements.[60] They are, however, significant in the history of Adventism since they offered a common hope and common expectation with a most uncommon theology and an alternative system of authority.

Between these three movements there are historical (and trans-Oceanic!) connections, both general and specific. They were all influenced by the Theosophical movement which emerged in the latter quarter of the nineteenth century, and by the mystical and magical traditions which had developed within normally conservative Freemasonry. All three viewed the first World War as part of a process of world purification prior to a new Age, and sought to establish the foundations of new age communities which could survive the process of transformation which the world was to undergo. They each looked to the establishment of a new Age and a new world following the coming of the Teacher whose imminent advent each proclaimed. In that coming new Age, the movement's members would hold special places of status and authority.

Each movement placed an emphasis on the Pacific region as the focus for the new age, developing a special anthropological explanation for changes in human evolution in this area.

Each believed it would grow from small beginnings into a movement of great world influence and significance, and each was wrong. Although two of the movements today continue in fragments, none is publicly known, or indeed recorded in more than passing comment in history.

Notes

1. Among the various Adventist movements of the late 19th and early 20th centuries were:

Christian Israelites	1850s onwards
Jehovah's Witnesses	1870s onwards
House of David	1903 onwards
Catholic Apostolic Church ("Irvingites")	1830s

   There were also movements which did not foreshadow the Coming, but declared that it had happened:

Agapemonites	1840s
Baha'is	1863
Walworth Jumpers	1870s
Mariavites	1920s

   cf. E. Gausted, (ed.): *The Rise of Adventism: religion and society in mid-19th century America,* New York, 1974.

2. The exception to the fundamentalist Protestant theme in Adventism in the late 19th century were the Catholic Apostolics ("Irvingites") who maintained an elaborate, hierarchical ministry, with priests, liturgy, sacraments, vestments and magnificent churches. Cf. R.A. Davenport, *Albury Apostles,* London, 1970.

3. The Catholic Apostolic Church was also an exception to the general principle that Adventist movements tend to avoid direct contact with orthodox Christianity; they directed specific appeals to the leaders of Roman Catholic and Anglican Churches as well as other religions and political leaders urging them to prepare for the Coming. See *ibid.,* App. C.

4. Texts of the pamphlets are found in various works, including F.A. Yates, *The Rosicrucian Enlightenment,* London, 1972, Appendix, pp. 235ff.

5. For details of the history of groups claiming descent from the Rosicrucians see F. King, *Ritual Magic in England,* London, 1970; C. McIntosh, *The Rosy Cross Unveiled,* Wellingborough, 1980; A.E. Waite, *The*

Brotherhood of the Rosy Cross, Secaucus, 1973.

6. Cf. e.g., Yates, *op.cit.,* esp. pp. 235ff. and on the search, see *infra.*

7. This was reflected in such works as H. Jennings, *The Rosicrucians, their rites and mysteries,* London, 1879, and in the work of Eliphas Levi, for which see C. McIntosh, *Eliphas Levi and the French Occult Revival,* London, 1972. Levi's work permeated into English occultism and had a wide influence. The fiction of authors like Bulwer Lytton and Marie Corelli also popularized the mysterious Rosicrucians.

8. cf. King, *op.cit.,* chapter 3; the rituals of the *S.R.I.A.,* together with its teaching papers and publications, were consulted in the Warburg Institute at the University of London.

9. For an example of the MS, allegedly discovered in London, see E. Howe, *The Magicians of the Golden Dawn,* London, 1972, Appendix 1.

10. Lists of members of the Temples of the Golden Dawn and movements deriving therefrom are published in I. Colquhoun, *Sword of Wisdom,* London, 1975. The original Temple (Isis-Urania, No.3) included amongst its members, at various times: Moina Bergson (Mrs MacGregor Mathers), Sir Henry Colville, Sir William Crookes, Aleister Crowley, Florence Farr, Maud Gonne, Annie Horniman, Sir Gerald Kelly, Arthur Machen, Baroness de Pallandt, "Fiona Macleod", A.E. Waite, Mrs Constance Wilde, and W.B. Yeats.

11. For a biography of Mathers, see Colquhoun, *op.cit.,* pp. ??

12. For material received via The Sphere, see King, *op.cit.,* Appendix C.

13. The Anglican Mystic, Evelyn Underhill (1875-1941) joined Waite's dissident Golden Dawn group in 1904, remaining in it for several years, and being markedly influenced by its teachings, as some of her mystical works of the period show in their early editions; later editions - e.g. of *Mysticism* - were revised to delete the more obviously "magical" approach. cf. C.J.R. Armstrong, *Evelyn Underhill,* London, 1975, and Colquhoun, *op. cit.,* pp. 229-31. The rituals used by Waite, and heavily revised by him, were consulted in the Archives of the Order of Ancient, Free and Accepted Masonry in London.

14. Cf. King, *op.cit.,* ch. 14 (entitled "Dr Felkin's Astral Junkies"!).

15. cf. R. Steiner, *An Autobiography,* New York, 1977. It must be remembered that Steiner (deliberately?) omits references to his magical activities in his

autobiography.
16. For an account of Steiner's approach to Theosophy, and later to Anthroposophy, see his *Theosophy*, New York, 1910.
17. For details of Steiner's involvement in magical orders, see King, *op.cit.*, ch. 11 and Appendix E.
18. For details of the Cromlech Temple, see *ibid.*, ch. 15, and Appendix F, and also F. King, (ed.): *Astral Projection, Magic and Alchemy*, London, 1971, pts. 8 and 9.
19. Cf. King, *op.cit.*, p.129, and Colquhoun, *op.cit.*, p.197; for details of the work of the Guild of St Raphael (without any mention of its magical origins), see Weatherhead, *Psychology, Religion and Healing*, London, 1963, pp.223-5.
20. The most influential of the rabidly antagonist ex-members was Miss C.W. Stoddart, who, under the pseudonym "Inquire Within", wrote two books "exposing" the Golden Dawn, its derivatives and all other occult and masonic movements as part of an international Jewish-Masonic-Communist-Occult conspiracy: cf. "Inquire Within": *Lightbearers of Darkness*, London, 1930, and *The Trail of the Serpent*, London, 1936.
21. The full texts of the original *Stella Matutina* rituals were published by Israel Regardie, a former secretary of Aleister Crowley; cf. his *The Golden Dawn*, Minnesota, 1971. A small *Stella Matutina* temple continues to function in New Zealand, and at least one Temple, associated with *S.R.I.A.* continues in London, from which an authority was issued for the establishment of a Temple in Australia. None of the continuing Temples is obviously adventist. Original *Stella Matutina* material was consulted in private collections in London, including the Gerald Yorke Collection at the Warbung Institute in the University of London.
22. For a biography of Ward, see P.F. Anson, *Bishops at Large*, London, 1964, pp. 282-3; The Catholic Apostolic Church: *The Orthodox Catholic Church in England, 1929-1979*, London, 1980, chapter IV, and *Who's Who* (1943).
23. cf. Ward, *The Confraternity of the Kingdom of Christ. Its message to the nation and to the individual*, New Barnet, 1934; *The Confraternity of the Kingdom of Christ. What it stands for and how it came into existence*, New Barnet, n.d., and Catholic Apostolic Church (1980), *op.cit.*, ch.4.
24. Much of this collection was later sold to pay for the removal of the

Confraternity from England to Cyprus in 1946, but some of it remains at the Abbey of Christ the King (New Barnet), and some of it was eventually brought to Australia where it is housed at the Confraternity's headquarters at Caboolture, Queensland; cf. D. Mackay, "Splendid treasures in the bush", in *Australian Womens Weekly*, May 11, 1977, p.27.

25. *Conf. King. God; What it stands for, op.cit.*, p.3.
26. The practice of adopting a new name "in religion" is common to the monastic orders; the adoption of a motto rather than a name was also a feature of the Golden Dawn, and *Stella Matutina*, and their later derivatives. A list of Confraternity names is held in the archives of the Catholic Apostolic Church (London); see Catholic Apostolic Church, *op.cit.*, pp. 10,17.
27. cf. *Ibid.*, chs. 1-3; Anson, *op.cit.*, pp. 276-8, and H.R.T. Brandreth, *Episcopi vagantes and the Anglican Church*, London, 1961, pp. 57, 67.
28. Full details are found in Catholic Apostolic Church, 1980, *op.cit.*
29. For details of Vilatte, cf. Anson, *op.cit.*, chs. 4 and 8, and Brandreth, *op.cit.*, ch. 4.
30. Cf. M. Seraphim, "Antioch's perfidy. The historical background to Antioch's repudiation of the Vilatte Succession", in *The Glastonbury Bulletin*, No. 57, June, 1980, pp.152-60.
31. For an indication of Vilatte's work and influence, see G. Tillett, *Joseph Rene Vilatte. A bibliographic study*, Sydney, 1980.
32. For Lloyd, cf. Anson, *op.cit.*, pp. 253-61.
33. For Sibley, Anderson and Harrington, cf. *Ibid.*, pp.276-81, and Catholic Apostolic Church, *op.cit.*, chapter II.
34. cf. Catholic Apostolic Church, *op.cit.*, pp.12-14; also I. Adamson, *A Man of Quality: a biography of the Honourable Mr Justice Cassels*, London, 1964, pp. 224-30.
35. In Catholic Apostolic Church, *op.cit.*, p.13, it is suggested that Ward and his wife believed Dorothy Lough was to be the mother of the Coming Lord; Archbishop Peter Strong, of the Orthodox Catholic Church in Sydney, a member of the C.K.C. at the time, denies this.
36. From interviews with three of the original members of the Confraternity.
37. For details of Gardner's association with Ward, cf. J. Bracelin, *Gerald Gardner: witch*, London, 1960, pp. 156-8 (although there are important errors

of fact in this account), and G.J. Tillett, "Gerald Gardner. Some historical fragments", in *The Australian Wiccan*, No.14, April, 1981, pp. 5-7. Also Catholic Apostolic Church, *op.cit.*, pp. 17-8, note 12.

38. For details of the theology of the Confraternity, see *Ibid.*, ch.10; also Ward, *The Psychic Powers of Christ*, London, 1936, and *The Kingdom of the Wise: Life's Problems*, London, 1929.

39. cf. Catholic Apostolic Church, *op.cit.*, pp. 57-8.

40. The subsidiary organizations included: The Temple of the Rosy Cross, The Ritual of the Mystic Star, The Guild of the Mysteries of God, The Liberal Catholic Church, The Co-Masonic Order (British Federation), The League of Redemption, The Order of the Servants of the Lord, The Order of the New Age, The Order of the Round Table, The Brothers of Service.

41. Cf. S. Weeraperuma, *A bibliography of the life and teachings of Jiddu Krishnamurti*, Leiden, 1974.

42. Cf. B. Campbell, *Ancient Wisdom Revived. A history of the Theosophical movement*, Berkeley, 1980; and A.B. Kuhn, *Theosophy. A modern revival of ancient wisdom*, New York, 1930. For biographies of Blavatsky and Olcott, see M. Meade, *Madame Blavatsky. The woman behind the myth*, New York, 1980; and H. Murphett, *Hammer on the mountain. The life of Henry Steel Olcott*, Wheaton, 1972, respectively.

43. For a biography of Annie Besant, see A. Nethercot, *The first five lives of Annie Besant*, London, 1961, and *The last four lives of Annie Besant*, London, 1963. For a biography of Leadbeater, see G.J. Tillett, *The Elder Brother. A biography of Charles Webster Leadbeater*, London, 1981.

44. For accounts of Leadbeater's Christianity, see his *The Christian Creed*, London, 1899; 3rd edition, St Alban Press, Sydney, 1978, *The Science of the Sacraments*, Los Angeles, 1920, *The Hidden Side of Christian Festivals*, Los Angeles, 1920, and *A Christian Gnosis*, Sydney, 1981.

45. Cf. R.B. Clarke, *The Boyhood of J . Krishnamurti*, Bombay, 1977, and M. Lutyens, *Krishnamurti. The years of awakening*, London, 1975, chapters 1-5.

46. For details of the teachings regarding the Masters and the Hierarchy, cf. Leadbeater, *The Masters and the Path*, Adyar, 1925.

47. Cf. Besant, *Esoteric Christianity*, Adyar, 1966, and Leadbeater, *op.cit.*

48. For details of the training programme, cf. Clarke, *op.cit.*, pp.5-15, and

Lutyens, *op.cit.*, pp.25-8, 40-5.
49. Very little has ever been published about the Temple of the Rosy Cross; information about it was obtained from interviews with former members.
50. Cf. Wedgwood, *Universal Co-Masonry. What is it?* Sydney, n.d., and Leadbeater, *Glimpses of Masonic History*, Adyar, 1926, ch. 12.
51. Cf. Wedgwood, *Beginnings of the Liberal Catholic Church,* Ojai, 1976, A. Cockerham, *The Apostolic Succession in the Liberal Catholic Church,* Sydney, 1966, and T.H. Redfern, "The Theosophical Movement and the Liberal Catholic Church", in *The Liberal Catholic,* 27/5 (January, 1951) and 6 (April, 1951), pp. 135-41 and 180-185.
52. Cf. *The Three World Movements. Convention Addresses 1925,* Adyar, 1926.
53. Cf. Besant and Leadbeater, *Man: Whence, How and Whither,* Adyar, 1913, and Leadbeater, *The Beginnings of the Sixth Root Race,* Adyar, 1931.
54. Cf. Tillett, *op.cit.,* and Lutyens, *op.cit.,* ch. 30.
55. Cf. *Ibid.,* pp. 223-4.
56. See Krishnamurti, *The Dissolution of the Order of the Star,* Ommen, 1929, and Lutyens, *op.cit.,* chs. 33 - 34.
57. Cf. The Liberal Catholic Church: *Statement of Principles and Summary of Doctrine,* 2nd edition (1920), 3rd edition (1925) and 4th edition (1926), London, 1920, 1925 and 1926; and Liberal Catholic Church: *Summary of the Proceedings of the Third Episcopal Synod,* London, n.d.
58. Cf. Leadbeater, "Art thou he that should come?", in *The Australian Theosophist,* 8/1 (April 15, 1930), pp. 19-25.
59. Membership figures for the three movements discussed are difficult to obtain, but the following estimates, drawn from official records, are approximations:
Stella Matutina 100 in England up to the time the Felkins moved to New Zealand.
Confraternity of the Kingdom of Christ 8 fully professed and 43 other members prior to the move to Cyprus (not including members of the Orthodox Catholic Church not also members of the Confraternity, or supporters attending, but not belonging to either).
Order of the Star in the East 30,000 at its peak in the mid-1920s; the Theosophical Society had 45,000 members at its peak in 1928.
60. Amongst the more recent esoteric adventist movements, many of which

derive from the concepts of the Theosophical Society, are the groups based on the teachings of Alice Bailey (from 1919 onwards), and Benjamin Creme (who claims to have succeeded her). Cf. Alice Bailey, *The Reappearance of the Christ*, New York, 1948.

Melanesia and Eastern Indonesia

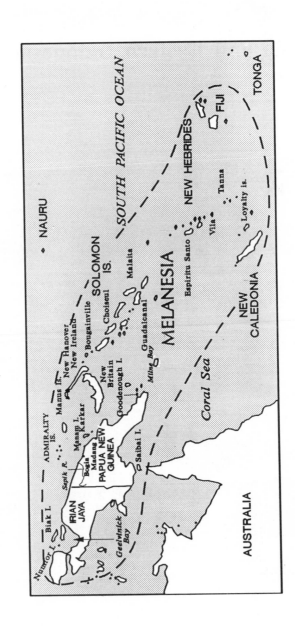

Map 2. Melanesia

Chapter Four

Journeys of Transformation: the Discovery and Disclosure of Cosmic Secrets in Melanesia

Roderic Lacey

When the anthropologist Thomas G. Harding went to the Siassi Islands of New Guinea in September 1963 to begin his inquiry into the ancient and complex trading network in this region, one of his chief informants on Mandok Island in the Siassi group was Aibung.[1] Just over twelve years later, in December 1975 Aibung's son, Lew Allace, as an undergraduate student at the University of Papua New Guinea, returned home to Mandok to begin a fieldwork project for his studies in the oral history programme at the University. He was to continue the discourse begun more than a decade earlier between his father and Thomas Harding, and to record some valuable traditions of the Siassi trading network.[2] Aibung told his son an epic legend concerning the fantastic exploits and journeys of the family of Mala in which the foundations of this exchange and trade system were laid down.

Before sketching the outlines of this legend which tells of journeys and transformations by Mala the father, his mother, and his son also called Mala, the Siassi network needs to be placed in context. Harding's record of the evidence, which he gathered from eleven months' fieldwork in 1963-64, bore the title *Voyagers of the Vitiaz Strait*. Perhaps in this he was echoing the title and spirit of Bronislaw Malinowski's classic *The Argonauts of the Western Pacific*,[3] on the *kula* network in the Louisiade Archipelago to the southeast in the Papuan Province of Milne Bay. These echoes of ancient epic maritime journeys for trade and exchange have a certain currency among their European recorders. The early Lutheran missionary, Johann Flierl, wrote of Tami Island voyagers in the Siassi system as :

...the Phoenicians of all the coast as far as the Huon Gulf to the west and
as far as the Siassi Islands and the large island of Rook to the north...[4]

More recently, an archaeologist, in analyzing some of the dates for obsidian
blades quarried from Lou, the Admiralty or Manus group and distributed along
with other goods by traders or migrants as far afield as Malo Island in Vanuatu
- a distance of at least 2700 km. - aptly called his report 'The Loneliness of the
Long Distance Trader.'[5]

These images reflect a complex historical reality about Melanesia which is
becoming clearer to grasp with each decade. Ethnographic evidence is coming
to light, that trade, exchange and the flow and consumption of food and valuables in feasting and dancing were at the centre of many village economies in
Papua New Guinea.[6] Archaeologists are adding an acute sense of antiquity, distance in space, diversity and patterned similarities as they plot, recover and
date the ebb and flow of durable remnants such as obsidian flakes, pottery
sherds and other artefacts. More recent recordings of the movements and activities of culture heroes and heroines, such as Lew Allace's of the Mala tradition,
now have a specific and significant dimension in that they emerge from and
reflect this ancient and complex landscape of movement, innovation and the
flow of goods over land and sea and across barriers of language, culture and
history.

Voyages of the Culture-Heroes

The exploits and achievements of the three major protagonists in the legend
communicated by Aibung are intimately bound up with the conception and
growth of the Vitiaz-Siassi network. Here is a paraphrase of it (told in 1976).

Mala was the youngest of three brothers living on Mandok. He was
driven away from home by his two older brothers, having been charged
by one of them with a misdemeanour with that man's wife. He battled
for his rights to stay, but finally became an exile. He did not leave his
home island alone; he was accompanied by his mother; and after [strug-
gling with his brothers for] three days he prepared for the journey. He got
some stones, then soil from the hills, then soil from the beach and plants

of the beach such as *nakaiwa, tadded, palala, babir...* and put them on board the canoe.

Mother and son sailed their craft until their homeland was well out of sight.

[He] dropped the stones, then the sand, then the stones again and beach sands. He planted the plants and made a new home. His mother had a house for herself and he had one for himself.

A true emigrant, he had brought the essentials with which to transplant the culture of his homeland into a new place which he, as a creator hero, brought into being. In this new-old environment beyond the horizon they were able to live "with plenty to eat and drink, but no people to enjoy life with them".

To overcome their loneliness Mala set to work with his mother to fashion grass shirts, drums and head-dresses. Then, at dawn on a certain day, he went to the beach and made ten men and ten women from the sand. And he commanded the new people to dance the '*Singsing* of Sia' (which was to become one of the major items in the Vitiaz network). He also founded a new people and commanded these dancers to marry. He finally fashioned his own wife from the new sand and married her. He also shared a secret with his mother which led eventually to a new exile and to his mother herself becoming a voyaging culture bringer.

When he made that land he also created the fish *nangur* and *sup* which he put in the lake up the hill, with only a small trapdoor to it. He showed it to his mother. When they wanted to have fish his mother would go up with her basket and pick out the two biggest ones for the meal.

People were filled with curiosity as to how the old woman came by the fish. Her son's new wife bore two sons and their grandmother taught them how to make bows and arrows, telling them that "their father came from a land where they used bows and arrows, so that they were permitted to learn this skill, too". Their mother persuaded them to follow their grandmother up to the lake and learn her secret. When they saw how she came by the fish, they decided to make some bows and arrows and catch fish for themselves. This brought disaster, as the wall of the lake cracked open and fish and water poured out down to the sea.

Their grandmother tried to stem this tide of fish and then resolved to plunge into the water. In doing this she became a shark and led the fish to a new home, finally settling with them at Malai, where a dialect different to her own was spoken. Here she became a woman again, went ashore and negotiated with an old man who became her trading partner. In return for a new home, she gave him the rights to these fish, provided he prepared and cooked them in a particular way.

Meantime her son became an exile once more from his new home on Amandak because of the disaster his sons had brought by their foolish search and secret knowledge. He settled finally on Tarawe beach, met there a new wife, Gainor, but soon left her, because he broke some food tabus. Travelling to the west he came to Gom village where he enjoyed the company of the local women when they came on their daily errand of water gathering. The village men discovered this playfulness and resolved to kill him for his crimes. He escaped their blows by turning into an eel and slipping under an old man's feet.

His protector captured the eel and brought it home to his house wrapped in a mat. After the old man made a feast, during which he revealed that he had harboured their enemy, Mala was finally accepted as a member of Gom village. In the meantime, Gainor, made pregnant during her brief encounter with Mala, had brought forth a son whom she named Ampugim. When he reached maturity he married two wives and settled in his mother's village. The time came when a neighbouring village asked the Tarawe people to participate in an exchange dance and feast, and Ambugim was to be one of the key challengers in this feast. So the Tarawe men went to Gom to trade for *ngas* arm bands. His mother Gainor sent Ambugim with his fellow villagers on his mission, but warned him that she had no trading-partner with whom he could negotiate the *ngas* vine, because 'Your father was a drifter and he deserted us.'

In Gom he met his father who was now an old white-haired man and whom he did not know. In conversation with him, Ampugim gave his father a betelnut which the old man recognized as being 'sweat of Mala' and a pepper he knew as 'blood of Gainor.' He recognized his son in these gifts and, having chewed the betelnut, he began to sweat. Then he 'collected his sweat and sprinkled it on his son' and commanded him to gather his fellow villagers and return home. Before the young Mala (Ambugim) left, his father took a small role of *ngas* from his mat and gave it to him in return for his gifts. Next day at Gom, when the traders returned from their journey, young Mala found that his portion of vine was beautiful and long.

Soon his father's spirit came to him in a dream and he went with his wives to find the people of Gom in mourning and about to bury old Mala. When the villagers saw the young man,

> they called out, "Oh! wait and let his son see him for the last time." He jumped into the grave, opened the mat, and with his sharp fingernails removed his father's skin, put it in his walking-mat and jumped out. He told the mourners to resume their ceremony.

There follows a series of exploits made mysterious by Mala's assuming different disguises and identities by putting on his father's aged and scabby skin. These culminate in his winning the great challenge facing him and his people at the pig festival and dance. Once more, because of breaking conventions, he is driven into exile and travels to the east. He makes sure that he takes his father's skin with him on this journey. At Garau village he was invited to join the people in a feast. Once more he broke tabus, abused hospitality through his sexual exploits, and was soon journeying on until he arrived at a village called Birik. Here he once more played tricks with his identity by concealing himself in his father's skin.

In this final stage of his journey Mala emerges with the full powers of a culture bearer. As the men of the village prepare to fell a great tree,

> [he] shook the tree towards New Guinea and all the following valuables: bowls, pots, *muruk*, bows and arrows, dog's teeth, and plumes fell onto New Guinea. And coming back the tree fell towards New Britain and he went with it, taking.cockatoo plumes, *muruk*, boar's tusks, and black beads, to New Britain. (cf. also ch.1, second sect.).

In New Britain he took on the life style of the mountain hunters. with whom he lived. He then set about transforming their economy with gifts.

> There he showed the people to make all things that they used. He made a canoe and sold it to Aromot... The tree which fell was like a bridge. People crossed from Siassi to Kilenge [in New Britain]... At Aromot he changed the mast and Kilenge people asked him to go into the canoe and direct the mast to its place. He knew what was coming and put on some

lime and red juice of a tree. As the Kilenge people shot him the lime and juice poured out and he disappeared. The people of Kilenge sailed the canoe back...and there on the beach he made the wind change their course and they landed where he stood. They saw him and they could not believe their eyes... He took his pigs and brought back the canoe to Aromot and told them to make canoes like that and sail to outside places to get good things. So the trade system began.[7]

In the terms devised by Malinowski for interpreting the 'mythology of the *kula*' this myth of Mala is a legitimating 'charter' by which the mutually interdependent trading and exchange alliances between diverse economies, with people living in a diversity of ecological zones and producing a diversity of goods being welded together into an 'international' trading unit.[8] The unity is achieved through the journeys and exploits of the three protagonists. Aibung's narrative draws on the oral traditions of the different cultures welded together here. It should be noted that Harding recorded Aibung's network of genealogical ties extending beyond Mandok and Siassi into the Mainland and Bismark Archipelago which gave him access to a wide range of 'trade roads' and traditions.[9] One name suggested for Mala the elder is Kilibob, the name of a brother culture hero found in myths and legends told by people along the north coast of New Guinea including those in the Vitiaz Strait (cf. ch.1, second sect.). That complexity of traditions echoes and affirms the complexity of the trading network itself.

If the Tami Islanders can be seen as the "Phoenicians of all the coast" and the *kula* traders, and their founding heroes and heroines as the "Argonauts of the Western Pacific", then the protagonists are cultural parallels to Ulysses and their journeys to the Odyssey. The evidence from ethnographic records and from archaeological excavations has brought the rich diversity of inter-linking networks of trade and exchange to the light of day again, after these were swamped by colonial mining and plantation economies. The mass of oral traditions in the form of legends, songs, dances, chants and myths, recorded in earlier decades after the onset of the colonial era, and still present in many villages, now reveal that this Odyssey of the Mala protagonists is not isolated to this one region, but that hero traditions about journeys, transformations and innovation are a strong vein running through this rich variety of oral traditions. They reflect strands which continue into the colonial age and help us to gain insights for interpreting issues about identity and mobility in the past and present in this area of the Pacific.

Mala-Kilibob, with his shark-mother and Ambugim-Mala his son, are matched as types of culture hero by Tudava, the bringer of crops and agriculture in the Trobriands; by Dsari (or Jari) the Sepik heroine who taught about life-giving, fire and birth; by the Waropen heroes from north coast Irian Jaya who stole the art of metal smelting from the islands in the west;[10] by Manarmakeri the scabby-skinned hero from Biak in the same region who sought vainly to bring the vision of Koreri, the better life, to recalcitrant and unheeding coastal and river communities and then became transformed into a nationalist cult figure in the Dutch colonial era;[11] by the prodigious culture bearer of many names in the Papuan Gulf and hinterland, Iko-Sido-Hido-Souw;[12] and by Edai Siabo that hero of the Motu who gained the knowledge of trading and of building sea-going *lagatoi* canoes from a *dirava* spirit under the sea.[13] These are some of the more famed heroes and heroines in a galaxy of stars scattered through the oral traditions.

The legend about Edai Siabo, the 'discoverer' and bringer of the knowledge which made possible the *hiri* trading voyages between the Motu of Port Moresby and their partners living in the beach and river villages of the Gulf of Papua, is a good example of the themes found in these other traditions. The essential elements in this legend are: a journey-like death, a removal from his people and a return with new knowledge.[14] This is the sequence by which Edai Siabo brings a new and significant institution into the lives of the Motu, thus freeing them from the constraints of their ecological niche. Near Boera Edai Siabo's canoe became separated from those of his brothers off the Papuan coast. Suddenly the canoe was overturned and he found himself held in the stong grip of an underwater monster, which dragged him headfirst into a cave. There he was introduced to a whole new world and was taught new knowledge, especially as to the making of the many-hulled *lagatoi* canoes and the secrets of the long trading voyages which would take their builders and owners annually into the Gulf of Papua to exchange their pots and shells for sago and timber. His brothers, searching for his canoe, eventually found their brother's dead body wedged tightly in the deep cave mouth. After releasing him, and bringing his body home for the funeral rites, Edai Siabo awakened as if from a sleep or trance and told his brothers what had happened. He then taught them about *lagatoi* making by using a model of what he had been given under the sea. He also taught them how to make the trading voyages. Thus began the voyages of the *hiri*.[15]

The Melanesian culture hero, then, is typically the discoverer and of course more often revealer of cosmic secrets. The hero usually faces immense ordeals in the uncovering of hidden 'truths' and the undertaking of great tasks. Perhaps death will be an inevitable lot (as in the case of the so-called *dema* culture-bearing deities).[16] Despite variations, and despite clear differences in the ways in which narrative material is communicated, as well as relative disparities of world view and historico-cultural context, the many legends of these culture heroes do reflect a basic *typos* and continuity concerning the process of innovation.

Most of the examples I have thus far provided have been from coastal Melanesia, yet my own detailed research into the oral traditions of the Enga tribes, high in the New Guinea highlands and constituting the largest single language area in Melanesia, reveals parallel motifs, normally imbedded within clan migration traditions. Pesoto, for example, a leading 'man of knowledge' in the Piau clan, one of the largest descent groups of the Yanaitini phratry among the Mae Enga passed on to me a characteristic and pertinent story. It should be noted that Pesoto's powerful federation of clansmen hold sway over extensive sweet potato gardens straddling the Lai and Ambum valleys at an altitude above 6,000 feet and immediately to the west of Wabag (the Enga provincial headquarters).

> My ancestor, Yanaitini, was born at Tilyapausa, a place down the valley (near Wapenamanda).Yanaitini came to Tetemanda Yaumanda and buried some sweet potatoes there. Then he went up to Aipi Andaka to make salt. Having put in the *Aipi*, Yanaitini buried the sweet potatoes he had brought with him and returned.

> When Yanaitini had returned, the sweet potatoes he had buried had budded at Yaumanda. Consequently, Yanaitini cut down a *Waima* tree and left for Tilyapausa. The people there disliked his manners so they sent him away to some other place.

> As a result, Yanaitini returned to Yaumanda and settled down there permanently, after burning down the *Waima* tree he had cut down before (to make a new garden).

Then Yanaitini went back to Aipi Andaka to make salt. When he got there, someone reported that Monaini had taken away the sweet potatoes which he had buried during his first trip. When Yanaitini understood that Monaini had already gone, he returned to Yaumanda, promising to go sometime to attack Monaini.

At Yaumanda, Yanaitini lengthened his net loin cloth and prepared bundles of arrows to go and attack Monaini and remained there until he claimed another place called Yamnikutisa. Then Yanaitini returned to Yaumanda and married two women.[17]

This is a migration tradition of some significance because of the possible links it provides between the quarrelsome, convention-breaking pioneer Yanaitini and the spread of the sweet potato from east to west along the Lai Valley and beyond into the higher Lagaip Valley. In this instance, migration opened up territory for the birth of a new people and was also a mechanism for the diffusion of a new crop which became the base for their subsistence economy.

Hundreds of comparable traditions, together with the other sources of evidence already noted, also reveal Melanesians journeying as migrants in the 'pre-contact' and more distant past. In a review of many traditions of migration and clan foundation, made during the 1970s on the basis of evidence provided to the oral history programme at the University of Papua New Guinea, I listed the major causes for migration. These included quarrels between brothers; disputes over pigs, fish, land or the distribution of food at feasts; jealousy over wives; sorcery accusations; as well as the effects of disease, natural calamities or warfare.[18] This listing has further justification in the greater detailing of population mobility in the oral historical investigation of other historians at the above university.[19]

In Melanesia, significantly, local migration traditions have been, and today remain even more so, significant parts of the heritage of their owners. Through the legends, songs, chants and dances by which this knowledge is transmitted, the people have received from previous generations basic legal, political, social and economic charters by which rights and obligations between lineage groups within communities are defined and rights to specific resources and territories are defended.[20] This may help explain not only why these stories are so often formally disclosed and instilled in the context of initiation, but also so many

Melanesian institutions of initiation, or *rites de passage,* entail journeys bringing seclusion and ordeal. Some examples of such initiation journeys, through which young men and women were publicly transformed from childhood status to full citizenship of their communities, have been recorded by Bateson, Williams, Read, Hogbin, Lehner and Kigasung.[21] And once more some Enga material I have garnished is highly relevant.

In these rites, named *sangai* and *sandalu,* in different dialect communities sharing the Enga language, young bachelors and youths were initiated and purified. The elders who were the guardians of the sacred objects at the centre of these ceremonies, secretly led the candidates out of their familiar places of residence down in the valleys *(andakama)* into the house of seclusion hidden in the high ridge-top forests *(kakasa).* The initiates began the process by a journey into an unknown, secret and dangerous zone, removed from all the familiar surroundings of everyday life. Here in seclusion they underwent purification and cleansing in sacred springs, fasting, trials and a systematic transmission of significant knowledge for four to five days and nights. Once they had successfully completed their tasks, the young men clad themselves in their finery and began a return journey to their clan dancing ground where an emergence feast had been prepared for them. As the 'new men' came on to this dancing ground all strained to hear their songs. In these songs, cast in highly compressed and elaborate picture language, they conveyed to their assembled clansmen wisdom and insights about the community and its destiny which they had acquired in dreams which came to them in their seclusion up on the ridge tops. Through these rites the youths were transformed into mature men, brave warriors, productive husbands and cultivators and effective negotiators in exchanges, but they carried with them into the public arena knowledge essential for the survival and prosperity of their people.

The initiates had acquired this knowledge through the dreams which came to them in the seclusion house. These dreams were induced from the powers inherent in sacred ritual objects, either sacred plants *(sangai)* or sacred substance in bamboo containers *(sandalu).* Because these objects were so central and powerful in the transforming rites, it is not surprising that traditions about them were an essential strand in the bodies of knowledge taught by the elders to the young men during their time of seclusion in the forest.

In some *sangai* regions of Enga province I recorded elaborate and beautiful praise poems which commemorate how significant and specifically named *sangai* plants were won at great cost - by heroic ancestors two to three generations ago. These poems recount how the heroes heard of feasts and dances, or witnessed the effects of famed plants upon their owners. They then set out on long and difficult journeys from their homeland valleys, through high forests, across streams and over bridges into the areas of their owners. Their journeys often took them through enemy territories, where they put their lives at risk and often journey on at night guided by the light of bamboo torches. Finally, when successful negotiations were over, and a great price had been paid for the plants and their chants *(nemongo)*, the heroes would set out on their journey homeward, bringing these powerful new possessions to a safe hiding place near their own seclusion house, deep in the forest. There the plants were guarded, cultivated and given to initiates and, as a result, the new owners and their clansmen grew in strength, wisdom, bravery and wealth. These great consequences of daring journeys into the unknown to win this prize were sung about in the commemorative chants.

These more recent heroes do not slough off scabby skins as did Manarmakeri of Biak, or play tricks of identity with their father's skin as did Ambugim-Mala of Siassi. But like the Waropen heroes, they did venture beyond the security of their valley homesteads to win a great prize for their clansmen. Like the blind Homer singing of the journeys and exploits of Ulysses and other heroes of Troy, recent generations of Enga poets have praised these heroes and immortalized their deeds through the images of their commemorative chants. In fact these ancestor heroes, like those who founded new communities through migration or who introduced innovations through trade, take on the proportions of culture heroes in that the plants acquired transformed the communities of the new owners. So it can be argued that there are parallels and continuities between these three strands of traditions which sing of heroic journeys and transformations.

From Labouring to Leadership in New Journeys of Discovery

These insights from oral traditions, as well as from ethnography and archaeology, enable us to see significant continuities in other journeys in the colonial age and beyond. One stream of travellers who blend and intersect with culture heroes, traders, migrants and initiates on their journeys were the foreigners who came into Melanesia by sea and later journeyed over land, and along rivers in search of new places to 'discover' and map, new wealth to draw into their treasuries, new lands, resources and peoples to control or conquer, new heathen souls to convert to their religion. These travellers and their journeys cover several centuries of recorded history, beginning, at least for writers of European documents, as far back as the early decades after Portuguese and Spanish mariners had sailed into and across the ocean to which they gave the name 'Pacific'.[23]

The coming of the foreigners and the planting by them of their enclaves, stations and mines in this landscape opened up new pathways and possibilities for indigenous travellers. Young men of Papua New Guinea in particular often went with the foreigners as guides, interpreters, mediators and carriers of their cargo, making discoveries themselves, like the earlier heroes, by venturing into new worlds beyond the horizon on their own journeys of discovery, innovation and initiation. Often by becoming workers, policemen, evangelists and teachers they trod a razor-sharp path between worlds and became 'men in the middle'.[24] One way in which the new age with its new technology, religion, and systems of knowledge was spread over Papua New Guinea was through the journeys away from home into the enclaves and back again by young labourers who were launched out of their villages into a Melanesian 'diaspora'. This took them on whaling ships into the Pacific waters, as plantation workers to Samoa, Fiji and Queensland, as colonial soldiers and policemen to Ponape in Micronesia and even to Tanganyika, and more recently to the mines, plantations, ports and towns which were far from home but within the confines of the new colonial territories which became the modern nation of Papua New Guinea.[25]

This more recent diaspora of the colonial era had two earlier exotic precedents. (West) Papuan slaves are recorded as being part of the workforce building a Javanese temple 1000 years ago.[26] They were the predecessors of those slaves culled with spices and timber by the trading voyages of the Sultans of Tidore and Ternate (the *hongi*), continued by early Dutch rulers of the East Indies.[27] The Spanish captains Prado and Torres also captured fourteen young men and women in their raid on the south coast island of Mailu and took them either to Manila or home to Spain as prizes. These were the first Christians of the region. They were seized in August 1606. This was for these Mailuans a terrible and new initiation journey from which they never returned, having been kidnapped by ravening monsters from the sea.[28] That was a forestate of the many-pronged intrusions and their consequences for Melanesians especially during the second half of the nineteenth century and the first four decades of the current one. It was in that span, of course, that the opening up of a new age - as I have just been characterizing it - was most significantly and prevalently sensed.

Then came another invasion by foreigners, the armed warriors (on both sides) of the Pacific War of the 1940's. They set fire to the land and brought with them more people, more wealth, more instruments of destruction and tools for building than people had dreamed of. Into this machine were sucked more villagers and young workers than had ever been tapped before. From this holocaust emerge many epic journeys of escape and survival, and many young men filled with dreams and visions of making a new world out of the ashes of the past. Journeys and the potential for renewal, innovation and transformation multiply and expand for the survivors. A new period of high colonialism comes into being and, in just over a generation from 1945 to 1975, there is the move from colonial control to political independence, accompanied by moves towards 'self-sufficiency' and 'development'. To the earlier colonial patterns of diaspora and the epic journeys and visions of the Pacific War is added a continuing multiplication and diversity of journeys and opportunities for transformation, including the movement of young people to the emerging towns and cities in search of education and work.[29]

Given this pattern and framework of change over the last one hundred years, can we say that breaks with the village traditions and worldviews have been so frequent, widespread and dramatic that there are no real lines of continuity between what we have discovered in the traditions and what has gone on, particularly in the post-War generations? The numbers of travellers have increased, as have the distances of individual journeys; the range of opportunities has become more varied and as different in their quality as in the difference between pieces of cloth, beads and mirrors, or metal axes and modern machines and university degrees - each being representative of the goods and knowledge to be gained by those who ventured forth from their homes, across the beaches, beyond the horizon to the enclaves. But we would be blind to the significance of the traditions with which this exploration began, if we stayed at so superficial a level of comparison.

A closer study of the process of innovation resulting from journeys away and returns home by young workers who then struggled for the reform of village economies, reveals something more of the continuities existing between the movements and achievements of the heroes of the legends and more recent journeys of transformation. One finds new discovery turned into innovative initiative among a select number of individuals who took what they had experienced from work in the outsiders' world and attempted to forge a 'new road' (pidgin: *nupela rot)* for their own people. "When I came out of the bush I was like a fool", one Anton Misiyaiyai of Moseng (in the Sepik hinterland) told Bryant Allen of time as a labourer in the New Guinea islands,

> When I saw how the white men lived my head went around. I saw their houses. When I became a servant I saw inside their houses. I saw their beds and their chairs and tables. Their food and clothes. I thought all these things were good. I saw the stores too. I was amazed at the things in them. The knives and clothes and all the different sorts of food. I thought this was good, too.[30]

It was this very Anton, however, who returned to the Sepik with a vision of transforming his people's subsistence economy. He had been deeply impressed by the wealth and life-style of the Europeans; he had learnt the process of rice cultivation from peasant Japanese soldiers during their occupation of New Ireland; and he grasped the idea of commercial production and crop marketing. For years he struggled against colonial officials suspicious of such 'native upstarts', persisting despite constant frustration to found a Sepik Producers' Cooperative Association.[31] Anton's 'epic' can be compared with the story of other noteworthy young men who survived the Pacific war. As one recent history has put it of that particular generation of survivors,

In the 1950s Papua New Guinea could look back to the War as an awesome disruption that brought few permanent changes. But for many, there was no return to the 1930s. Communities on Manus, in Madang, the Sepik and the Gulf of Papua took their own initiative. Paliau, Yali and Kabu were revolutionaries who conceived plans in varying degrees of knowledge about the economic situation that they hoped to change. The soldiers returning to Toaripi [of coastal Papua] had been aware that the foreigners had power not just through wealth and knowledge, but through organization. The Toaripi were determined to do more for themselves by combining into larger units and drawing on more manpower and capital.[32]

To mention Paliau Maloat, Yali of Sor and (Tommy) Kabu is to name three famous personages long associated with Melanesian millenarism.[33] Now it is quite justifiable to contend that one can much better understand the emergence of most so-called 'cargo cultism' in the region (which can be considered cross-culturally as a species of millenarism)[34] by setting it against the backcloth we have just spent time reconstructing. The famous cult leaders of Melanesia, in fact, were almost invariably returnees from journeys far beyond the reaches of average villagers. Like Anton, they too were extremely impressed by the riches and capacities of the whites, and were prepared to carry out programmes of action to render what they had seen accessible to their own fellows. What is distinctive about these cult leaders, however, is that their own (and their followers') hopes of some kind of spiritual interventionism becomes at some time highly accentuated. In their efforts they were already comparable to the culture-heroes of the past, as the bearers of new skills and knowledge, or discoverers of a 'new road'; but more important still is that they become identified (or confused) with 'culture-heroship' by those who look to them as the key to the Cargo - the 'openers of the way' to spiritually-generated wealth. Whether through the ancestors or Jesus or the 'whiteman's religion', the coming of rich (sometimes unlimited) quantities of European-style goods was taken to be under their control (cf. ch.1). To complete this article (and to introduce matters raised by the next two chapters of this book), the cases of two renowned 'cargo cult heroes' of coastal and hinterland New Guinea will be considered in detail.

A 'wanderer' who chose a different path to renewal and innovation to Anton was a man to be called the 'Black King'. The major eye-witness account which relates the events surrounding the rise of this prophet, Mambu, on the northern New Guinea coast west of Madang, is from the pen of the German Catholic missionary, Georg Höltker, who realized the significance of the former's activities during the 1930s.

One Sunday towards the end of 1937, about a year after he had returned from a spell of contract labour in Rabaul, New Britain, Mambu came to the mission church at Bogia. He was much earlier than usual. He entered the church, removed the dust covers from the altar and tables near by, and proceeded to lay out the prayer books for Mass. Some minutes later the missionary sister, whose duty it was so to prepare the church, came in. She saw, with some surprise, that Mambu had done her work for her. She was puzzled, but she made no fuss. Mambu, meanwhile, remained quietly in the church until Mass commenced. Then he went out.

After Mass the missionary priest, who had heard of the morning's doings from the sister, sent for Mambu, and tried to get him to talk about what he had done, and why he had done it. But Mambu would say nothing.

Then the Angelus bell sounded.

Normally, a Catholic will stand with bowed head, repeating the Angelus prayer. Mambu fell straight to his knees and prayed with passionate fervour.

As the prayer ended Mambu rose, took his leave of the priest, and departed.

A few days afterwards there was another strange event in the mission. One of the missionary sisters woke up during the night, startled to find a Kanaka bending over her in the darkness. Very frightened as he started to clutch at her hands, she was about to call for help when the intruder, whatever his intention had been, slipped off into the night.[35]

This intruder, Höltker tells us, was "never positively identified", but natural connections between the third occurrence and the other two made Mambu the likely person.

Very soon after this nocturnal visitation, Mambu began his activities in Apingam, his own village (in the culture area). His own people, however, would have nothing to do with him, and after some trouble he took off for the Tangu settlements, further inland. "There, speaking in pidgin, he seems to have found a few followers". While the resident missionary was absent he managed to collect a sum of money - the 'head-tax' - which he said "should be given to him and not to the administration". When the missionary returned, however, he made sure that the money was returned to the donors and told Mambu he should leave. From this expulsion, Father Höltker recognized, "Mambu developed an implacable hatred for the mission". He took off into the Banara hinterland, beyond Parieknam, where he was welcomed, and where he settled into his task.

According to Höltker, Mambu's basic teaching was as follows:

At the present time, Mambu said, Kanakas (='natives') were being exploited by white men. But a new order, a new way of life was at hand which was dependent on no longer submitting to white men, whether they were missionaries, administrative officers, planters, or traders. The ancestors had the welfare of their offspring very much at heart. Even now some were in the interior of the volcano of Manam island [20 km. out opposite Bogia, manufacturing all kinds of goods for their descendants. Other ancestors, adopting the guise and appearance of white men, were hard at work in the lands where white men lived. Indeed, said Mambu, the ancestors had already despatched much cargo to Kanakas. Cloth for *laplaps,* axes, khaki shorts, bush- knives, torches, red pigment, and ready-made houses had been on their way for some time. But white men, who had been entrusted with the transport, were removing the labels and substituting their own. In this way, Mambu said, Kanakas were being robbed of their inheritance. Therefore, Kanakas were entitled to get back the cargo from white men by the use of force. The time was coming, however, when all such thievery and exploitation would cease. The ancestors would come with cargo for all. A huge harbour would be created in front of his (Mambu's) house in Suaru [on the coast], andthere the ships of the ancestors - laden with cargo - would make fast. When this time came, all work in the gardens should cease. Pigs, gardens - everything - should be destroyed.

Otherwise, the ancestors - who were going to bring plenty for all - would be angry and withhold the cargo.[36]

In the meantime, while waiting for a sign, his followers were expected to pay taxes to him as 'The Black King', for "the administration had no right to demand a tax". There was no longer any obligation to clean up the roads or do any carrying; and his people were not to attend mission schools or churches, or go to the whites' stations. Disobedience would mean being disallowed "the glories of the new age", and being "burnt up and consumed in a holocaust". Cult membership involved participation in ceremonies conducted by Mambu, who behaved like a substitute priest. He prayed to the dead - for payment; he sprinkled waters on the genitals when pairs of men or women came to stand in front of him for "a form of baptism"; he ruled that European clothes be worn and traditional clothing buried; he made unusual signs with a crucifix; and he remained celibate. What Höltker calls small "temples" were erected, each with a cross and red flag on to the pole at the top of its conical roof, but the purpose of such buildings as yet remains unknown.

Thus Mambu attempted to rule. He preferred the title *King bilong ol Kanaka* (the King of all Kanakas), and declared himself invulnerable against all threats to his person.

> Mambu caused trouble. Attendance at schools and churches dropped off alarmingly and administrative officers found their task increasingly difficult. So, action was taken. Mambu was imprisoned in Bogia, and later taken in chains to Madang.[37]

When the chained prophet did not return from prison (as he had actually promised), his followers became disillusioned, and, according to Höltker, the movement had entirely collapsed after about three months. By June 1938 'things had returned to normal'. The anthropologist Burridge, on the other hand, during his fieldwork in the region in the early 1950s, recorded an oral tradition in the making about a most significant journey which Mambu went on, after leaving for Madang bound in the colonial government's chains. This was told him after the people had suffered the effects of the Japanese invasion, the collapse of the colonial system, the bombardment and terror of modern warfare and the return of their pre-War colonial *mastas* - all of which gave them new perspectives on the impermanence of the old colonial system, and opportunities for rebuilding new ways of living, questioning their ancestral inheritance and forming new relationships with foreigners, whether from overseas or from other parts of Papua New Guinea.

Here is his record of the legend of Mambu current among the Tangu people in the 1950s. It places Mambu and his actions and promises in a perspective different from that in Höltker's account, and has turned him into a culture hero - suffering ordeals but holding the secrets of his people's future.

> Mambu, say Tangu today, was a Kanaka of the Bogia region who had been working in Rabaul. When he finished his contract he stowed away in a steamer bound for Australia. He was, however, discovered and hauled before the captain of the ship. The captain was very angry with Mambu for stowing away.
> He was about to have Mambu thrown overboard lest by going to Australia he should chance upon the secret of the white man when Mambu's former employer, his 'master' who was on the same ship, intervened and saved him. The same man, an Australian, saw Mambu safely to an Australian port.

Arrived in Australia, Mambu was clothed and fed. His master showed him the sights, gave him rice, spare clothing, beads, knives, canned goods, razor blades - heaps of good things. All this cargo was packed into cases and sent to the quayside for loading. The master's sister wrote a letter, stuck it into Mambu's hair, and told him to go down to the quay where he would find all his cargo marked with such-and-such a sign. Mambu was to board a certain ship together with his cargo and return to New Guinea. If there was any trouble, or if anyone questioned him, Mambu was to produce the letter.

Mambu boarded his ship. He survived several attempts by the captain to have him thrown overboard, but eventually he reached Bogia. If it had not been for the letter probably he would have been killed.

In Bogia, Mambu claimed that he knew the secret of white men, and that they, being jealous, were preventing Kanakas from obtaining it. Kanakas, said Mambu, should not submit to this. They should be strong and throw the white men out of New Guinea into the sea. And to make themselves strong Kanakas needed money. To this end Mambu travelled around the countryside collecting pennies and shillings. But for doing so Mambu was reported to the administration by a missionary and then gaoled. He was dangerous to white men and might destroy their over-lordship.

When the policemen came to arrest him, Mambu said to them: 'You can hit me - never mind! You can maltreat me - never mind! Later, you will understand!'

The policemen were awed, but took him to gaol. That night, though supposedly behind bars, Mambu was seen chewing betel in a nearby village. In some mystical way he had slipped out of his chains. The policemen - who knew of this escape - were too frightened to report the nocturnal excursion - and some informants say that there were several such forays - lest they be accused of neglect of duty. Nevertheless, Mambu could not escape his fate, and he was taken away to Madang. Before he left, however, he prophesied the coming war.

Mambu also performed another kind of 'miracle'. He produced for an informant, who had gone to 'try' him, a banker's packet or 'stick' of money out of thin air - money, moreover, that was actually used to buy an axe and some beads. He said to my astounded informant: 'You do not understand. You are like a child who has yet to learn much. You do not understand the things that I know'. Mambu then went on to claim that he was able to get more (money) whenever he wanted.[38]

In telling of Mambu's journeys from the colonial enclave in Rabaul town to the metropolitan centre in Sydney and then his successful return home again to Bogia, the Tangu people were, in the 1950s, lending a twofold legitimacy to the 'Black King's' revolutionary claims and teachings about a new way of living for them in the 1930s. His journey out to the source of wealth meant that Mambu became transformed into the mould of the ancient culture heroes of the region and part of the process by which the people were reshaping and extending these hero traditions in a colonial context, in which they were effectively cut off from participating in the wealth and power manifest in the actions and enclaves of the foreigners. Secondly, Mambu's claim that he had journeyed from Rabaul to Sydney, and had survived that journey and the return home, meant that he had seen with his own eyes the secrets and knowledge which foreigners were withholding from the villagers, few of whom could claim to have travelled beyond Madang or Rabaul. There is also the strong implication, no doubt influenced by mission teaching, that Mambu suffered like Jesus at the hands of the authorities, but that it was the sufferer who held on to and remains the key to the truth. (This implication has its echoes elsewhere; in the way the rejected Manarmakeri has been appealed to by the Biak islanders, for instance as a sufficient local equivalent to Jesus, and in the way Jesus had been depicted as being put to death by the Australian administration).[39]

Mambu's case considered, however, there is really no better illustration of a discoverer and innovator among cargo cult leaders than Yali of Sor, and no Melanesian life is more naturally evocative of a culture hero in modern guise.

Yali's life history and the shifting contexts of popular movements into which he moved on his return from the Pacific War have been presented in great detail by Peter Lawrence and others after him. The prime focus here will be upon two events in his experience as a serviceman in that War: his journey to Madang from Hollandia in West Papua (or Irian Jaya), and a number of journeys to Australia. But first, a brief sketch of his pre-War life, particularly as policeman and local reformer-prophet.

Yali was born around 1912 in a bush village in Ngaing, inland from the Rai coast, south of Madang. His father was a respected man of knowledge and warrior in their village. As a boy Yali was fully initiated into the Kabu Ceremony "but was never properly trained in garden ritual, sorcery, or other similar skills". He left home as a youth to seek work and remained away for a long period, so never filled this gap in local knowledge. The mission, government and plantation enclaves, developed on the coast from German times, were beginning to spread their influence into the hinterland soon after Yali's birth, so that, at the close of the 1914-18 war (which marked the end of German rule) young Ngaing men were being regularly recruited. His people were not as willing to be drawn into the spreading sphere of the Christian missions. This was largely because the Lutheran evangelists and elders in the region had decided that villagers should renounce the Kabu Ceremony and dance as a prerequisite for taking on the new religion. The Ngaing village elders were not prepared to follow such a road.

Journeying away to work in a growing mining enclave, put Yali in touch with a whole new network of influence and ideas. Around 1928 Yali was taken to Wau as an indentured labourer. He served as a bar boy and waiter in the hotel, enjoying the work and the alcohol surreptitiously supplied. Although having to fob off homosexual advances from certain whites, his relations with the colonials were good. It was in Wau, however, that

> Yali for the first time heard cargo talk and expressions of antagonism to Australian rule. Several natives, who had recently been in prison for participating in the Rabaul Strike of 1929, came to work on the goldfields. One of them was Tagarab of Milguk, who for a while cultivated Yali's acquaintance on the grounds that they were both from the same general area and virtually trade friends. Tagarab had a great deal to say about the Rabaul Strike. Although he did not emphasize its religious background, he described the general feeling among the police- men and labourers that their European employers were both underpaying them and holding back the cargo sent them by their ancestors. Yali claims to have taken very little interest in the affair.

Yali was at that stage more interested in "seeing the world", and Tagarab's talk did not leave him unsettled, nor with any anti-colonial antagonisms.[40]

On his return from this first contract in 1931, the young man Yali followed a path taken by many returned workers. He became a middleman between the new and old systems. He became the *tultul* (less senior headman) of Sor village, and as such was involved in the widening of both colonial and mission authority into the Rai Coast hinterland. On good relations with government officers he often accompanied them on patrol, and on one occasion in 1932 he helped Patrol Officer Nurton disperse 'cultists' at Sibog, a village "at which the Second Coming of the Lord and the arrival of cargo appear to have been prophesied."[41]

Yali also emerged as a cunning mediator for his people. At a time when there was increasing pressure from Lutheran missionaries to evangelize the Ngaing, who resisted their coming, he negotiated for the entry of another mission, largely because of what he had heard of their policies, while away in Wau. Some "Rabaul natives" he had met there expressed surprise about the Lutherans always urging Yali's people to convert by giving up the Kabu ceremony and dance. They told him about the Catholic Mission, "whose priests were quite lenient toward native religious ceremonies", so that when a Catholic priest made his appearance on the Rai coast, Yali was among those who first expressed interest, with the proviso that the Kabu festival was left intact. While the Catholic mission was establishing itself, however, he was not a very active participant in the new religion. He continued his work as a local official until tragedy struck. At the end of 1936 or early in 1937 his wife, to whom he was deeply attached, died. This led him to another series of journeys and a new and significant occupation, as well as to exposure to new ideas and influences.

He decided to leave home again, resigned his office as *Tultul* of Sor, and joined the Police Force. As a recruit, he went to the Police Training School at Rabaul and saw the earthquake. After his training he was drafted to Lae. He served at Wau, in the Markham Valley, and in the Huon Gulf area generally, during the next three years. He was in Lae at the outbreak of war in Europe in 1939 and, like many other natives, soon knew about it, in spite of the Administration's efforts to keep it secret, by picking up bits of careless European gossip.[42]

While working as a policeman, Yali had two kinds of experience which had much influence on his later life. First, he learnt the power and potential for corruption which came to those wearing the government's uniform and carrying the government's rifle. He openly divulged to Lawrence in the 1950s a number of instances where this potential was demonstrated, particularly the policemens' power over property and women. And in the Police Force he once again "heard cargo talk and expressions of dislike of Europeans". While grumbling over pay rates, his fellow policemen were convinced the secret of the Cargo was being withheld; it lay hidden somewhere "in Christianity", but the missionaries had failed to divulge it. And he heard suggestions that the spreading War might provide an opportunity of getting rid of the Australians and "replace them with other masters ... more likely to 'open the road of the cargo'".[43]

While still serving as a policeman in the new colonial town of Lae (which was being transformed into the colonial capital after the destruction of Rabaul by the 1937 volcanic eruption) he was hearing more and more rumours and predictions of the impending destruction of this town in the coming war. He was also becoming curious about the news he was receiving of more and more cargo movements among the people of Madang. Then he took another journey home. It is fascinating how his chosen route during three months leave in 1941 made him all the more aware of cargo cult activity near his own home area. He stopped at Bilbil on the coast and saw how members of the Latub cult had destroyed their property in anticipation of the supernatural coming of the Cargo. And after leave Yali was actually posted to Madang, from whence he accompanied a party to Karkar island, "to arrest the natives accused of instigating the Kukuaik Cargo Cult". One of these instigators was a mission worker who had prophesied Madang would be bombed, a presaging which had already motivated Tagarab to begin a separate cult on the mainland, and a soon-to-be fulfilled prediction which left Yali profoundly impressed.[43]

In the chaos and anarchy which followed the bombing and swift occupation of colonial towns like Madang and Lae on the north coast, Yali emerged as a highly skilled leader and organizer, helping workers to return home in an orderly and safe way. He now launched into his series of war journeys and exploits, from which he emerged as a new man and a hero in the eyes of the Madangs. When the Japanese arrived he witnessed the fall of Lae; he then made his way with Captain G.C. ('Blue') Harris to Finschhafen, and on to New Britain to help evacuate refugees; and then subsequently was appointed to be a coast-watcher at Talasea (west New Britain). It was in November 1942 that a party he was with was attacked by the Japanese, and suffering losses the remaining members were withdrawn. Harris and Yali, "by this time firm friends", reported to Port Moresby, "where Yali was promoted to the rank of Sergeant of Police" and promptly "sent to Queensland for six months' special training in jungle warfare.

In Peter Lawrence's book *Road belong Cargo* we have one of the most powerful and moving statements about the reaction of a non-literate, ingenuous yet enquiring Melanesian mind to the developed neighbouring country, with its innumerable goods, across the sea.

In Brisbane and Cairns, Yali saw things which he had never before even imagined: the wide streets lined with great buildings, and crawling with motor vehicles and pedestrians; huge bridges built of steel; endless miles of motor road; and whole stretches of country carrying innumerable livestock or planted with sugar cane and other crops. He was taken on visits to a sugar mill, where he saw the cane processed, and a brewery. He listened to the descriptions of other natives who saw factories where meat and fish were tinned. Again, he suddenly became more aware of those facets of European culture he had already experienced in New Guinea: the emphasis on cleanliness and hygiene; the houses in well-kept gardens neatly ordered along the streets; and the care with which the houses were furnished, and decorated with pictures on the walls and vases of flowers on the tables. In comparison, his own native culture - his rudimentary village with its drab, dirty, and disordered houses, the mean paths in the bush, the few pigs that made a man feel rich and important, and the diminutive patches of taro and yam - seemed ridiculous and contemptible. He was ashamed. But one thing he realized: whatever the ultimate secret of all this wealth - and this he understood in very much the same way as other natives - the Europeans had to work and organize their labour supply to obtain it. Again he compared this with native work habits and organization. He felt humiliated by what he considered the deficiencies of his own society.[44]

He then resigned and took on a new occupation as a member of the Australian Army, in the Coast Watching Service Section of the Allied Intelligence Bureau. It was sitting alongside other Melanesian recruits that he heard the promise of a white officer that, if they would help "win the war and get rid of the Japanese", they would be no longer "kept backward" but be helped to get houses with galvanised iron roofs, plank walls and floors, electric light, and motor vehicles, boats, good clothes, and good food.[45]

With these prospects not forgotten, Yali served the Australians with the greatest distinction, being involved in the recapture of Finschhafen, the training of recruits near Brisbane, and attaining to the highest rank ever achieved by a "native ... in the Australian Armed Forces", that of Sergeant-Major.[46]

Then a strategy was drawn up by which new attacks would be launched against the Japanese strongholds in Wewak and Madang, by landing a special commando force in Hollandia, the capital of occupied Dutch New Guinea. This was to be preceded by the landing of a special coastwatching force near Hollandia. It was made up of twelve men: Harris in command, Yali the senior native N.C.O., plus six other Europeans, three New Guinean soldiers, and an

Indonesian interpreter. They were landed from an American submarine late in March 1944, yet walked into a Japanese ambush, after losing much of their equipment in the heavy surf. Harris and four others were killed. Three Europeans, the Indonesian and the three New Guinean soldiers, including Yali, escaped. His nightmare journey, with one of these soldiers is parallel in its tragedy, endurance and resourcefulness to any legend of a culture-hero, and is one of the more memorable escape stories of the Pacific War.

Yali got away from the battle into the jungle with one Sgt. Buka, a Manus man (from the Admiralties). With neither food nor matches, with Yali in possession of a carbine, fifty rounds of ammunition, a bayonet and a compass, and with both able to tell the time from their wristwatches, they headed east following the coast. Existing on "the hearts of black palins, bush fruits, any vegetables they could find", as well as "the few animals they were able to shoot", and once looting a temporarily vacated Japanese outpost, they somehow managed to keep going. Yet only Yali survived the ordeal. Buka fell ill and disappeared in the vicinity of Vanimo. Earlier in their journey they had encountered a crocodile, and Yali was disinclined to kill it, considering that its presence so far away from any river indicated it was a local deity. Buka, though, a practising Catholic, and enjoining Yali to "think only of God", and "not ... about local deities", shot it for meat. Over the next day they carried the butchered crocodile meat along with them; yet they found themselves walking in circles, and Buka became frightened when Yali reproved him for "having no respect for the local deities". Buka became so ill out of fear that Yali had to carry him, until they were separated near the scene of a mopping up battle against the retreating Japanese. Yali went back to the place he had left his friend but could not find him. He had to press on to Vanimo, alone, and then on to Aitape, further into the Sepik region, where he reported to the Army by mid-1944.[47]

At Finschhafen he made a detailed report of his experience and recuperated in hospital for two months. His journeying was by no means ended. Back in Brisbane again he learnt more about life in the metropolis, visiting in particular the museum where he saw and pondered over collections of artefacts from Papua New Guinea, and stuffed animals he took to be the 'whiteman's totems'. In February 1945 he was able to travel still further from home, this time to Sydney. "Here he was shown over the Harbour Bridge, an aircraft repair shop, and the

Burns Philp stores and warehouses". Then came a posting to New Britain, followed by a few months home leave and service in Madang, Lae and Nadzab. His war service finally came to an end in November 1945.[48]

News of his return from Hollandia spread through those communities in Madang and the Rai Coast, torn by the turmoil of the Japanese occupation and War and already receptive to the dreams and promises of the return of their ancestors with the secret knowledge which would open the *rot bilong kago* (Road to the Cargo) for their people. At War's end, when he returned home with his great fame, he was seen as a ghost who journeyed out of the land of the dead, a prophet and reformer who could help the people improve their lives and as a culture hero returned to open the way. In his own mind, he emerged from a journey in which, though "not entirely blameless", he had somehow survived the onslaughts of hostile spirits (whereas his friend Buka had succumbed to them). He has emerged as one with deepened faith in the ancestral heritage, his life owing itself to the "respect for the old religion" he had shown in the jungle;[49] yet he was also committed to build a new world, after the image of what he had seen and heard in the foreign cities.

It was this Yali who, though for some years cooperating with the Australians in a work of post-War Rehabilitation, eventually fell disillusioned with both Mission and Administration, and who organized the largest 'cargo cult' movement in Melanesian history. The Wartime Australian promises he found to be hollow; the Cargo his people were clamouring for came neither via church nor colonial government. Remembering his journey, Yali chose the ancestors and tradition (pidgin: *pasin belong tumbuna*) as the true sources of money and the new goods it could buy. His followers went back to the Kabu and other indigenous ceremonies, while special innovative rituals were devised - focussed on tables, with cloths, cups, *croton* leaves in beer bottles, etc. - to bring about ancestral support.[49] The movement spread as far west as the border between the Madang district and the Sepik, and as far east as the Huon peninsula.[50] Its missionary-like representatives were even securing a brief following in the Eastern central highlands; and it was a grass-roots movement which could not be held together but by hard travelling.[51]

The travels of Mambu and Yali, whether as legend or 'fact', hardly stand alone in the history of cargo cult leaders. We are not to forget the experiences of islander Paliau Maloat, for one, involved as a constable in the opening up of the central highlands range; nor those of Irakau of Manam, whose escape journey from Buna in Papua was perhaps even more tortuous than Yali's from Hollandia.[52] Other tales may be told. Earlier ones, of men such as the Fuyughe adventurer Ona Asi (alias the prophet 'Bilalaf') who dared to cross the highest Papuan ridges to see for himself the *tidib* - the white, returning culture-heroes - he predicted would return.[53]

Thus in this essay we have explored linkages between journeys of transformation which are legendary and those which are factual. That there are parallels should not be so surprising. Most, certainly many legends or myths may well be based on unrecoverable historical events in any case; and these narratives are rarely so presented in traditional cultures that their content has no correspondence with the world of everyday life. The point is that the new heroes become crucial and magnetic precisely because they evoke the spirits of the past in their achievements, and look to a future of wealth and the freedom of possibility reminiscent of the 'time of the gods'. This is nowhere clearer than in the comparable journeys of discovery and consequent transformation by culture-heroes and men. The traditional stories of culture heroes contain archetypally compelling exploits - acts of daring, great journeys, encounters with the 'other side', extraordinary innovations - which are not to be neglected as data helpful in explaining the special qualities and expectations of Melanesians leadership, cargo cultist or otherwise.

Notes

1. T.G. Harding, *Voyages of the Vitiaz Strait; a study of a New Guinea trade system*, Seattle, 1967, pp. 158-60.

2. Allace, "Siassi Trade", in *Oral History*, 4/10 (1976), pp. 2-22.

3. London, 1922.

4. Flierl, *Forty-Five Years in New Guinea: a Memoir of Senior MIssionary John Flierl*, Chicago, 1931, p.18.

5. W.R. Ambrose, "The Loneliness of the Long Distance Trader in Melanesia", in *Mankind*, 11/3 (1978), pp. 326-33.

6. Thus cf. R.J. Lacey, "Agricultural Production on the Eve of Colonialism", in D. Denoon and C. Snowden (eds.), *A Time to Plant and a Time to Uproot; a history of agriculture in Papua New Guinea*, Port Moresby, 1981, pp. 65-77.

7. For the above material, including quotations, Allace, *loc. cit.*, pp. 2-12.

8. Malinowski, *op.cit.*, pp. 290-333.

9. Harding, *op.cit.*, p. 159.

10. Malinowski, *Coral Gardens and their Magic*, London, 1935, vol.1, pp.65-75 (Trobriands); G. Höltker, *Myths and Legends of the Monumbo and Ngaimbom Papuans of North-east New Guinea* (trans. G. Duigu), Port Moresby, 1974; *Myths and Legends from Murik Lakes*, Port Moresby, 1975, pt.1; M. Tamoane, "Kamoai of Darapap and the Legend of Tari", in G.W. Trompf (ed.), *Prophets of Melanesia*, Port Moresby, 1981 edn., pp. 107-121 (Sepik); G.J. Held, *The Papuas of Waropen*, Leiden, 1957 (Waropen).

11. Cf. esp. F.C. Kamma, *Koreri: messianic movements in the Biak-Numfor Culture Area*, The Hague, 1972, *passim*.

12. R. Wagner, *Habu: the innovation of meaning in Daribi religion*, Chicago, 1972, esp. ch.1.

13. See N. Oram, "Environment, Migration and Site Selection in the Port Moresby Coastal Area", in J.H. Winslow (ed.), *The Melanesian Environment*, Canberra, 1977, pp. 74-99, cf. C.G. Seligmann, *The Melanesians of British New Guinea*, Cambridge, 1910, pp. 97-100.

14. A shamanic motif (of being dragged to the depths and 'killed' [in other cases, as in Siberia, dismembered limb for limb]? [Editor].

15. For a Motuan's translation, K.B. Hitolo, "Goddess Helped the First Lakatoi

Builder", in *South Pacific Post,* 12 June, 1986, p.7. cf. N. Oram, 'Edea Siabo and the Founding of the Hiri Trading Expeditions: a multi-faceted approach to a Papuan Legend' (mimeograph, Centre for South West Pacific Studies, La Trobe University), Melbourne, 1983 [Editor].

16. For background, W. Flannery, "Appreciating Melanesian Myths", in N. Habel (ed.), *Powers, Plumes and Piglets; phenomena of Melanesian religion,* Adelaide, 1979, pp. 164-5; T. Aerts, "Melanesian Gods", in Bikmaus, 4/2 (1983), pp. 13-18; cf. (for background), J. van Baal, Dema, The Hague, 1966.

17. See A. Amean, P. Pato, K.T. Talyaga and M. Timothy, "An Enga Clan Tradition", in *Oral History,* 2/2 (1974), pp. 2-15.

18. Lacey, "Religious Change in a Precolonial Era", in *Point,* 2 (1978), pp. 180-1.

19. Cf., e.g. J. Waiko, "Binandere Oral Tradition: sources and problems", in Denoon and Lacey (eds.), *Oral Tradition in Melanesia,* Port Moresby, 1981, pp. 11-30; P. Swadling, L. Aitsi, G. Trompf and M. Hari, "Beyond the Early Oral Traditions of the Austronesian Speaking People of the Gulf and Western Central Provinces", in *Oral History,* 5/1 (1977), pp. 50ff.; W. Jogoga Opeba, "The Migration Traditions of the Sebaga Andere, Binandere and Jaua Tribes of the Orokaiva; the need for attention to a Religion and Ideology", in Denoon and Lacey (eds.), *op.cit.,* pp. 57ff.; Trompf and A. Kandwel, "The Epic of the Komblo", in *Oral History,* 10/1 (1982), pp. 88ff.

20. See Lacey, "Traditions of Origin and Migration: some Enga evidence", in Denoon and Lacey (eds.), *op.cit.,* pp. 45-56, cf. Waiko, *loc.cit.*

21. G. Bateson, *Naven,* Stanford, 1958; F.E. Williams, *Drama of Orokolo,* Oxford, 1940; K.E. Read, "Nama Cult of the Central Highlands, New Guinea", in *Oceania,* 23/1 (1952), pp. 40-54; I. Hogbin, *The Island of Menstruating Men,* Scranton, 1970; S. Lehner, "The Balum Cult of the Bukaua of Huon Gulf, New Guinea", in *Oceania,* 5/3 (1935), pp. 338-46; W. Kigasung, "The Value of Bukawa Initiation", in *Point,* 2 (1978), pp. 128-39.

22. For most of the material in the above paragraphs on the Enga, E. Kelly, 'Socialisation among the Kyaka People of the New Guinea Highlands' (unpublished typescript), Baiyer River, n.d.; Lacey, *Oral Traditions as History: an exploration of oral sources among the Enga of the New Guinea Highlands* ([Doctoral] dissert., microf., University of Wisconsin), Madison,

1975, pp. 199-244; G. Teske, "Christianising the *Sangai*", in Point 2, 1978), pp. 71-102.

23. Major surveys of the documentary sources of these journeys include, I. Hughes, *New Guinea Stone Age Trade*, Canberra, 1977, pp. 10-59; J.L. Whittaker, N.G. Gash, J.F. Hookey and Lacey (eds.), *Documents and Readings in New Guinea History prehistory to 1889*, Brisbane, 1982, pp. 173-309, cf. A. Wickmann, *Nova Guinea*, Leiden, 1909-12, 3 vols.

24. Pidgin: *Man namel*. Lacey, *Journeys and Transformations* (in preparation).

25. See esp. J. Griffin, H. Nelson and S. Firth, *Papua New Guinea: a political history*, Melbourne, 1979, ch. 4. For specific studies of Melanesians in far-flung areas, e.g. M. Meleisea, *O Tama Uli: Melanesians in Samoa*, Suva, 1980; C. Moore, *Melanesian Mackay*, Port Moresby, 1986 (Editor).

26. Hughes, *op.cit.*, p.17. Cf. also Trompf, "Introduction", in Trompf (ed.), *The Gospel is Not Western*, New York, 1987, p. 9 on the possibility of black Melanesian slaves going as far as Rome (Editor).

27. Whittaker, *et al.*, p. 207.

28. H.N. Stevens (ed.), *New Light on the Discovery of Australia as Revealed by the Journal of Captain Don Diego de Prado y Tovar*, London, 1930, pp. 154-7.

29. Esp. Griffin, *et al.*, *op.cit.*, chs. 10-13.

30. B.J. Allen, 'Information Flow and Innovation Diffusion in the East Sepik District, Papua New Guinea' (Doctoral dissert., Australian National University), Canberra, 1976, p.353 (quoted with kind permission).

31. *Ibid.*, pp. 362-4.

32. Griffin, *et al.*, *op. cit.*, p.99.

33. See P.Worsley, *The Trumpet shall sound*, London,1970 edn., pp. 193-204, 225-8.

34. Cf., e.g., Lacey, 'The Vailala Madness as a Millenarian Movement', and 'Tangu Millennial Ideology and Ritual' (unpublished typescript, University of Wisconsin Seminar), Madison, 1971.

35. Höltker, "Die Mambu-Bewegung in Neuguinea; Ein Beitrag Zum Prophetentum in Melanesien", in *Annali Lateranensi*, 5 (1941), pp. 181ff. (trans. by K. Burridge, in *Mambu a Melanesian Millennium*, London, 1960, p.183).

36. Using Burridge trans., pp. 184-5.
37. *Ibid.*, p. 186.
38. See *ibid.*, pp. 183-90.
39. Cf. H.M. Thimme, "Manamarkeri: theological evaluation of an old Biakmyth", in *Point*,1 (1977), pp. 21ff. (Biak); T. Schwartz, *The Paliau Movement in the Admiralty Islands 1946-1954 (Anthropological Papers of the American Museum of Natural History 49)*, New York, 1968, p.255 (Editor).
40. Lawrence, *Road belong Cargo*, Manchester, 1964, pp. 118-9.
41. *Ibid.*, p. 119.
42. *Ibid.*, pp. 121, cf. p.120 for earlier, short quotation.
43. *Ibid.*, p. 122, cf. also p.99, and R. McSwain, *The Past and Future People*, Melbourne, 1977, pp. 24ff., 84ff., 171ff.
44. Lawrence, *op.cit.*, p. 123 (both longer and the earlier shorter quotation).
45. *Ibid.*, p. 124.
46. *Ibid.*
47. *Ibid.*, pp. 125-6, 130-2. P. Lawrence has recently come to possess more information about Buka [Editor].
48. *Ibid.*, p. 126.
49. *Ibid.*, pp. 196-249, cf. L. Morauta, *Beyond the Village (London School of Economics Monographs on Social Anthropology)*, London and Canberra, 1974, pp. 39-43, 113-21; T. Ahrens, "New Buildings on Old Foundations: 'Lo-Bos' and Christian Congregations in Astrolabe Bay", in *Point*, 1 (1974), pp. 29ff.; etc.
50. Cf., e.g., A. Maburau, "Irakau of Manam", in C.E. Loeliger and Trompf (eds.), *New Religious Movements in Melanesia*, Suva and Port Moresby, 1985, pp.14-5; Wagner, 'The Outgrowth and Development of the Cargo Cult' (unpublished typescript), Kanosia, 1965, ch. 1B [Editor].
51. Cf. Trompf, "The Theology of Beig Wen, the Would-Be Successor to Yali", in *Catalyst*, 6/3 (1976), pp. 166-7, 172 (on Lagitamo Luka) [Editor].
52. Schwartz, *op.cit.*, pp. 240-6 (Paliau); Maburau, *loc. cit.*, p.11 (Irakau).
53. Trompf, "'Bilalaf'" in Trompf (ed.), *Prophets, op.cit.*, pp. 21-27.

Chapter Five

The Cultivation of Surprise and Excess

The Encounter of Cultures in the Sepik of Papua New Guinea

Patrick Gesch

There is a tendency to think of cargo cults as part of the orderly progress from a village religious worldview to an acceptably modern and Western scientific outlook.[1] Even an observer of the Yangoru (East Sepik) cargo cult could be persuaded that rational argument was the key to moving cultists along the line of progress. I think here of William Stent, as he wrote of a village friend who began to turn to business,

> His change in attitude towards the cult was gradual and the result of rational argument and reflection. It was a slow change.... He changed his system of belief without going through a dramatic conversion process. Even so, it is true, that for him, the world had changed. He no longer believed in cargoism.[2]

I certainly agree that cultists are reasonable people, but I believe a change of worldview such as Stent suggests, is the extraordinary exception rather than the rule. It seems to me that in a cargo cult, the forms of the modern Western world are assumed as an external set of activities, but it is the traditional religious worldview which remains the motive and key for evaluating success. People can learn from the experience of failure, but the setting aside of discredited cargo cult programmes does not of itself mean that a whole way of thinking has been set aside.

To illustrate this proposition, I wish to refer to the Mt. Rurun Movement, which has flourished in the Yangoru area of the East Sepik Province, Papua New Guinea, from about 1969 even up till the present day. Its climax occurred on the 7th July 1971, when the leaders Matias Yaliwan and Daniel Hawina of Ambukanja and Makimbanja villages removed cement markers from the mountain top to void the magical curses of white men, and rectify trespass on the place of the dominant spirit of the area. The movement gathered up to 200,000 followers, who subscribed at least $200,000 in the hope of participation in promised millennial blessings.

Yangoru is 100 kilometres due west of Wewak, which is on the central north-coast of Papua New Guinea. Yangoru lies in the densely populated belt of foothills on the inland slopes of the Prince Alexander Range. The area has much in common with the areas studied by Mead and Gerstner,[3] but has largely been untouched ethnographically until lately. The villages of Yangoru average a population of about 200 each, and are composed of dispersed hamlets throughout the bush, the borderlines of territory (demarcating perhaps 3 km square of land) being indistinguishable to outsiders. Livelihood comes from subsistence agriculture, supplemented by the beginnings of a coffee industry. Religion centres around kinds of spirits, an increasing reliance on magic, and vivid memories of the traditional initiation system. The Christian missions have been known since 1912, but missionaries have only been in residence since 1948, since which time most villagers have joined one of the Christian groups.

The missionaries represent the forward fringe of European culture in the district, sponsoring schools, trade stores, radio transmission, power generation, transport and other systems of modern technology. The government officers established a presence about 1935, but there has been very little of the work of white businessmen in the area. Most village men, however, even up to the present time, have averaged two years working in distant towns or plantations, there getting an impression of bulkstores filled with Western goods, the shuffling of papers and mail which makes merchandise appear, and the systems of transport, education, corporation employment and credit, which all go to make business happen, mysteriously.

Yangoru had known a series of cargo cults over the years, amongst the returnees from other New Guinea centres. The Mt. Rurun Movement, however, was far larger than anything known before.

The Mt. Rurun Movement has assumed many forms and programmes over the years. It was a clarion call that reverberated throughout much of the East and West Sepik Provinces (or along the hinterland of mainland New Guinea west of the Sepik River mouth), giving rise to a wide variety of inspired programmes on the local level. However, in the central villages of Malimbanja, Ambukanja and five others to be counted in for their leading loyalists, I propose that there were sixteen forms which can be thematized out of the course of the Movement. In the main sections of this article I will set these out as a progression from "traditional religious" to "modern economic, political, social and religious". My argument is however, that appearances of shifts towards modernity were more apparent than real, and were actually no progression at all. The modern Western forms were not what they seemed, because underlying and explaining them was the traditional religious worldview. This worldview can best be detected by the criteria of surprise and excess. Western activities were assumed as a working programme by the cultists; but always some *surprising* result was counted on - it was hard to say what might happen, but Jesus would come back, the old ways would collapse, or the lifestyle of the villagers would be expected to change in some dramatic way. The dramatic change was usually a matter of being flooded with an *excess* of something: goods, friends, soldiers or a clarity of understanding.[4]

It seems to me the traditional religious outlook can be distinguished from the modern scientific view by two major symptoms. First, the cultists expect a gratuitous and excessive result to their activities, a result defined as wonderful and personally enthralling. Second, this secret something is expected to be under the control of some persons and can be witheld by them. Such characteristics I understand to be anathema to science, if applied as intrinsic attributes. The problem with cultism is generally held to be the fact that they expect scientific-technological results from the use of religious means. What is the precise problem here, since it seems that religion remains in the world of Western technology? The difficulty seems to be a matter of being reconciled to using two different worldviews alternatively. Briefly my own view of the difference between the religious and scientific outlooks is as follows.

Science must always take a partial view, carefully defining and delimiting all kinds of conditions and the scope of research. Scientific achievements must be repeatable at any time and in any place where the conditions can be made to apply. The scientist must necessarily be fundamentally detached from the results of his experiments so that they can tell of universally valid relationships between things themselves. By contrast, religion claims that its whole validity rests on the relationship of the believer himself to the respondent of belief. Religion is thoroughly bound up with a holistic view of personality wherein values are found worthy of complete devotion, and trust in somebody else's experience is held to be an inadequate substitute for one's own unique experience.

Clearly there is a need and a use for the detached and partial outlook of science; but not everyone sees that a holistic, devoted view of anything, even of science itself, is not scientific but in fact, religious. The thrill of discovery in science, the conviction of the purity and value of method, the sense of integrity in empirical criteria - perhaps these things are not what we usually mean by the religious, but they are surely on a direct continuum with religious values and wonder. What is peculiarly scientific is the detached, parsimonious, verifiable application of method. What is peculiarly religious is devoted response to the awesome and Holy, the "tremendous yet fascinating mystery".[5]

With these distinctions in view, let us now move through the sixteen forms of the Mt. Rurun Movement in the manner I have proposed. In all of these programmes we will be able to see the world view of the traditional village religion resurgent. Sometimes the only indication that the traditional religious view is operating is that the modern forms are undertaken with the presupposition that a gratuitous, surprising or excessive result is expected from the activities. In the light of such a scheme, though, we can see that traditional religion is definitely surviving, and with great vigour. It invests the world with renewed levels of excitement; it accounts for the continuous willingness of cultists to undertake new proposals in the Movement; and it shows that the modern village lives with an enduring situation that "will not be solved or swept away with minor reforms or development projects".[6]

The Mt. Rurun Movement centred around the activity of Daniel Hawina and Matias Yaliwan over the last fifteen or so years. Although these two men are of different temperament, Hawina being much more the skilful manager and strong-minded 'bigman', and Yaliwan a more mysterious, reflective, if not psychologically unusual type, they shared a common disaffection with the colonial order and legitimated each other's claims to authority. They announced that the local spirit of the nearby Mt. Rurun (spelt variously, Turu or Hurun) was greatly offended by a cement survey marker which the American Air Photographic and Charting Service had unwarrantedly planted on the mountain top in 1962. Invoking a mixture of Christian and traditional religious symbols, they said the offending cement marker had to be removed on the seventh day of the seventh month of 1971. Its removal would allow the Spirit Rurun to restore the former prosperity of the bush, the streams and the gardens. However, the story reached the outside world with the banner headline of the Port Moresby *Post-Courier* (17/5/71): "Human sacrifice! 15,000 to watch cargo cult rites." Matias Yaliwan had had a dream while in prison that he was to be sacrificed in the manner of Jesus Christ, and three days afterwards was to rise from the dead, bringing access to the good times for all the people of Papua New Guinea. The press played a role in gathering the 15,000, and in focussing the interest of hundreds of thousands of Papua New Guinean people on the taking out of the marker on July 7th. Despite this great show of interest, the events of the day passed without incident; the markers were carried down the mountain with solemn indications of religious devotion, were handed over to the government officers at the patrol post, and then the people dispersed.

The Movement continued with the assumption of various programmes. I represent these programmes in the accompanying Figure 2 (on p 222). The first four forms are rather clearly the traditional village religion embracing a few novel ideas; the next five forms are taken from modern politics, but reveal the hope of surprising returns; three more refer to modern economic ventures; two others to general development programmes; and the last two are derived from Christian forms. My use of a circle in the Figure is neither meant to denote cyclical recurrence nor temporal sequence. It is meant rather to indicate that the tradition did not substantially alter relative to any of the sixteen forms, and to allow for the representation of overlapping of the forms, clusters of which coexisted at the same times. I have selected dominant themes which appeared at various times during the Movement, and my subsquent explanations will select supporting facts from out of the span of the Movement since 1969.[7]

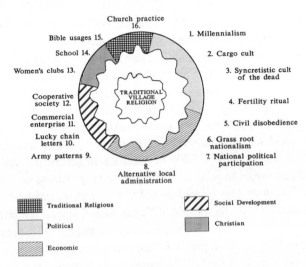

Figure 2. Forms Assumed in the Mt. Rurun Movement by Traditional Village Religion

Traditional Religious Forms

The first form assumed by the Mt. Rurun Movement is millennialism, which has also flourished in many other parts of Melanesia within the cargo cult tradition. An old man living very close to the top of Mt. Rurun identified the surveyors' contraption with its cement indicators as being an offence to the Spirit Rurun. His message was taken up by Hawina and Yaliwan, who organized a traditional festival in December 1969 to remove the iron framework from above the ground, and prepared the people for eschatological consequences following from the deed. Only two police arrests followed, so the leaders repeated their challenging proclamation in a widely publicized meeting in May 1971. The old man's complaint was now taken to be an offence against the spirit, and it was alleged that the whites had worked a magical bundle to deprive the people of their traditional prosperity; to remove this magic would be at the same time to appease the spirit and have the good times return. This was quickly taken up as a belief that much else would be transformed by taking out the cement markers. There would be an earthquake; darkness would come at noon; traditional food such as coconuts would fall from the trees; birds would fly upside down; whites and blacks would exchange colours; and there would be a tidal wave that would sweep over the mountain from the coast to the Yangoru side of the Prince Alexander Range - a wave to clean out the unrepentant whites and blacks. The stories of these overwhelming events to come seem to have been endlessly embellished, and became yet more wonderful the further one got away from Malimbanja village. The priest of Negrie Catholic Mission at the time remembers frequent explicit reference to the coming thousand-year peace time of the New Testament Apocalypse, thus showing how traditional cataclysmic notions could chime in with 'mission talk' about the End of the known world (cf. also fifth sect. below).

The second form assumed by the Movement was that of a cargo cult. I avoid use of this term to describe the whole Movement wherever possible, because the members reject it, and it is reductionistic. The main usefulness of the term is to connect the Yangoru events with the so-called 'cargo cult' tradition of Melanesia. The Mt. Rurun Movement was a cargo cult properly so-called, however, in its stories of whites who met the village dead at night and diverted technological goods intended for villagers to their own ends. It was said 400 American planes carrying 4,000 Americans and disgorging great amounts of cargo would come to the top of Mt. Rurun. As the cement marker was about to be removed from the mountain, stories were repeated that the larger goods of Western society would appear from the hole in the ground. More frequently money was to appear gratuitously, and the money theme was the more lasting one in the Mt. Rurun Movement. The surprising bestowal of Cargo was a religious theme having origins in the idea of traditional wealth being instituted by powerful spirits and brought along by ghosts of dead relatives to provide for their living descendants.

Thirdly the Movement was a syncretistic cult of the dead. Large amounts of money were collected before and after July 1971, and again around July 1972. The main destiny claimed for this money was that it should go to the War Memorial in Canberra - to invoke the spirits of the American and New Guinean war dead - so that the departed should send things freely from Australia. Attempts were made to associate various Christian churches with this money.

The Catholic Bishop of Wewak said he did not wish to appear as endorsing these beliefs. The Foursquare Gospel of Madang refused to be associated with these moneys, as also did the Jehovah's Witnesses. Besides these, Daniel Hawina is said to have approached the District Commissioner to forward this money to its destination. He too declined. The amount of money being collected was not inconsiderable. At the time of the taking out of the cement, Daniel was shown standing beside a box of money said to contain Aus$21,572. This was from membership fees of Aus$12 per family which were being collected to ensure participation in the coming good times. Again in July 1972, on the first anniversary of the removal of the marker, money was collected from the sale of memorial plots, and by this time the collection by Malimbanja alone was said to amount to nearly Aus$100,000. Daniel insisted the memorial plots were only little gardens to commemorate the men and the villages who had flooded in to join Malimbanja in their activities. But to the common eye they looked like the War Memorial cemeteries in Lae and Bomana, neatly laid out with colourful crotons and a head board for each plot. These plots were sold for Aus$10 each, there being perhaps 800 of them in Malimbanja itself, and more in other centres of the Movement. Sometimes, it was said, money was found on these plots.

Some youths were organized as "Workers", and they say they were instructed to stand at night with appointed girl associates, and removing their clothes, were to roam around watching for dead spirits in these memorial gardens. Were they to see one, they should seize it, and money would fall from its pockets. The traditional dead were being honoured, but in novel, coercive ways. The dead are responsible for bringing blessing and success to the work of men, and for presenting themselves in the bodily form of game animals for the hunt to help their descendants; but now they were being laid to siege. Very dramatic results were being expected of them.

Fourthly, the Movement involved a fertility ritual, one of the items most talked of by outsiders. The disappointment of nothing having happened on July 7th, 1971 was met by Daniel Hawina's declaration that something had indeed happened: he himself had been endowed with power. Anyone who wished to join in his good fortune should go home and complete a "power house". This was a rather vague notion, drawing on the traditional usage of having a house built to harbour the paraphernalia of magic that was involved in traditional wealth accumulation and distribution cycles.[8] The houses were then built in many parts of the Sepik Districts, but Daniel says he allowed some Madang visitors to run their own project at this stage - a "house country" where people were taken inside and, with the shaking of the house, sent away to the country where all good things originate.

Teams of "Flowers", young nubile girls, were organized at various places. Their job was said to be that of *paitim dis* (shaking the dishes) inside the power houses. On the one hand it was claimed that they necessarily must remain virginal or they would have no power to make money multiply in the dishes they were shaking. On the other hand there is considerable evidence that the ritual involved sexual intercourse, either with the official *komiti* (committee representative) of the village or with an assigned young Worker. There were a number of pregnancies reported as outcomes of this, and some young men tell me that it was insisted upon that they should sleep with their Flowers. The intercourse was connected with tipping a lot of coins backwards and forwards between two dishes. It was said that on some nights Aus$5, $4 or $1 extra might be found, but that it was certainly hard work. This understanding seemed to endure because it involved a non-refundable capital. Those who donated coins for the shaking were not guaranteed a quick return of the principal.

The Flowers had a further role in the carrying of red suitcases. This is a very popular focus for cargoism to assume in Papua New Guinea, since the contract labourers of early days were given red wooden suitcases to take their basic bedding materials and utensils off to the plantations.[9] On their return, their earnings were distributed from these cases. Now people were urged to buy the familiar red suitcase, to bring it to Malimbanja where it would be suitably charmed, and then to carry it home and wait for the appointed day which would see an outflow of great wealth when the case was opened. The whole event was surrounded by difficult observances. The box was to be carried from Malimbanja by a virgin girl with no one preceding her. She had to carry it undisturbed on her outstretched forearms, and was to speak to no one on the way, looking neither to right nor to left. The owner of the case was to wash only in warm water, to do no work and to sleep by the fire with his suitcase for as many days as the waiting took. When this exercise produced most unexciting results, people were told they had failed in their proper observances.

Political Forms

Moving over now to the arena of political forms for the Mt. Rurun Movement, we can refer to the fifth form as that of civil disobedience. Matiai Yaliwan long insisted to the world that this was the essential thrust of his activity. The Americans had come to the top of his mountain, had done their work and left behind the marker without adequately consulting anyone. If this were permitted to go on, it would be like allowing a rot to attack the principles of village self-administration and proper land rights. So a vision he had was appropriate in telling him to remove the marker, as it involved a naked act of trespass. The removal of the metal framework in December 1969 brought a swift retaliation from the government, and a gaoling for Matias and Daniel. Nevertheless they proceeded to the next removal of markers in July 1971, and the following year an excuse was found to put Daniel back in gaol. But the simple act of trespass referred to by Matias was obviously something more. The more resistance the government and the missionaries offered, the more people's conviction arose that along this path lay a surprising access to the great wealth and idealized life of the Europeans in general.

I lived and worked in the Yangoru area for a large part of the time from 1973-1983, and continually I felt that I was being asked for the secret of European prosperity. Why do Europeans never have disputes among themselves? Why are they never sick or with sores? If they have goods from factories, then why do villagers not have factories too? These were questions I was explicitly asked during the years. On a certain occasion, as I was leaving the area for an extended period, I spoke to a small village meeting, and I said I had a final announcement to make before the meeting dispersed. The local magistrate got very excited, and quietly insisted to everyone: "All right, be quiet now. Here it comes at last. Here it is now." He had often made it clear to me that he expected a real revelation from me. At this time I became exasperated and explained that my great announcement only had to do with a Parents and Citizens meeting for the local school. My experience was no isolated thing. Other European visitors to the area have also discovered themselves being asked, in moments of quiet friendliness with the villagers: "Are we Countrymen? Will you speak out the Secret to us now?" I have often pondered what I could possibly say that would satisfy the requests. To say that the secret of our success lies with schooling, the division of labour, and industrialization hardly grips people as a very satisfying answer.

It is obvious, however, that Daniel Hawina gave the people the answers they liked to hear. The dreams of Matias Yaliwan and the programmes of Daniel Hawina clearly responded to what the people were seeking. A dream is a revelation from the eternal times which suits the needs of the present; and what is revealed is a way of acting and a way of life that can be assumed with confidence to make all of life exciting and happy. This demand for the revelation of wonderfully satisfying programmes of action is an element that cargo cults share with enthusiastic movements in the West, both religious and political.

The sixth form of the Movement was its grass roots nationalism. On the national scene in Papua New Guinea, there is much juggling of Cabinet posts and allocation of budget moneys to create a sense of national unity which the people have not felt in the past. At the time of Independence in 1975, the Government waged a very effective campaign, using a series of widely distributed posters, to impress on people the message, *"Bung wantaim* - Unite!" This theme gave considerable force to the meaning of Independence, but it still remained largely an abstraction for the village. For the greater part, centralized government institutions meant little to the people; the named institutions did not seem very responsive to their demands; it was hard to understand where the government's money came from; and it was difficult to imagine that dealings in Port Moresby had much to do with life in the village. But with the Mt. Rurun Movement, people felt that a sense of national identity was definitely emerging. Daniel Hawina preached constantly that everybody was welcome to Malimbanja. Even people from Madang, from Papua and the Highlands could come, because the events on Mt Rurun concerned whites and blacks, men of all races. Malimbanja village, at the height of its activities, was said to resemble nothing so much as the cosmopolitan hubbub of a place like King's Cross in Sydney. But this dazzling cosmopolitan life was brought into village terms, at least for a while, and without losing its great fascination.

Matias Yaliwan had a dream that on his home ground, on a plot of land sold many decades previously to the Catholic Mission, God had created Adam and

Eve and thus all mankind. It was a great puzzle for people that there should be black and white men with greatly differing endowments and inclinations. Matias' suggestion that he "knew about blacks and whites" was held in much awe by the people. Matias withdrew from his home village to a position about twenty kilometres eastwards along the highway leading to Wewak. Here he gathered around himself something in the nature of a religious community. When I spoke to them in 1974, they told me that they met for prayers every morning and evening, that Matias withdrew into his house on the hill to pray, and that they did not go outside their enclosure for fear of being distracted from their project at hand. But most impressive for them was their sense of being a community drawn from many different areas. Families from Wewak were there, some Madang folk, there were West Sepik people present, such that it felt like a living experience of nationalism. The intermingling of people from across traditional boundaries was long a remarkable feature of the Mt. Rurun Movement. For the participants themselves it seemed nothing less than an eschatological age.

Largely consequent on this remarkable feeling of a ground-swell of unity among the peoples, the Movement entered its seventh phase, national political participation. At the end of 1971, there was a lot of talk about the significance of the new House of Assembly - to be elected in the following year. It was the first national parliament to be wholly elected by universal suffrage. People became aware that it had a lot to do also with the up-coming notions of Self-Government and Independence, which were known to be somehow critical events of the future. One of Matias' dreams, prior to July 1971, was that God had appointed him *gavman* ('Government') of Papua New Guinea. This title seemed to have rather holistic implications. It did not seem likely that he meant he would be the first among equals, that there would be others with whom he would share responsibility, or that he would consider himself representative of any community. His appointment as *gavman* was by divine right, and Matias was greatly puzzled by the refusal of some to accept this destiny he had been given. Matias seems to have done a limited amount of campaigning to get himself elected to the House of Assembly. Daniel was reported to have propagandized for Matias in other areas beyond the immediate Yangoru neighbourhood. That granted, however, there can be no doubt that the religiously surprising and excessive expectations of the Mt. Rurun Movement were the enthusiastic basis for 'the political campaign'.

Matias won the election with 83% of the vote, and large numbers of Peli Association members (as Daniel called his organization after 7/7/71) made a big impression on the election by abstaining from voting in other electorates (because they were not able to vote for Yaliwan). Once in the House of Assembly, he lost no time in announcing his position as *gavman* of Papua New Guinea. When this was ignored by the House, he continued for some time to participate in the routine matters of voting and making requests, but eventually felt himself to be very sick because of his frustration. He accused Daniel Hawina back in Malimbanja of making sorcery against him, as Daniel was making forceful demands to show results. Matias eventually resigned from the House, and moving away from his home village, formed a new Seven Association which drew the support of his most ardent followers. Daniel and the Peli Association hesitated for some time, but soon reaffirmed their unity with Matias. Matias thus had enough support to guarantee the election of his lacklustre secretary Linus Hepau to be his successor in the parliament. Linus went to Port Moresby and repeated the divine-right claims of Matias, praising him for being the only one who had shown the meaning of Self-Government and Independence to the people. But he was greeted with the same coolness as shown Matias, and little more came of this religious version of national politics.

Still in the political area, we can refer to some of the works of the Peli Association as an attempt to substitute for the Local Government Council. This is our eighth form. There was a certain amount of tension between the local council and Peli. Peli was clearly an institution that had the support of the people, and held a wide range of their hopes. The Council was there mostly by the demand of the Administration. The Council President Thomas Wolimpanku was a relative of Daniel and Matias, but twice his life was threatened when he demanded an end to the over-crowded conditions in Malimbanja caused by the Peli members' unexpected squatting. Daniel was brought to court twice on counts of not fulfilling his duty of working for the Council on Mondays, not paying his Council tax, and encouraging others to follow his example. Daniel asserted that this was due to the fact that he was indeed doing other work for the country. When councillors challenged him on what this other important work might be, he scornfully replied that such questions could only come from small boys. In 1973 and subsequent years Peli pointed out to its followers that there was little to show for the years of giving tax to the Council. Instead Aus$3 should be given to Peli every year. Many people claimed they did give this money, although the only improvement noticed from it was a steep unsure road down into Malimbanja itself, mostly done by hand-labour. There were also dramatic confrontations with police and government malarial spray teams when the sprayers were forbidden from entering Peli houses. Daniel was forced to back down on this. As a local administration, Peli relied on an open-ended hope for betterment among its followers, and some people never tired of subscribing to Peli plans.

Another aspect of Western life that was assumed as a form for the Mt. Rurun Movement, was the ninth form, army patterns. Around Yangoru, there is justifiable respect for the enormously transformative power of armies. The Japanese invaded the area during the Second World War, and were very demanding and punitive in their attitudes towards the villagers. When the Allies came in to reclaim the territory, there was a great deal of bombing, and many Japanese bones were left behind. I was long puzzled by a repeated question put to me: "Independence, what army is that? What country will come upon us?" The transforming power of independence was being impressed on the citizens, but the only model they had for such a political transformation, was that of occupation by a foreign power. There was now a question whether Independence meant the invasion of the Indonesians or of the Russians. In 1978, when concern about freedom fighters from Irian Jaya crossing over into Papua New Guinea was at a high level, some Irian Jaya people must have come to Malimbanja. I was told they were distributing epaulets and small flags, and a truckload of young men was sent on its way to travel up the coastal road to Irian Jaya to join in the fight. They soon turned back, but to take on an army uniform was the very model of a hope in an excessive return. Occasionally Yaliwan and some villagers liked to present themselves by coming to military attention or forming military lines. Some members of the House of Assembly worried about an alleged army around Peli headquarters. Sentries halted visitors and sought their credentials, but this "army" was probably little more than the clusters of men who continually hovered about the area, jealously guarding access to Daniel and Matias, and with a heightened curiosity in every turn of events.[10]

Economic Forms

We move on now to a more economic vein. Access to freely flowing money was long an emphasis of the Movement. A Papuan, Peter Koae, who was closely associated with Matias Yaliwan in 1971-2, was reported in the newspaper as saying that money was already flowing in by the sackful. If one put one's ear to the wall of the power house over there, the sound of money pouring out could be heard. Money was to pour out of the holes by the cement markers, was to multiply readily in the dishes as they were shaken, and was to be found in abundance in the memorial gardens. We can mention three specific forms of money experiment.

Our tenth form refers to the fascination of chain letters. "Australian Bonanza" was a type of chain letter that promised great financial return to anyone who sent off a dollar to the name at the top of the included list of addresses, and then sent the chain letter on to some of his own friends. The nationwide interest in this at the time of the Peli events brought a flurry of letters to the *Post-Courier,* asking for the banning of these false hopes by some. Others felt that such a clearly profitable venture should be taken over by the national government. The chain letters were taken up by the school children, whose special abilities in writing were also utilized by Peli to fill long ledgers with the names of subscribers. Once I was shown another kind of letter, which exercised a great appeal. I paraphrase it: "We have many good and important things which you can get from us by sending one dollar. However, if you are Papua New Guinean, do not try to get these special things from us, because they are meant only for Australians." Young people took this very seriously as a hope of success in a way comparable to the way Peli members invested hope in the Movement.

In the eleventh place, members of the Movement frequently turned to commercial enterprise, but always with a unique religious overtone to it. Some of the leaders of the Movement condemned rice growing and coffee planting. They said these were superficial deceptions to turn people aside from the direct path which could be found in money factories, and special parts of the Bible. Others, however, submerged themselves in various commercial enterprises in the hope of finding the mysterious secret concealed within them. Many small trade stores were started, selling goods at impossibly low prices, simply as an experiment to find out the truth of the statement that money comes from business. Peli purchased a large trade store in Yangoru for Aus$10,000 and it was widely hoped by Westerners that this would be turning the collected moneys to good use at last. However, there was no relationship between this enterprise and Western notions of approved business principles. Loans and a sense of community ownership soon ate into the stocks and income, and the enterprise vanished into thin air. In a similar way trucks were purchased for helping those who had paid membership fees to travel around, perhaps also to make a little income. They were over-exploited and soon were mechanically useless.

During all of this, villagers were making explicit statements that business and all the roads ventured upon by Peli were all of the same nature - as experiments to uncover a divine revelation. Those who thought abundance would flow from planting rice were disappointed; so they could try a trade store, coffee-growing, or perhaps *paitim dis* or the red suitcases. Each of these was presented to the villagers as a prescribed way of proceeding, and to each was promised the reward of a return that greatly exceeded the investment. People were cross and disappointed at not having the profit promised to them, but their only hope was to await the real revelation in which they could fully participate.

In the twelfth place, the Movement was frequently viewed as a cooperative society. As the 7th July 1971 approached, the word was urgently spread that the great out-pouring of this day would be available only to those who had paid their membership dues of Aus$12. People viewed this as being like the coffee cooperative society. They paid their membership dues to this, and at the end of the year received a surprising and almost unexplainable bonus for their investment. Now it was generally held that the Peli Association held the key to the coming good times; Daniel and Matias had uncovered the secret that was so long awaited. To share their rewards, dues were necessary. Again when the Peli Association adopted the form of a Christian denomination in 1978, dues were sought and obtained from those who felt that the return of the dead would not occur for those who did not invest. This time the membership in the area of Soli village was (PNG) K15 for each man and woman. The model was that of a cooperative society, but the motives and the hopes were definitely the religious ones of expecting to be surprised by a forthcoming excess.

Plate 5. Matias Yaliwan, Melanesian Apocalypticist

Plate 6. Yaliwan reading from the Pidgin New Testament at his Hideout

Forms Resulting from Social Development

A further two forms of the Movement we will consider as general development forms. A thirteenth phase was the women's clubs. A sister of the Catholic Mission at Negrie had been arranging and conducting meetings for women in the villages from 1972 onwards. However, in the beginning of 1975 it became apparent that her work was suddenly being treated with cult veneration. Whereas before the women were only grudgingly allowed time off garden work by the men for the sake of attending meetings, now there was a great deal of cooperation from the men which was quite unsolicited. The men proceeded to build meeting houses for the women, a man or two was appointed to watch over the activities of the club, and money was forthcoming for dress-making materials and sewing machines. The origin of cotton material and clothing features large in people's questions about European goods. However, after fewer than six months of zealous investment by the men, they were unable to suppress their boredom with women's affairs, and interest began to wane once more. The degree of surprising enthusiasm that had been shown for the women's clubs was the more accentuated by a return to the tedious process of negotiating attendance and all the affairs of the clubs.

As a fourteenth form of the Movement we should nominate the national school system. All over the country complaints are made that parents and children generally have quite different purposes and hopes in schooling than do the various administrations. In the Yangoru area, the hopes in a rather religious breakthrough are the more explicitly recognized. Here education is for the dramatic opening of access to wealth. The image of one's son sitting cleanly in an office seems the very picture of control over the abundance of these new times. The Education Department's policy of educating for a return to the village is almost universally scorned by the villages, and anyone who is dropped out anywhere along the educational system is said to have "failed". Books featured repeatedly in Daniel Hawina's list of special revelations which he made public to the press and the villagers. He had a book of the Jehovah's Witnesses, a copy of Agatha Christie's *Death Under the Sun,* and Matias Yaliwan carried around a copy of a *Reader's Digest* - all of which were said to have been delivered to the bearers by revelation in dreams from God. Accordingly, in 1970-1, there was considerable interest in an adult literacy programme presented by the school at Negrie. The adults took considerable pains to gain inside access to this activity which so obviously was the underpinning of the new times. But the enthusiasm of the adults faded with the arrival of newer programmes and more novel hopes; while the school children generously donated their long nights to the keeping of books for the Peli Association. Still the complaint can be heard, "I have paid and paid money for my children's schooling, and if he does not go on to finish high school, what return can I get on my investment?" The total amount invested in school fees for six years up to 1975 would have been about Aus$12. For this reason, schooling must be included in the list of searches made for the secret that controls access to the ready inflow of prosperity.[11]

Christian Forms

Some forms from Christianity were adopted by the Movement, but given special meanings according to the hopes of the village. In the fifteenth place, there were usages of the Bible. It was the Biblical account of Jesus who was the Road, opening the doors of heaven by his dying and rising again, which led to the frequently recurring theme of Yaliwan having to die. This story has surfaced from 1971 until 1980 at various times. Frequently the line drawings in the Book of Revelation in the *Nupela Testamen* were referred to and given a wholly Melanesian interpretation. The angel holding the key and the chain over the abyss was a very suitable image for the secret which must be discovered by the Movement. The eagle swooping down from heaven was taken as the *peli* hawk, the traditional totem of the Hawina family, which gave its name to the Peli Association. Daniel referred to himself as the *banis bilong sipsip* (door of the sheepfold), that is, the one "in the know". The creation of Adam and Eve, the animosity of the two brothers Cain and Abel (one white and the other black), authority from God, and the millennium, were all major themes of the Movement, drawn from the Bible of the missionaries. The image of an old man leading the procession with the markers down from the mountain-top while holding up a copy of the *Nupela Testamen*, was one that struck many reporters; as does also the continuing scene of the prophet Matias in seclusion, reading the

Bible. Daniel quotes Biblical themes, but he expresses his suspicion that the true Bible has not yet been sighted by the villagers, and it will make a strategic difference when this Bible is revealed. All of these Bible items were fitted into the context of the traditional religious viewpoint, searching for the hitherto withheld secret that would yield a radical change in the wellbeing of the village.

Sixteenth, the Movement identified itself with Church patterns. The all-national Seven Association of Yaliwan lived as a holy community with church and prayers. Various sacramental forms, taken mainly from Catholic practice, were used at different times: the profusion of uses of the number seven; there seem to have been Mass procedures in some places; and one vision of Malimbanja village was that it should be turned into another Lourdes devotional shrine. In 1978, however, Daniel's long term interest in the Christian denominations bore a special fruit. Daniel says he affiliated himself with many Christian churches over the years but none of them suited him very well. One of his close relatives and strongest allies was Markus Kenua who was simultaneously a leader in the local Catholic Church. Since Markus had only girl children, Daniel urged on him some further wives and a loosening of his attachment to the Church. Markus delivered a rebuttal to Daniel, "You ought to go and start your own Church, if you are man enough!" Malimbanja people remember this incident as not long preceding Daniel's return to the village one day with some representatives of the New Apostolic Church, which was new to the Sepik area.

The New Apostolic Church was brought by two white Canadian missionaries. Not able to stay the night, and not yet familiar with pidgin the two missionaries addressed the hastily assembled crowd in Malimbanja. Daniel conveyed their likely meaning to all the listeners. There were many points of similarity between the NAC and the villagers: an eschatological emphasis urging awareness of the coming crisis; a sacramental practice; the possibility of vicariously performing acts that were of benefit to the dead; an emphasis on international unity; and a hierarchy of appointees who functioned by inspiration and had little regard for school learning and Bible reading. Closely following settlements that were identified with the Peli Association, the NAC spread rapidly and widely throughout the Sepik Districts. The enthusiastic conversions of the people were reported joyfully in the missionaries' magazine. However, the missionary Apostles soon found it necessary to go on radio to announce that they had nothing in common with Matias Yaliwan and that cargo cult ideas were foreign to the NAC. For a long time local politicians tried to label the NAC with stirring up the old Movement, particularly as denying the payment of Council tax and doing due Council labour. Villagers generally held the belief that members of the NAC had joined up because they were thinking of a return on their former membership fees in Peli.

Daniel told me that here at last was a *real* church. The NAC were going to build a church in Malimbanja for free; he was given black trousers, white shirt and black tie, and an electronic watch free from the Apostles. The Canadians continued as if they were blithely unaware into whose hands they had fallen, but they became the subject of a very specific set of hopes. There is much evidence for believing that the New Apostolic Church was largely under the manipulation of Daniel and Peli leaders for their own purposes. There is no need to force the title of "cargo cult" on the NAC, since such a name and reputation have always been repudiated by the Peli Association. I have seen recent receipts for payments totalling nearly K25 which one family gave to village NAC leaders. The leaders would not acknowledge these payments to me, and it seems unlikely that they were authorized by the missionaries. The Canadian New Apostolic Church can be granted its full legitimacy as a Christian denomination; but as it appears in Malimbanja and other outposts of the Sepik, it is a form assumed by the Peli Association in connection with ideals of traditional village religion.[12]

Conclusions

We have now passed in review sixteen forms assumed by the Mt. Rurun Movement. They suggested themselves by appearing to be some kind of step by step progression from crude cargo cult notions and limited village beliefs through rationalistic ideals of politics, economics, social development and modern church. That, however, is a superficial impression. This is not only because the Movement did not undergo change in any simple, stage-by-stage fashion; but more because, basically, from the first form to the last, villagers' hopes remained of one kind. They wanted to uncover a secret that would give a new fullness of life - to life presently so awry and out of balance, as modern Western institutions mingle uneasily with the traditional ways. The old plus the new formed a constant problem for discussion and investigation. The desired future situation would come as a time of abundance and easy accessibility. This applied to all the marvels of technological civilization, to clothing, tinned foods, cement and corrugated iron houses, trucks, radios and planes; but it also applied to Western systems and values, and to a new sense of unity among peoples. Peli was greatly satisfying in providing a liberal feeling of brotherhood, at least as long as everyone seemed to have one shared purpose for being in Malimbanja. It was never possible to get a detailed vision of what the hoped-for new time of fullness would be like. I once asked if it would be a time of no disputes, and got the remarkable answer, "No, of course not. But it will be a time when disputes are easily settled."

What was hoped for amounted to the uncovering of a way of acting which would be nothing less than a spiritual revelation. People were ready to follow the dreams of Matias and Daniel, or they sought direct contact with the mountain spirits or the spirits of the dead. Any of these could produce the surprise that would tie all the confusions of life together. It was expected that this way-to-be-uncovered would bring a great excess, a marvellous entry into a new religious situation.

It is because of these notions of a surprising and excessive revelation that I have found it necessary to refer to the whole of the Mt. Rurun Movement as religious. This is not to deny vestigial steps along the way to specialization in science, economics and politics, but it is to say that the basic motivation was a hope for something more than simply the product of hard work. The hope that the "law of Yaliwan would break open" was the desire to feel the effects in life of something more than just the drudgery of one's own hard work, to uncover something wonderful which came like a gift. Yet to say that the people sat down idly just to wait for this gift does not represent the truth. If there were moments of intense expectation when people did not perform ordinary work in favour of continuous meetings and discussions, this should still count as a time of intense *activity;* and the workings of the Flowers and Workers with their *paitim dis* and memorial gardens were times of vigorous industry and experiment. The religious gift was to come as a way of acting, where results came abundantly and readily to hand. Daniel and Matias revealed programmes of action: building special houses, building a community situation to live in, casting one's vote in an election, and the subscribing of continuous sums of hard-earned cash in a situation where a full day's work might not produce K1 from business enterprise. The people wanted a graciously endowed programme of action, and they expected it to come as a religious revelation.

In this I believe we can see a broad area of common ground with what is called religious in the West. To become aware, to think, to reach out personally, and to change moral direction are all great mysteries of life - these are the things we Westerners ourselves do, but which yet are abilities that seem to be bestowed as gifts, and which we can only hope will continue into the future for us in ways which we cannot now describe and predict. The revelation we hope for in this matter is something we experience and do, not something separate from us which we talk about or look at as over there opposite us. Religious people believe that all of life is to be transformed by a new sense of purpose that ties together aspects of life previously experienced only as a burden. All of life thus serves as a vehicle for such religious hope, and illumination can be expected to come while working in any particular secular field.

To this extent the religious is all-embracing. Given the needs of assorted kinds of persons, it will not be always wide of the mark to say, "Sport is his religion", or "Politics is his religion". For some people these things seem truly to exist on a continuum of meaning with religion. These are the fields in which people can dedicate themselves with something like total personal concern, and in which they expect surprising revelations and an exceeding sense of fulness. One thing after another assumes a religious aura in such an outlook. On the other hand, the belief on which science is based is that some kinds of knowledge are not advanced by passionate adherence and investment of the total personality. Things are known scientifically and objectively by relating them to each other under specific conditions - a partial, detached, step-by-step methodical approach.

The coolly rationalizing people of the world can scorn eschatological visionaries, but cargo cultists and other men of religion are waiting for something necessarily discontinuous with the merely rational. They do not seek an investigation of a limited thing, the simple working-out of a person's industry, but an engrossing discovery of vital importance. They are cultivating the hope in what is surprising and excessive.[13]

It is ironic, of course, that missionaries to Papua New Guinea should at the same time be representative of the Western technological outlook, the bringers of a spiritualized religion, and agents of secularization as well. It is the missionary who is slow to add religious blessing to malaria medicine, the tin fish stocked in the trade store and the cranky carburetor. It is he who thinks money cannot be made to increase by washing, planting or marrying it. Yet at the same time it is he who preaches, "All things work together for the good of those who love God" (Rom. 8:28). The missionary wants to defend the scientific culture to which he belongs, at the same time as he fights the rearguard action of a battle between science and religion. The villagers are apparently already religiously impressed by so many technological things that come with the presence of the missionary and others. To assume control of their lives within the technological culture, the villagers are being pressed to adopt another viewpoint - the partial, detached outlook of the application of method, the willingness to discard discredited alternatives, and to relate things to each other before referring them to themselves - all of which does not very much impress. For all this seems a poor cousin to religious enthusiasm. Which is why the cargo cult tradition will probably continue to play a role in the development of Papua New Guinea for quite a while to come - if not as an explicitly ritual approach to acquiring Western technology, then at least as a constant pattern of interpreting modern events of some seriousness in traditional religious terms. It all comes to depend on what values, what purpose in life, is chosen by the people of either side of the fitful meeting of the two cultures.

Notes

1. Cf. M. Weinstock, "Notes on the Sepik Cargo Cult", in H. Barnes (ed.), *The Niugini Reader*, Melbourne, 1972, pp.37ff. Cf. also the notion of an 'Adjustment Movement' espoused by the editors of *Point*, 1 (1974).
2. W.R. Stent, "An Interpretation of a Cargo Cult", in *Oceania*, 47/3 (1977), p.216.
3. M. Mead, *The Mountain Arapesh 11: Arts and Supernaturalism* (1938), New York, 1970 edn.; A. Gerstner, "Ans dem Gemeinschaftsleben der Wewak-Bortein-Leute, Nordost-Neuguinea", in *Anthropos*, 48 (1953), pp. 413-57, 795-808.
4. Cf. also Gesch, "Cargo Cults: the Village-Christian Dialogue", in W. Flannery (ed.), *Religious Movements in Melanesia Today 3 (Point Series 4)*, Goroka, 1984, pp. 1ff.
5. For background to the abovem esp. B.J.F. Lonergan, *Insight*, New York, 1957 (on science), R. Otto, *The Idea of the Holy* (1917) (trans. J.W. Harvey), Harmondsworth, 1959, p. 26 ([translated] quotation; and on religion).
6. Thus B. Allen, personal communication, 1982. Cf. his 'Information Flow and Innovation Diffusion in the East Sepik District, Papua New Guinea' (doctoral dissert., Australian National University), Canberra, 1976, ch.7.
7. Cf. also Gesch, *Initiative and Initiation (Studia Instituti Anthropos 33)*, St. Augustin, 1985, ch. 14, pt.III, and the literature cited there.
8. Cf. also Gesch, "Magic as a Process of Social Discernment", in N. Habel (ed.), *Powers, Plumes and Piglets; phenomena of Melanesian Religion*, Adelaide, 1979, Part B, ch.2 [Editor].
9. Cf. also L. Morauta, *Beyond the Village (London School of Economics Monographs in Social Anthropology)*, London and Canberra, 1974, pp.43-45; Allen, *op.cit.*, pp. 265-6; A. Strathern, "The Red Box Money Cult in Mount Hagen, 1968-71", in *Oceania*, 53 (1979), pp. 88-102.
10. Police arrests were eventually made in 1986 in the Dreikikir area, west of Yangoru [Editor].
11. For elaboration on the third and fourth sections of this paper, see Gesch, *op.cit.*, esp. chs. 6, 13-14.

12. Cf. also S. Camp, "The Pali Association and the New Apostolic Church", in W. Flannery (ed.), *Religious Movements in Melanesia Today 1, (Point series)*, Goroka, 1983, pp. 78ff; G.W. Trompf, "Independent Churches in Melanesia", in *Oceania,* 54/1 (1983), pp. 66-7.

13. Cf. also Gesch, "Initiation and Cargo Cults: the Peli Case", Flannery (ed.), *op.cit.,* pp. 94ff. For theological side-light, note G.W. Hughes, *God of Surprises,* London, 1985 [Editor].

Chapter Six

Knowledge of Cargo, Knowledge of Cult: Truth and Power on Tanna, Vanuatu

Lamont Lindstrom

On Tanna, an island of southern Vanuata, some people claim that Cargo is just talk or even, more harshly, bad talk. This talk forms a stream of interpretative messages. Cargo talk began when James Cook introduced both European persons and goods to the island in 1774. Whether people appraise talk to be good or bad, true or false, reflects the degree to which they are willing to hear (consume) a particular message. Borrowing a term from Foucault, Cargo is "discourse", a field of effective statements. Every discourse erects structures of truth:

> Each society has its regime of truth, its 'general politics' of truth: that is, the types of discourse which it accepts and makes function as true; the mechanisms and instances which enable one to distinguish true and false statements, the means by which each is sanctioned; the techniques and procedures accorded value in the acquisition of truth; the status of those who are charged with saying what counts as true.[1]

People establish knowledge of cargo and also determine the truth or falseness of cargo within the terms of local "discursive formations."[2]

I discuss in this paper Tannese knowledge of Cargo, as produced, exchanged and consumed within Cargo talk. In many movements, including those of Tanna, knowledge is an end as well as a means. Cult members search not only for the requisite knowledge of Cargo (to obtain goods), but also for knowledge of knowledge (to become wise). Cults are regimes of truth which claim to provide access to further, deeper truths.

I am also concerned with the politics of truth - the ways in which a particular knowledge is deemed to be truth or false; the manner in which a discourse becomes "authoritative"; the way in which meaning is managed.[3] Here, we encounter questions of power. Foucault notes that a discourse establishes a particular regime of power, as well as truth:

> In any society, there are manifold relations of power which permeate, characterize and constitute the social body, and these relations of power cannot themselves be established, consolidated nor implemented without the production, accumulation, circulation and functioning of a discourse.[4]

There are two fields of power here: one socially external, the other internal. Cargo talk, setting itself up as a regime of truth, aims to control external beings and objects, Westerners and their goods. By knowing Cargo - if this knowledge is in discourse made true - one obtains power over it. Cargo talk includes, as discursive events, rituals which command the appearance of goods, or which induce externals to provide goods. In Cargo knowledge Melanesians have a machinery with which to master outsiders.

The significant field of power, however, is the internal. If a Cargo knowledge can be made to be true and authoritative, those individuals who control its production and exchange achieve political power. They are in command of the apparatus by which statements are deemed true or false; they determine who is allowed to discourse and who is not; they control the social consumption of knowledge, their own consumption as well as that of others. This sort of discourse is doubly authoritative. It "seeks continually to preempt the space of radically opposed utterances and so to prevent them from being uttered"[5] and it creates and maintains inequality within social (communicative or discursive) relations, given inequalities in the production and consumption of that knowledge determined to be true.

Finally, I discuss a second discourse - that of knowledge of cult. There is an extended body of description and exegesis of particular historical discursive events on Tanna, and elsewhere in Melanesia. This analytical discourse first brings scattered events together and composes a unity it labels "cultist". It then offers various truths as explanations for the unified events. These explanations - as they must - violate these events by reducing them to true essentials, or categorizing them into true taxonomies, or translating them into true universals. Thus, cargo cults are really ideological expressions of colonial relations of production;

they are millenarian; they are exemplars of human need of salvation or dignity. Although "cargo cult theory" is not as encompassing or culturally central, it does have certain similarities with that system of discourse Said labels "Orientalism". Both originated as Western attempts, dealing from a position of strength, to represent and contain the other. Possession of such knowledge implies that the known object is vulnerable to scrutiny; it implies ability "to dominate it, to have authority over it".[6]

Here, again, we are back to questions of power. Knowledge of cult, like knowledge of Cargo, supports both socially external and internal regimes of power. Externally, it sees, understands, and therefore denies autonomy to cultists by knowing them. An interesting competition exists at this point of controlling the external other. Melanesians attempt to master Europeans by knowing their Cargo. Europeans dominate Melanesians by knowing their cults.

It seems to me, however, that the important effects of discourses such as Orientalism or Cargoism are contained within socially internal fields of power: to know/control not so much the other as ourselves. Of course, both Orientalism and Cargoism emerge within colonial relations of economic and political inequality and sustain these relations by making them understandable and true. Both, however, also are part of dominant internal frameworks of discourse which circumscribe the normal and the expected. Melanesians, while abused for being cargoistic (and Orientals for being Oriental), are supposed - are known - to be such. This abuse is multiplied many times if a self (not an other) challenges politically and culturally authoritative truth; we are supposed not - are unknown - to do such. Concern to know and thus dominate the other by some authoritative discourse is part of the apparatus for the internal domination of ourselves (or of some of ourselves).

Tanna

This reticulation of knowledge, power, and truth makes clear a number of incidents of the last two centuries on Tanna, the southernmost island of Vanuata (formerly the New Hebrides). I bring together for this purpose a number of historical events to compose a working unity we know is rightly labelled cargoistic, or cultist. Tanna has a population of 17,000 people who speak five related Austronesian languages. Underneath this linguistic diversity lies a general cultural sameness. People live in usually small, scattered hamlets which encircle kava-drinking grounds. These central spaces are the most significant in the cultural landscape. Here, men gather daily to prepare and drink kava root *(Piper methysticum);* family groups and their supporters meet to exchange goods; and debaters convene to establish working truths, to settle disputes, and to take socially important decisions.[7]

Some decades after Cook's precipitating visit, in 1774, serious contact with Europeans, and Europeans' goods, began in the 1860s. Presbyterian missionaries (after a few spectacular failures) managed then to establish a continuing presence on the island. South Pacific labour traders, too, had begun sailing Vanuata waters searching for recruits to work the plantations, ranches and mines of Queensland, Fiji, New Caledonia and Samoa. Tanna provided many of the initial recruited labourers. As culture contact deepened, so did problems of control. Europeans aimed to subdue and regulate the Tannese. The Tannese, for their part, attempted to explain and thereby encompass Europeans within governing island systems of interpretation and authority.[8]

Technologies of control were both informational and physical. Cook knew his natives. Taking on water and other refreshments at the head of Port Resolution on east Tanna, he drew a line on the ground and posted armed guards to prevent its crossing by whom he knew or feared to be untamed people.[9] Islanders likewise knew Europeans. They knew them to be visiting ancestors and dealt with them accordingly. In 1839, for example, Mr. Harris, an aide to missionary John Williams (who called on Tanna a day before his subsequent martyrdom on Erromango to the north), was surprised by a Tannese man on the beach. The latter, after convincing the unsuspecting Harris to open his mouth, spat down his throat. Spitting is an important ritual technique to control sometimes dangerous ancestors, as Williams and Harris were known to be.[10]

With increasing frequency of contact, ruling interpretation shifted in subsequent interaction between Europeans and islanders as did the mechanics of attempted control. In the establishment of cross-cultural understandings, naval men-of-war, guns, and exchange of words (argument) replaced ritual lines drawn on the ground or spitting. Knowledge of shared humanity, however, remained for a while problematic. As Sahlins has noted, "we are the only people who think themselves risen from savages; everyone else believes they descend from gods".[11]

Supplementing knowledge of Europeans, knowledge of their goods acquired exchange value which increased along with that of the goods themselves. Ruling truths, as elsewhere in Melanesia, account for production of European goods, as they account for production of traditional goods, in terms of ancestral generation. Agnes Watt, wife of a nineteenth century Presbyterian missionary working in the southeast, described an event in which ruling island interpretations of Cargo production appear:

> There was an old woman to the west of us who professed to have communication with the unseen world. Many who had lost relatives sought unto her; and she brought beads, turkey-red, tobacco, pipes, and knives from the departed. One man, a very sensible fellow in many respects, brought a knife he had got from a deceased son-in-law; I forget the maker's name, but it was a Sheffield-made knife. In vain we showed him the maker's name, and told him it was all a hoax, that the old witch was befooling him. He declared that he heard his son-in-law speak to him, to tell him to stretch forth his hand in the direction of the voice and he would receive the knife. He did so, and there was the knife- now was not that proof positive? Day by day new messages came from the dead; some sending for goods and others giving back return presents. As one piece of turkey-red is much the same as another; why, the poor deluded creatures actually believed that that very piece of turkey-red of that pipe which had been buried with their relative, was now sent back from Ipai (Hades)! Of course, we were branded as deceiving the people.[12]

Here truth grapples with truth. Christian (European) interpretation attempts to define its opposition as befuddlement, hoax, and delusion. It, in turn, must invalidate opposed proofs and sensibilities as well as avoid charges of deception.

Traditional and in-coming systems of knowledge compete to establish regimes of truth - to draw the limits of delusion. This competition (here between the Watts and a knowledgeable female spirit medium, or "clever" in Vanuatu Pidgin English) also concerns regimes of power. That knowledge which establishes greatest exchange value becomes an important resource within local political competition. The social consumption of a knowledge which succeeds in becoming truth establishes political inequalities between knowledge consumers and knowledge producers/controllers.

Just after the turn of the century, consumption of Christian knowledge expanded greatly on Tanna. Its increased exchange (and therefore truth) value perhaps reflects the end of the Australian labour market and the return of workers to Tanna, as well as growing European colonial and economic presence in the archipelago. Younger men, who achieved a measure of control over Christian/European knowledge by taking positions of deacon and elder within the mission hierarchy, also emerged as "chiefs" within forming Christian political organizations. These new political relations spurred a spatial reorganization as people moved down to live in large Christian villages near coastal mission stations. Christian chiefs, in control of true knowledge, elaborated a number of rules, enforced by informal police and courts, known as Tanna Law.[13] This law made illegal a number of activities (defined to be delusive by the emerging regime of truth) including kava drinking, dancing, polygyny, etc.

Although there always existed a number of alternative knowledges, this new regime of truth/power maintained its exchange value until 1940. Its final collapse was apparent on May 11, 1941, when only a handful of worshippers attended the Presbyterian churches on the island - their absence signalling refusal to consume this knowledge and the loss of its exchange and truth value.[14] What precipitated invalidation of ruling truths was the emergence of an alternative which since has been known as the John Frum Movement.[15] A mysterious figure speaking in a strange voice appeared in the night at a kava-drinking ground in southwest Tanna. He claimed the name of John Frum and urged people to more cooperative effort in clearing land for gardens, building houses, etc. He, at first, also commanded obedience to government officials and missionaries working on the island. His message soon changed, however, into one challenging ruling truths. People say the voice ordered them to revive traditional dancing and kava drinking.

Government officials assumed that a small group of devious men were conspiring to make fools of fellow islanders. In their discourse, they made out the advent of John Frum to be mass delusion. Condominium agent Nichols described the apparition of John Frum as both a "hoax" and a "racket". He arrested two men, one of whom confessed to acting the part of John Frum.[16] The

Condominium government exiled these men to other islands for a number of years. This capture of the purported impersonator, and revelation of the truth, did not, however, reestablish the exchange value of European wisdom. New John Frum truths maintained value even though these initial deportations were the first of many as cultist activity broke out in a number of other areas of the island. People, still today, debate whether John Frum is man or spirit. In traditional regimes of truth, however, this matters little. People know well that ancestors and spiritual culture heroes commonly appear at night to communicate messages.

John Frum's message soon developed millenarian tones in addition to its cultural revitalism. The message proclaimed the coming of a new age. It told people to discard European money, to kill introduced animals, and to abandon houses and gardens as all these things would be replaced with new goods. John Frum reportedly also warned that Tanna would overturn and emerge joined with neighbouring islands; that mountains would flatten and valleys fill; that Europeans would vacate the island; and that anyone arrested would gain freedom. Many people did kill animals, quit productive labour, and discarded their money. Some threw this into the sea while others participated in a run on trade stores to spend their cash before this too lost exchange/truth value.[17]

In 1942, shortly after the emergence of John Frum discourse, the American military arrived in the archipelago to establish two huge supply bases supporting the war effort to the north. The Americans recruited around 1,000 Tannese men to serve as labourers assisting the unloading of cargo ships and storage of military supplies at Port Vila. Soon after repatriation of American troops in 1946, John Frum cultists began to predict the return of American soldiers either by ship, submarine, or from the bowels of the central mountain range.[18] Cult messages manifested concern with obtaining material goods in addition to freedom from the colonial powers with American assistance. These messages have retained exchange (truth) value for the last 45 years, a remarkble record in Melanesia where timespans of the social consumption of a particular cultist interpretative knowledge tend to be rather short.

John Frum truth has engendered several emergent political organizations on the island. The movement is now a powerful combined church and political party.[19] Political institutionalization became possible when government suppression of cultists ended in the mid 1950s. The most successful of these organizations is headquartered at Sulphur Bay, a village of East Tanna. This group attempted, unsuccessfuilly, to withdraw from newly independent Vanuata in 1980.[20] Although somewhat chastized because of its failures during the politics of national independence, John Frum interpretative knowledge and the men who control this are still strong truth-competitors on the island.

Other bodies of knowledge which advance claims to truth include now revitalized Christian organizations; a group known as the "Four Corners" movement (sparked by a French colon who offered himself as Tanna's King;[21] and the Prince Philip people. The latter's message, essentially, is that Prince Philip of Great Britain will serve to mediate the enrichment and enlightenment of Tanna. Monolithic power and hegemonic discursive formations (insofar as these existed during the Tanna Law period of Christian truth, or the cultist period of John Frum truth) has for the present broken down in the context of a number of competing messages on the island. Each of these messages, to the extent of their social consumption, establishes mini-regimes of power and chequered regimes of truth. Neighbouring villages often consume different messages and are part of different political organizations within which this knowledge is exchanged. Each defines its competitors as holding monstrous and delusive error in order to protect its own regime of truth (the greater part of this truth competition occurring in gossip, private statements and indirect speaking).

Knowledge of Cargo

Whether or not a problem is worth, or demands, an answer depends both on a society's system of culturally informed interests and on the problem's own impinging force to define new interests. After initial contact, Europeans and European goods became problematic for the Tannese. They demanded answers. The exchange value of these answers - of interpretative knowledge of a Christian sort, or a John Frum sort, or a Prince Philip sort - depends both on the utility and increasing nuisance of Europeans and their goods, on the one hand, and also on traditional island interests and the local value of knowledge and goods, on the other.

To follow the events summarized above, in which regimes of truth are translated into regimes of power, we need to understand the exchange value of knowledge in Melanesia, as well as its social consumption. Lawrence [22] remarks that Melanesians, as do Westerners, recognize the key importance of knowledge for material production. The means of production, whether one is producing taro, a canoe, or an automobile, subsume knowledge as well as resources and labour power. This knowledge is created and maintained by ancestors and other supernatural actors. A person, however, may have access to knowledge by various devices and use it to his advantage.

Lawrence divides productive knowledge into two categories: empirical and ritual. Although this division may not exactly model Melanesian epistemology, it does reflect important differences in means of accessing knowledge.[23] Empirical knowledge is available to everyone and is learned in open, communicative relations. Ritual knowledge which supports production, on the other hand, exists as restricted individual or group property protected by secrecy. A knower teaches this privately only to an appropriate heir. Ritual productive knowledge may also be transmitted along other, restricted channels (such as dreaming) to which only certain individuals claim legitimate access. People consider the application of both sorts of knowledge (maintaining Lawrence's analytical distinction, here) essential for successful productive action.

We can understand many features of cargo cults in terms of people's more complex desire for knowledge of Cargo, or as their attempts to apply knowledge to produce cargo, rather than in terms of a simple cupidity for the goods in themselves. Desire for knowledge of Cargo, rather than for just the always perishable goods makes good sense given traditional productive technologies. These allow for more-or-less continual production and replacement of goods. Storage and conservation are rare in the Melanesian environment. A field is only a temporary clearing in a slash-and-burn fallow cycle; a house lasts less than a decade; tools and clothing must be constantly renewed. Productive technologies need allow for continuous manufacture and replacement of goods. Goods which, because of special conservation, survive longer than the average (such as ritual exchange tokens including shell and stone valuables), possess value by virtue of the impossibility of reproducing an exact replacement. A material good, in general, is less valuable than the knowledge by which it is produced.

We see this concern with knowledge of Cargo, rather than just cargo *per se,* in a number of Melanesian cults. Burridge[24] records that followers credited Mambu, a Papua New Guinea cult prophet, with great learning and understanding. Similarly, Worsley notes that Vailala cult leaders "were credited with special powers and accorded great respect, though many of them declared that any wisdom they possessed in their stomachs was not their own, but emanated from ancestors".[25] Strathern, describing the Red Box cult of highland New Guinea, notes that people, in addition to desire for cash, wished "to know money's true origins and so to manage its supply for themselves".[26] Mitchell, speaking of the Mount Turu cult, writes: "It wasn't just material goods they desired, they wanted to know!".[27] Stent, discussing the enigma of money for Yamikum cultists, suggests "it was in the solution of that puzzle that the cultists believed, rather like the alchemists of old, that the key of 'true knowledge' would be found".[28] Knowledge of something provides several sorts of power over that thing, including the power to produce, and reproduce, it.

Dreaming, Telephoning, Reading

Given Melanesian cultural interest in knowledge, as an ingredient of productive technology, claims to control access to requisite knowledge become a basis of power. Where might knowledge of Cargo be obtained? In local discourse, people achieve knowledge from external sources. Melanesians have an inspirational rather than creational conception of knowledge.[29] People know knowers not to invent or create their ideas. Instead, knowers receive these from supernatural or external sources. Knowledge is passed down rather than made up.

Dreaming is a major channel of knowledge transmission.[30] As people sleep, they enter into communication with ancestors and spirits and learn various sorts of socially valuable information including novel medicinal recipes, new songs, the location of lost objects, the course of the future, sources of ancestral displeasure, or innovative edicts for social behaviour. John Frum leaders, similarly, claim access to that knowledge (empirical/ritual) which supports the production of Cargo. Their spirit/culture-hero, John Frum, teaches requisite knowledge to leaders as they dream. These dreams become messages. According to local truths, they belong to movement prophets as transmitters rather than as innovators. The messages of leaders are exchange tokens which, insofar as they are consumed by followers, evince and maintain a particular regime of truth which accounts for Cargo.

Parallel devices for transmission of transmission of knowledge include the telegraph poles, radio wires and antennae erected in various movements[31] and, more recently, telephones. John Frum leaders, for example, ritually manipulate on occasion a telephone constructed of large, white bell-shaped datura flowers. By means of this apparatus, leaders symbolize their control of valuable knowledge they derive from their abilities to communicate with knowledge sources (receive and send messages).

Reading, similarly, serves as another means of knowledge access. Like dreaming, it is a channel of knowledge transmission. External knowledge reaches people by means of middleman prophet readers. Here we see the (to us mystified) importance of "books", letters and writing in many cults.[32] Leaders have hidden away books - which only they are capable of reading - that provide knowledge of Cargo. Describing the Vailala movement, Worsley notes "'Reading' by wholly illiterate natives was common in this movement; they would hold Bibles in their hands, often trembling and twitching the while. One man walked into a White man's house smoking a cigarette, with the Gospel of Luke in his hand and a pencil and paper, on which he made marks which he said were a 'letter'".[33]

On Tanna, within Christian regimes of truth, Christian texts have also served as major channels of access to knowledge. During the nineteenth century, before Christian knowledge established exchange value, people scrupulously avoided contact with books. This refusal to read/consume Christian knowledge marked people's continuing commitment to traditional discourse and different truths. In 1860 the missionary John Paton commented that "the Tannese had a superstitious dread of books, and especially of God's Book". He also reports the burial of Christian texts.[34]

Towards the turn of the century, several self-made Tannese missionaries appeared. One of these, named Johnny Pata, had learned to read in Tonga. He returned to Tanna and established a "school". In his presentation of messages, he manipulated various symbols, including European clothing, Sabbath rest, and three books he had obtained during his sojourns abroad.[35] As Christian knowledge established social exchange value, book ownership and reading skills became instruments within the new regimes of power. Paton's son Frank, who established a mission on the opposite coast of the island in the 1890s, noted that "the people were eager for books, and as soon as it became known that I had hymn-books with me, a rush was made for the tent, and they were all sold out in a few seconds".[36] Books, like dreaming, provided access to new answers with growing social exchange value.

The establishment of cargoist "schools", also makes sense in these terms.[37] Leaders, controlling access to the source of knowledge, institutionalize the transmission of messages to followers in schools. Neloiag, for example, who attracted followers with his version of the John Frum message in the early 1940s, established a school wherein he instructed these followers. His book was an American photo-illustrated war brochure.[38] More recently, Lispet, daughter of one of the founders of the John Frum movement at Sulphur Bay, has organized a school in which she instructs students to read a language she claims belongs to John Frum. She herself learned this language communing with John Frum in the privacy of her house. Every morning (in 1981-82), she convened a class in which she instructed children and adults to read and write arcana.

Dreaming, telephoning and reading are means of accessing sources of suspected powerful knowledge. Cultists ritually elaborate these activities. They thus symbolically indicate their acquisition of knowledge they know to be essential in the production of Cargo. Relations of hierarchy within cultist organizations, in part, depend on the establishment of inequalities to these means of knowledge production (or access). Power depends, as well, on appropriation of the means of message interpretation and management of truth.

Knowledge of Knowledge

Control of knowledge production, exchange and consumption is a significant dimension of inequality in Melanesia.[39] If a person commands a body of knowledge, and if this has social exchange value, he attracts followers (knowledge consumers) with whom he exchanges information and interpretation. These informational transactions may generate political relations of inequality between the wise and the ignorant. Lawrence, describing the qualities of Madang leaders, notes: "The leaders were men who 'really knew' and who could direct the activities of others - those who did not 'really know' - to the best advantage. It was popular conviction of this ability that enabled the particularly successful leader, who had an outstanding personality and had never been defeated by unforeseen circumstances, to lure followers away from his less fortunate rivals".[40]

Given this political exchange value of knowledge in Melanesia, the major concern of some movements is the achievement of wisdom in general (knowledge of knowledge) rather than some plane load of material goods (knowledge of cargo). Where concern with wisdom replaces a narrow desire for cargo, leaders frequently evince a range of special knowledges - of which geographic is a common example. Tannese leaders attempt to map out spatial relations between their island, America and other key places including South America, Honolulu, and Europe.[41]

Although cargo acquisition has been an element of John Frum ideology in certain of the movement's phases, a broader concern for the achievement of wisdom appears in cult message and ritual. Leaders speak of the instant knowledge supporters will receive following the return to the archipelago of American forces. They devise rituals which will transmit this knowledge. These schemes have included bathing in a local stream, hypodermic injections, and covering, for a few seconds, a man's head with a fathom length of calico cloth.

In the late 1950s, Sulphur Bay movement leaders travelled to each supporting group in the organization and installed spiritual Americans - who people knew to have arrived by submarine - in "offices" complete with table and chairs. Supporters constructed these near local kava-drinking grounds. Several days of dancing marked the opening of each office building. Local men in the middle reaches of the cultist regime of power, called "wire-men" (symbolizing their place within the network of information flow), enjoyed the duty of providing the American occupant of the office pork and other food. The Americans, as everyone knew, would in return make local supporters wise by setting a hat on their heads.

Knowledge of knowledge, where this has exchange value, is a political resource.[42] The power of knowers depends on the extent to which they are able to control the production and exchange of knowledge. This control - which determines an inequal relationship between knowledge producer and knowledge consumer - is the basis of hierarchy in cult organizations. Although prophets transmit messages, they often intimate that they command even more powerful, restricted, and secret information. They also keep secret the means of producing their messages (the techniques by which they contact knowledge sources). By thus controlling discourse and knowledge exchange, leaders appropriate the administration of meaning and the interpretation of truth. Nachman describes ambitious Nissan islanders who transacted interpretations of problematic events: "such men could offer others a new 'truth' and attract followers to themselves at the expense of rival big-men".[43]

Semantic opacity and the use of nonsensical words (such as John Frum's language as taught by Lispet) is a common form of cult secrecy.[44] Here, rather than protecting the means of knowledge production, this sort of secrecy permits knowers to control interpretation and the management of truth. Knowers, who are able to provide interpretations of nonsensical linguistic forms, create and thereby control meaning. Semantic opacity occurs, for example, in the songs John Frum leaders receive in dreams. They teach these songs to followers who sing them during weekly Friday night meetings at cult headquarters. Many songs contain strings of nonsensical words, which knowers identify to be John Frum's language. Followers depend on leaders to provide new songs and to interpret these meaningfully. They also depend on received interpretation of meaningless drill team marching commands (used during cult celebratory marches). This sort of knowledge exchange maintains both inequality in interpretative control and in political relationship.

The social consumption of interpretative and explanatory knowledge engenders regimes of power. Power survives only as long as knowledge maintains truth (exchange) value. In-coming Europeans, knowledge, and goods are problems which furnish exchange value to several bodies of explanatory knowledge on Tanna. Islanders hope to know, and therefore control, these ingressive, penetrating forces. Knowledge of knowledge, and knowledge of Cargo, while targeted towards the external other, are tokens within internal political networks of consumption. A successful system of discourse (widely consumed) converts answers into truths, didactic relations into hierarchy, and knowers into leaders. Concern to control the other through knowledge thus effects local regimes of truth, and emergent internal relations of power.[45]

Knowledge of Cult

I restrain myself from calling this concluding section "knowledge of knowledge of knowledge" (or Western truths of Melanesian truths regarding our knowledge). Nevertheless, cargo cult accountings are, in Wagner's phrase,[46] the "interpretation of interpretation". These interpretations are accommodated within a discourse which encircles and comprehends a scattering of Melanesian actions and conversations. Given the inherent inequalities within colonial relations (which determined the privileged vantage point of cult knowers *vis-à-vis* cargo knowers), knowledge of cult (like Orientalism) was part of the apparatus which maintained these colonial inequalities. Colonial authorities, apprised of cults, invariably acted on this knowledge to suppress activity and speech they knew to be cultist. On Tanna, for example, colonial authority, encountering activity it first defined to be cultist in 1940, initiated a vigorous programme of repression. During the following decade and a half, it arrested and exiled to northern islands more than 140 "cultists".[47] Cults were known to endanger public order, after all. In the late 1950s, repression subsided in terms of a revised interpretation: cultists were now perceived to be more crazed and unsophisticated (as all Melanesians are known to be) than dangerous. Authority allowed exiled leaders to return, permanently, to their homes. It kept them, however, under its eye.

Worsley points out that cargo cult discourse gained exchange value in Western societies after World War Two: "'Explanations' of the Cargo phenomenon now became very popular. Most observers regarded the movements as preponderantly religious phenomena, and stressed the savage irrationality of the Melanesian".[48] This knowledge of the other, and the truths it allows, also allows power over the other whether this is the power to suppress physically or the power safely to ignore. It first seizes aspects of Melanesian discourse and behaviour. It then combines these into a unity it calls "cult". It submits this unity to a definitional apparatus of truth/falsity (or, rather, what it can say and what it cannot). It, finally, generates series of interpretations which account for and monitor the "cultist".

Can we say this interpretation of interpretation is true? Is our knowledge of cult more genuine than their knowledge of cargo? Here we encounter the problem of translation which is always the epistemological bedevilment of anthropology and cross-cultural understanding. How can one culture be explained in the terms of another? If we could forego translation and listen directly to cultist discourse (which is impossible since some act of selection is always necessary) we would probably find this discourse incomplete, false or even useless. Acceptable knowledge of cult depends on the appropriation of one discourse (knowledge of cargo) by another. The truths established by one regime must be bent to fit the sovereignty of another. Keesing, for example, suggests that cult knowledge of the Maasina Rule of Malaita misperceives the true essence of the movement:

> Contemporary observers over-emphasized the millenarian content of the movement and underplayed the rational political goals and strategies: in so doing, Europeans sustained their racist stereotypes about the simple credulity of "the natives", dismissed a frontal challenge to the legitimacy of pre-war style colonial rule, and in the end rationalized their own political blunders.[49]

Our truths about the religiosity of Melanesian "cultists" distort the real essentials. On the other hand, perhaps the reduction of millenarian content to political essentials is also one of the unavoidable truths generated by our discourse. Asad,[50] wary of this trap too, suggests we regard as problematic "the whole business of looking for and reproducing the essential meanings of another society's discourse (its 'authentic culture')." Even the terms of our discourse (such as "cult", "cargo", and "knowledge") perhaps cease to exist when they leave the bounds of truth established by that discourse. As Wagner supposes, "what we call 'cult' or 'movement' is nothing less than the ordinary form of ritual and interpretative innovation in Melanesian societies".[51]

Although we may be unsure of the degree to which we can really know the other, and how this real knowledge might be recognized, let alone obtained, we can be more certain of the validity and significance of knowledge of cult within our own discursive regimes of truth and power. Knowledge of Cargo, and knowledge of cult, each attempt to comprehend and therefore establish power over external others. In doing so, however, they inform internal regimes of power.

Thus, the powerful on Tanna who appropriate the means of production of knowledge and the management of truth, attract followers who consume their interpretations. Within emergent cult organizations, inequality in knowledge exchange maintains political relations of hierarchy. This power inequality is sustained by the successful production and consumption of further truths.

Similarly, although knowledge of cult emerges as part of the apparatus by which Westerners know and control Melanesians, it is also part of a discourse which creates and maintains a complex internal regime of power in the West. Although the ostensive purpose is to know the other (in this case Melanesian cultists), this knowledge is taken and reapplied within Western societies. It speaks to and maintains elaborate systems of truth and normality. Any person or group challenging ruling truths with heretical words or acts is liable to be dismissed (known) as "cultist", or "cargoistic", or Melanesian-like in general. On this side of the Pacific, we apprehend cults with metaphors of otherness, disease, etc. Cults are external; they spread, corrupt; they must be observed, monitored, combated and controlled.

The internal, controlling powers of "Cargoism" as a ruling discourse in the West is, of course, particularly apparent in religious contexts. Religious talk and acts which violate Western normality may be "known", and thereby diffused, in terms of Cargoism. The mass appeal of the messages of Oral Roberts, for example, a fellow townsman of mine, is often "explained" as a form of wayward American cargo cultism.

In the 1970s, Roberts began emphasizing financial blessings in addition to his earlier message of faith healing. He regularly circulates messages about

> God's Financial Plan. When you read it, I know you just can't miss seeing the money God has for you, and how to receive it and use it for His glory. In other words, I want you to see that God wants to bless you financially, so He can make you a financial blessing.[52]

Drawing on Malachi 3:10-12 and III John 2, Roberts suggests that God wants to "prosper" the faithful.[53] To learn the secrets of the financial plan, of course, one must turn to Roberts who controls access to God's knowledge.

In context of the deindustrialization of the American economy, money often presents people with keen problems for which Roberts has answers:

[Money] represents your total being spiritually, mentally, financially even emotionally. You can get sick financially, and you can get sick over your finances. I know. I've been there. You are delicately tuned to money. Every person is, or he doesn't eat. You have to have money. God knows that. Even Jesus had to have money, and He always got it.[54]

The problem is the devil: "the devil is stealing your money from you ... the devil has been stealing from some of us so much that we can't even pay our bills".[55] Here his message converges with common Melanesian explanations for the unequal distribution of Cargo: whites have stolen the Cargo which Melanesian ancestors meant for their descendents to receive. Roberts' statements are known - are accounted for, tamed, and controlled - by ruling truths as "cultic". Roberts recognizes this and, in fact, makes good use within the organization of his discursive denigration and persecution by outside powers.

The political utility of cargoism within Western regimes of power and truth, however, extends far beyond mere religious contexts. The discourse of cargoism recognizes, knows and controls more of us than just irregular Oklahoma prophets. Instances of the use of Cargo knowledge as a controlling device abound in everyday American spoken and written discourse.

The chairman and chief executive officer of a multinational corporation, to take one example, denounces "cargo cult mentality in America": "like South Pacific islanders who thought that talking into little boxes made the planes come, the U.S. is responding to its problems with magic rituals instead of rational planning and hard work".[56] Similarly, a national newspaper columnist rebukes our cargoistic approach to reducing poverty in which the poor are taught "like New Guinea's pitiful 'cargo cultists,' to become mere clients".[57]

The common accusation that anthropology is the handmaiden of colonialism, insofar as it provides knowledge of outsiders by which these might be controlled, is incomplete. Knowledge and definition of the other (including knowledge of cult) only takes place within a wider discourse of knowledge of self, and how that self ought properly to be constituted and behave. The "real" purpose of anthropology, in this vein, is not to know/control the far-away other, but to maintain regimes of power and structures of inequality at home.

These two discourses - knowledge of Cargo and knowledge of cult - engender regimes of both truth and power. We understand the exchange value (truth) of John Frum messages, and cargo cult exegeses, in terms of governing systems of discourse. Similarly, although both knowledges attempt to pin down an alien, external other, we should also investigate their functions to preserve regimes of power within the societies of their articulation. We might call this final level of investigative discourse (carrying the above to an extreme) knowledge of knowledge of knowledge of knowledge.

Notes

I carried out fieldwork on Tanna during 1978-79, 1982 and 1983. I would like to thank the Institute of Culture and Communication of the East-West Center, Fulbright Hays, the English-Speaking Union of the United States, the Departments of Anthropology at the Research School of Pacific Studies, Australian National University, the University of California at Berkeley, the University of Tulsa, and all friends on Tanna for the assistance I received and the welcome I experienced during these periods.

1. M. Foucault, *The Archaeology of Knowledge* (trans. A.M.S. Smith), New York, 1972, p.27. This interpretation of Cargo as a discursive regime of truth recalls K.O. Burridge's original characterization of Tangu understandings of Cargo as a "myth dream" (in *Mambu; a Melanesian Millennium*, London, 1960, chs. 5-7).
2. Cf. J. Fabian, "The Anthropology of Religious Movements: From Explanation to Interpretation", in *Social Research*, 46 (1979), p.28. My use of the terms "discourse" (as a unity of statements about Cargo and about cults) and "power" (as directional and interpersonal) no doubt distorts some of the subtleties of Foucault's argument.
3. See A.P. Cohen and J.L. Comaroff, "The Management of Meaning: On the Phenomenology of Political Transactions", in B. Kapferer (ed.), *Transaction and Meaning; Directions in the Anthropology of Exchange and Symbolic Behaviour*, Philadelphia, 1976.
4. Foucault, *Power/Knowledge: Selected Interviews and Other Writings, 1972-1977* (trans. and ed. C. Gordon), New York, 1980, p.93.
5. T. Asad, "Anthropology and the Analysis of Ideology", in *Man*, 14 (1979), p.621.
6. E.W. Said, *Orientalism*, New York, 1978, p.6.
7. Cf. M. Lindstrom, "Speech and Kava on Tanna", in M. Allen (ed.), Vanuata: *Politics, Economics and Ritual in Island Melanesia*, New York, 1981, ch. 15.
8. See R. Adams, *In the Land of Strangers*, Canberra, 1983.
9. J.C. Beaglehole (ed.), *The Journals of Captain James Cook on his Voyage of*

Discovery, vol.2: *The Voyage of the Resolution and Adventure, 1772-1775*, Cambridge, 1961, p.485.

10. Lindstrom. "Spitting on Tanna," in *Oceania*, 50 (1980), pp. 228-34. On Williams' death, cf., e.g., J. Garrett, *To Live Among the Stars; Christian origins in Oceania*, Geneva and Suva, 1982, pp. 164-7.

11. M. Sahlins, *Culture and Practical Reason*, Chicago, 1976, pp. 52-3.

12. A. Watt, *Twenty-Five Years Mission Life on Tanna, New Hebrides*, Paisley, 1896, p.214.

13. J. Guiart, *Un siècle et demi des contacts cultural à Tanna, Nouvelle Hébrides*, Paris, 1956, pp. 130-8.

14. Cf. M.H. Campbell, 'A Century of Presbyterian Mission Education in the New Hebrides: Presbyterian Mission Educational Enterprises and their Relevance to the Needs of a Changing Society, 1848-1948' (Masters dissert., University of Melbourne), Melbourne, 1974, esp. p.118.

15. See esp. Guiart, "John Frum Movement on Tanna", in *Oceania*, 22 (1951), pp. 165-75; *Un siècle, op.cit.;* Lindstrom, "Cult and Culture: American Dreams in Vanuata", in *Pacific Studies*, 4 (1981), pp.101-23.

16. See Guiart, op.cit., p.408, for Nichols' statement. A photograph of Manchevi, one of these two, who confessed, appears in H. Luke, *From a South Seas Diary, 1938-1942*, London, 1945, plate 75.

17. G.L. Barrow, 'The Story of JonFrum' (unpublished typed Report to the Western Pacific High Commission), n.p., 1952, p.4; P. O'Reilly, "Prophetisme aux Nouvelles-Hébrides: Le Mouvement JonFrum à Tanna", in *Le Monde non-Chrétien*, 10 (1949), p.195; Guiart, *op.cit.*, p.159, cf. also H. Priday, "JonFrum is New Hebridean Cargo Cult", in *Pacific Islands Monthly*, Jan. 1950, pp. 67-70; Feb., 1950, pp. 59-64; D. Marsh, "The Surprising Gospels of John Frum: He Who Swept Sin Away", in *Ibid.*, Oct., 1968, pp. 83-90. The repudiation of money in Jonfrumism - much different from the concern to increase money, as found elsewhere in Melanesia (note, e.g. A. Strathern, "The Red Box Money Cult in Mount Hagen, 1968-71", in *Oceania*, 50 [1979], pp. 88-107; W.R. Stent, "An Interpretation of a Cargo Cult", in ibid, 47 [1977], pp. 187-219, cf. Burridge, *New Heaven, New Earth*, Oxford, 1969, pp. 41, 145), perhaps relates to a general restriction of exchange on Tanna, to that of identities (pig for pig) rather than equivalences

(pig for money). Cf. Lindstrom, "Doctor, Lawyer, Wise Man, Priest: Big-Men and Knowledge in Melanesia", in *Man,* 19 (1984), pp. 291-309.

18. Guiart, *op.cit.,* pp. 182-3.

19. Lindstrom, "Cultural Politics: National Concerns in Bush Arenas on Tanna (Vanuatu)", in G. Cronin (ed.), *Emerging Political Cultures in the Pacific,* Lae, 1983, ch. 5; cf. also G.W. Trompf, "Independent Churches in Melanesia", in *Oceania,* 54 /1 (1983), p. 69.

20. Lindstrom, "Cult and Culture", *loc. cit.* See also J. Jupp and M. Sawer, " The New Hebrides Prepares for Independence", in *Current Affairs Bulletin,* 56/11 (1980), pp. 22ff.

21. See Guiart, "Le mouvement 'four corner' à Tanna", in *Journal de la Société des Océanistes,* 46 (1975), pp. 107-111.

22. P. Lawrence, *Road belong Cargo,* Manchester, 1964, pp. 29-31.

23. See *ibid.,* p.30, yet for questioning, P. Gesch, *Initiative and Initiation (Studia Instituti Anthropos 33),* St. Augustin, 1985, p.305.

24. *New Heaven, op.cit.,* p.67.

25. P. Worsley, *The Trumpet Shall Sound,* London, New York, 1968 edn., p.78.

26. Strathern, *loc. cit.,* p.96.

27. W.E. Mitchell, *The Bamboo Fire; an Anthropologist in New Guinea,* New York, 1978, p. 152.

28. Stent, *loc.cit.,* p.213.

29. Lawrence, *op.cit.,* p.30.

30. M. Stephen, "Dreams of Change: the Innovative Role of Altered States of Consciousness in Traditional Melanesian Religion", in *Oceania,* 50 (1979), pp. 3-22; "Dreaming is Another Power! the Social Significance of Dreams among the Mekeo of Papua New Guinea", in *Oceania,* 53 (1982), pp. 106-22; Gesch, *op.cit.,* pp. 42-4.

31. Cf., e.g. Worsley, *op.cit.,* pp. 55, 200.

32. *Ibid.,* pp. 28, 71, 82; Burridge, *Mambu, op.cit.,* p.5; Gesch, *op.cit.,* pp. 51-2, 134.

33. Worsley, *op.cit.,* p.87.

34. J. Paton, *Missionary to the New Hebrides, an Autobiography,* London, 1890, pp. 202, 283.

35. Watt, *op.cit.,* pp. 128, 247.

36. F. Paton, *Lomai of Lemakel: hero of the New Hebrides*, London, 1903, p.165.
37. Worsley, *op.cit.*, pp. 70, 87, 159.
38. Guiart, *op.cit.*, p. 187.
39. Lindstrom, "Doctor, Lawyer, etc.", *loc. cit.*
40. Lawrence, *op.cit.*, p.31.
41. Note also Burridge, *Mambu, op.cit.*, p.10, on a Manam Islander's map of the world.
42. Thus M.R. Crick, "Anthropology of Knowledge", in *Annual Review of Anthropology*, 11 (1982), pp. 287-313, cf. Lindstrom, *loc. cit.*
43. S. Nachman, "The Validation of Leadership on Nissan", in *Oceania*, 52 (1982), pp. 199-220, cf. also R. Keesing, *Kwaio Religion*, New York, 1982.
44. See Worsley, op.cit., pp. 23, 25, 61, 85 for examples.
45. My argument that regimes of truth create and maintain emergent regimes of power reflects Worsley's interpretation of the integratory functions of cargo cults (*op.cit.*, p.227).
46. R. Wagner, "The Talk of Koriki; a Daribi Contact Cult", in *Social Research*, 46 (1979), pp. 140-165.
47. E. Rice, *John Frum He Come*, New York, 1974, pp. 251-62.
48. *Op.cit.*, p.205.
49. Keesing, "Politico-Religious Movements and Anti-Colonialism on Malaita: Maasina Rule in Historical Perspective", in *Oceania*, 48 (1978), p.243.
50. *Loc.cit.*, p. 623.
51. *Ibid.*, p. 164; cf. also Said, *op.cit.*, p.325.
52. Roberts, *If You Need to be Blessed Financially, Do These Things*, Tulsa, 1982, p.4.
53. *Ibid.*, p.7.
54. Roberts, *Flood Stage: Opening the Windows of Heaven*, Tulsa, 1981, p. 164.
55. Roberts, *How to Get into the Flood Stage of God's Financial Supply*, Tulsa, 1982, p.3.
56. R.F. Mettler, "The Cargo Cult Mentality in America", in *Business Week*, Sept. 22, 1980, p.22.
57. W. Rasberry, "Tapping the Poor's Capacity to Produce", in *Tulsa World*, Jan. 7, 1986, *passim*.

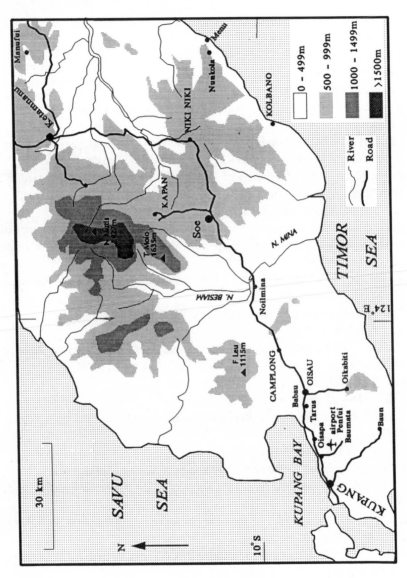

Map 3. Western Timor

Chapter Seven

Spirit Movements in Timor

Graham Brookes

Introduction

This article attempts to describe two Spirit Movements, each occurring this century on the island of Timor and among the people usually referred to as the Atoni. The first movement occurred during the second World War Japanese occupation of Timor, the second in close time proximity to the attempted, so called Communist coup of 1965. An earlier movement occurred on the nearby small island of Kisar, some 25 km north of the eastern tip of Timor. Beginning in 1920 the overt phenomena of that earlier movement are best explained in terms of cause to war, cyclone, famine and death during the world-wide 1918 influenza epidemic. This article does not attempt to trace the likely connections between that earlier movement and the two that are described.

When the two Spirit movements under investigation were in full flight, the Atoni were subsistence farmers, as is still basically the case. The nature of Timor's soil and climate, together with the practice of shifting agriculture among limestone outcrops allow the Atoni to produce poor crops of rice, millet and maize, the staple food source. The end of every dry season in recent times has been characterized either as a period of 'ordinary famine' or 'extraordinary famine'. A single continuing theme expressed culturally from the time of the foundation of the Dutch outpost on Timor in 1613 to the present day is the repetitive statement of the area's deficiency in natural resources.[1]

The traditional religion of the Atoni was one rich in ritual act accompanied by many hymn-prayers to 'the Lord of Heaven'. The people lived, not in fear of an unknown world, but in close relationship to a hidden one, which combined with the physical world forms into an inseparable whole. The very order of the world has its roots in the hidden one. The hidden world is neither invisible - because the Atoni sometimes see much of it in their visions and they sometimes hear voices from it - nor some kind of 'hereafter', because to the Atoni it is a real world, complete with ancestors, which surrounds them while at the same time being hidden in the sense that it is mysterious and sacred. A great deal of material has been published about the Atoni's traditional religion. Unfortunately most of it is only available in old magazine articles and in Dutch, but works by H.G. Shulte Nordholt and Pieter Middelkoop are accessible.[2]

To propagate their faith and to gain a share in the lucrative sandalwood trade, the Portuguese gravitated toward Timor and the Lesser Sunda Islands, after their conquest of Malacca in 1511. The extent of early Portuguese relations with the Atoni is difficult to assess; it is often forgotten that the Portuguese arrived on independent trading vessels. Jesuit and Dominican missions to the Timor area began in the Hispanic dominated sixteenth century, so that when the Dutch landed at Kupang at the beginning of the seventeenth century, there were some 25,000 adherents of Catholicism on Timor.

The Dutch came as officers and representatives of a single tightly organized trading company, the East Indies Company or VOC. As for the history of Protestant activities on Timor, these are usually dated from 1614, the year Mattheus van den Broeke was appointed to Timor with his first duty and responsibility to act as pastor to the employees of the VOC stationed at the Kupang 'factory'. The demise of the VOC on December 31, 1799, however, also brought an end to the first period of Dutch missionary endeavour, the period known as that of *Oud-Hollandse Zending* . It was a period when conversion meant denationalization: to become a Christian was to become a black Dutchman.

In 1787 the *Nederlandsch Zendings Genootschap* (NZG), was established but it was not until 1819 that Timor received its first missionary sent by this board. Despite the fact that NZG efforts had been expended on Timor for 35 years, though, when it closed its work there in 1854 the Gospel had not spread beyond Kupang and its environs. Ambonese missionaries were fervent servants but very often considered themselves more the pioneers of a new civilization of which Christianity formed a part.

The *Indische Kerk* established in 1817 was virtually a state instrumentality -

the instrumentality that looked after spiritual matters. Its aim was to expand religious knowledge, promote Christian morals, care for the interests of Christianity in general and the Protestant church in particular, and to cultivate love for the Government and country. What was important was that members be obedient and loyal citizens of the Dutch Indies Government. Fortunately, however, there were some outstanding people, both servants of the government and of the *Kerk*, who were able to lead the church in Timor. 'Native teachers' were trained in a school for Evangelists which was opened in 1902, moreover, and they became responsible for the spread of the Gospel throughout western Timor.

One of the most remarkable of modern missionaries, Dr. Pieter Middelkoop, arrived in Timor in 1922. Except during the years of Japanese occupation he continued to work on Timor until 1957. He tells that in 1930 the whole area of Molo, Amanuban and Amanatun was inhabited by 'pagan' people - the number of baptized Christians numbering about 500. By 1957, though, the total Christian membership for this area - inhabited almost solely by Atoni - had grown to some 80,000.[3] The period of Japanese occupation saw the church left without any of its expatriate leaders. This eventuality had been foreseen and in January 1942 the de jure leadership of the church had been placed in native hands. But it was a time of great confusion. It is something of a miracle that the majority of church workers remained faithful, refused to work for the Japanese, and continued to serve their congregations. In fact the church grew rapidly during the Occupation years. Following the Japanese withdrawal from Timor a missionary by the name of Dr. E. Durkstra returned to Timor as the appointed Superintendent. He appointed a committee to work towards the independence of the church. The Protestant Evangelical Church of Timor (GMIT) became independent on 31 October, 1947. Membership of the church grew rapidly. In the area left by Middelkoop in 1957, when the membership was 80,000, there was growth to 120,000 by 1960 and to over 153,000 adherents in 1971.

The article describes the conditions in which the two Spirit Movements occurred within the context of church growth among the Atoni. In many ways the movements highlight the fact that a great many, perhaps the majority of church members, still lived in and were influenced by the atmosphere of the primal Timorese village, which is still only half a century out of a completely indigenous ('animistic') religious sphere. In the indigenous situation belief in miracles, and in the visible, physical acts of the spirits and demons, as well as the vivid manifestation of power in curse and blessing, the unquestionable authority of functionaries related to the world of the spirits and demons, were all "practically universally held and experienced".[4]

The term Spirit movement has been used to refer to the movements described in this article. Spirit movement is an accurate translation of the Indonesian *gerakan Roh*. It could be translated as a movement of the Spirit. The term *gerakan kebangunan rohani* is also used by Indonesians.[5] This means 'a movement of spiritual growth'. But those words are also used to describe other activities such as, for example, an evangelistic campaign. I have chosen to use the term 'Spirit movement', though, because it arises from the special experience of the Christians involved. Conceptually, indeed, it described that part of their experience which they regard as definitive. Unless certain phenomena are experienced the event is, by definition, not called a 'Spirit movement'. What permits the Timorese to regard a particular movement as a Spirit movement is that in their estimate one or more people have been obviously 'moved by the Holy Spirit'. That movement is experienced through dreams or visions or some auditory experience - by the very experiences concerning which the Timorese say 'the spirit and the heavens have ordained it'. From that dynamic moving there is no possibility of unpunished escape. Obedience is imperative.

War-Time Movements

Between 20 and 22 February, 1942, the Japanese landed on the south coast of Timor without experiencing any opposition. As they moved westward they were engaged in some short but bloody conflicts with the small Australian contingent. Because of the overwhelming advantage held by the Japanese both in men and equipment, the fighting did not last long; the Japanese were soon in effective control as the occupying power.

The attitude of the Japanese towards the Atoni and institutions such as the Church that served them varied from one area to another. Generally the occupying forces were firm but not cruel. Nevertheless,for everyone it was a time of great difficulty and suffering. Practically all supplies from outside were cut off and the people had to live entirely from the meagre resources of the land. The Japanese forces also had to be fed. Large numbers of cattle were slaughtered to feed the Japanese, gardens were wantonly destroyed, food producing trees were cut down for timber and fuel, and the land generally impoverished.[6]

In 1944, the Japanese requisitioned the total corn and rice harvests, leaving the people only tuberous roots and other forest products to eat. For the Atoni the need to provide for the occupying forces meant that their annually experienced "period of usual hunger" *(lapar biasa)* became an extended one of "extraordinary hunger" *(lapar luar biasa)*, or famine. Many Christian Atoni interpreted the experience of occupation and extended famine as signs of the imminent *parousia* according to their reading of biblical passages such as Luke 21:10f.[7]

During the occupation of Timor an intense Spirit Movement was experienced.[8] The movement began and was mainly concentrated in and around Nunkolo, a small village just a few kilometres from the south coast of Timor in the eastern Amanuban area.

At Nunkolo two specific problems arose. The Japanese throughout Timor demanded the provision of young women to serve the needs of the soldiers. It is a striking feature of the Nunkolo movement that only in this area were the Japanese demands refused. Here the people made a firm stand and succeeded in hiding their young women from the occupying army.[9]

The second problem was the consumption of alcoholic drinks at celebrations held by the Japanese at which Christians were expected to participate. The Protestant pastors at Nunkolo, J. Sine and his assistant L. Hauoni appealed in their sermons that people might not drink at these celebrations since the use of alcohol had been a chronic problem at Nunkolo.

Knowing that the Japanese disliked abstinence and were suspicious towards those who refused to drink with them, the school teachers at Nunkolo were upset and nervous about the pastors' appeal. The teachers planned to lodge a complaint against them. Mrs Juliana Mnao, the wife of one of the school teachers, overheard the teachers hatching their plot against the ministers. She became increasingly uneasy until in her great anxiety she began hearing a voice calling her. Mrs Mnao, who first heard the voice on 27 August 1943, and thereafter on two other occasions, believed that God was calling her to become his messenger. She emerged as the leading prophetess of the Nunkolo Spirit Movement. Her public activities seem to have started around mid-October 1943 and lasted until New Year's Day 1944.

On the evening of the 17 October 1943, Mrs Mnao heard a voice saying:

> The school and church labourers are living in disagreement. Let them come, one after the other, four families in all. Let them kneel and pour out their hearts and pray together.[10]

They came in obedience to Mrs Mnao's summons. They ventilated their grievances. Alternating between prayer and hymn singing they remained together until dawn.

On Tuesday, 19 October, during the morning prayers, Mrs Mnao experienced an ecstatic state. The voice ordered her to tell Pst. Sine that although the people came faithfully to church they did so half-heartedly. Screaming, she protested to him and his congregation: "You have made my house an auction hall!" She then ordered a complete re-arrangement of worship times, strictly segregating the Sunday School children together with the unbaptized, newly converted from the baptized members. On the same day many who wanted to become Christians surrendered their sacred objects *(le'u)* which they had received from their ancestors. In the Nunkolo region these items were traditionally hung in the church. However, the voice charged Mrs Mnao to inform the people that the objects should not remain in the church but should be incinerated immediately.[11] Here we have two excellent examples of new actions and behaviour patterns being immediately adopted by church members at the dictation of a prophet.

Prophets frequently engage in revealing hidden sin and prophesying about general calamities in the world. Examples in the activities of Mrs Mnao are not difficult to find.

On one Saturday evening the voice impressed upon Mrs Mnao the importance of preparation on the part of those who on the following day would celebrate the Lord's Supper. At the preparatory service, Mrs Mnao placed her ear close to the participants' chests, listening to "what welled up in their hearts".[12] She publicly announced each person's sins and charged the congregation to settle their differences. Listening at people's chests to hear "what welled up in their hearts" became one of Mrs Mnao's characteristic activities. This "sin sniffing", as it has been called elsewhere can be paralleled from recent Spirit Movements to the east, in New Guinea, and we will have more to say about its appearance in later Timorese phenomena.[13]

Mrs Mnao and some of the other prophets who arose during the Nunkolo movement were convinced of the imminent return of Jesus Christ. The teams that formed around the prophets took every opportunity to call Christians to confession and repentance. Many people accepted the call; some rejected it. This consistent call to a devout and holy life and away from the problem sins of the day (drunkenness, fornication and gambling) became a characteristic of the Movement. Informants from whom a great deal of information concerning the movement was obtained continually used the Indonesian *pembersihan* (purification) to describe the aim of Mrs Mnao's challenging activities.

Mrs Mnao's behaviour sometimes became quite excessive. She frequently resorted to slapping people in an effort to have them confess. Usually she began by slapping her husband, Simon, and then proceeded down the row of people at whose chests she had been listening.

Belief in the efficacy of the curse provides a deep-rooted and wide-spread latent source of fear for the Atoni. Mrs Mnao and other prophets of the Nunkolo movement frequently resorted to curse as punishment for those who aroused her displeasure. The following story is typical.[14]

One day a man named Thomas Tamelan was in Nunkolo. Mrs Mnao demanded that he should kneel and bow his head to the earth. He refused. Mrs Mnao convinced him that he should pray aloud and then she said, "The prayer was good, but he doesn't humble himself; that's no good". Tamelan disagreed and a quarrel began. Tamelan's answers to Mrs Mnao's questions so displeased her that she announced that he would die, if not within three months, then certainly within six months.[15] Indignant, Thomas left in haste. He arrived home and there read the Bible with his family, then prayed that God's truth and justice would prevail and the curse be cancelled.

About two hours later, Pst. Sine arrived with a group of people to fetch Tamelan back to Nunkolo. They threatened that if he did not accompany them his father would die that same night. So certain were they of the power of this curse that Mrs Mnao had even ordered Pdt. Hauoni's wife to provide a body wrapping for the elder Tamelan. Whilst Thomas was making up his mind whether to accompany Mrs Mnao's ambassadors back to Nunkolo, Pst. Sine went to the father and told him of the curse caused by the disobedience of his children, especially Thomas, which would result in his death.

After long consideration Thomas reluctantly decided to accompany the group back to Nunkolo. There he was commanded to recite the Ten Commandments and the Apostles' Creed. His recitation pleased Mrs Mnao, but still she declared that his heart was not right. Altercations continued throughout the night during which Mrs Mnao slapped Thomas several times.

After daybreak all of them, including Thomas, returned to Pst. Sine's house. There, amid gales of laughter, Mrs Mnao recounted how she had treated Tamelan. When Thomas himself saw her behaviour, he surmised, "She's crazy".[16]

Through the use of curse, exhibitions of anger, corporal punishment and sheer charismatic magnetism Juliana Mnao encouraged many people to confess to their wrongdoings, to repent and to live a devout and holy (pious) life in preparation for the *parousia* . Those who obeyed Mrs Mnao's call to confession and repentance were regarded as the "elect". Soon after the beginning of her public activities Juliana Mnao had named a watering place the "Pool of Siloam". The prophet commanded her followers to take mud from this pond and to rub it on their faces so that they would be recognised as the elect.[17]

If Juliana Mnao seemed to cast her own rôle in the mould of John the Baptist - undertaking the task of one preparing people for the coming of the Lord - there was another prophet-leader to follow soon after who quite clearly saw herself as greater than the one who preceded her.

The prophet Maria Banoenaek was identified as God by one of her 'team' members, Neeltje, who identified herself as Jesus. A third team member, Juliana, was identified as the Holy Spirit. The rest of the 'team' were angels. Maria heard a voice calling her to obedience. Her first task, on 3 November, 1943, was to call the Christians of Nunkolo together for confession.[18]

The voice then ordered that a team should be elected to carry a message to the village of Manufui (also known as Eno Nitas). A team consisting of two men and three women were chosen. As they travelled to Manufui the voice said: "Don't go to Manufui because they won't receive you there".[19] The team turned back and travelled instead to the village of Menu where the area command of the Japanese was established. Having arrived in Menu the team called the people, one by one, for confession.

The team walked to the beach at Menu. Its members later confessed that they had been ordered by the voice to walk over the water but that they had not dared. Only much later did the story emerge that the team actually attempted to cross the sea to Australia on a piece of wood.[20] Several of the team members pushed a log into the sea, climbed aboard and closed their eyes expecting that, upon opening their eyes after a decent interval, they would find themselves in Australia. Middelkoop comments, "the discovery of these naive Christians was that having closed their eyes and waited several times, much to their disappointment they were still in the same place".[21]

On the day following their great disappointment, however, Maria's team was enlarged to nine persons and it started again on the visit to Manufui. As the voice had prophesied, there the minister and his congregation put up a stout resistance. A quarrel arose in consequence, during which the prophetic band, in obedience to the voice, kicked the pulpit, broke two plates and ripped the copy of the scriptures to shreds. The following morning peace was restored and the team promised to give new plates and to replace the Scriptures.[22]

This particular team seems to have had little if any charisma. They were unable to witness effectively at Menu, and by their excessive behaviour at Manufui they nearly caused a riot. There was little appeal in their work and message. Villagers and their ministers were willing to suspend judgement for a short time; the team leaders could have been whom they claimed to be. But it was not long before many people were offended. The voice had commanded the team to "stamp your feet and announce a sign from heaven",[23] but nothing followed. The villagers' conclusion, then, as expressed by the minister at Manufui, was that "it was all evil".[24]

The Nunkolo Spirit Movement was brought to an end by the excesses of the prophets and their bands. On New Year's Day, 1944, a tumult developed in the Nunkolo church. "Everyone brought his own message; everyone spoke at once. There was much confusion. After that virtually all the Christians of Nunkolo did not believe in the movement",[25] so that the mounting expectations of some Divine Transformation was dissipated from that time.

Because of the questionable nature of much of the behaviour and many of the claims of those involved in the movement, the Presbytery Committee called for an investigation of the movement after the departure of the Japanese. Following this investigation all those leaders of the movement whose appointments were controlled by the church were removed to other places. Nearly all who were moved, however, carried the message concerning what had happened at Nunkolo, and the challenge of holy living, to their new appointments. Working quietly in their immediate circles, these people widened the influence of the Nunkolo movement in a way more closely akin to a Christian Revival Movement, with millenarian features being subdued.

Pst. Sine was transferred to the village of Baumata, a small village about fifteen kilometers from the city of Kupang. When he arrived in Baumara Pst. Sine found a congregation consisting almost entirely of nominal Christians. Preaching of the Gospel in Dawanese[26] had been neglected. Because of the situation during the war years when the Japanese chose the village for a large encampment, the Christians of Baumata had not been well served. Many had returned to pre-Christian practices. Tribal worship places, though neglected, still stood; nominal Christians were serving as ritual leaders at these places. All of my informants are agreed that there was a great deal of sickness which they saw as God's "cane" *(rotan Tuhan)* wielded in punishment.

It is clear that the revival at Baumara began with the destruction of the many ritual places. Under the leadership of Pst. Sine all such places were pulled down; the wood and carvings burnt; the silver and gold buried. The destruction of these places eliminated the continuing influence they exercised while they remained.

Immediately upon the razing of the ritual places people began to return to the church. There was something of a "people movement" which included Christians who had returned to primal practices and those who newly desired to become Christians.

Unlike the Nunkolo Movement there was never any emphasis on public confession in the Baumata Revival. However, people began calling the minister and elders in cases of sickness. Challenged to take stock of their lives, they whispered their sins to the servants of God. Many people still witness to having experienced a newness of life at that time.

The influence of revival and renewal, experienced by the Baumara Christians in the late nineteen-forties and early nineteen-fifties, continues to the present on their own witness. The revival resulted in a new religious fervour; the practices of Christianity, Bible study, prayer and confession, were followed faithfully. The position and work of the church elders, functioning as a team with the minister, were emphasised. Minister and elders lived in an intense fellowship of prayer and faith. This example influenced the lives of many Christians and attracted many who, leaving their primal practices and "cutting their hair" as a sign of severing their relationship with the primal powers, became Christians.

Post-War Developments

The British Sociologist, Bryan R. Wilson has said that:

Once charismatic leadership has occurred among a people it is capable of periodic recrudescence, and may, apparently, be reactivated without the experience of new processes of social change which appear to be the first stimulant of charismatic claims.[27]

If this is the case, then perhaps the conditions that prevailed in Timor during 1965 may be seen simply as the catalyst that encouraged the reactivation of charismatic leadership.

1965 was a year that saw widespread famine in Timor. In December 1965 Pst. Y.M.E. Daniel, the Presbytery chairman at So'e, wrote to P. Middelkoop:

The number of inhabitants of the area of Amanuban is about 200,000 to 250,000, among whom about 170,000 are famine stricken. The cause of this famine is the fact that the rains came pouring down very early, in August. Nobody had prepared his plantation; nowhere had the necessary burning of undergrowth before the rains came down taken place. In consequence of the continuous rains people planted their corn in unprepared soil. After a few weeks the rains stopped again and the dry monsoon set in again. Consequently the new crop perished. Many people planted two or three times. Those planted for a third time reaped a very limited crop. The prices of food are increasing enormously.[28]

In addition to the economic pressures experienced by all Indonesians for over a decade to 1966 and the conditions of drought and famine experienced by the Atoni and other groups living on Timor, the people of Indonesia were under severe political pressure which amounted to a clash of cultures and climaxed in what could only be regarded as a situation of open warfare. The people of South Central Timor were under particularly severe pressure. Official government policy was expressed as NASAKOM, an acrostically derived word standing for *NASionalisme-Agama- KOMunisme,* Nationalism, Religion, Communism. The new doctrine, the brain-child of then President Sukarno, promised a resourceful blending into a viable alliance for national development of the three forces which had wrestled for Indonesian independence. In Timor many Church members joined the Communist Party or its organisations and "in some places threatened to take over control of church organisation".[29] By 1965 the Indonesian Communist Party (PKI) and its subsidiary among the farmers, The Indonesian Peasants' Brigade, were practically in control of many villages and districts. In the tragic events that followed the attempted coup thousands of people saw the church as the only safe fortress. "The death of so many victims created great anxiety in the congregations. Churches were full to overflowing."[30]

Cosmic signs became visible when, in early September, 1965, the Ikeya-Seki comet appeared in the sky. Visible only in the southern latitudes of Indonesia in the hours before dawn, this comet first formed a small speck drawing a slim tail. Each night, however, throughout September the comet grew larger, filling the night sky, almost from end to end. To the Atoni the comet was the harbinger of the end of an era that would be ushered in with war and bloodshed.

Each year on 26 September, special services are held in the So'e church of *Gereja Masehi Injili di Timor,* The Protestant Evangelical Church of Timor. Many hundreds of people gather to celebrate "the beginning of the Timor Revival". In fact the events of the *qerakan Roh,* or Spirit Movement as the Indonesians call it, had started before 26 September, 1965, but on that date several pre-existing streams met and were directed as participants would claim, by the renewing work of God's Holy Spirit.

Several events contributed a formative and catalyzing influence to begin the Timor Spirit Movement. As the result of a vision in which a woman had seen Jesus speaking with the Samaritan woman at the well at Sychar and there offering her "living water" (John 4:1-26), there began a small prayer group which consistently prayed for "the water that...will become...a spring which will provide...eternal life." Pst. Daniel formed an *Organisasi Pekabaran Injil*

(Organisation for Evangelism) and a *Badan Pergumulan* (Prayer Group) at So'e. The prayer group consisted of the ministers of So'e, together with their wives, and church elders and deacons. Their aim was prayerful "wrestling without ceasing" and their prayer was that God would "wipe away the tears of his threatened people", not only in Timor, but throughout Indonesia.[31]

The Assembly of the Protestant Church signed an agreement in 1964 for co-operative work with *Yayasan Perseketuan Pekabaran Injil Indonesia* (The Indonesian Missionary Fellowship) which had its headquarters at Batu, not far from Malang, in East Java. As a result of the co-operative agreement with what is popularly called simply "Batu", the Dutch rector of the Indonesian Gospel Institute *(Institut Injil Indonesia)*, the Rev. Detmar Scheunemann, visited Timor in July, 1965. He was accompanied by a team of the institute's students. They began their ministry in Kupang and later moved to So'e. The team also conducted evangelistic campaigns in several other parishes.

The emphasis of the Batu team was on personal piety, the abolition of *le'u* objects, books of incantations, etc., so that Christians could have power to follow Christ and to become his witnesses. Scheunemann brought a unique knowledge of the hold over "the powers of darkness". He was able to place before the people well articulated, penetrating insights into the dangers of the Timorese *le'u*. In fact the surrender of amulets, charms, magic potions and other objects - those very things which had a powerful hold on the Atoni - became a feature of the Spirit movement which was soon to begin.

Teams of young evangelists were in existence as early as August, 1965. These teams were the result of the work of Miss H. Tunli'u. Miss Tunli'u, director of the secondary schools at So'e, was in Kupang for the school vacation when the Batu team arrived; she attended many of their meetings. Miss Tunli'u felt stimulated and challenged by the Batu team, and she continued a close association with them after their arrival in So'e on 22 August, 1965. The director of the Batu team said on one occasion that the team was already desirous of returning to Batu "but some great event is going to happen in So'e."

Actually this statement of Scheunemann acted as a stimulation for a spiritual movement. What is more, the statement was addressed to Miss Tunli'u who had on several occasions benefited from the ministry of the Batu team led by Scheunemann.[32]

Later Miss Tunli'u became a student at the Batu Institute and from there, on 12 December, 1965, she wrote to P. Middelkoop.

...On 16 August, 1965, while attending a church service I felt myself moved by the Spirit and heard a voice calling me, saying, "This is the moment to surrender yourself and to follow the course at Batu in order to become a missionary. The Lord who calls you is faithful and true, He will fulfil it." Then I asked the Lord, "Is it really your voice? Or is it only a wish?" Then again I felt moved by the Spirit and the voice of the Lord came to me. "For God is at work in you, to will and to work for His good pleasure." (Phil. 2:13) ... Then a great joy filled my heart and I remembered what happened when I was staying at your house near the well in So'e in 1956. I am convinced that the Lord Jesus, at that time, had already called me.[33]

Moved by the Spirit, Hennie Tunli'u began to testify to her calling and her message spread quickly among the people of So'e. Her witness and work among the young people created prayer groups, fellowships and evangelistic teams.

Following the service on 26 September, 1965, in which many people caught the spirit of renewal and dedicated themselves to Christian witness, the number of teams increased rapidly. By December 23 there were 49 teams[34] and by January 20 1966, the total had grown to at least 75.[35] Generally speaking the teams consisted of 5 -10 people, with some reaching a membership of as many as 20 persons. These teams were made up primarily of younger people, including many school teachers. Most of the team members came from around So'e and the South Central Timor area. Many of the teams were led by women.

Although the teams were given an identifying number, there remains uncertainty as to the total which were formed. Teams formed as a person who believed himself or herself to have been "called" by the Spirit and as the Spirit revealed the names of those who were to join the group. Teams broke up as leaders were unable to sustain their claim to charismatic leadership, many of the members joining or forming other teams. The highest total of teams at work at any one time appears to have been around 100, with a total membership of perhaps 6-700 persons.

There is no doubt that very great enthusiasm reigned. Many team members simply left their jobs and went in obedience to the call. The schools in So'e could not function normally for several months because many of the teachers and students were away with the teams.

Unlike the Nunkolo movement, which possessed only two major teams, and was therefore easier to summarize, the diverse activities of the So'e teams are too complex to recount in a limited space. For that reason the work of two representative teams, yet each of them engaged in only one of their campaigns, will be described.

Team Number 17, like most teams, originated from the South Central Timor area; its leader was Mrs Wilhelmina Boimau and the membership consisted of both males and females. Most of the ten team members came from the village of Kolbano, not far from Nunkolo. The team proclaimed its task as a mission of "divine healing" *(kesebuhan Ilahi)*. The call for divine healing also carried with it a negative message which was directed primarily against the drinking of alcohol and the use of magical objects.

Mrs Boimau was illiterate, but she depended on the assistance of her "secretary" who always sat beside her. All the members of the team admired Mrs Boimau because, according to them, she had received an extraordinary "charisma": she was always in contact with God. The members mixed their metaphors a little, suggesting that it was as if there were a gramophone which gave announcements to her from above. The secretary, however, claimed that the messages were "telephoned" from heaven. The secretary was always at his leader's side, well prepared with pencil and paper, to note the messages from above which the latter whispered to him. This occurred at all times, even during meetings. The secretary frequently displayed his notes which consisted of hundreds of Bible verses. He was proud to announce that all of them had been "telephoned" from heaven to the respected Mrs. Boimau.

The team was very dependent on what they called "visions and revelations". For the team as a whole to receive a revelation presented some problems. They had to pray together and then wait together until their desires materialised or the answer was given. They were happy to wait for several days, during which time they would not permit themselves to be separated. This way, they said, they would be prepared to take immediate action when their prayer was answered.

One vision, recounted by Mrs. Boimau with pride, was that before long Indonesia would govern the whole world and that President Suharto would become president of the world. This particular vision plucked a rather sensitive chord among many of her hearers. Indonesia, at that stage only recently independent, was sensitive about continuing colonialism. She was in fact anti-colonialist. As a result it just could not be accepted that Indonesia would try to dominate other nations. Appealing to this apparent contradiction, many people refuted and rejected Mrs Boimau's "vision".

Those who in their own estimate were willing "to test the spirits" and to declare them false, and those who judged Mrs Boimau's prophecies to be false, however, were confronted with great anger. The viewpoint of team 17 was that all the "revelations" they received were from God. Those who derided the actions or statements of the team, they claimed, or who rejected the orders received by revelation through the team leader could expect to experience God's curse through illness or accident. Team 17 frequently suggested that the curse would manifest itself in falling from a horse or having one's house destroyed by fire.

The members of Team 17 also regarded themselves as having received special gifts for healing. Healing problems became the burden of the team's work. Its members taught that medicine and medical care were no longer needed. Healing, or whatever expression of wellbeing was desired, could be had by praying providing the prayer was uttered in faith. This included the solution to the problems of tropical hygiene, so that if a person or members of his family were suffering from head lice there was no need to use toxic applications. "Just pray and the lice will disappear," the team said.

Mrs Boimau's secretary listed all the healings that occurred under the team's ministry. He frequently and proudly exhibited the list, and on one occasion made the claim that, "It's obvious that our work brings great satisfaction and has already saved the island of Roti from danger."[36] Pst. J.E. Manoeain, the chairman of Central Roti Presbytery, reported that Team 17's list for the village of Messina showed that 88 people had been healed there. When Pst. Manoeain made an investigation, he concluded that no one had been healed.[37]

Everywhere Team 17 journeyed, they elected and ordained new teams by the "authority" received by Mrs Boimau. New team leaders were immediately accorded the same exaggerated respect enjoyed by Mrs Boimau.

Pst. Manoeain summarised the message of Team 17:

...My impression is that everywhere they work inspirations, revelations and visions which they have "received" become the emphases of their preaching and conversations with the congregations: not the contents of the Bible.[38]

This observation accords well with the fact that Atoni conceptions attach profound significance to the immanent mystery of things.

The second representative team was a large one, in excess of forty people led by Pst. Y.M.E. Daniel, the chairman of the So'e Presbytery. This team travelled widely in Timor. The team consisted of both young and old, men and women, subsistence farmers, school teachers, students and government employees. Most of the team publicly witnessed that they had been called to their work by various means, leaving their places of work in order to carry the message of revival throughout Timor. Generally speaking this team was well received and, led by Pst. Daniel, a rather phlegmatic man, there were very few instances which resulted in negative reactions.

Everywhere the team went the message proclaimed was a call to repentance and conversion. This message was given some large measure of urgency by the proclaimed belief that Christ was soon to return; it was further extended and the urgency built upon, by the warning that once Christ returns the door to conversion will be closed.

If the team's preaching was generally acceptable and attractive, the same could not be said for its "witnessing". By "witnessing" *(bersaksi)*, the team meant the giving of personal testimonies. The witness tended strongly towards "telling stories of miracles, visions and dreams". Many of the stories were quite clearly fabrications or the spiritualization of common events. The team's "witness" brought negative reactions, particularly in non-Atoni congregations, and tended to destroy the mostly positive attitude created by their leader's preaching. There were also other teams whose total message consisted of the re-telling, with much elaboration, of "stories of miracles". This was so great a problem with many teams that they had to be "invited" to go back to where they had come from.[39]

The team led by Pst. Daniel, like nearly all other teams, encouraged the surrender and destruction of all potions, items of magic, and so on. This might well be seen as one of the most characteristic marks of the Timor Spirit Movement.

One member of the team led by Pst. Daniel, Frans Selan, claimed to have received the gift of visions and the ability to "divine" the sins of others. Apparently Selan himself was rather cautious about publicizing his visions. His brother-in-law, Mel Tari, using the typically undifferentiating method of retelling visions (thus giving the impression that he was reporting actual events), frequently caused amazement. This led to many researchers, including missiologist George Peters, being met with incredulity when they enquired concerning some of the supposed miracles.[40] Mel Tari later wrote two books in which many of the stories are the contents of visions rather than actual historical events.[41] Stories of the miraculous provision of food are common to Tari's books, to the unwritten record of the Timor Movement and to the Nunkolo Movement.[42] In fact, the stories of the miraculous provision of food should not surprise. We recall that both Spirit Movements occurred at times of widespread and desperate famine. The phenomenon of hungry and hallucinated people reporting their visions as real events was not unknown in the ancient world, and one must not forget the inspiration provided by the relevant Gospel stories (Mk. 6:32-44, etc.).[43]

Selan was not the only member of the team who claimed to experience visions. The other members were not reticent about announcing their visions whether they occurred during prayer or during their "witnessing". While this sort of behaviour was accepted among the Timorese, it found little acceptance in city congregations or in those consisting of other ethnic groups.[44] As one church member said, "Maybe they were having visions; all of us have them at times. But what was the use of announcing them? None of us saw what they saw - where was the edification in their stories?"[45]

Selan's gift of the ability to "divine" people's sins frequently amazed, frightened and encouraged many people to repent. On one occasion Selan "uncovered" the secrets of a church member, naming three sins. The man, Mesak Samai, was challenged with having stolen coconuts as a boy on the island of Alor. This was not particularly amazing; after all, most small boys steal coconuts. However, Samai's amazement grew as Selan, with his eyes closed "as though seeing it all in his mind's eyes", described exactly the method used to steal the coconuts. Samai's second sin was that he had broken into several homes to steal potions to experiment with; he wanted to see if he could use them with no ill-effect. The accused wondered whether someone had told Selan about these things, but then his third sin was uncovered and he was, on his own witness, somewhat floored. For two weeks Samai had been planning murder and he had not told a soul. His plan was uncovered, and he confessed the truth of the charge.

Mesak Samai had also attempted to prevent or, at least obstruct, the work of Pst. Daniel's team. He fell ill, accepting that his illness was a punishment from God. Later, following the confession of his sin, he recovered. Pdt. Daniel counselled him, challenging him to surrender his *le' u* and describing "the way to holiness in living". Samai repented and later joined the team. Later, his name changed to John, he led a team to Namosain and worked there for three years.[46]

In addition to the specific descriptions of the work and outlook of the two teams described above, there are some general observations which contribute to a fuller understanding of the Timor Spirit Movement.

The majority of teams were first established as *kelompok doa* (prayer groups). These groups were formed in one of two ways:

1. Whenever someone experienced a vision, dream or voice which was interpreted as a call to evangelistic endeavour, the person concerned would attempt to convince others to form a team, obtaining the names of those to be approached by "revelation". The person making the claim to charismatic leadership remained the leader as long as he or she could retain the respect of the team members.

2. People who repented and confessed their faith during revivalist meetings were formed into one or more prayer groups for nurture. Usually it was not long before someone in the group experienced a vision or voice and thus claimed priority as group leader.

In order to obtain directions from God concerning what they would do, or to obtain a solution to some problem, the teams prayed or "wrestled" for hours on end. Frequently a member of the team would experience a vision during the long period of emotional "wrestling". For example, during a chain prayer for healing conducted by a team in So'e, a member of the team received a vision of a hill in the house of the sick person. The hill was seen as symbolic of unconfessed sins.[47]

The teams were convinced that they could depend on God's guidance and that they would receive all that they needed from him. All decisions were dependent on God's leading and it was believed that God was making his will known through the phenomena of vision, dream and audition. The teams depended on these phenomena for travelling instructions; for permission to witness and for the content of their witness. The Bible lessons to be used, sermon text and even hymns were not chosen by the preacher but, rather, received by "revelation". A widespread saying was *Usi es an etu* (God will supply it).

The prayer groups prayed for those who had repented in order that they might not sin again. In the Spirit movement this was called a *doa putus* which carries the double meaning of "a prayer of decision" and a "severing prayer". The groups also prayed for evangelists and evangelism, the church, the government, etc. They also prayed in order to prevent natural disasters such as land-slides.

Most of the prayers were aimed at "having God do something"; for example, to cause a miracle to occur. Seen from the point of view of the lengthy times spent in prayer, the content of many of the prayers, and the emotional energy spent during prayer meetings, it is clear that the prayers generally had the characteristic of attempting to force God, or at least bargain with God, in order that the requests made should be fulfilled.

Some prayer groups remained simply as prayer groups; the vast majority, however, also became evangelistic teams. These teams saw their main task as "witnessing" even if many teams also claimed a healing ministry. By witnessing the teams meant telling stories about what they had experienced (dreams, visions, etc.), or witnessing to God's Word, whether that Word was received from dreams and visions or from the Scriptures.

The content of the teams' witness revolved around sin, the Day of Judgment, repentance, and the *parousia*. The aim of the teams' witness was "to win many souls for the Lamb of God". Following repentance, the teams encouraged the repentant to lead a spiritual life. By "spiritual life" was meant avoiding the world and its delights. Smoking, dancing, drinking alcohol, chewing betel-nut, recreations such as films, etc., were all things which "poisoned the spiritual life". The reason advanced by the teams for this asceticism was that the body is "the temple of the Holy Spirit" and must not be soiled.

The teams aimed not only at witnessing but also at "spiritual revival, awakening" *(kebangunan rohani)* . In revivalist meetings conducted by the teams, people involved in the Spirit movement told of their dreams, visions, auditions and other experiences. The stress in stories of visions and dreams fell on the sinfulness of humans, repentance, the last judgment and everlasting punishment. To what I consider to be the emotional, highly suggestion-prone mentality of the

Atoni (and other tribal groups), these themes provided a powerful influence. Repentance, confession and "surrender to God" were the frequent results of the revivalist meetings. The meetings tended to stimulate emotion rather than to build up faith and belief.

Some teams gave themselves almost entirely to healing and exorcism. At the beginning of the movement, only a few people appeared as healers. As the movement gained momentum, "divine healing" became an interest of nearly all teams and an integral part of their work. The practice of "divine healing" required that the person seeking healing first confessed his or her sins. The sick person was then reminded that faith was a necessary requirement for healing. Only then was the prayer offered. If it became apparent during the worship or prayer for healing that there was no result, then "lack of faith" on the part of the sick person was advanced to explain the failure. This was based on the text Lk. 8:48.

Healing teams forbade the use of pharmaceutical medicines - "because they are the possession of the world and the devil". Hospitals and nursing care were also regarded as having no further use. Those who obtained assistance from doctors, hospitals or clinics, were regarded as lacking in faith.

Those involved in the Spirit Movement made a direct causal link between sin and sickness; because sin causes sickness therefore the cause of sin, often an evil spirit, had to be exorcised. This exorcism required special "wrestling" and prayer. In practice demons were also exorcised from places where natural disasters were known to occur. After investigations designed to find the cause of a disaster such as a land-slide the certain conclusion was that a *setan* or demon lived at the place. The demon had to be exorcised by special prayer. Demons were also exorcized from those places which were regarded as having supernatural (magical) properties; for example, from certain large trees or large rocks.

Some few teams limited their activities solely to the production of "miracles". These activities increased dramatically as Western miracle seekers flocked to Timor to witness for themselves the miracles that had been reported in some parts of the Western religious press. By the end of 1967, however, most teams had ceased to exist. A small number of teams who gave themselves to holding rallies for spiritual awakening *(kebangunan rohani)* continued their activities to the benefit of the Protestant church until the sensitive pre-election period of 1971 brought such mobility temporarily to an end.

Revivalism or Millenarism?

During the late sixties and again in the more settled atmosphere following the 1971 election Western reporters, researchers and miracle seekers flocked to Indonesia and to Timor in particular. Their presence and interests coupled with the fact that Western writing concerning the Spirit Movement had begun to filter into Indonesia gave widespread currency to the word "revival". Many people began referring to the Spirit Movement they had experienced as "a revival".

This is not the place to attempt to discover a definition of revival; indeed the variety of revival suggests that any definition would need to be supremely simple, having already worked its way through the complexities of events to the essence of the event.

A study of numerous revivals suggests a short list of results that we would hope to find flowing from any revival. The history of revivals suggests that we should hope to see most, if not all, of the following:

i. An increase in religious fervour or, in other words, a quickening of the spiritual life of the congregation or church experiencing revival.

ii. Real and meaningful church growth either as a result of the extension of the church to the non-Christian or the growth of real discipleship and dedication among previously nominal Christians.

iii. Flowing directly from the previous point, we would hope to see a real effort being made in teaching for Christian formation (nurturing, discipling) of the new Christians or the newly re-dedicated Christians.

iv. A revitalised and effective evangelism which might show itself as a renewed and dedicated interest in local mission or in the provision of personnel or support for more widespread mission.

v. The dedication of the revived congregations to whatever meaningful social action was both needed and open to them in their own context. This social action would be planned, long-term and seen as a true part of Christian ministry.

There is an obvious exception to the fifth point. Expectations of the imminent return of Christ do not lead to long-range programmes of social reform. This point is evidenced in the Timor Spirit Movement where the only action of social reform was the encouragement of rich team members to share their riches with needy team members.[48]

Of the movements described in this article only the Baumata Revival, described in passing as an outcome of the Nunkolo Spirit Movement, exhibited most of the results of revival listed above. The Christians of Timor do not recognize the Baumata Revival as a *gerakan Roh* or Spirit Movement. The quiet, steady, unspectacular revival events at Baumata do not fit the Timorese people's concept of a Spirit movement. It was not a *gerakan*, it was not a dynamic, spectacular movement; and, therefore, it remains unrecognized. The Timorese concept of a Spirit Movement requires that one or more people are "moved by the Holy Spirit" *(digerakkan oleh Roh Kudus itu)* and can, as a result, make a claim to supernatural power which can be recognized. As Wilson points out, "charisma is not a personality attribute, it is the social recognition of a claim".[49]

We have seen that the movement of the Spirit is experienced through dream or vision or an auditory experience. Concerning these experiences the people of Timor say, "The spirits and the heavens have ordained it" *(Nitu ma neno es anlek)*. While leader-prophets need to manifest particular qualities, to perform miracles or to demonstrate ecstasy in order to retain leadership, it is the initial experience that permits the claim to charismatic leadership that is important.

Evidence points to the conclusion that 'revival' might be one suitable term to describe these movements. That, of course, is a category likely to be welcomed by enthusiastic Christians who project the image of a world-wide revival, and who wish to fit the Timorese experience into the paradigm of the missionary 'success story'.[50] On the other hand, there were strong indigenous elements in the activities I have described which speak more of continuity from tradition. The prophetesses in the church groups, for instance, recall the role of specialists in pre-Christian religion; the groups' pursuit of visible and concrete manifestations of power smacks strongly of traditional Atoni expectations about the direct intervention of spirits (cf. also chs.1, 6 above); while the participants' concern to secure bodily and material security might just as easily be deemed a feature of primal religion as anything. These indigenous constituents, of course, were blended with Christianity, for in the group activities we considered, the Bible and its stories had already become a new tradition (reinforced both by mnemonic oral teaching and steadily increased literacy), and the millennial hopes of the Christian message filled in a gap which was apparently left untouched by the old religion. But to talk of these activities as Christian revivals, when the creative adaptation of *tradition* to them is so significant, and when Christianity is so young among the people in any case, seems inappropriate. For this reason, and because of the special emphasis on the gifts of the Spirit, I prefer the category 'Spirit Movement' to describe them.

Later on, mind you, during the 1970's, the American propagandists of the Christian Missionary Alliance cultivated the spiritistic tendencies of the Atoni in such a way as to produce revivalism after their own conservative image. The American missionaries in this Alliance drew off Atoni from interest in the Protestant Church of Timor, and the Atoni separatism which resulted manifested itself with some of the phenomena we have already discussed. But not, we must insist, as authentically. In the activities I have covered in this paper the attempts to integrate tradition and the Christian way were genuine expressions of Timorese innovation. What happened under the Alliance during the 'seventies was orchestrated by Americans and Europeans, and Timorese leaders were encouraged into a sad mimicry of Western revivalist styles.[51] Money was offered to those who were more adept at the kind of leadership best reproducing those styles. Cargoistic elements - or an interest in the greater chances of acquiring new commodities through fulfilling American expectations - only enter the story of Atoni 'Holy Spirit' activity at this later stage.

The activities during the War and in the early post-War period, by comparison, reflect more purely millenarian rather than cargoistic hopes. The crises of the War and the famine of 1965 both required, in the minds of Atoni religious leaders, an intensification of the spiritual life. The call to this fervour satisfied a need, one which came with these crises and could not be met by missionaries of the Protestant Church. Part and parcel of being caught up in the works of the Spirit, in the fulfilment of this need, was the expectation that the Last Things were around the corner. The exercise of faith by the Atoni in this Parousia had its own rewards; there was no projecting of abundant Cargo to be provided for those hitherto deprived of it, and, though there was definitely an element of protest in the Spirit activities which was against arid and stolid qualities of the Protestant Church, the fervour erupted within the ambience of that church. Only during the 1970's were there manipulations to divert spiritistic tendencies into separatism. Before that we have the less obtrusive kind of millenarism, which is not to be forgotten in the Third World, if studies are to be complete. It is a kind less locked into protest activity and more muted by other religious concerns (in the Atoni case to do with ther Spirit's gifts). For these reasons it is often neglected by social scientists in not having other-than-religious dimensions, or in apparently lacking obvious impact.

Notes

1. F.J. Ormeling's book, *The Timor Problem: A Geographical Interpretation of an Underdeveloped Island,* Djakarta, 1956, remains the best description of this facet of life in Timor.

2. Easily available to the English reader is H.G. Schulte Nordholt's, *The Political System of the Atoni of Timor,* The Hague, 1971. Still available in some libraries are the works of Pieter Middelkoop, long-term missionary in Timor. His book, *Curse, Retribution and Enmity: as data in Natural Religion, especially in Timor, confronted with the Scripture,* Amsterdam, 1960, and his monograph, *Headhunting in Timor and its Historical Implications (Oceania Linguistic Monographs 8 [a],[b],[c]),* Sydney, 1963, both provide a great deal of information.

3. On Atoni ethnography, cf., esp. H.G.S. Nordholt, *The Political System of the Atoni of Timor (Verhandelingen van het Koninklijk Instituut voor Taal-, Land- en Volkenkunde 60),* The Hague, 1971.

4. Frank L. Cooley, "The Revival in Timor", *The South East Asia Journal of Theology,* 14/2 (1973), pp.82-3.

5. The people of Timor use the descriptive term *gerakan Roh* which is faithfully translated as Spirit Movement. *Roh* is capitalized to indicate the Timorese belief that these movements are the work of the Holy Spirit. Due to my prior research on Timor, and that of Pieter Middelkoop before me, Spirit or Holy Spirit Movement (cf. Dutch: *Geestesbeweging)* is now being used as a category in other indigenous Pacific contexts, due especially to the work of John Barr (who has himself researched on Timor for the Research and Development Commission of the Protestant Church of Timor since 1984). Cf. Barr (with G.W. Trompf), "Independent Churches and Recent Ecstatic Phenomena in Melanesia", in *Oceania,* 54/1 (1983), pp.48ff.; Barr, "A Survey of Ecstatic Phenomena in Holy Spirit Movements in Melanesia", in *ibid.,* 54/2, pp.109ff.; "Foreword" in W. Flannery (ed.), *Religious Movements in Melanesia Today, 2 (Point Series 2),* Goroka, 1983, pp. vff.; "Spiritistic Tendencies in Melanesia", in *ibid.,* pp. 1ff., "The Age of the Spirit", in *ibid. (Point Ser. 3),* Goroka, 1984, pp. 158ff.; A. Matiabe, "Revival Movements

'Beyond the Ranges', Southern Highlands", in W. Flannery (ed.), *Religious Movements in Melanesia: a selection*, Goroka, 1983, ch.3; J. Kale, "The Religious Movement among the Kyaka Enga" in C.E. Loeliger and Trompf (eds.), *New Religious Movements in Melanesia*, Port Moresby and Suva, 1986, pp. 45ff.; S. Namunu, "Spirits in Melanesian Christianity and Spirit in Christianity", in Trompf (ed.), *The Gospel is Not Western*, Maryknoll, 1987, pp. 109ff; M. Maeliau, "Searching for a Melanesian Way of Worship", in *ibid.*, pp.119ff.

6. G.S. Dicker, 'The Proclamation of the Gospel in Timor', (Theol. M. dissert., Melbourne College of Divinity), Melbourne, 1965, p. 42.

7. Lk. 21:10f reads: "Then he said to them: 'Nation will rise against nation, and kingdom against kingdom. There will be great earthquakes, famines and pestilence in various places, and fearful events and great signs from heaven". (NIV).

8. The source of information concerning this movement which is nearest to the event is Pieter Middelkoop, "De Geestesbeweging in Noenkolo op Timor", [The Spirit movement at Nunkolo in Timor], *De Heerbaan*, 4/9 (September, 1951), pp. 244-252; 4/10 (October, 1951), pp. 272-276; 4/11 (November, 1951), pp.301-306; 5/4 (July-August, 1952), pp.172-177; 5/6 (November-December, 1952), pp. 320-324. The Movement is also covered in my Masters qualifying thesis, 'Spirit Movements in Timor - A Survey' (Melbourne College of Divinity), Melbourne, 1977.

9. P. Middelkoop, *loc.cit.*, 4/9 (1951), p.244.

10. P. Middelkoop, 'Two Revival Movements in Timor Compared', (Typescript, 1 October, 1970), p.2, cf. also p.7.

11. *ibid.*, p.2.

12. Middelkoop, *loc.cit.*, 4/9, p.248.

13. See esp. G. Cramb and M. Kolo, "Revival among the W. Highlands/Enga Baptists", in W. Flannery, *op.cit.*, (Ser.2), p.99; J. Kale, *loc.cit.*, pp. 51ff.

14. The account depends heavily on the record contained in Middelkoop, *loc.cit.*, 5/4, p.177f.

15. This was Mrs Mnao's characteristic curse-formula.

16. Middelkoop, *loc.cit.*, p.177.

17. *ibid.*, p.175.

18. *ibid.*, 4/10, p.273.
19. *ibid.*
20. *ibid.*, 5/4, p.176.
21. *ibid.*, p.177.
22. *ibid.*, 4/10, p.276.
23. *ibid.*, p.275.
24. *ibid.*, 4/11, p.304.
25. *ibid.*, 5/4, p.176.
26. Dawanese is one of the class of assorted languages referred to as "the Timor-Ambon Group". The word *Dawan* is not Timorese. There is a distinct possibility that the Belunese people called the Atoni *dawan*, or highlander.
27. Wilson, *The Noble Savages: The Primitive Origins of Charisma and its Contemporary Survival*, Berkeley and Los Angeles, 1975, p.27.
28. Y.M.E. Daniel, letter to P. Middelkoop, quoted in Pieter Middelkoop, 'Een nieuwe Opwekkingsbeweging op Timor', in *De Heerbaan*, 20/4 (1967), p.220.
29. Frank L. Cooley, *Indonesia: Church and Society*, New York, 1968, p.84.9
30. M.A. Noach, *Langkah Pertama: Suatu Tinjauan terhadap Periode 25 Tahun GMIT - 31 Oktober, 1947 - 31 Oktober, 1972*, Kupang, 1972, p.23. For background, R. Mortimer, *Indonesian Communism under Sukarno: ideology and politics, 1959-1965*, Ithaca, 1974.
31. I. Toto, 'Kegerakan Roh di Timor Tengah Selatan' (unpublished type- script written at the request of the present author), Kupang, 1978, p. 1.
32. J.A. Telnoni, 'Gerakan Roh di Timor: suatu Tinjauan Missiologis' (Exit dissert., Akademi Theologia Kupang), Kupang,1976, p.6.
33. Quoted in P. Middelkoop, *loc.cit.*, 20/4 (1967), pp. 225, 226.
34. I. Toto, letter to P. Middelkoop, in *ibid.*, p.221.
35. A. Radja Haba, letter to P. Middelkoop in *ibid.*, p. 223.
36. Letter from Pst. J.E. Manoeain to Majelis Sinode GMIT, dated 5 February, 1966.
37. *ibid.*
38. *ibid.*
39. Interview with Pst. M. Jakob, April, 1976.
40. See, e.g., George Peters, *Indonesia Revival: focus on Timor*, Grand Rapids,

1973, p.85.

41. See Mel Tari, as told to Cliff Dudley, *Like a Mighty Wind*, Carol Stream, 1971, and Mel and Nona Tari, *The Gentle Breeze of Jesus*, Carol Stream, 1974

42. See, e.g., M. and N. Tari, *op.cit.*, pp. 57-59.

43. Visions, no less than dreams, can be wish fulfilling. This fact is echoed in Isa. 19:8 , "It shall even be as when an hungry man dreameth, and, behold, he eateth, ...or as when a thirsty man dreameth, and, behold, he drinketh..." (We await the important history of ideas by R. Banks on religion as projection [Editor]).

44. Timorese conceptions find little sympathetic accord with, for example, Rotinese conceptions of the world.

45. Interview with Mr D. Gjari, a Sabunese at Nunhila, April, 1977.

46. Interview with Mr M. Samai, April, 1977.

47. Telnoni, *op.cit.*, p.11.

48. A good example of this point was that a rich Chinese woman who was a member of Team 49. (I. Toto, ' *op.cit.*, p.2).

49. Wilson, *op.cit.*, p.5

50. For background to the hope of a world wide (evangelical) revival, see esp. W.N. Gunson, "Victorian Christianity in the South Seas", in *Journal of Religious History*, 18/2 (1974), p.189. cf. also Barr, "Survey, etc.", loc.cit., pp. 111ff. and the literature cited in the bibliography, pp. 122ff. [Editor].

51. For the signs of this, see K. Koch, *The Revival in Indonesia*, Schweickhardt, 1972, pp. 121ff.

Black America and Africa

Chapter Eight

One Love - One Heart - One Destiny

A Report on the Ras Tafarian Movement in Jamaica

Karlene Faith

Introduction

The original version of this essay was written in 1969 when I was first drawn to the Ras Tafarians, a religious-political subculture of Jamaica, West Indies. I had learned that this group considered themselves patriots of Ethiopia, East Africa, and that they worshipped Ethopian Emperor Haile Selassie as a living deity. This was a matter of interest to me because I had previously lived in Ethiopia, working as an administrator with the U.S. Peace Corps.

One of the poorest countries in the world, Ethiopia had a feudal land system until 1974. 90% of the 28-million population resided in rural areas, where 55% of the land was owned by the government and the remainder was owned by the Ethopian Orthodox Church, headed by the imperial family. Haile Selassie ruled the country for 46 years. He was the world's oldest and longest-reigning monarch. More pointedly, he was one of the world's richest individuals - until a military junta, in September 1974, led a land reform revolution. Selassie died shortly thereafter, an impoverished prisoner within his own palace.

The Ethiopian rebels who eventually overthrew Selassie espoused many of the same principles as the Jamaican Ras Tafarians concerning justice and social equity; and yet it was Selassie to whom the Ras Tafarians gave their allegiance. This contradiction intrigued me and I went to Jamaica to learn firsthand the basis of the Ras Tafarians' belief system. During the months I lived on the island I was fully engaged as a participant-observer in the life of Ras Tarafi brethren and their families.[1] Over the course of the study my interest extended to include economic and domestic patterns, as well as customs and attitudes related to religious and political ideology.

The Ras Tafarians of Jamaica do not live homogeneously in a single location. In the urban centres, especially in Kingston, there are large populations of Ras Tafarians who occupy crowded "shanty-town" residential sections. However, my investigation was concentrated on rural variants of the movement and in no instance did I find more than ten Ras Tafarians residing in a single non-urban locale. Communication channels are poor and the insulated life of the average rural Ras Tafarian keeps him separated not only from the rest of Jamaican society (a separation which is generally desired and nurtured by both groups) but from his Ras Tafari brethren as well. It was not uncommon to discover two groups of Ras Tafarians living within a dozen miles of one another who had never had occasion to make contact or acquaintance. Such scattered and diffuse residential patterns provided the study with certain logistical difficulties; countless hours were spent driving on narrow island roads in search of research subjects.

Related to the geographic diffusion, and in part resulting from it, is the fact that Ras Tafarians do not conform to a single religious, political or lifestyle pattern. The differences among them are many and pronounced, and I soon realized that the multivariate characteristics within the movement defy cross-application. In preparing the descriptive material of Part II it was necessary, therefore, that I distinguish between the types of Ras Tafarians I encountered, insofar as they could be "typed" at all.

In Part I I have reviewed the major historical factors of the movement as it rose and developed beginning in the 1930s. For this part I relied heavily on studies which were conducted prior to and including the year 1960. All statements have, however, been confirmed and supplemented by information conveyed to me by Ras Tafarians. Where Ras Tafarians have objected to certain aspects of previous studies as containing incomplete or false information, I have either substituted their emphasis or correction, or indicated the conflict of viewpoint.

History and Background of the Ras Tafari Movement

A. *1930 to 1960:* Although Ras Tafarians fail to agree completely as to actual dates, events or personages which mark the beginning of the movement, the most commonly accepted point of origin is the 1930 coronation of "Ras Tafari" as Emperor Haile Selassie of Ethiopia.[2] Contained in Rev. 5, 17 and 19 are references to a Holy King who would rise from the mountains of Zion bearing the title King of Kings and Lord of Lords. "For he is Lord of Lords, and King of Kings: and they that are with him are called, and chosen, and faithful." (Rev. 17:14) For an undetermined period prior to the coronation of Haile Selassie there existed a small number of Jamaicans whose knowledge and interest in Biblical prophecy had sustained in them the belief that such a King would one day appear on African soil. And when Haile Selassie assumed the leadership of Ethiopia, a country which has traditionally represented for black expatriates the whole of the African continent, with the attendant connotation of ancestral and spiritual homeland, they were quick to identify him as the Lord for whom they had been waiting. Their faith in his spiritual authority was reinforced by the title which he assumed, i.e. His Imperial Majesty, King of Kings, Lord of Lords, Conquering Lion of the Tribe of Judah, coupled with his own declaration of himself as having descended genealogically from the kings of Israel through the union of King Solomon and the Queen of Sheba.[3]

It was also in the 1930's that the success of Marcus Garvey and the Universal Negro Improvement Association had reached its apex. Garvey achieved his most spectacular influence among the black population of the United States, but the black nationalistic philosophy which he promoted gained followers throughout the world, including his Jamaican homeland. Proclaiming "Africa for the Africans - at home and abroad", and "One God, one aim, one destiny", Marcus Garvey advocated a Back to Africa programme.[4] He encouraged worldwide black populations to leave the oppressed areas that had held them since the earliest days of captivity into slavery and to return to the home of their ancestors. Garvey instilled in his followers an exhilarating new sense of dignity and self-pride. Through his design for a reunited black race, bearing political, economic and religious autonomy, he established a boldly prescient philosophy which Ras Tafarians have manifested in their teachings through these past several decades of human rights struggles. And Ras Tafarians can be counted among the forerunners of the various black nationalistic movements in the Americas, Asia and Africa who today rate Marcus Garvey as their leading prophet.

The degraded status which follows Ras Tafarians even today found its roots at least in part in the activities of one Leonard P. Howell. Although Howell was just one of several world-travelled Jamaicans who independently claimed the divinity of Haile Selassie, Howell was the first to arouse a substantial following of an organized faith. With his appeal concentrated on the frustrated poor of Jamaica's lower social stratum, Howell exploited a then-popular interest in the Order of Niyabingi - an organization of unclear origin and purpose of which Haile Selassie was ostensibly the founder and leader. *Niyabingi* was translated by Jamaicans to mean "Death to the black and white oppressor"[5] and the aggressive stance of Howell's followers was readily vulnerable to the violence which this slogan induced and justified. Howell was arraigned and imprisoned several times on charges of assault and sedition, the latter charge based on his reported sale of 5,000 photographs of Haile Selassie which he sold for one shilling each under the pretense that the photographs represented passports to Africa. In 1940, during one of his periods of release from prison, Howell had established a farm near Sligoville which he named Pinnacle, on which the 600 communal residents raised *ganja,* i.e. *cannabis sativa* (aka marijuana), known to Ras Tafarians and other poor Jamaicans most popularly as "the herb".[6] For more than a decade the community suffered conflict with authorities who protested their illegal cultivation of *ganja* and their purported harassment of neighbouring Jamaicans. Finally in 1954 the settlement was broken up by police, with Howell ultimately confined to the Bellevue mental hospital in Kingston.

Despite the depression which resulted in imprisonment for many of Howell's followers, Ras Tafari activity continued to gain impetus and had grown sufficiently, even apart from Howell's followers, to warrant a formal study - which was conducted in 1954 by Professor George Simpson. Simpson grouped the Ras Tafarians of his investigation into two basic pattern groups. The first of these strove for moderation of racial views within the disciplined framework of the Ethiopian World Federation, an organization founded at the instigation of Haile Selassie by Dr Malaku E. Bayen, of which the purpose was to enlist world-wide support and assistance on Ethiopia's behalf. The second type is "the informal activist groups. These are to be found in the most poverty stricken areas. Their members grow their hair and beard long and unkempt, are more aggressive and extremist in their racial views and are generally considered by the rest of society, and to a large extent by themselves, as the only true Ras Tafarians."[7] Professor Simpson concluded that "Ras Tafari groups form, split and dissolve, and some individuals accept cult beliefs without attaching themselves to an organization. In contrast to a revivalist group, which is dominated by a leader, a Ras Tafari band is extremely democratic."[8]

The hostility engendered by conflict between the police and the more activist members of the Ras Tafari movement resulted in repeated clashes and street demonstrations, with the public fear mounting steadily. Religious and political aspirations among the Ras Tafarians remained diffuse and ambiguous, but the emphases which came to represent most clearly the Ras Tafari doctrine, in the mind of the public as well as for the majority of Ras Tafarians, were first that Ras Tafari (i.e. Haile Selassie) was the Living God, and secondly that repatriation to Ethiopia was the way of redemption for the black race. Between 1955 and 1958 there were numerous unsuccessful attempts to organize departures by ship for Africa, of which a large 1958 gathering resulted in the most serious clash with the police in the history of the Ras Tafarians, with uncounted serious injuries and arrests.

Then in August, 1959, the Rev. Claudius Henry organized a large gathering in Kingston. Rev. Henry and his supporters, who are discussed in Part II, refer to the event as a Decision Day, a momentous occasion which would (and reportedly did) provide the followers of Haile Selassie with an opportunity for casting their faith as a multitude. Threaded through the various reports of what happened is a tremendous amount of ambiguity and contradiction. It is suggested by Ras Tafari brethren that Rev. Henry did not deliberately deceive his followers but rather was scapegoated by religious rivals. Nevertheless, 15,000 people are purported to have purchased false passports to Africa, leaving their homes with the expectation that upon their arrival in Kingston they would be embarking by ship for the African continent. Rev. Henry was ultimately imprisoned on charges of fraud and once again the Ras Tafari leadership was temporarily repressed.[9]

B. *1960 to 1969:* Subsequent to this fiasco there were repeated occasions of brutal police harassment against Ras Tafarians. Their long plaited locks were shaven, they were beaten, their homes were destroyed, and they were often unjustly imprisoned.[10] There were doubtless occasions of retaliatory disturbances on the part of Ras Tafari brethren which provoked the police into ever-stricter controls and justified to them their own abuses against the Ras Tafarians. It seems true that in most instances the Jamaican middle-class prejudice against the Ras Tafarians as a 'bizarre, dangerous, long-haired drug-using cult' has been nurtured, if not deliberately promoted, by unfair police brutality against them.

The Ras Tafarians' most common response to these abuses has been to withdraw insofar as possible from the larger Jamaican society. They have boycotted political elections, the consequences of which seem irrelevant to their needs. Their contempt for the establishment has prompted many of them to move further away from the urban centers to isolated environs where harassment against them is less pronounced. In addition to the relatively peaceful atmosphere in the countryside, which facilitates the meditative quality of Ras Tafari life at its purest, rural Ras Tafari brethren also have less difficulty finding means of supporting themselves and contributing to the support of their communal families. Ras Tafarians have supplied Jamaica with the proverbial "last to be hired, first to be fired", and unemployment and poverty have been chronic conditions for urban Ras Tafarians. In the countryside, however, there are opportunities for small-scale fishing and farming activities which, in addition to the cultivation of *ganja* and limited employment by government departments, significantly reduce the problems of poverty which are so commonly experienced in Kingston and other urban centers.

It was during 1960 that the Jamaican Prime Minister Norman Manley is reported by Ras Tafarians to have made a public broadcast to find ways of protecting the larger society of the island against the alleged violence and subversion of the Ras Tafarians. To this the latter 'retaliated' in a surprising and remarkable way, and the recourse was to have profound consequences for the movement. A small group of Ras Tafari brethren arranged through the University College of West Indies (UCWI) at Kingston for a trio of respected scholars to undertake a comprehensive, rapid survey which would explain the realities of the movement, dispel the myths, and hopefully result in improved governmental treatment and social acceptance.

Upon its completion the report was received in all quarters with great interest and debate. It refuted the image of the Ras Tafarian as a social rebel who refused to work or be educated, whose mental faculties were crippled by excessive *ganja* intake, whose dreams of returning to Africa were based on delusion, and whose only immediate interest was in the disruption of Jamaican society. In its place, the study produced the profile of the Ras Tafarian as a peaceful citizen, devoted to his religion, eager to improve his educational and living standards, and wanting to have an equal share of the benefits accorded to the rest of Jamaican society. The study revealed that the movement contained widely diverse ideological variances but that the violent and subversive elements were in fact only marginal phenomena which did not represent or have roots in basic Ras Tafarian thought and aspirations.

Professors Smith, Nettleford and Augier concluded the UCWI report with a list of recommendations which would implement programs for the improvement of living conditions, the cessation of police brutality, and the establishment of educational and social facilities. Also included in the recommendations was the suggestion that the government of Jamaica arrange for a mission to Africa to include Ras Tafari brethren. Such a mission, they believed, could explore realistically whatever possibilities might exist for immigration to that continent.

In November, 1960, just four months after the publication of the study, the following article appeared in the London *Times:*

> Mr Norman Manley, the Premier of Jamaica, has announced that ten persons are to be selected fora government-financed delegation to go to Africato investigate the possibilities of migration there from Jamaica. Mr Manley has had talks with Ras Tafarians, the religious sect advocating a return to Africa, and other groups who are interested in the project.

The delegation, including three Ras Tafari brethren, proceeded to the African continent in 1961 where they spent nine weeks touring, including nine days in Ethiopia. They received an audience with Emperor Haile Selassie who was "so touched by the gifts they had brought for him from Jamaica that he offered to pay all the mission's expenses in Ethiopia."[11] His Imperial Majesty, however, also impressed upon his Ras Tafari visitors that he would not welcome unskilled immigrants to Ethiopia. He confirmed that an offer had been made in 1955 through the Ethiopian World Federation for 500 acres of fertile Ethiopian land to be given to skilled immigrants who would live and work on the land in an ambitious, communal spirit.[12] Upon visiting the land the delegation was disappointed to discover that there were no homes on it - "just pure land" - and to date no action has been taken to secure land rights for Ras Tafari immigrants. But despite the failure to meet with any tangible success in formulating immigration plans, the African mission was a very real triumph for the Ras Tafarians. Just as the UCWI report had given the movement a status it had never before enjoyed, so did the mission enhance Ras Tafarian prestige to an unprecedented degree. As a people long ignored or feared the Ras Tafarians were now beginning to be seen as a viable and significant Jamaican subculture.

Finally, the 1966 visit by Haile Selassie to Jamaica demonstrated conclusively that the Ras Tafari movement could no longer be ignored. The *New York Times* reported from Kingston as follows (on 21 April, 1966):

His Imperial Majesty Haile Selassie I of Ethiopia was mobbed by thousands of adherents of a cult that worships him as a living God when he arrived here today for an official visit to Jamaica on a tour of the Caribbean. The cult is known as the Rastafarians. They regard His Imperial Majesty as their messiah and hope for the day when they can migrate to Ethiopia. The worshippers broke through police cordons and hemmed the Emperor in his plane for nearly half an hour. Waving green, red and yellow banners with such inscriptions as "Hail to the Lord, Annointed and Conquering Lion of Judah," they swept up to the steps of the plane in thousands.

Ras Tafarians themselves, and other eye witnesses, report that police attempts to control the enthusiastic and overwhelming large numbers of Ras Tafarians (estimates given at 15,000), who had travelled from every corner of the island to see their messiah, were so ineffective that they finally gave up their effort and let the Ras Tafarians control the day. [13] All was not chaos, however. During the course of the Emperor's visit, Ras Tafarians were included in the various official audiences which greeted him. Ras Tafarians were being recognized, identified, welcomed into receptions, listened to. And these three events - the report, the mission to Africa, and the visit to Jamaica by Haile Selassie - served the development of Ras Tafari prestige among Jamaicans and, by pointing up their numbers and strength, brought the effect of solidifying and uniting the brethren themselves.

C. *Recent Trends:* Clinton Black's monograph, one of the most widely read and respected accounts of Jamaican history, and which was revised in 1965, fails to give a single mention of the Ras Tafarian movement.[14] Yet a 1969 editorial in the island's only newspaper, the *Daily Gleaner,* suggests that Jamaicans do well to rid themselves of the compulsion to imitate everything British and to take a lesson from the Ras Tafarians. As the island's dispossessed, it reads, they have evolved the "only real piece of (indigenous) culture Jamaica has experienced." (29 June, 1969) Katrin Norris, in speaking of the search for identity that presently plagues Jamaican society, cites the Ras Tafarians as the only group which has escaped the cultural schizophrenia Jamaica is experiencing as a newly independent nation which has so long struggled for success as British imitators:

> The only group which has stepped out of the chase are the Rastafarians, who at least have the mental comfort and in many cases the dignity that goes with the courage of their convictions.[15]

Orlando Patterson, a professor of Sociology at the University College of West Indies, has written a popularly received novel describing the hypocrisy of an apathetic Jamaican society, which somehow manages to ignore the victimization and despair as well as the beauty and courage of life in a Ras Tafarian shanty town.[16] In the same year, Patterson wrote a scholarly article on the Ras Tafarians as a millenarian cult in which he describes himself as "a querying sociological outsider, and on the other hand one who feels a deep sympathy for and a reckless sense of identity with these pursuers of the millennium."[17]

There was in Jamaica, by 1969, an urgently rising call for black power. Representing that movement was a weekly paper, *Abeng,* which calls attention to problems of colonial and imperialistic aggressions on the island, problems of developing nations at an international level, and to abuse of Jamaica's poor and dispossessed, including and especially the urban Ras Tafarians. Ras Tafarians have authored many of the published articles and letters of this paper and also participated in protests and demonstrations against social injustices.[18]

Early in my own research it became clear to me that the Ras Tafari movement and the rising black consciousness among disenchanted youth and black power advocates are phenomena which are inextricably entwined, at least at the urban level where political interest and activity are strongest. There is an increasing recognition that the Ras Tafarians have, for nearly four decades, been addressing themselves with a prescience and a persistence which couples utter faith with the rejection of a society which is based on the assumption of white superiority. The majority of those Ras Tafarians among whom I conducted my research, admittedly, are rural brethren whose lives are insulated by the religious devotion which dominates their interest, as well as a physical isolation. Their knowledge of other approaches to Ras Tafari faith, their concern for the island's political and social problems, is in most instances negligible or at least a very personalized one. Nonetheless, no review of the historical trends of the movement would be complete if it should fail to mention this significant development as it is occurring in urban, and especially in the Kingston, areas.

"We are all Rastas. All black people are Ras Tafarians if they are conscious at all in terms of status and recognition for the Negro." The words belong to one of the most respected scholars in Jamaica, Rex Nettleford, who was one of the three UCWI professors to conduct the 1960 study.[19] And the unguarded enthusiasm with which he evaluates and supports the current trends in the Ras Tafari movement - the growing recognition of them by other Jamaicans, their own increased sense of purpose and solidarity, their refusal to remain subjected to a marginal share in Jamaican life - reflect an understanding and acceptance of Ras Tafari philosophy which has increased particularly among Jamaican youth and intellectuals, but which is shifting as well to the periphery of Jamaican middle classes. That the Ras Tafarians remain a startlingly oppressed group, who are still discriminated against and abused, there can be no doubt. Nevertheless, an account of the historical rise of the movement must fairly take cognizance of the positive attitudinal changes that have been and are continuing to be made.

Ras Tafari Life and Doctrine: Four Perspectives

Estimates of the total population of the Ras Tafari movement have reanged from 15,000 to 30,000, although one of Jamaica's most prosperous businessmen has ventured a confident, off-the-record, estimate of 45,000.[20] Additionally, there is an ever-increasing number of 'sympathizers', who identify with the movement and in many cases even uproot their lives and desert their families to reestablish themselves in the midst of Ras Tafari brethren.

With the exception of the brethren who are attached to one of Rev Henry's parishes, the Ras Tafarians have no hierarchy of office or authority. They do not meet on a regularly scheduled basis and although there continue to be occasional rallies in Kingston, which hundreds and even thousands of Ras Tafarians might attend, such as the annual July celebration of the birthday of Haile Selassie, such events do not take place in rural Jamaica. The interaction among rural Ras Tafarians is indeed negligible, as has been previously mentioned. On the other hand, chance encounters between Ras Tafari brethren produce a spontaneous rush of warm exchange, and even those never meeting before can fall into warm embrace and intimate conversation.

The Old Testament of the Bible is studied and revered with profound devotion, and it is the total guiding force for the lives of most followers of the faith. Its passages are quoted freely and lucidly, and Biblical phraseology has been adopted for general conversational use, casting on the Ras Tafarian an impression of poetic wisdom. Just as there is no formal leadership among most Ras Tafari groups, neither is there an interpretative authority of Biblical doctrine. Nevertheless, most Ras Tafarians seem to agree on which of the Bible's books and chapters deserve the greatest attention and credence.[21]

In distinguishing between the various Ras Tafarian approaches to life and thought I have arbitrarily divided the Ras Tafarians into four major groups. All four groups contain at least some characteristic common to other groups, but all are distinguished in at least one major way that precludes their being grouped together. Conversely, many Ras Tafarians would fit neatly into none of these four groups, but to list the entire gamut of varying approaches to Ras Tafari life and doctrine would seriously encroach upon the clarity and more limited purpose of this study.

During the course of the research I spent prolonged periods of time, in conversation and sharing of activities as well as in formal interview, with approximately one hundred individual Ras Tafarians, and I encountered and observed several hundred more in less personal situations. Although I did not formally select specific persons to serve as informants, I have selected four individuals (one from each major group) and drawn from their comments and biographical data for the purpose of elucidating and personalizing the description of the major group which they represent. These individuals[22] were selected for this purpose because in each instance they revealed particularly strong devotion to their special approach within the movement, and because they were able to articulate or otherwise demonstrate their ideas and feelings with expressive clarity. It is also true that each of them is accorded respect by his fellow Ras Tafari brethren, and each represents an individual who has earned unique status among his peers, if not a position of formal leadership (as in the single case of Rev. Henry) by virtue of his special personality traits or his superior knowledge of the Bible.

A. *Ras Julian Trevor*

I had just the day before landed by plane in Montego Bay for my first visit to Jamaica and my first anthropological field experience. Now, having squished barefoot across a broad expanse of muddy clay, I stood staring at the neat white cottage which was the largest and best-constructed of the buildings in the fenced-in compound before me. I had been told by giggling Jamaican teenagers that in this house I would find some Ras Tafarians, so I continued to stand there, feeling benumbed and uncertain and thinking simply, "So this is where Ras Tafarians live." The place seemed deserted and I had almost decided to postpone my first attempt to acquaint myself with the Ras Tafarians when there emerged from one of the small buildings a man whose long, twisted locks stood from his head in every direction and whose unsmiling face seemed more threatening with each step as he walked slowly toward me. He was carrying a saw, and I remembered warnings I had received about the hatred "Rastas" feel toward white people and the violence with which they allegedly expressed that hatred. But as he came closer to me, with the fence still between us, I heard myself beginning to speak to him in a voice that barely betrayed the intimidation I felt so keenly. I introduced myself by explaining that my experience of living in Ethiopia as a first-hand witness of Haile Selassie in relation to the Ethiopian people had given me a great curiosity about the Ras Tafarians, who were said to worship "His Imperial Majesty" as the "Living God." And with that he spoke - slowly and deliberately, and piercing my vision with his: "Haile Selassie - he's nothing to me." (At which he spat upon the ground). "He's a man, same as me. A man. No more."

It is as a perpetual contradiction that the Ras Tafarian movement can best be characterized, and it is fitting that this study should have begun with the ultimate contradiction. I had arrived in Jamaica with just two firm assumptions about Ras Tafarian beliefs: Haile Selassie is a Living God, and those who worship him seek repatriation to Ethiopia. Yet the first Ras Tafarian I encountered, with the first words he spoke, knocked those assumptions right out from under me. In the weeks ahead I had many long and friendly conversations with this same man, and with the eight brethren with whom he shares his home. None of them believe in Haile Selassie, all of them regard themselves as the only true "Ras Tafarians", all of them are voracious students of the Bible and eloquently share their knowledge of it. All of them have given up the conventional trappings of a family life to come together and live communally as a self-contained, self-supported, mystical band of fishermen. And none of them realized that just three miles north there lived yet another group of "Ras Tafarians" who share almost precisely their philosophy and their life style.

It is in this second Ras Tafari camp that I came to know Ras Julian Trevor and to learn from him and his brethren what it means when a Ras Tafarian says, upon greeting a friend or a stranger alike, "Peace and love, sister".

With his six brothers and four sisters Ras Trevor was raised without a father,[23] and contribution by the children was necessary to the sustenance of his hardworking mother's household. While still in school at age 10, Julian got his first job, "as a kind of garden boy for a white man". While a teenager, having long since dropped out of school, Julian went to Kingston where he learned the wicked ways of the city. "I was going on doing all the evil, having many women, gambling, stealing, telling lies, fighting my brothers and sisters every minute. Then the Lord came into my mind and showed me that all those things are evil".

A point which was reiterated by virtually every Ras Tafarian with whom I talked is that conversion to the faith does not, cannot, come as a result of proselytizing. One person cannot teach another to have faith. Conversion itself is a false concept. One is either among the called, the chosen, or one is not. But unlike the Calvinist, a Ras Tafarian *knows* at some point in his life - and usually his knowledge occurs during a period of extreme 'wickedness' - that he is among the chosen. Thus Ras Trevor believes from his experience that "no one is ever influenced by another man to accept the faith. It is the Lord Himself who calls.

The Lord chooses who he wants - it is not man's decision to accept or deny. The Lord decides who is the elect. And we know".

As he began to grow in the faith and to follow the teachings of the Bible, Ras Trevor's life style began to change in drastic ways. The Bible explains that when a man gives himself unto the Lord, he separates from himself all the habits with which wicked men indulge themselves. For the Ras Tafarian the act of separation which has the most serious social consequence is that which commands that "All the days of the vow of his separation there shall no razor come upon his head: - he shall be holy, and shall let the locks of the hair of his head grow". (Num. 6:5)

Ras Trevor accepted this (originally Nazirite) edict, and as his locks began to grow, his position in the general community began to decline. He was unable to find work, he was arrested on false pretenses, and while in jail he was beaten and his head was shaven. Upon his release he obtained a job as a tractor driver on a government farm, where harassment resumed as his locks began to grow back. His employers tried to force him to shave, but "God said 'No' and finally the government people came to accept me". Ras Trevor has remained with his job for nearly fifteen years, and is considered by them to be one of their staunchest workers, never missing a day in his seven-day work week.

The domestic life of Ras Trevor and his brethren is monastic in character, with a purely communal cooperation in the sharing of household duties and possessions. A total commitment to the Lord requires that a man abandon women and marriage: "there be eunuchs which have made themselves eunuchs for the Kingdom of Heaven's sake. He that is able to receive it, let him receive it". (Matt. 19:6) Thus, as one enters the faith, one leaves one's family. Many of the brethren in Ras Trevor's home, before becoming Ras Tafarians, had engaged in common law marriages and had fathered children; they see their children from time to time, giving them money and food and showing affection for them, but they have dismissed all familial identification with them. Their lives centre around their home, and they are absent from it only for the time they must spend cultivating vegetables or pursuing jobs which provide them with salaries sufficient to accommodate their modest needs. They built their stucco cottage themselves, and have furnished it simply but tastefully. The bright colours of the walls, the general neatness and good state of repair of their home and furnishings, the cooperative manner with which meals are prepared and served, all reflect the cheer, order and discipline with which they conduct their lives.

As the men gather for their evening meal they issue prolonged praises to the Lord and later the quiet time is devoted to reading and discussing the Bible. One of the oft-cited verses is "When my father and mother forsake me, then the Lord will take me up". (Ps. 27:10) Having been rejected by their parents (not an insignificant factor in the decision to leave their families behind), and estranged from their friends for the disgrace brought upon them by their strange appearance and way of life, they console each other by reinforcing the faith that binds them and always seek the Biblical explanation for whatever tragedy befalls them.

The brethren sought not to impress or convert me, but rather to share with me the joy which their faith has brought to them. At no time did I recognize any sign of self-consciousness, either at my presence or in their own relationships. Indeed, their most striking quality was the consideration which they showed one another, caring always for the other's needs and completely respectful of what each had to say. The fellow with the stammer and slow thought processes was listened to by the others with attentiveness and concern, and they discreetly explained his difficulties to me, asking that I show special patience with him.

The object of their worship, whom they call God and the Lord interchangeably, is not a tangible personal figure in their lives, but rather an all-encompassing world force. And when they offer "Thou shalt love no God before me" they explain that "God is all men but no man is God". They acknowledge Haile Selassie as the figure who inspired the movement toward Ras Tafarianism, and they consider their own approach as an offshoot of that movement. But they do not consider him to be God, they do not seek repatriation to Ethiopia, and indeed they accept the name "Ras Tafarian" only because society attaches it to them. "That is a name the world bestows upon us. God is our leader, and we are servants of the living God. Worshippers of Haile Selassie are members of a temporal organization - they do not have substantial wisdom".

Jacob was the first man to be made in God's image and he reveals that God is black: "I am black; astonishment hath taken hold on me" (Jer. 8:21). They do not adhere to the idea that all white people are evil, as is commonly considered as basic to Ras Tafarian thought. The oppressor may be white, but he may also be black. Just such an oppressor is the government of Jamaica, which is criticized by Ras Trevor and his brethren for the abuse laid by it upon the needy and the poor. At the same time, however, having endured a lifetime of persecution, they have come to appreciate the lessened hostility which the police express toward them.

> It is only for *ganja* that they can now persecute us - only for the herbs. We must therefore keep their eyes from it. The Lord made herbs and cattle for the use of men. Herbs are a medicine for your body. The government does not want you to use it because then you will not use their doctors. They know it is not dangerous. Herbs make you peaceful. The government does not want you to be peaceful. They want you to be violent so that they can lock you up and get you to work for the government without salary. They want you to drink rum, which makes you crazy and violent, so they can arrest you.

The apocalyptic passages in the Bible are referred to with a gentle optimism for the day when "God will speak to the world and all wickedness will cease. There will be no more earthly kingdom. We shall witness a new purified earth and it shall be heaven. So it is written". And they know themselves to be a special and chosen vanguard of the ultimate peace which God will cast on the world. Just as the world in which they live cannot accept them, neither do they aspire to an identification with that world. "We do not choose the things of the world. We are in the world, but we are not of the world. We are a peculiar, separated people, bcause the faith chose us".

When I questioned them about their reputation for violence they cited many instances of false accusations of inciting trouble, and insisted they had always "turned the other cheek" and sought peaceful resolution. "We are peaceful with our brethren, just speaking the word of God. Peace and love, sister". The answer turned out to be as superfluous as the question!

B. *The Reverend Claudius Vivian Henry, Repairer of the Breach*

> Plot to Overthrow Government - 25 Arrested in Jamaica - Police said today that they arrested a 57-year old clergyman and 24 other persons after the discovery of six homemade bombs, dynamite, shotguns, revolvers and other small arms in four police raids. They said that the clergyman, the Rev. Claudius Henry, leader of the 'Rastafari' cult, who have long matted hair and beards and believe the drug marihuana is ordained by the Bible for man's use, had been charged under the treason

law. The treason charge is said to be the first in the British colony since 1865. In peacetime the maximum penalty is life imprisonment. The police said that the series of raids had also disclosed letters between Mr Henry and Dr Castro, the Cuban Prime Minister. *(New York Times,* April 12, 1960)

Rev. Claudius Henry was convicted of the treason charge and he subsequently spent seven years in prison. He was the most notorious individual connected with the Ras Tafarians; mention of his name among non-Rastafarians invariably evoked references to the "Castro-Marxist influences" on the movement and stories of Rev Henry's alleged efforts to overthrow the government and generally disrupt Jamaican society.

To my surprise, upon meeting Rev. Henry, I found myself encountering a man who from the first greeting conveyed unusual warmth and humility. In the weeks that followed I spent many days in the company of Rev. Henry, his wife and his followers. The serenity that seemed to me to pervade the lives of all rural Ras Tafari brethren was nowhere more in evidence than in the presence of Rev. Henry and the believers of his particular approach to Ras Tafari faith.

The essential facts of Rev. Henry's early life are that he was raised by his parents as one of sixteen children in a small Jamaican village. The family lived a frugal, impoverished existence, and sought solace in a devoted faith to the teachings of the Anglican church which they attended. Claudius felt himself privileged to be able to attend school, and he showed promise as a student. His primary energy, however, was directed toward his religious activities and in disciplining his life as a 'God-fearer'.

At 17 Claudius was to receive the first of many visionary experiences, and at 21 he finally confided these experiences to his Anglican minister. The visions indicated that a male Saviour would reappear on Earth who, just as Christ before him, would lead the world into the promise of salvation. Through the medium of his visions Claudius was led to consider the meaning of Hebrews 9:28, which runs: "So Christ was once offered to bear the sins of many; and unto them that look for him shall he appear the second time without sin unto salvation". The minister in whom Claudius confided was confounded by the intensity of this young man, and it was probably at his instigation that Claudius was apprehended by authorities in 1935 on charges of lunacy. He was visited by several doctors during his internment, including the head physician of the Jamaican Ministry of Health. This doctor, after listening carefully to the content of the visions, decided that he could not in good conscience hold such a "man of simple and profound faith" any longer.

There are two sections in the Bible which Rev. Henry interprets as literal and personal commandments and which have been the dictating creeds for his life. The first of these is found in Psalms 87:1-6:

> His foundation is in the holy mountains. The Lord loveth the gates of Zion more than all the dwellings of Jacob. Glorious things are spoken of thee, O city of God. Selah. I will make mention of Rahab and Babylon to them that know me: behold Philistia, and Tyre, with *Ethiopia; this man was born there. And of Zion it shall be said,* This and that man was born in her: *and the highest himself shall establish her.* The Lord shall count, when he writeth up the people, that his man was born there. Selah.

This man, whose appearance Rev Henry had been anticipating, at last came, as he understood it, in the person of Haile Selassie, Henry subsequently announcing the Emperor as the Living God for whom the world had been waiting.

Of perhaps even greater significance for the direction which Rev. Henry's life was the message he derived from Isaiah 58. He was directed to this passage in a vision which occurred during his arraignment for lunacy. In this vision God was the instructor:

> They are planning to send you to a lunatic asylum, but you will not go there. Make up your mind to stay here for three days, not drinking water or eating bread. When you go home take your Bible and read Isaiah 58. What is written there will be bestowed on you if you are to do accordingly.

The passage which Rev. Henry read became his creed. It runs, in part, as follows:

> Is not this the fast that I have chosen? To loose the bands of wickedness, to undo the heavy burdens, and to let the oppressed go free, and that ye break every yoke? Is it not to deal thy bread to the hungry, and that thou bring the poor that are cast out to thy house? When thou seest the naked,

that thou cover him; and thy righteousness shall go before thee; the glory of the Lord shall be thy reward. And they that shall be of thee shall build the old waste places: thou shalt raise up the foundations of many generations; and thou shalt be called *The repairer of the breach.* Then shalt thou delight thyself in the Lord; and *I will cause thee to ride upon the high places of the earth, and feed thee with the heritage of Jacob thy father:* for the mouth of the Lord hath spoken it.

Thus did Rev. Henry feel himself to be personally and directly called to serve as the appointed "repairer of the breach" and to devote his lifetime to rescuing Jamaica's outcaste from neglect and oppression.

A significant turning-point in Rev. Henry's life occurred during the twelve years (1945-1957) Henry spent as an immigrant to America. It was in the United States that he was able to receive the religious instruction which led to his ordination as a minister,[24] and which gave him the resources and the impetus to return to Jamaica with the task of recovering his people from a life of material and spiritual destitution. Rev. Henry had recognized his affinity with those in Jamaica who called themselves Ras Tafarians and who worshipped, as did he, the living presence of Haile Selassie. A conversation with the Ethiopian Consul General in New York, however, had convinced him that the adherents to the Ras Tafari movement were lacking the knowledge which could lead to true salvation and were instead engaged in habits which served only to make them appear eccentric. Rev. Henry had accepted the Ras Tafari devotion to the philosophy of Marcus Garvey and their Garveyist aspirations to return to Africa. A brief 1957 journey to Ethiopia, however, convinced him that Ethiopia was not prepared for any mass immigration and that ideologically Jamaica *was already* a part of Africa, needing only to preserve its own identity and improve its own conditions with the efforts of its own people. Upon his return to Jamaica he therefore intended to organize the Ras Tafarians into a more stable, doctrinal movement and to promote among them social improvement programmes to develop their economic welfare.

When he returned to Jamaica it was with a renewed sense of purpose. By 1959 he had organized 20,000 Ras Tafarians,[25] and it was this following which produced the mass rally that led to his first arrest, on charges of fraud. After his release from prison he found himself confronted with factions within the Ras

Tafari movement and the events which followed led to his ultimate arrest for treason. Rev. Henry and his followers deny unequivocally the charges made at that arrest, and they explain that while there were internal dissidents of the movement who may have deliberately sought to discredit him in an effort to assume his authority, the most probable culprit was the government itself. Ras Tafarians commonly believe that the government plants spies and phony instigators in the movement to create factions, to cause public disturbances, and to arouse general suspicions and hostility against the movement. Thus, members of Rev. Henry's faith believe implicitly in his innocence, and are convinced that it was the government itself which placed the ammunition and the unmailed letters addressed to Castro, implicating Rev. Henry, leading to his and his wife's arrest, and resulting in the temporary and severe disruption of his programme.

During his imprisonment on treason charges, a prison stay which lasted seven years, Rev. Henry's son, Julius Henry, felt inspired to leave his New York home to return to Jamaica with the hope of gaining his father's release. He brought two black American comrades with him and in the events which followed all three were arrested, convicted and executed by hanging on charges of conspiracy to overthrow the Jamaican government.[26] The grief which engulfed Rev. Henry as he learned of this outrage from the confines of his own prison cell firmed his resolve to bring positive change to Jamaican society through the process of religious faith and industrious social reform. Recognizing himself as the appointed "repairer of the breach", he accepted his son's death as a prophetic sign that, just as Christ had been murdered by those traitors who feared God's power on earth, so would the loss of his son provide redemption for the faithful who remained.

Upon his early release from prison in 1966 Rev. Henry issued the following statement:

> I, the undersigned, adopt this medium to indicate to Government, Government agencies and the people of Jamaica in general, that my recent incarceration, notwithstanding the humiliation and embarrassment, have left me void of animosity, vindictiveness or hatred. It was most unfortunate that my purpose then, my aims and objects were wrongly evaluated and resulted in my incarceration. However, please be it understood that the height of my ambition is to be able to continue my work based on a social and religious aspect and to establish an organization founded on peace and love, geared to help the less fortunate, regardless of creed,

colour or national origin, of which there are thousands whom I am sure will adhere to conform to the laws and high principles of our Government. I am humbly appealing to be given the opportunity to prove to all concerned, my honesty of purpose and I further appeal for the assistance and cooperation of those in authority to help me to achieve these aims. The formation of this organization, be it firmly and emphatically understood that it is to be strictly a welfare organization - NON-POLITI-CAL - NON-VIOLENT.[27]

Rev. Henry has since been engaged in the arduous process of reorganization and in 1969 there were over 4,000 followers attending regular church services in four parishes across the island, identifiable by special shirts imprinted with a picture of the Black Christ and the motto 'Black Power for Peace'. Pooling their limited personal resources, adherents have constructed church buildings and have established programmes which nurture the physical and spiritual well-being of their membership. The most ambitious of these projects has been the construction of a rural school near Mandeville, a modern and attractive compound, which bears the name 'Ethiopian Peacemaker's School of Ancient Traditional Bible History'. The school, which opened in 1969, provides tuition-free education to 87 children who could otherwise not afford to attend classes, and offers them a general academic curriculum in addition to religious instruction.

Rev. Henry's wife was arrested and imprisoned at the same time as her husband. Thereafter she provided important assistance in the governing of the school.[28] Students are brought from surrounding districts in buses supplied by the organization, and the parents play a significant role in the school's operation by any material contributions they can afford along with time and energy.

In many significant respects, the Ras Tafarians who follow Rev. Henry bear little in common with other Ras Tafari brethren. In their effort to be integrated with Jamaican society they observe that society's standards with unusual propriety and care. Their hair is closely trimmed, and rarely is a 'Locksman' seen in one of his congregations. Rev. Henry's followers reject the use of *ganja*, on societal rather than on moral grounds. They seek employment through regular channels and their family unit comprises two parents and offspring, together with grandparents and other kin who may seek or require the sharing of their home. This emphasis on family ties is atypical, not just for Ras Tafarians, but for Jamaican society in general.

The adulation which Rev. Henry is accorded by his followers often approaches idolatry, and he is regularly likened to Jesus Christ, Moses, Marcus Garvey, and even Haile Selassie. The government and the Jamaican public, however, have been slow to acknowledge the value of his work. To the contrary, the years 1966-69 saw a continuing series of raids and harassments. The most discouraging of these occurred on June 5, 1968, the day which was to commemorate the opening of a new parish church in the St. Elizabeth district. Followers of Rev. Henry had crowded into three buses and two trucks and were proceeding toward St. Elizabeth when they were stopped *en route* by police who for six hours conducted a search of all persons and vehicles. Neither Rev. Henry nor any of his followers offered resistance and they were finally allowed to continue. When they arrived in St. Elizabeth, however, they were met by over 100 policemen who greeted them with tear gas, holding them off at gunpoint. Before the disturbance had ended the church and all the adjoining buildings were completely destroyed and many of the people had suffered severe beatings at the hands of the police. The incident at least caused a large public outcry, and harassment temporarily diminished.

Rev Henry, meanwhile, continued to propagate his beliefs with the conviction that ultimately his faith will bear fruitful results not only for Jamaica but for the world. As he put it,

> We are nearing a wonderful change in the world. It is not possible that the world could remain in this condition for very much longer. God, who lives and works in man, is bringing about a universal change to save suffering humanity. This is a year [i.e., 1969] of great trouble, but 1972 will end this dispensation. We will experience the beginning of a new creation. The world is made up of two things - good and evil. Good will take its course and will replace evil. Mankind will adapt itself to doing good, and we will go back to year one. A new beginning. Haile Selassie will have a large part to play in this. He bears in his body the same spirit that operated in Jesus Christ. All men bear this spirit but in most of us this spirit is dormant. Isaiah 9:6 tells us 'For unto us a child is born, unto us a son is given: and the government shall be upon his shoulder: and his name shall be called Wonderful, Counsellor, the Mighty God, the Everlasting Father, the Prince of Peace'. So will Haile Selassie reign on this earth as the Prince of Peace. Haile Selassie is the one!

C. *Ras Mosiah and Sister Gloria*

In the preceding sections A and B we have examined first the lives of Ras Julian Trevor and his brethren, who reject the divinity of Haile Selassie and the validity of repatriation, and secondly we have considered the approach of Rev. Henry and his followers, who acknowledge Haile Selassie as a deity, who accept a firm and authoritative leadership, and who reject repatriation to Ethiopia while concentrating on improving their lives by conforming to the ideals of Jamaican society. In this third section we are introduced to a family who form an interesting composite of all other approaches to Ras Tafari faith. Originally followers of Rev. Henry, they have since removed themselves from formal parish life, choosing to maintain the habits that Rev. Henry's parishioners have abandoned, such as allowing their hair to grow. At the same time, they respect Rev. Henry's faith, they agree that their responsibility is to themselves as citizens of Jamaica rather than Ethiopia, and they sustain a solid family unit.

It was nine years before that Ras Mosiah came to have the faith of the Ras Tafari. "I am not a believer. I do not just *believe* that His Imperial Majesty Haile Selassie is the Returned Messiah. I *know*." He met Sister Gloria, one of the very few lockswomen I encountered, in Rev. Henry's church in Clarendon. When Rev. Henry was imprisoned and his following was dispersed, Ras Mosiah and Sister Gloria were among the many Ras Tafarians who established a life for themselves - maintaining their faith and their customs - without hope or intent of ever returning to Rev. Henry's fold. It is true that both of them would like to feel free to occasionally attend the latter's services, but they cannot bear the stigma there of being among the few with locks.

Their locks have great symbolic significance for both Ras Mosiah and Sister Gloria. "To wear locks means to have taken a vow - it means giving up your soul to God; 'there shall be no razor come upon his head'." And yet, when asked if the wearing of locks was necessary to having the true faith of Ras Tafari, Ras Mosiah replied, "There can be a true Rasta man without locks. Because the whole armour of God does not lay only upon the locks, but in the heart. You serve God with your whole heart and it does not matter if you have locks. But for me there must be locks." [29]

Ras Mosiah and Sister Gloria have three small aughters and live as a private domestic unit in a small wattle-and-daub house on the shaded periphery of a small fishing village. Above their bed are photographs of Haile Selassie and his wife, Itegue Menen, and wrapped around the photographs are strands of "black power" beads, mad from locally gathered seeds. Decorating the walls of the room are red, gold and green stream-ers, signifying the Ethiopian flag. And parallel to these are streamers of black and gold, honouring the Jamaican flag.

Mosiah, like Ras Trevor, is exceptional in that he has acquired a government job, working for the Public Works Department. However, he also cultivates *ganja* in the forest near his home, and there is constant traffic of customers to his home to buy the herb.[30] Always Mosiah would offer me a smoke in his chillum pipe, and when I declined he would admonish, "You must begin to use it. It is the way to the tree of life. It is the Healing of the Nation. Nothing chose from the herbs given by God should be taken from us. Eventually even the birds feed on the seeds. You burn herbs. And you boil it and drink it as tea. When I have my little herbs I could never think of anything evil - only good. And I can meditate on the mountain of Zion."

Where Mosiah is stern and sober, Gloria is a warmly affectionate young woman, who quietly tends to her children's needs and lovingly meets her husband's demands. She is intensely quiet, but not afraid, and when Mosiah defers to her, she speaks clearly of her faith and her life in the village. Her children were all born at home, with the help of a midwife. Like all the Ras Tafarians with whom I spoke, she and Mosiah speak disparagingly of government efforts to promote family planning. "It fights against the will of God. Only God can make life and we have no right to stop it".

Ras Tafarians are commonly said to refute the value of education, but invariably the attitudes conveyed to me were consistent with the following comment of Ras Mosiah: "We want education for our girl so she can write the message, as you do. Writing is such a great thing, and one must be able to read. We are being robbed of that. The government just talks, and no action." Rasta children often do attempt to attend public classes, but they are usually put down by school officials and the other children alike. Often they are forced to cut their locks, or physically punished without provocation. Thus Rasta families tend not to send their children to public schools and attempt instead to provide them with the rudiments of learning at home. That they are successful is evident in the ease with which children are able to read from the Bible.

Plate 7. A Rastaman teaching Amharmic

Plate 8. A Rural Rastawoman and Brethren

Mosiah and Gloria spoke often, but without apparent bitterness, of the harsh treatment which they have received at the hands of authorities. They formerly lived in a large Ras Tafarian camp which was broken up by police in 1966. Four children, including their one-year-old daughter, were taken away. They were never able to locate their child and do not yet know what became of her. The adults were stripped and beaten, their camp was destroyed, and all the inhabitants were sent to prisons in Kingston and Spanish Town. Mosiah spent 18 months in the Kingston prison, where he was shaven and continually tortured.

The social indignities which Mosiah and Gloria have suffered are reflected upon and accepted with philosophical equanimity. Among the adjustments which they have had to make is the acceptance of their families' rejection of them. "The prophet says there shall be one from a family. It is as in ancient times. And it is God who must select." Indeed, I never found an instance in which a Ras Tafarian was *not* the single member of his or her primary family to have adopted the faith. Mosiah reiterates the common view that faith is "an inborn conception" which one is born with, and which not everyone can have.

Ras Mosiah and Sister Gloria hold a quiet confidence in the future and, echoing Rev Henry, they looked to 1972 as the year when

> There will be great changes in the world. Haile Selassie is the returned Messiah, but the Scripture says you must find your own vine and fig tree, wherever you are. You don't have to be in Africa. There will be a new dispensation. God's kingdom will come to power. This will be the great battle of Armageddon. After this battle the survivors shall live with God forever and forever. The whole earth will be Africa - anywhere you want to go. Because righteousness will cover the world.

They acknowledge Marcus Garvey as the forerunner of Selassie and of him Mosiah avowed, "He was a very great prophet, like John the Baptist. He taught us that we are of one unity. We must love all our brethren, black and white. One love. One heart. The joy of the Ras Tafari would be if everyone could light the star - One light. One love. One heart." I heard this family sing in a low, barely audible voice the chant *"Niyabingi, Niyabingi"* (death to the black and white oppressors), yet this retribution is not understood to be in their hands, but an outcome of the divinely planned eschatological future.

D. *Ras Chaka*

The Ras Tafari[31] did not begin with Haile Selassie. It had been going on since the beginning of time - for ever. The coronation was the beginning of the celebration of the arrival of the Ras Tafari. 1930 was the time when Ras Tafarians became conscious of the fulfilment of the book of Revelation toward the Returned Messiah. Because Christ said he was going to prepare a place for us that where He is there will 'I and I' [32] be also.

The above statement belongs to Ras Chaka, a young Jamaican who spent five years living and working in New York City. He left New York upon losing his job for refusing to cut his locks. And in the few years since his return to Jamaica he has adopted a complete identification with the Ras Tafari movement. Ras Chaka is a skilled artist; he researched and wrote a lengthy and articulate essay on the subject of slavery; he is the father of two small sons who live with him; and he is a beloved, though unofficial, leader of the large group of young Jamaicans who share his small country home. Above all, however, Ras Chaka is an ardent and altogether committed member of that large (though unorganized) group of Ras Tafarians who believe implicitly in the divinity of Haile Selassie and whose life's purpose is dedicated to the adulation of His Imperial Majesty and the ultimate goal of repatriation to Ethiopia.

Unlike his more mystical brethren, who wait in silent expectation for that glorious reunion with the Returned Messiah, Ras Chaka is an energetic spokesperson for his faith. He travels around the island, acquainting himself with his brethren, expressing his faith with the aid of a sophisticated knowledge of the Scriptures, and punctuating his praises to Haile Selassie with loud denunciation of Babylon. [33]

The Ras Tafarians whom Ras Chaka represents, more than any other single group within the movement, conform closely to the stereotypical attitudes and behavioural patterns that the wider Jamaican society attributes to Ras Tafarians in general. Unlike the group for whom Ras Trevor spoke, Ras Chaka and his brethren expressed emphatic belief in the divinity of Selassie:

Haile Selassie is Alpha and Omega. Beginning without End. First without Last. Protectorate of our Human Faith. The Architect and Builder of the

Universe. Mighty Creator. The Earth's Rightful Ruler. The Returned Messiah. Prince of Peace. Negus Negusti. King of Kings. Lord of Lords.

The Bible names seventy-two such titles as belonging to the Divine God, and Ras Chaka recited them all interchangeably in his references to Haile Selassie.

Unlike Rev Henry's followers, Ras Chaka denies the legitimacy of a leader for the Ras Tafari movement. "I and I, Ras TafarI, we do not want any leader. Selassie-I can lead us anywhere. Selassie-I is a lamp unto my feet and a light to my path. I follow no temporal man; I follow the internal power that supports me. Jah,[34] Selassie-I, Ras TafarI." And unlike Ras Mosiah and Sister Gloria, for whom Ethiopia has primarily symbolic significance, Ras Chaka believes in and plans literally for the day when all of the chosen will make their way to African soil: "Ethiopia is heaven. All Ras Tafarians will gather on the shores of Ethiopia - the land of our fathers. Open the gate and let me repatriate." It is not known just how and when such repatriation will occur, and there is little discussion of practical problems inherent in such a journey. But that it will happen, and that it will happen soon, there is no doubt.

The unemployment that plagues urban Ras Tafarians is felt less acutely by Ras Chaka and his rural brethren, of whatever persuasion their Ras Tafarian faith might take them. Some are fishermen, and many are tillers of the soil. On small plots of land they grow their own crops and vegetables, and raise their own goats. All produce which is not needed for their own consumption is carried to a village market to be sold. They own scant material possessions and even those few Ras Tafarians who have a job or work privately as artists, craftsmen, or as *ganja* dealers, share their incomes with their brethren and acquire only the barest essentials for themselves.

Lives are kept as simple and unemcumbered as possible, tastes are unpretentious, and the only objects which they prize highly are those which enhance or symbolize their faith: a red-gold-green Ethiopian flag, which they wave as a banner or display on the walls of their home; photographs of Haile Selassie which are framed and prominently displayed; the Bible; miscellaneous literature related to Africa, Ethiopia and Haile Selassie; Amharic textbooks, which they study assiduously in an effort to "recapture" their native language; a variety of drums which they paint in the colours of the Ethiopian flag and play in accompaniment to the songs which they sing in jubilant exhortation of their beloved Haile Selassie; and perhaps most importantly, their pipe.

The use of *ganja* is a sacred ritual among all Ras Tafarians excepting those of Rev Henry's faith. Says Ras Chaka:

> The herb is a natural thing. God said he created every green herb of the field that bears seeds, and it was good. It is a spiritual plant and it is divine. It has a lot to do with our meditation toward the Almighty. It does not show you who is the Almighty, but it puts you in a meditative mood. By locking off the outside world we can have our meditation. It is the Healing of the Nation. Our pipe is our Holy Chalice. We smoke with humility to God. We smoke with love. Jah, Ras TafarI. One happiness. One destiny. One love. Ras TafarI. The Almighty God.

While the Rasta men are smoking, the women who associate with them (only a few of whom may identify themselves as Rasta women) move together and smoke from their own special pipe. To do so is "right in the black house of David."

Such brethren reject both the cloistered life of Ras Trevor and the conventional marriages of Rev. Henry's followers and Mosiah and Gloria.

> To take care of only one wife and not look after the rest - that is bondage. Everyone that love I, I love them also. The trouble of the world is that one takes care of only one; but if you take only one wife there might be 100 without one to care for them. And then there is jealousy. Ras Tafarians are not going to stand up before the pastor and get married. True love is marriage, and marriage is true love - wherever you love, whenever you love, whoever you love.

Thus families exist only insofar as attachments and needs remain, and the children are cared for in the same communal spirit as is conducted all aspects of domestic life. "The young must be fed. The sick must be nourished. The naked need have clothes. All should be loved."

The subject of birth control invariably causes an irate response from Ras Tafarians.

> Birth control is introduced by the oppressor and utilized by white-hearted members of our race. It is a most murderous and ungodly attitude, created

to degrade and attenuate our health, dignity and rapid reproduction. Family planning is educated murder. It slows down the reproduction of the black race.

We have alluded earlier to the discouragement experienced by Ras Tafarians who endeavour to keep their children in public schools. Such efforts generally result in failure because the child simply cannot withstand the taunts and punishments of classmates and teachers. The abuse is particularly directed, of course, toward those children who have adopted their parents' habit of allowing their hair to grow in long, matted or twisted plaits.[35]

The question of hair is an important one to all Ras Tafarians. Not only are the locks the most conspicuous badge of identification, it is also one of their most significant concerns as members of the faith. As Ras Chaka put it,

> My body is a living temple of the living God, to keep the living truth. The locks are the secret covenant against wrongs. To accept this glory of Ras Tafarī you have to put away the razor, scissors, shame and sin and disgrace. When you use the comb you take-off your body.

Frequently discussed, however, are those many adherents to the Ras Tafari faith who do not grow locks. They explain that such persons are "just becoming awakened to the facts - when they fully understand and realize their faith, when they no longer have doubt, they will then begin to show full locks."

It is commonly accepted that early Ras Tafarians began to grow their locks after having seen photographs of African warriors, whose full plaited locks were their most distinguishing physical trait. Says Ras Chaka:

> We the black people of Africa are very much accustomed to such locks. There is nothing strange in it to us. Even the slaves who came, came in that attire. It is we, the black people, who are the sheep of God's pasture; we are the only people who carry wool on our heads.

To supply the scriptural legitimacy of the custom they cite Num. 6:5, "There shall be no razor come upon his head", and Lev. 21:5, "They shall not make baldness upon their head, neither shall they shave off the corner of their beard, nor make any cuttings in their flesh". To wear locks is to make a statement of one's faith; it is to offer oneself in total commitment to the teachings of the Bible and to the divinity of Haile Selassie. It is to deliberately and unequivocally separate oneself, physically and spiritually, from the evil forces of Babylon.

At the same time, however, Ras Tafarians agree that there are men who use their locks for false purposes and that such men cannot be properly called Ras Tafarians, despite their outward appearance. "He might be a madman who just does not cut his hair and comb it. And as in any organization, there are wolves in sheep's clothing." The wolves referred to are those disparate personalities who wear locks as a shield for illegal activity. Such men might be active criminals, or they might represent a government conspiracy against the movement with individuals posing as Ras Tafarians who infiltrate the movement, provoking internal disruptions and giving cause for arrests. Still others might grow locks to earn the trust of brethren whom they would then exploit for propagandist interests, such as, in Ras Chaka's words, "the planting of Marxist revolutionary ideas."[36] On the other hand, most "false locksmen" are seen as well-intentioned individuals who would like to have faith, or who want for various innocent reasons to identify with the movement, but who are not able to believe they are not among the chosen.

Pride in appearance, pride in an African heritage, and a keen sense of self-worth are marked characteristics of all the Ras Tafarians I came to know, and these are especially evident among Ras Chaka and those of his persuasion. It is their religious faith which gives them their particular sense of worth and esteem and they have been affected by the teachings of Marcus Garvey, whom they recognize as an important prophet and whose advocacy of dignity and autonomy for the black race has become an inherent part of their philosophy. To extol the virtue of blackness is not necessarily to negate the non-coloured peoples of the world, but a history of slavery and colonialism has done nothing to deter the hatred that is felt toward the white oppressor. The word *Niyabingi* ('death to the black and white oppressors) (see above) has become a kind of password among many Ras Tafarians. Generally (and without exception in terms of my own experience) this does not imply an active effort or intention to obliterate white people through sheer physical force and destruction. Rather, it suggests the *inevitable* fall of Babylon on the day that repatriation occurs and/or wickedness is replaced by good. Ras Chaka thus remarks,

On the great day of repatriation, the white oppressors and the white-hearted traitors will be devoured. They will burn. Their cities will be
destroyed. Babylon will fall and we, the chosen, will rejoice in heaven, on
the shores of Ethiopia.[37]

It is perhaps such verbal attacks on the white oppressor and Jamaican society
that have helped to perpetuate the fear that middle-class Jamaicans so often display in the presence of Ras Tafarians. On several occasions, while walking with
urban Ras Tafarian friends through busy city streets, I would witness the fum-
bling efforts of a passer-by to move from our path, his face showing unmistak-
able terror. (A terror perhaps compounded by my own very unlikely presence in
the group). The younger of the brethren in our midst would immediately exploit
this fear by shrieking "Blood and Fire - *Niyabingi!!*" and the frightened person
would scurry away as the young mischief-makers would howl with gleeful
laughter. Such incidents, however, do not constitute violence, and I know of no
instance where, without distinct and direct provocation, physical violence has
been imposed by a Ras Tafarian against another member of society, however
threateningly they may verbally indicate such intentions.

A concern for the world's oppressed peoples is an underlying theme among
Ras Chaka and his brethren. And it is thus not surprising that there has recently
been an increasing rapport building up between Ras Tafarians and those
Jamaicans who identify with a black power movement. Of that movement, Ras
Chaka says,

The black power people are coming to a consciousness of the black man,
a consciousness which the Ras Tafarian has always had. But the concept
of the Ras Tafarians means that Haile Selassie is the Almighty God. Black
power, you see, is still seeking that light, still searching for their path. The
Black Panthers, Malcolm X, etc. are all seeking a black goal, a goal which
will take some form of redemption from oppression and slavery. By seeking they will find that Ras TafarI is the Almighty God, for if you ask it
shall be given unto you. Knock and it shall be opened. But they haven't
found that yet. They will. The truth will be accomplished all over the
world. Ras Tafarians are the pioneers of black consciousness and can be a
medium of inspiration - a medium for Peace and Love.

Conclusions

This essay illustrates the heterogeneous nature of the Rastafarianism and the conjoint difficulties that one can expect to encounter in analyzing the meaning and significance of that movement. Earlier studies have posited certain definitive conclusions and while these studies must be credited with having contributed significantly to our knowledge of the Ras Tafaris it will be seen that not all of their conclusions can be applied without qualification to the movement as a whole.

Professor Simpson concluded in 1955 that

> The social-psychological functions of the Ras Tafari movement... include: compensation for the humiliations and deprivations of a lowly social station; emotional warmth and friendship of the leader and like-minded believers; hope for a better life in the other world; recreation; opportunities for self-expression through singing, speech-making, procession-leading, and costume-wearing; recognition through office- holding or as a speaker, musician, organizer or fund-raiser; and economic assistance at such critical times as serious illness, death in the family, and court trials.[37]

There is little in the above statement which corresponds to the data which I present in the preceding pages. And the few weeks which Professor Simpson spent in observation of the movement could have afforded him little opportunity for acquainting himself with the non-urban Ras Tafarians with whom I spent the bulk of the research and among whom I observed no instance of "procession-leading, costume-wearing, fund-raising or (except with Rev. Henry) speech-making and leadership."

The previously discussed 1960 survey conducted by Professors Smith, Augier and Nettleford[38] has received much-deserved attention for its descriptive value and comprehensive statement of recommendations. And despite the failure of the government to have taken those recommendations seriously in practice, apart from the mission to Africa and the somewhat diminished police brutality, the merits of this report are unquestioned. Nowhere else is there such a precise, perceptive and detailed report on the doctrines and conditions of the Ras Tafari movement. Yet even this study is limited in that the authors, for reasons of time and funding, were unable to move beyond the urban boundaries. Much of their findings is consequently inapplicable to the very large Ras Tafari population scattered throughout the rural areas of the island. Additionally, one of the basic premises accorded by them to Ras Tafari doctrine, i.e. Ethiopia is the black homeland, and repatriation will occur shortly, is no longer accepted by all Ras Tafarians as a literal truth.

The 1964 article by Orlando Patterson is founded on the conviction that the Ras Tafari movement, which he describes as an expression of "aggressive withdrawal", is based on a millenarian philosophy of hope - hope for the return to the Promised Land. "One can live in, and desire to live in, and only in, hope... The moment - the crisis, the burden, the humiliation, the despair... is resolved in pure expectation, sheer possibility."[39] I would suggest that this thesis is correct; the Ras Tafarian, in all the forms, does indeed live each day with eyes cast on a horizon of hope for the future. One must again take cognizance of the fact, however, that for a great number of Ras Tafarians Ethiopia has become a "homeland" only in the most figurative sense, and that for a significant number repatriation has likewise assumed a more symbolic than literal quality, as seen in the sections on Ras Trevor, Ras Mosiah and Sister Gloria, and Rev. Henry. This recognized, Dr Patterson is nevertheless correct in defining the Ras Tafari movement as a millenarian expression.

The apocalyptic emphasis of the Ras Tafarians finds clear classificatory definition in the 1962 discussion by Yonina Talmon the nature of millenarian movements.[40] The first characteristic which Dr Talmon delineates as important to such a movement is a linear attitude toward time. It is through a linear process that changes will occur and the millennium is an imminent occurrence which is tensely planned and prepared for. And while most millenarian movements reject the past, Talmon allows for those exceptions - the Ras Tafarians for one - who view the future as a return to a mythical 'golden age'. At the risk of extreme redundancy it must again be mentioned that this aspect of a millenarian definition can only apply to those brethren who, like Ras Chaka, actually anticipate a return to African soil.

A second feature described by Dr Talmon is that there is sometimes an absence of leadership in millenarian movements. While Rev. Henry here provides us with a clearcut exception, it is unquestionably true that Ras Tafarians are strongly collective in orientation (collective insofar as their physical and ideological diffusion can allow) and they follow a purely democratic system of organization. Thirdly, the Ras Tafarian is increasingly conforming to Talmon's observation that "there is a strong activist militant ingredient in the millenarian ideology", although two distinct qualifications must here be made. First, the statement is extended to indicate that the activist elements of the movement often outweigh the passive elements. This would be distinctly untrue of the Ras Tafarians, with the activist element a new, though increasing, phenomenon. The second qualification is that the activist element of the movement is confined almost exclusively to the urban area and is thus not wholly relevant to a discussion of the rural brethren who constitute the primary focus of this study.

A last point is that although many millenarian movements, like many nativistic movements, are messianic, there are those exceptions which allow the leader to function as a source of symbolic identification, even though exerting no authority or self-initiated leadership. Clearly this is true of most Ras Tafarians, and the peculiar deification-from-a-distance which the Ras Tafarians accorded Haile Selassie, without his acknowledgement or consent, may well emerge as the most unique feature of the religion.

An additional speculative comparison between the Ras Tafarians and the hypothetical millenarians, as posited by Talmon, is the possibility of viewing a millenarian movement as a prototype of modern revolutionary movements, employing neo-Marxian (or popularized Marxist) theory as an effective vehicle upon which to attach an analysis of social change. I have elsewhere referred to the fact that the Ras Tafarians have been credited (or discredited) with Marxian tendencies, and I have emphasized that if this is the case it must apply strictly to individuals in those urban centres with which this study has only been peripherally concerned. However, it behoves us to ask whether there are authentic Marxist influences on the movement, or whether the label has been imposed by over-zealous sociological observers, whose negative inferences do justice neither to authentic Marxist theory or practice, nor to the Ras Tafarians themselves. I consider the latter applies.

David Aberle writes that "no cult movement fits neatly into any one compartment alone"[41] and given the extremely heterogeneous quality of the Ras Tafari movement, we would do well to avoid inflexible definitions. Indeed, if the definition of a "cult" implies "*ritual* observances involved in the worship of, or communion with, particular supernatural persons or objects or their symbolic representations - a stable set of beliefs and myths centering around the rites -"[42] then we also cannot assign the label of "cult" to the Ras Tafarians, who have a marked absence of rituals or rites (unless *ganja* smoking be taken as such).

Nonetheless, whether a cult or not, if a basic characteristic of a millenarian movement is a planned, desired and dramatic change, the Ras Tafarians can surely be appropriately described by this categorical distinction. The single thread which runs through the doctrinal heart of all Ras Tafari life is the implicit faith that great changes will occur. For some, like Ras Chaka, this means a literal return to Ethiopia. For others it means a destruction of Babylon and a simultaneous victory for Ethiopia, as symbolic of heaven. For yet others it is simply an inevitable change in which the masses will revolt, governments will be overthrown, and the oppressed will assume the commanding role. "The meek shall inherit the earth" becomes, then, a militant cry for power.

The conviction that goodness will replace evil is likewise inherent in the Ras Tafarian's anticipation of change. Just as is the belief that the black peoples of the earth represent good, and the white oppressor represents evil. In both cases, however, exceptions are acknowledged. There are white-hearted blacks, to be sure, but so are there black-hearted whites. Ultimately it becomes a sometimes difficult task of revealing the content of one's heart, rather than the colour of one's skin, that determines the judgement of which side one stands upon while waiting for the apocalypse.

The real concern of the Ras Tafarian, then, is not how or when the apocalypse will occur, but rather in separating oneself from those evil forces which have allowed the world to dichotomize its people into relegated ranks of oppressed and oppressor. For some Ras Tafarians this concern is expressed through efforts toward justice for Jamaica's dispossessed. For others it becomes a philosophical issue of universal proportions, both on a contemporary and a historical level. For yet others the focus is strictly on a Biblical world-view in which events of 2,000 years ago receive literal transference and application to events of today,
as fulfilment of scriptural prophecy and with no heed paid to the historical developments and reversals of the time spanned in between.

Of whatever stance or persuasion, certainly the most pervasive and distinctive quality of Ras Tafari life is the utterly sincere and profound devotion of its members to religious thought and practice. The Ras Tafarians have been recognized as having political significance, particularly at the urban level and certainly as a potentiality of the movement, but it is first and foremost as a religious experience that the Ras Tafari movement sustains and perpetuates its self-identity. For the individual Ras Tafarian this sense of identity can, of course, assume a variety of qualities. The essential character of those Ras Tafarians met through this survey, however, revealed a peculiar strength and confidence - both in themselves and in the future of society and the world - which is unique among members of the wider Jamaican society. Nurtured and sustained by a keen sense of high self-esteem and unquestioned worth as one of God's chosen few, the Ras Tafarian has borne the ability to withstand humiliation and deprivation with an attendant psychological refusal to succumb to a position of inferiority.

If there are lessons to be learned from the Ras Tafarians they will not come from the asking of such questions as "What is the rationale behind the deification of Haile Selassie?" or "How can they expect to be transported en masse to Ethiopia?" These and similar questions and intellectual provocations are dismissed by the Ras Tafarians as simple admittances to a lack of faith. The real significance of the Ras Tafari movement is that it has endured and it has survived, and it shows every promise of continuing to grow and developing ever-new manifestations, without ever losing that unwavering faith that is so basic to Ras Tafari life and doctrine. A people who is not only unwilling to submit to the pressures of an aggrieved majority, but who is able to stand aloof from those pressures in a way that shields their beliefs and preserves their integrity can and should be enthusiastically recognized. That recognition should come in the form of social acceptance of Ras Tafarians within Jamaican society; it should also serve as an illustrative model for all oppressed peoples who strive to retain their unique character in the face of hostility and rejection. For those of us who desire to learn from the remarkable experience and beliefs of Ras Tafarians, we must first seek the right questions in the hope that relevant answers and solutions can grow from them.

Epilogue

During the decade following this study the island of Jamaica was plagued with political ferment and economic deterioration. Hunger was commonplace. Death and rage spilled on to the streets of Kingston, where a majority of the city's 3/4 million population was (and remains) in dire need of jobs, food, housing, schooling, and medical care. Gang warfare and unauthorized expressions of rivalry between the People's National Party (PNP) and the Jamaica Labour Party (JLP) resulted in the random killings of at least 400 people in 1980 alone. A series of assassination attempts were committed against real or symbolically powerful public figures on every side of the political arena. Michael Manley survived at least one attempt on his life during his term as PNP Prime Minister, and likewise Edward Seaga, head of the JLP, whose party was returned to office during the 1980 election. Prior to the election a U.S. diplomat to Jamaica, believed by many Jamaicans to be a covert representative of the USA Central Intelligence Agency, was the target of heavy gunfire into his house and the explosion of a bomb on his lawn.[43]

Bob Marley was another prominent Jamaican who was wounded but who survived gunfire that blasted into his home. What distinguished Bob Marley from other assassination targets was that he was a Ras Tafarian. He was also the leading international ambassador of Jamaican reggae music, before dying of cancer on May 11, 1981.

Reggae is indigenous to Jamaica but it carries the musical influence of centuries of traditions from Africa and South America, and it is kin to the popular music forms that have evolved in the Afro-American community in the United States. Since the early 1970s, reggae music has had phenomenal success as an imported popular art form on every continent. Through this music the Ras Tafarian faith has affected the consciousness of youth culture and progressive political communities in many countries - most significantly through Bob Marley's recordings and global concert tours. Albums are the most concrete evidence of this phenomenon, and these are referred to subsequently. It would be redundant to list them here, I believe.

The most important development in Ras Tafarian life and thought in the past decade has been the evolving synthesis of political and spiritual concerns. In

1969 the Jamaican Black Power movement was gaining momentum as a renegade political force on behalf of Jamaica's poor masses and as a base of political theory among progressive intellectuals. Simultaneously the Ras Tafarians were gathering young followers who were seeking a spiritual bonding and release from material frustrations. In the earliest days of Jamaican history runaway slaves had fashioned a system of communication through the rugged mountains whereby they used a cow horn, called an *Abeng,* to call coded messages to one another. *Abeng,* to reiterate, is the name given to a Black Power movement newspaper, which was passed hand to hand across the island and which featured many writings by Ras Tafarians - including political analysis as well as Ras Tafarian history, philosophical essays, poetry, and Amharic language instruction. The Kingston-based journal was bringing together the voices of Black Power, for whom the memory and writings of Marcus Garvey offered inspiration, and the voices of Ras Tafarians, who likewise looked to Garvey as the prophet of their movement. The *Abeng* office was bombed and vandalized repeatedly, but persisted in carrying the message of rebellion across the island. Reggae artists have carried that message across continents and political lines. The music combines the Ras Tafarian faith that good will overcome evil with the Black Power commitment to active confrontation against economic and political injustice.

Politics pervade Jamaican reality and many Ras Tafarians throughout the island found a political voice through reggae. In every revolutionary movement the people create and discover their own music. The unique significance of reggae is that it moved beyond the small island which gave birth to it and entered the sound waves of every English-speaking country in the world. The message seems universally clear, as shown in the following lyrics, excerpted from albums by Bob Marley and the Wailers:

> A hungry mob is a angry mob
> A rain a fall but the dirt it tough
> A pot a cook but the food no' nough
> A hungry mob is a angry mob.[45]

> Get up, stand up
> Stand up for your rights
> Get up, stand up

Don't give up the fight[46]

From the very day we left the shores
    of our father's land
We've been trampled on, oh now
Now we know everything we got to rebel
Somebody got to pay for the work
We've done. Rebel.[46]

The political message of Bob Marley's music is direct and explicit. The spiritual message reaches deeply into the apocalyptic premises that have sustained the Ras Tafarian movement:

I hear the words of the Rasta Man say
Babylon you throne gone down, gone down[47]

Let righteousness cover the earth
like the water cover the sea
Lightning, thunder, brimstone and fire[47]

Now the fire is burning
Out of control, panic in the city
Wicked weeping for their gold
Everywhere the fire is burning
Destroying and melting their gold
Destroying and wasting their souls[47]

Reggae lyrics acknowledge the pain that all Ras Tafarians have suffered, but it also states the optimistic refusal to be defeated by suffering:

Fear not for mighty dread
Cause I'll be there at your side
And down there, down there in the ghetto
And down there, we suffer
But I and I hang on in there
And I and I, I naw leggo
So Jah seh[48]

Hear the children crying
but I know they're not crying in vain

now the times are changing
love buds come to bloom again[48]

The musical synthesis of millenarian conviction and active defiance reflects the remarkable influence which Ras Tafarians have had in the past decade not only in Jamaica but on international cultural and political consciousness. The many bodies of the Rastas may not yet have crossed the oceans, but the voice of their millennial dreaming certainly has.

Notes

1. The Ras Tafari movement is primarily comprised of and pervasively dominated by men. This reality may well be challenged as the international
   women's liberation movement continues to gain momentum and definition.
   However, during the period of the research and writing of this study, Jamaica
   women, including those who identified with the Ras Tafarian movement,
   were very much subject to the gender-based restrictions on participation,
   expression and influence within a society based on patriarchal traditions and
   assumptions. Thus, my use of male gender pronouns throughout this paper
   reflects the masculine predominance within the Ras Tafarian movement in
   1969. Cf. also Plate 8.
2. The word 'Ras', translated from Amharic as 'governor', refers to the political
   title carried by Tafari Makonnen prior to his coronation as Emperor, at which
   time he adopted the name Haile Selassie.
3. D.L. Levine, *Wax and Gold: tradition and innovation in Ethiopian culture*,
   Chicago, 1965, p.151.
4. Cf. A.J. Garvey, *Garvey and Garveyism*, Kingston, 1963.
5. Opinion among present-day Ras Tafarians is varied with regard to Howell,
   with some revering his name and honouring his intentions, others considering
   him irrelevant, and still others having never heard of him. On Niyabingi, see
   M.G. Smith, B. Augier and R. Nettleford, *The Tastafari Movement in
   Kingston, Jamaica*, Kingston, 1960, p.7.
6. For an excellent account of *ganja* use among working class Jamaicans see V.
   Rubin and L. Comitas, *Ganja in Jamaica: The Effects of Marijuana Use*,
   New York, 1976. This medical anthropological research offers a multidisci-
   plinary analysis of the cultural, physiological and psychological parameters
   of *ganja* use. It is a thorough and well-documented report which dispels the
   negative stereotypes and prejudicial myths which have plagued marijuana
   users for the past century, stressing the harmless and beneficial qualities of
   cannabis sativa in its various forms.
7. Quoted in O. Patterson, "Ras Tafari: the Cult of Outcasts", in *New Society*, 12
   (Nov. 1964), p. 16.
8. G.E. Simpson, "Political Cultism in West Kingston, Jamaica", in *Social and*

Economic Studies, June 1955, pp. 133-49.

9. For additional details on the life and activities of Rev. Henry, who remains today an important personage of the Ras Tafari movement, see second sect., B.

10. Smith *et al., loc.cit.*, p.16.

11. K. Norris, *Jamaica: the Search for an Identity*, London, 1962, p.56.

12. Smith, *et al., loc. cit.*, p.39. See the Foreword of this book, however, on the current existence of a Rastafarian community in Ethiopia.

13. It was not only the Ras Tafarians who were impressed when, after weeks of steady rainfall, the appearance of Haile Selassie and the emergence of the sun coincided at precisely the same moment!

14. C.V. Black, *History of Jamaica* (1953), London and Glasgow, 1965.

15. Norris, *op.cit.*, p.100.

16. Patterson, *The Children of Sisyphys*, Kingston, 1968.

17. Patterson, loc.cit., p.15.

18. *Abeng* is the name given to the cow horns which were used by the Maroons, a revolutionary group of runaway slaves who, early in Jamaica's history, established themselves in the most remote and rugged hills, sending messages across to each other by codes devised with the use of their cow horns.Jamaica received independence from Britain in 1962. Although there is no longer official outside control of the island, neo-colonialist phenomena remain nevertheless, causing disenchantment and arousing protest by black power conscious Jamaicans. School children, for example, still use textbooks which are designed for British children and which generally make no mention of Jamaican history or culture. Likewise, the bauxite and tourist industries, which comprise the largest revenues for the island, are held by American and Canadian business interests.

19. Dr Nettleford has offered a major contribution to the process of educating the larger Jamaican society about the reality and substance of Ras Tafari life with the publication of his book *Mirror, Mirror: Identity, Race and Protest in Jamaica* (Kingston, 1970). In this work he analyzes the Rastafarians' importance in having "forced the society into self-examination" and influencing "the traditional (Jamaican) power elites towards a social philosophy that dare not ignore (the Ras Tafarians) and their aspirations". (p.111, and cf. p.61 for

quotation in the text). Other studies to note include S. Kitzinger, "The Rastafarian Brethren of Jamaica", in *Comparative Studies in Society and History*, (1966), pp. 33-39; L. Barrett, *The Rastafarians*, Boston, 1977; T. Nicholas and B. Sparrow, *Rastafari; a way of life*, Garden City, 1979.

20. The 1960 census as published by the Jamaican Department of Statistics shows a total island population of 1,600,000. This means that the Ras Tafarians would comprise a maximum of 2.8% of the total population, with the figure more apt to be close to 1.9%.

21. Professor Simpson has listed the following passages as Ras Tafari favourites and his list is compatible with my own findings: Numbers 6; Isaiah 43, 44, 47, 34, 3 and 9; Proverbs 8; Jeremiah 50, 51, 9, 8 and 2; Amos 9 and 3; Malachi 1; Revelation 18, 17, 6, 5, 22 and 19; James 5; Lamentations 5; Joel 3 and 34; Zechariah 8 and 14; Micah 4; Deuteronomy 28, 30 and 4; Ezekiel 37 and 48; Daniel 2, 7 and 12; Leviticus 25; Psalms 87, 27, 68, 48, 97, 99, 140 and 135; Genesis 2 and 18; Habakkuk 2 and 3; and the First Epistle of John 4. (Simpson, *loc.cit.*:p.137)

22. With the exception of Rev Henry, whose reputation is so public and well-known that attempts at anonymity would be futile and without benefit, I have used pseudonyms to protect them from any possibility of negative repercussion.

23. For an excellent account of the marriage customs of Jamaican society refer to Madeline Kerr's *Personality and Conflict in Jamaica, London, 1952*, and likewise, Judith Blake's *Family Structure in Jamaica*, London, 1953. These studies examine the phenomenon of a society in which the father is often absent, marriage is seldom legally finalized, and family units are frequently based on ties other than kinship.

24. Rev. Henry was ordained in Cleveland as a Baptist minister. However, he did not maintain an affiliation or doctrinal acceptance of this denomination, despite his oft-expressed gratitude for their supplying him with professional tools.

25. The figure, supplied by Rev. Henry, is substantiated by general opinion.

26. The confusions which abound in the contradictory reports of this incident defy clarification in the absence of more thorough investigation.

27. This document was printed by Rev. Henry's "Ethiopian Peacemaker's School

of Ancient Traditional Bible History", and given to me by the author himself.

28. Mrs Henry died mysteriously while *en route* to shopping on February 26, 1970. It appeared to Rev. Henry and members of the organization that she had been violently assaulted. The police declined to investigate.

29. I was frequently told by members of Rev. Henry's churches and by assorted other trimmed Ras Tafarians, that locks are essential to faith but that the abuses by the government against locksmen necessitate, for one's protection, the "wearing of my locks in my heart".

30. *Ganja* use is popular among workers within Jamaican society, and Ras Tafarians find themselves in demand as *ganja* cultivators. There are periodic public outcries against this increased "drug" habit, with debates over whether or not the *ganja* plant contains the staminate, or male plant. Ras Tafarians are greatly amused over "this question of sex" of their "little herb" and enjoy entertaining themselves with references to "Jamaica's sex problem".

31. The capitalized "I" represents the vocal emphasis which Ras Chaka and those who share his faith place on the last syllable as they chant "Ras TafarI - Ras TafarI - Ras TafarI is our God and King!" It derives and/or is derived from the phrase "I and I". (see n.32).

32. With the phrase "I and I" the Ras Tafarian addresses himself to the totality of his harmonious universe, of which Haile Selassie is the guide and the source of all power and inspiration. "'I and I' means every individual person and the internal power that reigns within I. I and Selassie; Selassie and I; you in me; me in you; I and I - the God in Man".

33. "Babylon" is the word used by all Ras Tafarians to denote evil and the oppressor. It can refer to a life of wickedness, an oppressive individual, the police, the government, an imperialist nation, or a "white-hearted" black Jamaican, i.e. one who allows the white oppressor to dictate his actions and beliefs.

34. The word "Jah", which is frequently used in chants and prayers. means Jehovah (or Yahweh) God.

35. One of the most abiding myths about Ras Tafarians is that they use cow dung or other substances to alter the colour or to control the strength and position of their locks. From all reports by Ras Tafarians and from my own observations, this is untrue. Particular care is taken to wash their locks regularly.

Upon rinsing away the soap, the locks are twisted by hand to release excess water and this twisting causes the hair to dry in separate, twisted plaits. A reddish cast is often noticed toward the ends of the hair and it was explained that the harsh Jamaican sun, after many years of exposure to it, causes this burnt-reddish hue.

36. Although the urban situation is apt to differ greatly from that observed in rural Jamaica, in no instance did I encounter a Ras Tafarian who was a self-avowed Marxist, nor did I encounter any individual who felt himself a target for Marxist, Communist, or Castro-inspired revolutionary activity. To the contrary, there seemed to be a distinct *naiveté* of political ideology of all forms, and a relative unconcern. When Ras Tafarians described "Marxist infiltrators" they were repeating to me what had come to them as hearsay.

37. Simpson, "The Rastafari Movement in Jamaica", in *Social Forces*, 34/2, (1955) p.170.

38. Smith *et al., op.cit.,* 1960.

39. Patterson, *loc.cit.,* p.17.

40. Y. Talmon, "Pursuit of the Millennium: The Relation Between Religious and Social Change", *Archives Européennes de Sociologie*, 3 (1962) pp.125-148.

41. D. Aberle, "A Note on Relative Deprivation Theory as Applied to Millenarian and Other Cult Movements", in S. N. Thrupp (ed.), *Millennial Dreams in Action*, New York, 1970 edn., pp. 209, 214. (Note also an article by Simpson in this collection).

42. *Dictionary of Anthropology* (ed. C. Winick), Littlefield, 1966, p. 143, s.v. 'cult'.

43. *San Francisco Chronicle:* Nov. 4, 1977; Jan. 10, 1979; Jan.11, 1979; Feb. 6, 1979; April 29, 1980; July 6, 1980; Oct. 15, 1980.

44. For background, esp. L.K. Johnson, "Jamaican Rebel Music", in *Race and Class*, 17/4 (1976), pp.397ff. (cf. his *Boss Culture*, London, 1975); S. Davis and P. Simon, *Reggae Bloodlines: in Search of the Music and Culture of Jamaica*, New York, 1977; A. Boot and V. Goldman, *Bob Marley: Soul Rebel - Natural Mystic*, New York, 1982.

45. NATTY DREAD, Bob Marley and the Wailers, "Them Belly Full (But We Hungry)", Islands Records Ltd., 1974.

46. BURNIN', The Wailers, "Get Up, stand up", Island Records Ltd., 1973;

SURVIVAL, Bob Marley and the Wailers, "Babylon System", Island Records Inc., 1979.

47. BURNIN', The Wailers, "Rasta Man Chant", Island Records Ltd., 1973; NATTY DREAD, Bob Marley and the Wailers, "Revolution", Island Records Ltd., 1974; SURVIVAL, Bob Marley and the Wailers, "Ride Natty Ride", Island Records Inc., 1979.

48. NATTY DREAD, Bob Marley and the Wailers, "So Jah Seh", Island Records Ltd., 1974; BURNIN', The Wailers, "Hallelujah Time", Island Records Ltd., 1973.

Chapter Nine

The Black Muslims in American Society: from Millenarian Protest to Trans-Continental Relationships

Dennis Walker

Elijah Muhammad led the Black Muslim protest movement in the U.S.A. from the Black 'Nation of Islam's' first emergence in 1930 to his death on 25th February, 1975. Under Elijah's leadership, elements from authentic Islam and from the Arabic language focussed the ghettoed, poor blacks' rejection of racial discrimination and lack of privilege in American society. Elijah Muhammad's very special development of Islamic elements, however, went with serious deviations from comprehensive orthodox Islam. He made whimsical changes to the Islamic precepts he kept: the Ramadan fast, for instance, conveniently became a December fast, corresponding to the Christians' Christmas festive season in the U.S.A. Elijah and his followers also asserted that he was the "Messenger of Allah" in the last days, a claim at variance with the Arabian Prophet Muhammad's status as God's final prophet. The Black Muslims under Elijah certainly did creditable work in restoring pride and self-respect to poverty-stricken, ill-educated blacks who had been spiritually pounded and atomized by white racism in America. But Elijah's confrontationist stance against the whites went so far that it broke with Islam's universalist thrust. Elijah used to teach that whites are "devils" who by nature could not be Muslims, and that God, "Allah", would soon judge and incinerate them for their crimes against black humanity.[1]

Following Elijah Muhammad's death on 25th February, 1975, his son Warith ud-Deen Muhammad became Chief Imam of the movement. Warith had a fair knowledge of Arabic and orthodox Islam. In a tactful but firm and final way he swept away all the mythologies and misunderstandings that had dogged the Black Muslims' actualization of Islam under Elijah. Warith declared that

Muhammad of Arabia was God's last and culminating prophet to humanity. Warith also ended the understandable racial rejection of whites by his father. Whites were no longer inherently devils and any of them converting to Islam would be admitted to membership in his sect's mosques. "There will be no such category as a white Muslim or a black Muslim", Warith declared in June 1975, "All will be Muslims. All children of God."[2] However, the Black Muslims under Warith continue to protest perceived aggressions and oppression by racist whites in North America, in Africa, and by Zionist Israelis in the Middle East against oppressed co-religionists and fellow blacks.

In the fourteen years of his leadership, Warith ud-Deen Muhammad has synthesized the range of functions that a viable black Islamic movement must discharge in North America: successful missionary propagation of Islam among urban blacks, but with a simultaneous deflation of those tensions with Negro Christianity built up by his father's hard-hitting approach. As well as better relations with Black Christians, Warith has striven to construct good relations between his black Islamic sect and white Americans. He has encouraged Black Muslim adherents to see themselves as American citizens and seize every opportunity that the white-dominated American system offers to them. We will see, however, that the earlier millennial thrust of the Black Muslims has begun to be reactivated from the mid-'eighties, in spite of his apparent moderations.

The Black Muslims' Original Millenarianism

Until 1975 most Black Muslims conceived America's blacks to have descended from the black tribe of Shabazz in the Holy City of Mecca, Hijaz, Arabia., They believed this to be the original homeland of all the world's blacks. About 6,800 years ago, according to this mythology, one Yacub, a dissident member of the hitherto harmonious black community in Mecca, initiated the greatest of evils. Precocious Yacub entered school when he was four; by the time he was eight he had graduated from all existing colleges and universities. His boasting and divisive talk irritated the Meccan authorities so much that they exiled him and 59,999 of his followers to the island of Patmos in the Aegean Sea. There, Yacub plotted revenge. He was a scientist skilled in genetics, and started breeding and

cross-breeding humans. This genetic grafting, carried on by successive generations of his followers for centuries after his death, culminated in the creation of
the artificial white devils. Almighty God Himself, Allah, had decreed this creation of the inherently evil white devils in order to test the blacks through sufferings and tribulations. The white devils, at first walking on all fours, living in
caves and trees and coupling with the beasts, stayed on Patmos for 600 years
before they escaped to the mainland of Asia. Within six months of their arrival in
Arabia, the white devils' underhand trickery ignited factional fighting among the
'original' blacks. Once realizing the whites were responsible for their problems,
however, the blacks mounted camels and drove them from Mecca, chained on
their bare feet, across the burning sands of Arabia to the caves of Europe. There
the white cavemen developed the Western civilization that has conquered the
world, and slaughtered and enslaved black humanity. Allah gave the white cavemen 6,000 years to perpetuate their follies and evils. By 1914 their time was up,
but he gave them an unspecified period of reprieve in which to reform and atone
for their crimes against the blacks. Predictably, they recklessly persisted in their
devilry.[3]

Since the moment when Almighty God supposedly appeared incarnate in the
person of the 'revealer' Wali Fard Muhammad to the blacks of Paradise Valley,
Detroit, Michigan, in 1930, divine intervention to judge, destroy, crush and incinerate the evil white world, white America first, has been a daily possibility. As
the headlines of a 1965 issue of the sect's *Muhammad Speaks* puts it, "Falling,
Falling the Old World!" with a warning by Messenger Elijah Muhammad following:

> Though in appearance America seems steadfast, she is moving towards
> the ultimate end. Salvation must come to the so-called Negro. The time of
> the ending of this world is now....The end is predicted and hinted in many
> places. Daniel (in the Bible), however, gives you a better knowledge of it
> than in any other place. And, the Qur'an's prophecy is exact. Do not
> expect ten years. The fall will be within a few days.[4]

While this was an extreme and urgent millenarian twinge, until Elijah's death
in 1975 the bulk of his followers did think of him as "the Messenger of Allah" in
the Last Days. From the mid-'fifties to the early 'seventies, Black Muslims even

took seriously reports of flying saucers, which were predicted to figure in the Final Judgement. When, by A.D. 2000 at the latest, Allah was to annihilate all white Americans, and all Negroes who chose to live with them in their modern Babylon, huge tidal waves, storms, hurricanes and epidemics would be but a prelude to a more decisive event from the heavens. A huge half-mile-long Mother space ship would drift across the sky, releasing fifteen 'baby planes', whose pilots had been brought up to destroy the world and who had never smiled. These babyplanes would pour down an unbroken stream of incendiary bombs and poisonous gases on to the North American continent, igniting violent fires that would burn for 310 years, and destroying all save those blacks who believed in black Islam. To these elect ones the babyplanes would drop leaflets in Arabic and English, directing them to routes by which to avoid the flames. After this Last Judgement, the righteous blacks would inherit authority over the whole globe, bringing "the New Islam", the final Age of eternal peace and happiness.[5]

Elijah's protest eschatology hardly lacked its paradoxes and concealed ambivalences. While the prophecies anticipated the destruction of white America, they themselves were more a homegrown mutation of Protestant apocalypticism than a transplanting of Islamic conceptions out of the Arab world. Steeped from childhood in the popular black Protestant fundamentalism against which he revolted, Elijah's 1965 outburst derived much more from the Book of Daniel than the Qur'an. His vision of the Final Judgement, moreover, played on underlying racial fury against the white enemy, which was pent up as corrosive self-hatred in the blacks. But it was left unclear as to whether the blacks themselves would hit back at the white Satans in the forthcoming Armageddon, or whether Allah the Executioner would do all the fighting necessary. This eschatology, paradoxically, heightened black expectations to flashpoint yet simultaneously dampened down and controlled all the rage of the black lumpen psyche, then channeling it into the arduous endeavor to become economic competitors of whites.

The Drive for a New Economy and a New Language under Elijah Muhammad

Although Elijah prophesied doom against the white devils, he did not see it contradictory to call for the building of a self-contained communal capitalist economy as an expression of separate black nationhood. He proclaimed "hard work, thrift, and the accumulation of wealth" as religio-national obligations, and during the late 1950s and early 1960s publicized success stories of entrepreneurial initiative, the most vivid among them being about a converted "mechanic on the street" who as a Black Muslim came to own a five-storey garage and five towing trucks.[6] Millenarist predictions of the impending incineration of the whites were thus meant to give ghetto blacks confidence to compete with them economically. It fuelled a gruelling process of self- Westernization that would assimilate them into the very patterns lived by those whom Elijah denounced as doomed white devils. His "Economic Blue Print for the Black Man" invoked "communalism": true Muslims would never boycott the businesses of their Muslim or black brothers; a bowl of soup would be shared by half between two black brothers; the blacks should work as hard "in a collective manner" as their covert models the white devils; members of Black Muslim temples would be required to give one tenth of their weekly or yearly earnings to the new Nation. The supportive, if authoritarian ethos created under the Nation appealed to the rather underpaid, unions-rejecting employees in Black Muslim grocery, clothing, dressmaking, drycleaning and other firms, because they felt they were working in their "own businesses" or were involved in "black ownership".[7]

By the mid-'seventies the Muslim endeavor to construct a black cooperative capitalist economy had been successful enough to win them respectability among middle class blacks and intellectuals, who had long been disdainful of the hitherto lumpen movement. By 1974, for instance, we find a confident challenge of Charles 67X as editor of *Muhammad Speaks* to "the educated blacks", with their "stench of marijuana", wife-swapping, be-bop dancing, expensive habits, and their intellectualizing presumption that "only ghetto dwellers need to live by a decent moral code, and as though they need no moral reform." The challenge signalled that the Nation of Islam was now intermeshing with the black bourgeoisie and intelligentsia. In this very same context it was announced that the

"Educational Seminar for the Muhammad University of Islam, College Division" (in Chicago) had brought together hundreds of followers of Elijah who had certificates and degrees.

> The fact that Muslim physicians, dentists, attorneys, pharmacists, mathematicians, educators, social scientists, and every other type of professional dignitary imaginable, now follow Messenger Muhammad should be cause for open-minded consideration on the part of every black 'thinker'.

Charles 67X was resentfully aware here that some members of "the bourgeoisie ... don't want the rest of us around", but he was increasingly viewing them as future recruits nonetheless.[8] Along with these drives toward a new economy and widening class appeal came the steady infiltration of the Arabic language and Arab practices into the movement. Under Elijah Black Muslim belief, terminology and practice were still strikingly non-Middle Eastern and American. Even up to the time of his death, and despite his own requests for change, places of worship were called 'temples' rather than mosques.[9] Although it was his son Wallace (thenceforth Warith) who secured the decisive transition to the acceptance of a comprehensive Islam, however, detached atoms of Arabic vocabulary did enter and cumulatively permeate the sect's life under Elijah as focii of parochial anti-white and millenarian sentiment. Arabic etymology was early applied to the name of the incarnate man-god Fard, for example, being interpreted as 'independent' (rather than 'individual' or 'separate') and taken to point to a future black state. Elijah also extolled Arabic as "the mother language of all the languages....and the last".[10] All this laid the basis for transformed attitudes toward language - the acceptance of the greeting "As-Salaam Alaikum", for instance, as an expression of new identity rather than "talking gibberish" - and lessened the sense of subservience to the tongue of white Anglo-Saxon domination. Before 1975 Arabic and Islamic motifs addressed parochial torments and needs not intelligible to real Muslims outside the unique American context. Yet precisely because of their intimately American functions these motifs were implanted at the very emotional heart of Black American experience at the street level. In April 1962, for instance, Black Muslims banded together to resist some brutal pistol-whipping against two of their number by the Los Angeles police. By collectively shouting "Allahu Akbar!" they unnerved the police and more detonated violence by them. Arabic was also used in Black Muslim rhetoric and in debate with Christian clergy - and in the naming of children, as the name of Malcolm X's third daughter, Ilyasah, well testifies.[11]

By the time Elijah lay on his death-bed, Arabization was even affecting ceremonial life. "By holy contract under Islamic law", in 1975, "two of Minister Louis Farrakhan's daughters" were married "to a grandson and nephew respectively of the Honorable Elijah", with the men of the wedding party donning fezzes and with hoods covering the women. The elegant suits and dresses may have approximated to mainstream American stylishness, as did the giving of rings and the cutting of the cake, but there was a definite attempt to meet traditional Islamic religious requirements; and America-resident Palestinian professor 'Ali Baghdadi "masterfully performed the ceremony in Arabic and English to give the wedding...a new meaning".[12] The overall impression of these shifts under Elijah, however, are that they were doctrinally superficial. Despite Malcolm X's urgent drive to fuse the sect with global Islam, Black Muslims remained cultural Americans who were only romantically attracted to Arab culture. Millenarian visions outweighed acculturative factors, but the seeds of what was to come under Elijah's son and successor Warith had been sown nonetheless.

Theological Adjustments up to 1975: the Emergence of Warith

The sweeping changes Warith introduced in the Black Muslim movement looked revolutionary to the wider American and black public at the time. In reality, the transformation of 1975 and onwards resolved pre-existing tendencies to mutuate the sect's Protestant-looking millenarism into a conventional, humdrum, orthodox Islam. As followers prospered and the class configuration of adherence altered, both the blatant racism and projection of an eschatological incineration of the white devils became less acceptable. Accordingly, a variety of highly-placed leaders in the sect patiently emptied Elijah's more worrying concepts of their content, though without repudiating them outright during his declining years. Wallace (later Warith) was not the only son of Elijah who phased out his father's demonization of the whites while the beloved founder-figurehead was still alive. Herbert (later Jabeer) refined it with even defter sophistry. Some years before formally converting to Islam after his defeat of Sonny Liston in 1966, Cassius Clay (thenceforth Muhammad Ali) discussed the concept of while devilshness with Herbert, who was then one of his father's powerful deputies. For Herbert, "a devil" was watered down to

> one who truly leads people from Allah....a mental attitude born out of false pride and self-exalting lies...one who goes against the natural order of creation...The Holy Quran teaches us: "No Associate has He'

Thus even a black who denied that God was the "Greatest" could become a devil. This was a new view of whites as people who committed crimes against the blacks because the Devil exercised possession of their minds rather than because they themselves were inherently devils by nature. When Herbert stated to Cassius Clay that "God has the power to destroy the devil without destroying the people", he had already dropped talk of Elijah's a final incineration by God-despatched space-ships. The Nation of Islam was no "hate sect", and "Muslims in America do not hate anybody". The White Establishment, Herbert maintained, might have taught blacks to hate themselves, but the struggle of the Muslims was now directed against the inferior "conditions" imposed on blacks.

> The history of oppressed people shows that they must learn to appreciate themselves, to love themselves.....My father teaches that we must have pride and respect for ourselves.....Whites who treat us with respect are not looked upon as devils, not by my father.[13]

Herbert Muhammad at least paid lip-service to his father's ideology; but his brother Warith was well known for his open, public rejections of Elijah's deviations from Islamic orthodoxy, even prior to his father's death in 1975. At several points Warith's rebelliousness actually landed him outside the sect. His drive to change the Black Muslim movement initially derived from Jamil Diyab, a Palestinian immigrant who was finally expelled from the movement and then denounced Elijah as a heretic. Doing very well at Arabic as a young student, under an Egyptian teaching in the University of Islam (the Black Muslim secondary school), Wallace was taught by Diyab and influenced by his understanding of the Qur'an. Appointed to teach science, mathematics and Arabic rather than religion, Diyab discreetly made him to "look for new meanings" in the holy

Plate 9. Two Black Muslim Cartoons

book which were not consonant with the protest millenarianism of Fard and Elijah.[14] Once appointed to be the Minister of the Nation of Islam's Philadelphia Temple from 1958, Wallace-Warith strove for the formation of a broad-based front supportive of such mainstream black civil rights movements as the NAACP. By 1964, he had temporarily broken with his father and the Nation of Islam leadership, and was encouraging Malcolm X - suspended from the movement in the same year - to carry through a conjunction with the normative Arabian Islam of Mecca. The Nation of Islam's "only possible salvation, he told Malcolm, lay in "accepting and projecting a better understanding of orthodox Islam".[15]

When Warith returned to the fold he was reappointed as a prominent Minister. In the last years of his father's life he preached soothing messages of a gentle, disembodied, cherishing God, unconnected with the perceived incarnation of Wali Fard Muhammad, and consciously eschewed all talk of white devils. His was a bland, still rather contentless, version of Islam, extolling Allah's benificence in the creation and natural phenomena. For two years before February 1975, it was regarded as an oppositionist theology, with Wallace's name rarely appearing in the Nation's official organ *Muhammad Speaks*. Wallace's cheerful, non-confrontationalist religion, however, spoke to the growing sector of the sect which had achieved material prosperity, become middle class, and had been tinctured with Arabic and standard Islamic texts from the Qur'an and the Prophet Muhammad's sayings *(hadith)*. It was this strengthening neo-bourgeois grouping, in fact, which made sure than Wallace was chosen as his father's successor in February 1975, with an implied mandate to take the movement in a different direction.[16]

Relations with Other Faiths, especially Christianity, under Warith's Leadership

Under Warith ud-Deen Muhammad's leadership, the Black Muslims have won a constant stream of converts from black Protestant Christianity to Islam. U.S. prisons have been one main recruiting ground. The Black Muslims perform valuable services to the U.S. society: they convert blacks to Islam in prisons and then take charge of their rehabilitation after release. Few of these converts relapse into crime once they leave prison. In general, U.S. urban blacks almost completely lack the ill-feeling against Islam wide-spread among white American Christians and Jews. Thus, Black Christians appreciate this success in rehabilitating black prisoners and drug addicts, in establishing an alternative network of black Islamic schools and in establishing black businesses to bail blacks out of poverty. White anti-Islamic Christian organizations try to involve black American Christian clergy in projects to counter black Muslim propagation of Islam *(da'wa)*, but few have consented to participate.

The widespread respect and acceptance which the Black Muslims command from Christian or non-religious Afro-Americans is very important for their security as a vulnerable religious minority. The Black Muslims have a self-confident attitude towards black or white Christians - and take the initiative to arrange occasions that bring black Muslims together with other faiths. Such social meetings, usually called Interfaith Assemblies, have defused tensions between Muslim and Christian by providing pleasant social contact. At the same time black converts to Islam are made through the interactions.[17]

But Black Muslim leaders and spokesmen also participated in inter- religious structures and occasions determined by non-Muslims. Imam Akbar Majied, for example, as representative of the American Muslim Mission engaged in religious dialogue with representatives of the Christian, Jewish and Islamic communities on "Brotherhood and Understanding" in January 1984.[18] The Black Muslims' greater openness to Christians and Jews, which had its origin in 1975, has contributed greatly to their integration into general American society (in which most whites follow variants of Christianity and Judaism). But the openness has been particularly effective in helping the Black Muslims to tighten the poly-sectarian black political and ethnic community.

While he lived, Elijah talked of a proud self-sufficient black community, but did little to weld it in co-operation with Christian black leaders. Elijah's vitriolic and contemptuous denunciations of Christianity as the religion of slavery and a tool of white domination made it psychologically difficult for black Christian clergymen to co-operate with him. Imam Warith's less abrasive, more accepting attitude, in contrast, has served to forge a united black community.

Many black civil rights leaders of the United States in the 1950s and 1960s were black Christian clergymen. Although still registering the religious difference, Black Muslims under Warith can now join company with Christian fellow-blacks in honouring these Christian leaders, whom they once lambasted as puppets of the whites. Imam Ibrahim Pasha, as Southern Regional Imam, participated on behalf of the Black Muslims in the January 1984 thirteenth observance of Reverend Martin Luther King's birthday, showing that the "struggle and fight for justice and human dignity" by the "Bilalians[19]/Afro-Americans" is "not being limited by religion, economics or class differences".[20] Along with these concessions came Warith's narrowing down of Black Islam's critique of Christianity.

For Elijah the whites gave the black the "poisoned book" and required him to join the "slave religion", which teaches him to love his oppressor and to pray for them who persecute him. It even teaches him that it is God's will that he be the white man's slave! For Elijah Muhammad, the Bible is "the graveyard of my poor people", enjoining them to love their enemies and bless those who curse them (cf. Matt. 5:34-4, 39-40) In his analysis, further, the black Christian preacher is the whites' most effective tool for keeping the so-called Negroes pacified and controlled, for he tells convincing lies against nature as well as against God. Throughout nature, God has made provision for every creature to protect itself against its enemies; but the black preacher has taught *his* people to stand still and turn the other cheek. He urges them to fight on foreign battlefields to save the white man from his enemies; but once home again, they must no longer be men. Instead, they must patiently present themselves to be murdered by those they have saved. Thus the black preacher is the greatest hindrance to the blacks' progress and equality.[21]

Now Christianity as an ideological emblem had a crucial function in the Civil Rights strategy of such leaders as Martin Luther King during the 1950s and 1960s The bond of common Christianity shared by America's whites and blacks was a crucial psychological weapon with which the black civil rights leaders morally pressured whites to release blacks from subordination and marginalization. But Elijah Muhammad and his Black Muslims derided the specific aims of the Civil Rights movement. For them the desegregation of white eating facilities, stores, places of entertainment, etc., was meaningless or harmful to the blacks. Whereas the long-oppressed blacks should have been developing their own separate business and economy, desegregation would have them spending more money than ever before in the businesses of the white devils. The American blacks would be transferring their $20 billion dollars annual income even more to their white exploiters. Elijah denounced the Civil Rights movement's tactics of blended Christian-Gandhian non-violence as an open invitation to whites to violently repress blacks. The Christian black puppet "leaders" were disarming blacks and drugging them with cosmetic civil rights gains that obscured the real needs of the black poor.

The Black Muslim newspaper *Muhammad Speaks* continued to snipe at Christianity as an instrument of the satanic white oppressors right up to the death of Elijah Muhammad on 25 February 1975. The paper carried savage caricatures and cartoons that depicted black clergymen as fawning, bought lackies of white bloodsucking merchants (cf. plate 9). After Elijah died, however, Warith and his editors quickly toned down such broadsides. He moderated the critique of Christianity in the context of American society, and courted the goodwill of the American white majority instead of denouncing them as satans. His new moderate stance toward Christianity was widely welcomed in the ghettos and suburbs alike as an essential step towards welding the U.S.A.'s blacks into a coherent political nation.

Even as early as 1977, in a speech given when consolidating his leadership and transforming Elijah's quasi-Islamic cult into a Sunni Muslim movement, Warith moved towards friendlier relations with the Christians. On one hand, he stated the uncompromising orthodox Sunni Muslim position that he had developed from the Qur'an. "The truth of Prophet Muhammad, which is that the truth of the Holy Qur'an shall prevail over all the falsehoods of the world, though the enemies (the idolatrists and the polytheists) may be adverse". On the other hand, however, while he urged his followers to make the truth of Qur'anic revelation "recognized" in America, he was careful to suggest that pious Christians and Jews would not be among the "enemies" who would oppose this. For

> Whether we call ourselves Jews, Muslims or Christians or other names, we all belong to one family if we believe in one God and if we accept the revealed scriptures that came to prophets of God....It is no need for us to be working against each other when there are so many evil doers, real devils, in the world. [22]

Such overtures towards the Christians has had real impact (a) in integrating

America's now multi-sectarian black community, and (b) in America's nation-building. In regard to the black community, his stress on the affinities (rather than differences) of Christianity and Islam has served as a good formula for much interfaith contact between Black Muslim Imams and adherents, and Black Christian clergy and congregations. With the past divisive antagonism defused, churches and mosques *(masajid)* have worked well together in relief activities in the depressed areas.

Not that Warith has dispensed with a Black Islamic critique of Christianity. The truth is that Warith has only contracted rather than ended it. A barrage of propaganda is still kept up to stress how intertwined white racism against blacks and Christianity in its Western versions have been. And while public critiques of Christianity's core theological tenets of the incarnate man-god (Jesus) and divine Trinity have been moderated, the Black Muslims continue to characterize churches as places whose religious art saps the self-respect of blacks and paralyzes their will like heroin to resist racism. Warith has time and again argued that "as long as 'white' (Caucasian) people think that their physical image is in the world as the image of God, and as long as non-Caucasians and Caucasians worship a Caucasian symbolic image of God on the cross", there will be trouble. "If we don't want dope in our communities, how much more should we be against a Caucasian image of God that makes Bilalians think inferior and act inferior" and fosters an "artificial" superiority complex in whites?

Along these lines Warith has launched the Committee for the Removal of All Images that Attempt to Portray the Divine (C.R.A.I.D.), in June 1977. His concentration of the attack upon the images of Christianity rather than its central doctrines has served the Black Muslims well. Various traditional black Christian churches still contain statues of alleged man-god Jesus and the apostles of Christianity, representing them as white. With the C.R.A.I.D. campaigns Imam Warith has thrown the black churches in the ghettos on the defensive without conspicuously putting the Black Muslims in the confrontationist, divisive position of attacking Christianity *per se*.[8] Warith has been able to associate the C.R.A.I.D. campaign with activities some Afro-American mental health professionals had initiated to warn how white religious images can damage blacks psychologically.[23] The campaign even picked up on themes going back to Marcus Garvey, the chaplain-general of the Universal Negro Improvement Association in the 1920s, who urged black Christians to "burn all pictures of white Madonnas and white Christs" because they perpetuated subservience. Warith's approach also chimed in with the sort of teaching articulated with Rev. Albert Cleage, who, as Malcolm X's friend in the 1960s, developed a theology of Christ as the political liberator of non-white people against white Rome.

As a result of C.R.A.I.D. conventions, Black Muslim leaders reached many black congregations within Christian structures. For the Dallas-Fort Worth area, where the campaign seems to have been most successful, Imam Qasim Ahmad was able to claim "good support from many reverends, preachers and pastors", because they were "working on common goals". Blacks were affected in Christian services by the Black Muslim ensemble led by song-writer Wali Ali, and joined in the refrain which questioned "why we pray to a Caucasian man". It was while giving a talk in a Methodist Church and in the context of a C.R.A.I.D. convention in Dallas, in fact, that Warith took his coalitionist tendencies to their limits, calling for "Muslim-Christian unity in the effort to make life better for the people".[24]

The Black Muslims' Struggle Against Ghetto Decay, Crime and Black Lumpen Sub-Culture

During Elijah Muhammad's leadership, as already indicated, the Black Muslims sustained the most uninhibited, never-ending torrent of denunciations of whites. However, various scholars viewed much of this tirade as a verbal screen behind which the Black Muslims installed a far-reaching critique of the ethos, sub-culture and life-style of the black ghettos' lumpen-proletariat poor. The real target of the Black Muslims' attacks has thus been black popular culture, which they wanted to eliminate as a barrier to the achievement of material prosperity in the mainstream of America's society and economy. In this sense the Black Muslim movement has always tried to make poor Black Americans *more* not less like the white Americans it denounced. Under Chief Imam Warith's leadership from early 1975, the Black Muslims have continued their pursuit of this prosperity, but it is a goal they now see more clearly will take much longer and be much harder to achieve in America than they had conceived under Elijah. The rejection of the black urban lumpen life-styles, formerly implicit under Elijah, is frankly, explicitly and systematically analyzed under Warith. In 1984 the *American Muslim Journal* publicized Dr Thomas Sowell's book *The Economics and Politics of Race*. In this work, so the Black Muslim journal told its Afro-American readers, Sowell had shown that Asians and Jews were over-achievers in U.S. society, succeeding economically despite the handicap of racial dislike they faced from white Christian Americans. In contrast, Bilalians (Blacks), Puerto Ricans and Mexicans had a 'cultural flaw' that prevented them from succeeding materially and in careers in the U.S.A. - and which consigned them to poverty.[25] Warith's contention, however, is that this traditional weakness can be overcome, that the criminality and constantly depressed state of black ghetto life can be ended, and that Black Muslims can integrate themselves in the mainstream of American society, not withdraw from it.

Concerning their efforts to combat criminal behaviour, U.S. prison authorities do allow Black Muslim Imams to visit their facilities, counsel prisoners and provide literature to black converts in the prisons. However, the conversions to Islam clearly worry some prison authorities. In 1984, the Graham Correctional Center in Hillsboro, Illinois, denied converted Black Muslim prisoners their religious right to perform "Jumah (Friday collective) prayer". The "Muslim ummat" (congregation) in the prison therefore filed suit against the institution to win their right to practise the rituals of Islam in full. Prison authorities do intermittently impose restrictions upon the practice of comprehensive Islam - with its rituals and dietary prohibitions - by incarcerated blacks. Under Warith's less confrontationist leadership the Black Muslim work to register protests and secure benefits for the blacks has produced an accelerating spread among black prisoners. For some critics the frequent use of Arabic phrases smacks of middle class intellectuals, but it is actually one point of attraction among lumpen blacks incarcerated in U.S. prisons.[26]

The black Muslims' techniques in reclaiming criminalized *lumpen* black ghetto elements are becoming increasingly sophisticated. They are building up an original analytical literature on criminality, penned on their own account to serve the reclamatory mission and proselytizing needs of their evangelical brand of Islam. Black Muslim Sydney Sharif, for instance, has written a book *Crime and Corrections, an Islamic Perspective,* rated as "one of the best sellers" at Kazi's Bookstore, which services the sect.[27] The Black Muslims, in fact, have never used

Islam as a means to withdraw from the terrible problems facing urban blacks into escapist spiritual self-consolation. They have always taken care to hold Islam out to American Blacks as the religion that offers specific solutions to their problems.

Elijah Muhammad was adept at putting the Black Muslims on parade in Negro neighbourhoods. This was to ensure that Islamic practice was woven inextricably into the daily life and needs of urban Afro-Americans in general, not just the lives of the believers and converts. The Black Muslims' observance of the holy fasting month of Ramadan in the city of Camden, New Jersey, in 1984 instances this pattern. At the end of a Zuhr (Noon) prayer, Resident Imam Fareed Munir reminded those in the *masjid* that "we are obliged to not just read our Qur'ans but also to live the Qur'an physically". Comprehensive Islam, he asserted, required "the believers ... as citizens of the city ... to voice and demonstrate their concerns regarding the mental and physical decay taking place in the city". He thereupon led 80 members of the Camden *masjid* on a "Moral Walk" through the streets of Camden - "up the main street to the notorious Kaighns Avenue Strip". Under the "benign neglect" that black ghettos have all-too-often experienced in the U.S.A., the block-long Kaighns Strip "is proliferated with trash of all types - paper, liquor bottles, drug paraphernalia and people of the same persuasion. Over the past few years a number of people have been killed on the strip". After Imam Munir formed a circle of the believers, "the believers recited Al-Fatihah and immediately afterwards began cleaning the entire block". The Black Muslim *masjid* security team stood by throughout the cleaning to safeguard the Imam and particularly Muslim sisters from neighbourhood thugs.

During their parade through the black areas of Camden, the Black Muslims held up placards: "Imam W.D. Muhammad is Our Moral Leader", "Save Our Children: No More Dope", "No More Prostitution". Over an amplifier, Imam Munir denounced deviant features of lumpen-proletariat black ghetto life-style and bade for the support of the non-Muslim bystanders. "The good people of the City of Camden are not the criminals - the pimps, prostitutes, junkies and freaks are the criminals". Showing their support, numerous non-Muslim black passers-by joined the march and helped the Muslims clean up the block.

The Ramadan march in Camden showed the credibility and respect which the Black Muslims have won among the urban black poor in the U.S.A. They present an Islam that holds out the promise that an integrated, viable black community can cohere in ghettoes blasted by the urban blight and social ills. Their Arabic formulae and rituals are emblems which focus both challenge and hostility towards existing (but for them less desirable) black lumpen behavioural patterns and culture. Having cleaned up the Negro slum in Camden, the Muslim men, women and children "with tools and signs in hand ... proceeded back to the *masjid*, reciting in unison, the Takbir and Kalima: *Allah-u-Akbar, Allah-u-Akbar, La Ilaha Illal-lah*". Such Arabic slogans mirror the Black Muslims' creative tension with the milieu in which their sect congealed, their simultaneous sense of belonging in - but determination to transform - the Black ghettos. Their hostility to other existing sub-cultures is obvious, potentially violent and readily perceived by the ghetto non-Muslim *lumpen* populations they are determined to reclaim. "One very ignorant man began to voice some discontent with the Muslims taking over the Strip and cleaning it" but "quieted down" when Imam Munir warned that the "peaceful" Black Muslims nonetheless knew how to handle "trouble". Before leaving the cleaned strip, Imam Munir warned the local residents that the Muslims "would be monitoring" it and had "another strategy" if the "riff-raff" dirtied it again.[28]

The Black Muslims' drive to eliminate crime from black communities in America has already cost a martyr. Activist Richard Walker Karriem preached Islam's reformatory truths to the pimps, prostitutes, drug pushers and homosexuals in the notorious Farish Street area of Jackson, Mississippi. On 7 January 1984, the criminal element murdered Karriem. After burying Karriem, Imam Ali Shamsid-Deen of the Jackson mosque led the attending Muslims in a protest march down Farish Street. The marchers' slogans against pimps, prostitutes, drugs and homosexuals drew support from some onlookers and also hostile shouts from others. A mass walk and rally "Call for Decency" followed on 18th February. At newspapers and television stations the Black Muslims chanted "Decency - Yes! Corruption - No! Pimps and prostitutes have got to go!" The Black Muslims' pressure and militancy greatly impressed Jackson Mayor Dale Danks: an at least "temporary and cosmetic" intensification of police patrolling in Farish Street followed. In other cities, such as Brooklyn, New York, members of local Black Muslim congregations have attempted to facilitate police raids on drug trafficking in black ghettos and have even set up armed guards to ensure drug dealers do not return to their old haunts; but lack of police response makes the Muslims suspicious that the drug peddling involves elements in the police force itself.[29]

How have the Black Muslims addressed the economic and social problems in the United States, more generally speaking? It was during the 1930s that Islam took root among unemployed, semi-literate blacks in the great industrial cities of the Northern U.S.A., in the modality of a protest religion. Despite their initial black nationalist rhetoric against the white devils, however, their real enterprise was the reformation and transformation of the American Negroes. While suggesting to black Americans that they were separating from white Americans, the Black Muslims really assimilated blacks to many of the main patterns of American society. In the economic sphere, the Black Muslim leadership tried to inculcate in converts the white Anglo-Saxon Protestant work ethic, the American entrepreneurial, go-getter spirit, and material acquisitiveness. Elijah Muhammad founded a $95 million empire of interlocking Black Muslim small businesses and farms. It was a black co-operative capitalism with Islamic emblems.

Upon Warith's succession in February 1975, the push to enter the mainstream of American life became more patent. He now abolished the national flag of a white crescent on red background which Elijah had propagated. Black Muslim adherents now had to salute America's national flag, the stars and stripes. When Warith was lifted on the shoulders of Black Muslims shouting *Allah-u Akbar,* and thus proclaimed Chief Imam, the American economy was still performing strongly and made prospects for taking his movement into the economic mainstream look bright. Warith's integrationism and American patriotism seemed an appropriate strategy for black Americans. The rise of oil prices from 1973 onwards, however, gradually sank the U.S. into economic depression; and the effects on urban lower-class blacks were severe.

By mid-1982, Reaganomics were in full swing and it had become very difficult for many Black Muslims to believe that mainstream, white American society had the well-being of under-privileged blacks at heart. The operation of the untrammelled free-market forces under the Reagan administration devastated the Black Muslims' property holdings, businesses and living conditions. The sect may have continued to celebrate New World Patriotism Day in June 1982, as in previous years, and its members continued to affirm that the United States' system would reward even very poor American blacks prepared to participate in it;

but the tone of Chief Imam Warith Deen Muhammad's speeches and statements became markedly sombre, in keeping with the grim conditions facing lower-class urban American blacks, the Black Muslims' main constituency.

Warith chose "The Dignity of Work" as the theme for the 1982 Annual New World Patriotism Day Parade. This theme expressed (a) the Black Muslims' tenacious determination to challenge the U.S. system positively, or to make it yield returns to Afro-Americans; and (b) the harsh reality that employment opportunities continued to elude many U.S. blacks. In Chicago, several members of the New World Patriotism Coalition interviewed him about the meaning of the theme that "human dignity requires lawful employment", and his replies were significant. "I accept that times are bad, very bad for poor working people", he stated, "the figures they give for the unemployed is said not to be accurate for the general work-force of the country. For African-Americans, I think, it is even more inaccurate".

Warith also stressed a theme which had been central in Black Muslim communications under his father Elijah, prior to 1975 - that uneducated, poverty-stricken American blacks have to take at least some responsibility for their own fate, to try to lift themselves up by their own exertions. They should *not* passively wait for the white-dominated U.S. system to bestow opportunities and resources upon them. Unemployed blacks should create lawful work for themselves. "There are so many ideas we could come up with", he contended, and offered practical suggestions. He was particularly concerned with giving "the elderly something to do. They need to be in the company of other people. They are lonely because most of us are too busy for them". He suggested that even black Americans of modest means should employ "an elderly person to help us out a couple of days". "I know we could use an elderly person to assist for a day or so in my home. Not to do housework, just to be in the home, or to answer the phone, to take the calls". This procedure would help younger poor Afro-Americans by making them "free to improve their own financial situations so that they would not be a burden on the society. At the same time the elderly person will have something to do that is rewarding to them".

For younger blacks faced with poverty, Imam Muhammad counselled a resolute, earnest, unflagging initiative. The focus for this resolute determination to meaningfully relate to American society had to be families, despite the very unfavourable conditions in which blacks were trying to reconstruct families. Imam Muhammad recalled his own period of poverty when he had left the Black Muslims' "Nation of Islam" in protest at the policies of his father, Elijah. Warith, with his wife and children, had been on his own then.

> I remember when times were hard in the early 60s for me ... I couldn't find a job, anywhere. But I was determined to keep the respect of my family, my wife, and the respect that I had for myself. So I went out and washed windows. I went to a hotel on the North side. I wasn't a professional window washer, but they accepted to let me wash windows, and I made a little more money.[30]

Imam Warith here reiterated a core theme that the 'sect' had always maintained since their emergence in 1930. Labour, lawful work that does not harm others and is socially recognized, is essential for all male black Americans. Throughout all the permutations of their attitudes to white mainstream society, the Black Muslims have always maintained their drive to reconstitute patriarchal families and win jobs for their male members. Indeed, in all the periods of their movement, they have invested work, jobs - and resultant ultimate economic affluence - with religious significance. To be dependent and on welfare is death.

When Elijah Muhammad led, he had taught his followers to expect little from the system. In altering this policy, and in desperately hoping that the U.S. system could still be made to meet the blacks' vital needs, his son Warith had been optimistic about more participatory solutions. By 1982, however, his optimism had largely dribbled away. He could no longer ignore the fact that the American capitalist system was not eliminating the ghettos and their attendant problems. His approach, though, was to try to extend the U.S. capitalist system, somehow modify it and tinker around with it, so that it would incorporate the black poor, rather than return to his fathers implacable rejection. In his talk on work at the Patriotism Day Parade, he was groping for new expedients to make the system function for blacks. He had already discussed with followers the use of "I love America" pageantry and publicity of the Patriotism Day Parades to "reach out to ... big companies". He thus toyed with a strategy in which "some of those foundations established by the big companies that have done so much already to help human beings live a better life would come out and identify with this grass-roots cry to society for help". He believed that it was in the enlightened self-interest of

the great capitalist American companies to respond to the Black Muslims' positive challenge to the system. Most "people without money, people without jobs,
people without high culture base" "just start screaming and tearing the place
down". Under Warith's leadership, the Black Muslims, though surrounded by
such depressing conditions in the ghettos, were "trying to find a way to bring
sensible remedies to the situation". Not that he was after financial contributions
to his sect from the American capitalist big companies: what he wanted was that
the companies "fund programs" that would increase jobs for Afro-Americans and
draw the black American private enterprise that existed into the mainstream
American economy. The alternative to some such partnership between white capitalism and blacks, Warith hinted, would be a property-destroying violent Black
Nationalist protest movement.

Imam Warith, admittedly, could hardly overlook the suspicion and hostility of
the powers-that-be towards attempts at innovation or modification to the system,
yet he pressed on to suggest that "the establishment or the government" should
subsidize the part-time employment by blacks of the black elderly. "Every time
you suggest an idea like this", he recognized, "people think you are Socialist,
people think you are Communist. But I think that's intentionally done to frighten
us away from insisting that society be sensitive to social change". Warith has
been only too well aware, furthermore, of pressures to insist that America conform to Friedmanite paradigms, and thus to free market forces regardless of the
consequences to blacks.[31]

Despite the set-back inflicted by recession and Reagonomics upon the Black
Muslims' drive to build up Black private enterprise, acquire property and achieve
prosperity, the sect has doggedly persevered with its quest. Of its three mort-
gaged farms in the South of U.S.A., the sect has lost two. However, it has completely paid off the third, a 4300 acre farm near Albany, Georgia, which is now
fully the property of the Black Muslims. The Black Muslims' campaigns of collective buying and selling of essential commodities, mainly food, have significantly lowered the followers' expenditure on food, cushioning them against the
inflation. Small businesses run by sect members are picking up again as well as
the U.S. economy revives.

Black Muslim Attitudes to Israel and Middle Eastern Affairs

Support for the Palestinians in their struggle against Israel has been the sect's main trans-continental Pan-Islamic endeavor. Part of the background to this is the deterioration of black-Jewish relations in the United States, especially since the 1950s, but a curiously superficial conjoining of the Palestinians' plight and that of the American lumpen blacks has made relations peculiarly bitter during the 1980s.[32] The Black Muslims have deduced that the United States' bankrolling of an expansionist-looking Israel has siphoned away funds from America's own poverty-stricken blacks. "This year", wrote Black Muslim columnist Munir Umrani, "Israel, which is actually Occupied Palestine, is supposed to pay you, the U.S. tax-payer, US$945 million you probably didn't know you were owed", but "the U.S. won't get a penny back". Umrani, whose Black Muslim terminology deliberately denies the right of a Zionist state of Israel to exist, angrily observed that the U.S. Congress would vote Israel all the additional funds it needed in 1985 whether it complied with the economic austerity programme President Reagan supported or not.

> If Israel really wanted to clean up the economic mess it is in ... [it] could save money by ending it's brutal occupation of Southern Lebanon. The Israelis are reportedly spending more than US$1 million a day to stay in Lebanon. But why should they care? U.S. citizens will silently foot the bill.[33]

United States Black Muslims extensively participate in anti-Israel, pro-Palestine gatherings occasions organized by Arab-Americans.[34] Their attendance at such political functions has not only deepened the Black Muslims' anti-Israeli stance, but the contact with Arab-Americans has also modestly tinctured Black Muslims with the colouring of Arab or Palestinian national culture and Arab experiences only tenuously related to Islam as such.

The Black Muslims' strong solidarity with the struggles of all Muslim peoples in the Third World, moreover, has persisted. This fellow-feeling for Afro-Asian Muslim peoples has occasionally caused tensions with white America, although the political stances by sect leaders are not always straightforward. During the Iranian-American crisis following the overthrow of the Shah, for example, they adopted an ambivalent, if sometimes critical stance towards American policies. In November 1978 Muhammad Ali said that he was on his way to Lebanon to help mediate in the crisis caused by the holding of American hostages in Teheran. In this case Ali was voicing the sense U.S. Black Muslims have had of standing between two worlds, to reconcile America and the Muslim world. But then in the interview Ali openly urged the U.S.A. to send the Shah back to Iran (as Khomeini demanded) on grounds that the country was "harbouring a thief" who had stolen $US 17 billion dollars from the Iranian people.[35] A conference of Black Muslim scholars in Detroit in the same month similarly vilified the Shah as a criminal who should be handed back, while simultaneously calling on Iran to release the U.S. embassy hostages.

Black Muslim attitudes to Islamic nations are not as uniform as the rhetoric sometimes suggests, and it is important to appreciate points of discrimination and emphasis, not only within the mainstream of the movement itself, but also in peripheral and splinter-group positions (as the coming sections will illustrate).

Black Muslim Attitudes to Africa

In some ways, the U.S. Black Muslims under Warith interact and identify more with West Asian Arabs than with Black Africans. This fulfils a pattern already prefigured under Elijah who valued the Arab world more than the West Africa from which most American blacks originated during the slave-trade. However, because two-thirds of speakers of Arabic reside in the Nile Valley and North Africa, the Arab World and Africa overlap. The Black Muslims in any case have built up interactions and contacts with Black Africans that in part develop previous millenarian concerns and in part present novel problems and tensions:

(a) Religio-Cultural and social reconnection. Black American Muslims achieve reconnection or contacts with the Black African world and cultures from which the slave master wrenched their forefathers.

(b) The contacts with Blacks on the African continent establish new economic pan-continental relationship. Thus, modern communications and the world's economic integration actualize the strong thrust of the old millenarian ideology to express the transcontinental religious-racial community economically.

(c) The Black Muslims' special identification with *Muslim* black African communities in the 1980s entails some tensions in their contacts with non-Muslim
Christian Africans, ascendant in the new African states.

In his best-selling 'faction' novel *Roots,* which subsequently led to two popular television series, Alex Haley romanticized Black Africa, especially Muslim
areas of West Africa. He stressed that black Americans' relationship with the
lands from which their enslaved forefathers were taken away in chains had never
been broken. The U.S.A.'s black Muslims have developed Hailey's theme with
vigour on their own account. Early in 1984 the sect's press highlighted the
American Black Muslim Barkary Taal's two vacations with his wife in West
Africa, during which they visited the Muslim village in Gambia to which Taal
believed he had traced his family origin. "Ironically, his African ancestors greeted him in the very same tribal village to which the celebrated author of *Roots,*
Alex Haley, traced his ancestral lineage: the Islamic village of Juffure in Gambia,
West Africa." West Africans repeatedly identified Taal as a long-lost Mandinka
on the basis of a nickname his grandmother called him and because of his high
cheekbones. In Juffure, an old female *griot* (or traditional reciter) identified Taal
as "lost blood" descended from a villager, kidnapped by white slavers from a
reading of Taal's palm, intuition and old genealogies. Taal knew that this data did
not meet "Western man's understanding of life ... fingerprints or photographs".
At least one native of Juffure benefited from the reconnection - Taal's "21-year-
old ancestral nephew" who went to America and lived with him while attending
adult education classes.

Taal's encounter with West Africa reflects the deep, widespread need felt by
Afro-Americans to revive a continuous racial and cultural community with some
group in Africa. The cultural genocide of slavery, and the later subsequent white
American racism that was almost worse, almost snapped the U.S. blacks' sense
of community with Africa, making it almost impossible to reconstruct the unbroken trans-oceanic links most white ethnic groups in America kept up with their
communities and areas of origin in Europe. Taal and his wife came to Africa
fired by passionate hopes of refusion: on coming down from the plane, Taal
shared Malcolm X's impulse to kiss the Mother Continent's soil. If the American
black Muslim was white-hot, his Gambian Muslim hosts coolly manipulated his
psychological needs, evoked a blatantly fictitious joint origin, to keep the stream

of black American pilgrim-tourists coming to Juffure, along with chances of development. Yet the U.S. Black Muslim tourists sought by the calculating villagers of Juffure would be much more compatible with Juffure's mores than non-Muslims, or Christian Afro-Americans. Taal and his wife were captivated by the colourful clothes and ceremonies of the Gambian village. But a specific ideological affinity drew him to Juffure - Islam. "Many [Afro-Americans] have visited Juffure, but no one has come back to speak of the Islamic spiritual feeling of Juffure - that's the key. The Mandinkas are a very spiritual people".[36]

Even more than grass-roots Gambian peasants, African officials in the U.S.A. are aware of the growing emotional need Afro-Americans feel for the continent of origin, Africa. Like Juffure's villagers, the African officials fan it in order to draw black Americans into long-term semi-intimate relations that will improve the economic and material prospects of black Africans. African diplomats and officials in the U.S.A. are respectful of the Black Muslims in this context as long-standing pioneers of black capitalism in North America, and thus potential investors. For their part, Black Muslim journalists astutely monitor and publicize in the sect's media all overtures from African officials for new economic relations between Black Americans and Africans. Along with notes on Tanzanian and Ghanaian expressions of interest, for example, the Egyptian Counsellor Dr Hussein Hassouna was quoted as saying that "the door is open for whoever wants to come and ... [Egypt] is ideal for Bilalian [Black] businessmen because they can relate to the culture".[37] The Nigerians opened a Consulate in Atlanta in 1982, seeking ready access to the black business classes of a city where Afro-Americans had recorded many successes. Moses Ihonde, as Nigeria's Consul-General in Atlanta, was soon to be interviewed by *World Muslim News* about his strong bid for economic ventures by U.S. Black Muslims early in 1982. To make his country attractive to them, he stressed that "Nigeria is a country of predominently Muslim population though there is a large number of Christians there also", with "no conflict between Muslims and Christians". He asked Black Muslims to be mindful, however, of "the advanced technology" to which U.S. blacks, in company with other Americans, had access, and observed that it created "impatience" and the demand for "immediate return on your investment" that made it hard for U.S. blacks, just like other U.S. investors, to stay on in Nigeria.[38] Black Muslim concern for these opportunities and new culturo-spiritual connections with black Africa reflect the sect's widening of contacts under Warith's leadership.

Black Muslim Attitudes to Arabs and African Muslims: Akbar Muhammad

What, then, of attitudes to the Arabs evident during the recent changes in the Black Muslim movement? From the evidence of his Islamic sermons Warith never learned to read any but elementary Arabic texts fluently, although what he did grasp of the language had a very strong psychological influence on him. However, there were some members of the Nation of Islam even during Elijah's period who achieved active bilingual mastery of Arabic to an academic level, and were able to interact extensively with Arabs in the Arab countries. One such adherent was Akbar Muhammad, the most scholarly of Elijah's sons. The United Arab Republic government of President Nasser granted Akbar a scholarship to study Arabic and Islam at al-Azhar, the Harvard of the Islamic world. While in Egypt, he imbibed on face value the verbally militant pan-African or pan-Afro-Asian anti-imperialism made so prominent in the Arabic press and political life there at that time. This Egyptian pan-Arab influence caused Akbar to deviate from the fierce but also politically cautious millenarian nationalism of his father Elijah. After seeing Afro-Asian solidarity conferences in Cairo, Akbar began to hope that, instead of waiting for Allah and a Mother Ship to incinerate the whites, the American blacks could liberate themselves by resorting to direct action. Though blacks were a minority, the continent-spanning militant unity of the non-white oppressed would make such resistance practicable in America. On his return to the U.S.A. in 1963, he stressed that the Muslims of Asia and Africa in general, and those in Egypt in particular, sympathized with and supported the American blacks. "Spokesmen from African states" in Egypt, he told a street rally of Harlem residents, had personally reassured him that "if you unite, they are ready to help us win our freedom. They are ready to help us with arms, men and know-how!".[39]

At this stage Akbar still viewed the Arab world in which he had been immersed positively. He was uncritically excited by new euphoric claims in the African states and independence movements that white supremacy even in far-off America could be ended. He still substantially maintained his father's millenarian nationalism, yet Arab and black African influences were pulling it towards a conventional political national movement. He had made an epic journey across continents, languages, civilizations, races and back but the different elements that the Black Muslims asserted still seemed to hang more or less harmoniously together: parochial American racism, the unique American Negro sub-culture, Islam as the emblem for protest against White supremacy in America, the Arab world, black Africa.

Then things all started to fall apart quickly. Back in America, Akbar found it less and less easy to put his two experiences together. Suddenly he moved closer to white America, which he no longer saw to be so alien, and repudiated his father. In January 1965, still only aged 25 years, he announced his defection from the sect, openly disowning his father's nationalist and anti-white views. He even charged that most leaders in the sect's temples no longer really shared Elijah's views, but stayed on in their positions just to keep drawing their salaries.[40] Once out of the sect, and with excellent credentials in Arabic, an academic career in Islamic Studies and African history soon fell open to him at the State University of New York at Binghamton. Akbar never really came back to the Black Muslim community, not even after his father's death, when Warith, his moderate brother, steered the sect in a different direction. With hurt feelings in a 1984 television interview, Warith lamented Akbar's refusal to return.

Like some other Black Muslims, Akbar Muhammad did not find long-term interactions with either the blacks or the Arabs of the African mother-continent of origin invariably ecstatic or harmonious. He found neither the Arab world nor the Black Africa extending beneath it quite as utopian as his sect's millenarian mythologies of exile projected. And however much he immersed himself in Arabic and its vast literature, he found it harder, as he reacted culturally against it, to regard Arabic as the natural element for Black Americans. Tensions arising in his attempt to reconcile continents and disparate cultures warped his perceptions of classical Arab Islam.

By 1977 Akbar Muhammad came close to denouncing Islam itself as an ideology that had failed to create a humane society integrating blacks with fair-skinned Arabs in the Middle East. He showed himself alienated from the Arabs when he reviewed the Sudanese academic Abduh Badawi's *The Black Poets and*

Their Characteristics in Arabic Poetry. This 1973 Arabic work focussed upon the careers of twenty-three black poets, mostly of Ethiopian, Nubian, or Sudanese origin, who lived in various Arabic-speaking Islamic states between the seventh and thirteenth centuries. But the light-complexioned Arab poets who were these poets' contemporaries, Akbar made plain, as well as the Arab literary historians, had denied these peripheralized black poets any recognition - out of "a somewhat pervasive contempt for the dark complexion". At the time of this review, Akbar was also preparing annotated translations of two relatively pro-Black works, *Tanwir al-Ghabash fi Fadl al-Sudan wa'l-Habash* (The Lightening of the Darkness on the Merits of the Blacks and Ethiopians) by Ibn al-Jawzi and *Raf' Sha'n al-Hubshan* (The Raising of the Status of the Ethiopians) by al-Suyuti. Tongue-in-cheek, Akbar quoted al-Jawzi to show that such Arab defenders of Negroes themselves had a racist distaste for the complexion and features of those blacks whose moral or intellectual quality they defended: "Islam also had its liberals".

By 1977 Akbar Muhammad clearly regarded the Arabs as historically unfriendly and racist to blacks in the Arab world. He spoke about "Blacks" and "Arabs" as mutually exclusive social groups, assuming that no Arabic-speaking Black could be an Arab. Akbar did not characterize Islam as an ideology with any strong thrust to over-ride racial divisions within states. The Arab-Islamist Egyptian 'Abd-al-'Aziz Kamil argued for a synthesis between blacks and the mainstream of the Arab-Islamic civilization both in mediaeval Arabic-Islamic thought and society and in modern Africa; Akbar dismissed him as "representative of a tradition of Muslim religious self-protection against social expressions of the non-Islamic, a tradition characterized by half-truths and irrelevant analogies". Instead Akbar praised Bernard Lewis who, in his *Race and Colour in Islam* "employs a cross-disciplinary approach and produces an interesting attempt to correct the picture drawn by mythmakers that historically Muslim society was free of social prejudice". In 1977 Akbar saw Bernard Lewis as "a well-known Arabist and Islamist" and his booklet on Islam and colour as scholarship. (However, Lewis doubled as an activist international Zionist polemicist and many Arab and Muslim academics retorted that Lewis's booklet was only expedient propaganda to take steam from the tightening relations between the Arabs and pro-Muslim black Nationalists in the U.S.A., which might threaten

Israel's interests).[41]

By 1977, then, Akbar Muhammad perceived Islam's classical golden age or Islam's Arab heartlands as no friendly sanctuary for blacks from the colonialism and racism that blacks faced from white Christian Westerners in North America and sub-Saharan Africa. Rather, he now tended to equate Muslim Arabs and white Americans as both racist. He did not see Islam as something that had made much difference for blacks in history. His view of the history of blacks in the Arab heartlands probably warped the past, accentuating racial tensions that had only been secondary in their classical Arab contexts. But in his concern to present English versions of primary Arabic texts about blacks in classical Islam, Akbar had achieved a paradoxical triumph for the erstwhile Black Muslim mythology's role in restoring North American blacks to the knowledge of their own heritage across the ocean.

Akbar Muhammad extended his bleak alienated vision down the Sahara to Islamic Black Africa itself. The Guinean (Mandingo) Muslim reformer and military adventurer Samory Touré (*ca.* 1830-1900) founded a powerful kingdom in West Africa and resisted French colonial expansion from 1883 to 1898. At its height in the early 1880s, Samory's rule extended from the Upper Volta region in the west to the Fouta Djallon in the east. When a French military column ejected his forces from the Soudan, he tried to establish his kingdom in the upper Ivory Coast colony, where he pillaged Kong (1897) and Bondoukou (1898). Pursued by French troops, he was captured on the upper reaches of the Cavally River on September 29, 1898. He died in exile. The French colonialists and French historians hated and feared Samory and stressed the slaughter and devastation he inflicted not on the French and their local allies alone but also on his fellow Africans and Muslims.[42]

Akbar constructed a realistic vision of pre-colonial West Africa that clashed with many themes of both the old Black Muslim mythologies about the Mother Continent and newer pan-African ones. The old Nation of Islam myths which depicted West Africa's blacks without differentiation as Muslims who were descended from immigrants from the black and Arabian holy city of Mecca, were dropped. According to Akbar's 1977 study, the Gyaman kingdom, of which Bondoukou was a part and which Samory invaded, was predominantly animist, Islam being only a minority religion of immigrant Dyula traders concentrated in

Bondoukou.[43] The harmony of African Muslims and non-Muslim ethnic groups, within the parochial, cohesive, unit of Gyamon showed that local and economic interests constituted African states, not religions. West Africa overall was not cohesive in the period leading up to the European conquests. With sharp documentation Akbar characterized West Africans as rather divided into warring mini-states and empires some of which courted the intervention of expanding Britain or France to beat back a rival Black State.[44]

The image Dr Akbar Muhammad offered Afro-Americans of Samory was closer to that French imperial apologists gave than to the celebration of historians loyal to African nationalism. Samory was a disliked invader by animist and Muslim residents of Gyaman alike. For Akbar, the pattern of ethnic divisions and fragmentation he had perceived in the classical Arab heartlands now startlingly held among Muslim black Africans also. It was not the case that the Black Africans had been a harmonious, humane community before the Satanic whites came and divided Africans. On the other hand, Akbar's realistic vision of Muslim and other West Africans at the time of the West's colonial conquests was paradoxically a triumph of the U.S. Black Muslim transcontinental impulse. Despite all the false steps and disappointments it had inflicted on those blacks who pursued it, and against all socio-economic and cultural odds, Black Islam had encouraged lumpen blacks in the U.S.A. to find sources of inspiration in Africa and Asia, and to reconnect themselves with Islam there. Akbar had achieved a realistic conjunction with the Arab world and black Africa, and offered American blacks instances of Islamic cultural achievements in black Africa.

Be that as it may, however, the Black Muslim milieux engender their own unique life-long ghetto into the psyches and lives of those who grow up within them. Having learnt Arabic, having encountered, and lost faith in, two very different versions of Islam, having had encounters with Arabs and Africans more often grief-instilling than happy, there yet can be no refusion with America or with non-Muslim African-Americans for such as Akbar Muhammad. From U.S. academia, his interactions with Arabs, as often unpleasant as cordial, continue. Unable to participate on a day-to-day basis in his brother Warith's Islamic sect, Akbar still passes through it from time to time reading papers at Muslim conferences, contributing barely acceptable semi-alienated articles to the sect's various magazines.

Despite repeated bitter and critical remarks about Islamic communities, Akbar cannot turn his back on Islam and put it behind him forever. In 1980 he announced in Jeddah's *Journal of Muslim Minority Affairs* his intention to write a general history of Islam in America, starting with the first attraction of white theosophists to it in the 19th century. His characterizations of North America's still developing multi-ethnic Muslim community, however, remained as bitter, alienated and unhappy as ever. In his writings he emphasized the persistent power of racial and national-ethnic divisions among American Muslims and the slowness of the integration that Islamic theory was supposed to actualize.[45] On the other hand, he recently classified America as among the most

> tolerant countries in the world with respect to freedom of expression and religious practice. Despite this society's many democratic shortcomings and lack of will to make its practices more congruent with its ideals, America's legal guarantees of basic freedoms foster Islamization. Muslim visitors and immigrants appreciate this fact much more than many other American Muslims, whose vision is often blurred by particular inadequacies and injustices in the American system...

Indeed, on considering the opinions of Arab, Pakistani, Iranian and other immigrants he had encountered in the U.S.A., he knew

> many Muslims in America believe that they enjoy more freedom of speech, assembly, and religious and ideological expression than do their coreligionists and countrymen in the Muslim world.[46]

Thus by 1985 Akbar had radically de-idealized the image he once had of the Arabo-Muslim world during his youth in Nasser's Egypt. His realistic perception of the Arab, Muslim and African countries made the U.S.A. look sectionally more positive than it could appear to Black Muslims, whose experiences and commitments to Islam remained more hemmed in by the torments of an America that became much more contemptuous, racist, violent or indifferent to its Blacks in the 1970s and 1980s.

The case of Akbar Muhammad, however, reminds one of a still greater source of turbulence on the edges of the Black Muslim movement, that stormy petrel Chief Minister Louis Abdul Haleem Farrakhan Muhammad, a man whose vitriole against Israel and the Jews must be set in contrast to the restrained realism that Warith strove to clamp down in the early years of his incumbency at least.

1984: Farrakhan and the Jews

I have written about Farrakhan's neo-millenarianism and nationalist thought elsewhere.[47] Here our attention will concentrate on those of his pronouncements and activities which brought him to the forefront of the movement and wider public life, especially his denunciations of the Jews and Israel (from 1984). Farrakhan had a natural furious, communal component in his personality which the dichotomies of Black Muslim ideology had sharpened. Playing on the past ill-treatment of ghetto blacks by many white American Jews, and also on the widespread resentment among American blacks of the American Jews' extraterritorial state in the Middle East, his anti-Jewish sentiments spoke to pre-existing social experiences of lumpen, but also middle-class upwardly mobile Afro-Americans, most of whom remained Christian. If Farrakhan was the spokesman for his people, however, his personal ambition also fuelled his denunciations: at least some of his anti-Semitic verbal excesses did not lack an element of calculation. In the life-time of the Honourable Elijah Muhammad, Farrakhan had gradually become the outstanding representative for the Nation of Islam, enjoying prominence and something like respectability in white American society.[48] It had been hard after Elijah's death when he was reduced to just one of several deputies under Warith, and so Farrakhan set aside Warith's authority to become a leader again in his own right. If he had behind him only a secondary splinter group, with Warith still regarded as the leader of Black Islam in the U.S.A. by blacks, whites and Arab states alike, at least he had some independent power and manoeuvrability.

In 1984, Farrakhan became a warm-up orator and his followers were working for Christian clergyman Rev. Jesse Jackson's campaign for nomination as the Democratic Party's candidate for the U.S. Presidency. By this means Farrakhan gradually secured prominence in black ethnic politics. His denunciations of Jews made him stand out even more as a champion of black ethnicity, at a time when Warith, in stark contrast, stuck to a dual policy of dialogue with American Jews and retaining recognition from the Arab states. Farrakhan was supposed to help and support Jackson's political campaign. There were elements of loyalty and personal friendship here. But from the beginning there was a latent competitiveness in Farrakhan's attitudes. Whether consciously or not he felt driven to catch attention and win primacy in the black community, undoubtedly expecting to be elevated in the minds of the black American community as the equal partner to Jackson, or perhaps to surpass him.

Farrakhan's following, though, was and remains but a limited cult. He lacked the institutions, contacts and resources to communicate with the public and governments of the Arab states available to Warith's much larger sect. Farrakhan was also handicapped in being less prepared to modify his group's version of Islam to make it fit into Arab Islamic norms, even if his vocal anti-Semitism and controversy with American Jews compensated somewhat for this religious lack of orthodoxy. Jackson's campaign, despite Jackson's own moderacy, gave him the chance for high exposure he needed. He had to grab screaming headlines around the world, projecting the tone of almost incoherent rage against the state of Israel, and Judaism in general, in order to detonate the desired hysteria from American Jewish organizations that made him the international celebrity he craved to become.

Farrakhan needed recognition and funding from the Arabs. If the Jewish attacks he provoked focussed on him as one of the most militant opponents of Israel in the United States, the Arabs would pay to bring him and his colleagues to their countries. It would make international travel very cheap for him and other leading figures in his cult. He could then visit the black African countries and various black minorities around the world. He had a mild interest in encountering such overseas blacks as an extension of his still somewhat millenarian black nationalism, or the vision of a recovered black American identity. Farrakhan had met Arabs, especially refugee Palestinians who had migrated to America, on and off over decades since becoming a Black Muslim. Despite such links, though, he hardly showed much empathy for the ethos and priorities of Palestinians and Arabs. He did not have to; once he came under attacks from American Zionists, the Arabs automatically rallied to him, just as he expected.[49]

Farrakhan and Eastern Muslims

During Elijah Muhammad's period of leadership from the 1950s to1975, organizations of immigrant orthodox Muslims in the U.S.A. often denigrated heresies he presented as Islam. For the most part, Elijah defied such orthodox Muslim bodies in America, but his succesor Warith was bent on Sunnification and transformed theological relationships. As for Louis Farrakhan's splinter group, because it maintained some of Elijah's old teachings and practices, Warith tried to delegitimize Farrakhan's claim to be an Islamic leader. Farrakhan, for one thing, had re-enlivened the belief that Elijah was the Messenger of God, and his followers asserted that much in the Bible allegedly referring to Jesus was really about Elijah instead.[50]

A piquant reversal of roles occurred when Ted Koppal's T.V. programme 'Nightline' respectfully interviewed Farrakhan in 1984 as an important Black Muslim leader in America. In response, Warith wanted to bring representatives of immigrant Pakistani, Indian, Albanian and other orthodox Muslim groups on to Ted Koppal's show to cast doubt on Farrakhan's doctrinal position, and deny he really subscribed to the religion of Al-Islam as given by the Prophet Muhammad in Arabia 1400 years ago.[51] But by the 1980s the immigrant Muslim communities in America were much larger and militant than in the 1950s and 1960s, and no immigrant U.S. Muslim leader has ever repudiated Farrakhan. Farrakhan, in any case, was becoming a frequently televised national figure in the U.S.A. in the context of his involvement with Jesse Jackson and the resultant Black-Jewish conflict. It was natural that immigrant Arab and other Muslims in the U.S.A. joined the blacks to rally behind Farrakhan, when the Zionists targetted him; and this made it hard for Warith to delegitimize him Islamically in the ongoing polarization.

Symptomatic of Farrakhan's increasing legitimacy among immigrant Afro-Asian Muslims in the U.S.A. was a press conference organized at the end of 1984 by the immigrant-led Muslim Development Corporation at Howard Inn in Washington DC. The press conference was attended by journalists from all over the Muslim world. Farrakhan mouthed the blatantly tongue-in-cheek orthodox Islamic doctrinal noises and the denunciations of Israel that his audience wanted to hear. Playing down his resurrection of Elijah's cult rhetoric, he stressed his bid to carry his community into the mainstream of Islam. He said that the "Nation of Islam", as he had revived it, believed in the Holy Quran as the final word of Allah and in the Prophet Muhammad as the last Prophet. They did not look upon Elijah as the founder of a new religion, but only the innovator of a methodology to bring the blacks gradually into mainstream Islam. Farrakhan also denied the media charge that he was a racist, and said Islam "does not countenance race, caste or colour". "Unfortunately", he went on to assert, "we live in a colour-conscious society; and if we preach we should love our colour, it is to express our love of Allah who created us like this".

While condemning the American government for its policies in the Middle East and for accepting the very existence of Israel, Farrakhan alleged that Muslim oil money was being used against Muslims. The money deposited by Arabs in Jewish-owned banks in the U.S.A. was being used to destroy Arabs, and he pleaded for this money to be withdrawn to "bail the blacks out of the depths of poverty and encourage them to move towards mainstream Islam". In a return to the old time separatist slogans of the dead Elijah, he even argued that the U.S. blacks have the right to a separate homeland of their own if they are continuously treated as second class citizens.[52]

Farrakhan had not moved as close to the Sunni Islam of "the East" as Warith, who was still politically cautious and less adventuristic. Yet Farrakhan had retained and developed some of the transcontinental millenarianism of Elijah's old Nation of Islam - the expectation that a trans-oceanic connection with the Islamic centre of power and wealth will suddenly bring prosperity and sovereignty "from the East" to poverty-stricken, abused blacks in America. In his 'cult of the Cargo', he laid claim to some of the capital that their Arab co-religionists were transferring across the seas to America, and in his semi-millenarian worldview fused religion, economics, black ethnicity, and the parallel emancipation of both Black American and Arab nations from the perceived global Jewish enemy.

On the other hand, Farrakhan's views are not quite so straightforward, and a combination of public pressures and his own international experiences have forced him to make some realistic-looking caveats. If Elijah claimed it necessary that the blacks should secede economically and politically from the white-dominated core of America, an interview with the BBC in late 1985 drew from Farrakhan some different projections.

As long as we have to depend on the whites of this nation to feed, clothe, shelter and educate us, and also give us jobs, then we will never be able to earn their respect, nor become self-respecting.

He alluded to Elijah's old plan for a "three year economic savings", and proposed that since "Black folks in America spend nearly $400 million a year on toothpaste, nearly $700 to $800 million a year on mouthwash, soaps and other detergents", they should produce these commodities themselves and set up their own system of distribution. Starting small, but growing, the blacks would thus be enabled to start farming and buy factories. Inevitably this meant coming to terms with the whites, rather than seceding. It meant productivity rather than pariahship in the whole society. There was undeniable force in Farrakhan's claim that he was only trying to achieve for blacks the same combination of separate communal institutions, ethnic economic units and participation in the American mainstream that other American ethnic groups such as the Jews had built for themselves in American life.

When challenged in the same interview about the Jews, he alleged that they over-controlled retail distribution outlets, and had economically coerced at least one black capitalist partner into withdrawing from collaboration in his projects. The rich powerful Jews were trying to destroy his sect's constructive economic endeavours. He denied, however, that he was anti-Semitic, for the Arabs as well as the Jews were Semitic people, and thus he himself had a Semitic dimension. He was, rather, only "against Zionism", and he stressed quite accurately that none of his speeches had ever incited any black audience to make a physical attack any specific Jew, Jewish store or Jewish synagogue. He had just been as a potential friend of American Jews

pointing out a fault that has to be corrected, otherwise these things fester and grow up into an ugly thing that could become violent down the road.[53]

Overall, Farrakhan and his supporters are ambivalent to Christian and Jewish whites whom they assail. They admire the ethnic self-organization, institutions and economic dynamism of the American Jewish enemy, and strive to duplicate it, and with a different configuration of the factors one day may become friends with them again. On the other hand, while Farrakhan envisaged the incinerations of Judgement Day or economic separation from America, he covertly held open the possibility that his cult's racialist economics and political participation would lead Blacks into America's mainstream.

As for attitudes resulting from his travels, on his 1986 visit to Ghana, where he gave a significant address to the university, Farrakhan experienced and responded to the realities of black Africa in a way not consonant with Elijah's idealized image of global black unity, 'the East' and Mother Africa. He found latter-day Ghana was fragmented, run-down, underdeveloped and - a word he used time and time again to describe it - "poor", and became fully aware of the depth of the division and ill-feeling between African Muslims and the much better-educated, privileged, politically more powerful Christians in this and other sub-Saharan black societies . As a result, he chose to mute the Nation of Islam's past vituperative antipathy to Christianity and the Bible, and insisted that Christianity and Islam were virtually just two labels for the same spirit, as all Africans united to liberate and develop their continent from Cairo to the Cape. At the same time he quite misread Flight-Lieutenant Jerry Rawling's military-based regime as a sincere attempt at Islam-like egalitarian nationalist government.[54]

If this response was perhaps in part contextual, in other encounters Farrakhan's eyes were opened still further to the ethnic divisions, poverty and oppression faced by people of colour across the globe. When attending a Conference on the world's "Persecuted Nationalties" in Libya in March 1986, the month following his Ghana trip, Farrakhan heard a speech by V.T. Rajshekar, editor of *Dalit Voice* of Karnataka, about India's Untouchables. Rajshekar castigated the Brahmanical Caste-Hindu racist oppression against the 120 million "Black Untouchables" in India, reiterating a dubious African pedigree for Untouchables that U.S. Black Muslim ideologue Clyde-Ahmed Winters had earlier published in *Dalit Voice*. The Indian hailed the conversions of American Blacks from Christianity to the more militant Islam as a decisive stride in Afro-American self-emancipation and as internationally significant. Farrakhan, who was present, embraced Rajshekar after his address. Farrakhan said he was "stunned on hearing the speech: he had made a study of the problems of Blacks in every part of the world but this was the first time that he was hearing about the existence of discrimination, segregation and persecution of blacks (Untouchables) in India: that these Indian Blacks were also of African origin and also that these Blacks exceed the population of whole Europe."[55]

Like Akbar Muhammad, and the critical articles on Black African dictatorships in Warith's journals, Farrakhan's responses to India instances U.S. Black Muslim awareness of oppression, ethnic divisions and poverty in those African societies mythologized and idealized under Elijah. Disillusionment and the painful achievement of differentiating visions here mark a progression in the U.S. Black Muslim consciousness - from the original trans-continental protest mythology to actualized trans- continental relationships with Africans and Arabs. In much more recent exchanges, however, this time with Amerindian groups, and in particular the Hopi, Farrakhan's hopes for the countless poor and oppressed have reinforced that aspect of his approach which is decidedly less realistic, and which is basically an Elijah-inspired neo-millenarism. Even in September 1985, his journal *Final Call* reported that Farrakhan had been "beamed up on board a space craft" to hear the voice of Elijah Muhammad expose a military plot by President Reagan; and there were claims that God's "angelic hosts" were working to support Farrakhan "in conjunction with an Intergalactic Federation of Star Brothers" as the modern Babylon's "final days" approached. Common UFO sightings were soon reckoned to be nothing other than glimpses of babyships swarming over the Earth in a cyclic rhythm with Farrakhan's activities.[56] It was in mid-1986, however, and in dialogue with Hopi Indians, that Farrakhan learnt about the myth of the coming appearance of a Great Wheel at Judgement Day (through which vehicle those Hopi who had strayed from tradition would be punished by God). In joint prayer and dream sessions American Indians and Black Muslims began realizing a common sense of the "present testing trials" under the white, Christian "invading strangers", and the shared hope of a Final Solution. These experiences were hospitably publicized in *Final Call*.[57] Farrakhan, then, while playing down the Armageddon scenario in his public rhetoric, as well as Elijah's projection of Judgement Day to destroy the whites, has not completely repressed the millenarian impetus in the ranks of the sectlet.

Conclusion

Chief Imam Warith ud-Deen Muhammad has proven a dynamic, realistic, adapt-
able leader, one who has skilfully brought the sect's followers into reasonable
conformity with the beliefs and practices of standard Sunni Islam, so that it has
irrevocably repudiated all heretical beliefs or practices that persisted under his
father Elijah.

Warith has also stressed that withdrawal from, or confrontation with, mainstream U.S. society is not the answer to ethnic disparities. Instead, he urges his
followers and those blacks who have not embraced Islam to pursue a sort of
street-wise "patriotism". Warith has strongly argued that American society is
only sectionally oppressive or evil, that Black suffering is tragic, because it
negates the very real potential for a humane society that America possesses.
Warith has tried to synthesize the God-revealed Qur'an's guidance with the man-
made ideological bases of American life. "Our patriotism is an acceptance of
what supports human excellence. We see in the U.S. Constitution something that
is compatible with our religion and with the concept of man in our Holy Book
Qur'an". "American democracy" and its idea that "every man is created equal" is
a political ideology that the Qur'an itself motivates Warith and his followers to
actualize now in American society, after so many false starts. These hopeful
claims have been made while nonetheless bringing home to his poor urban black
audience the pain and abjectness of their conditions. The 30 million African-
American people are "a race of consumers. We have no normal economic role in
America. We are a constrained colony of consumptive spenders who are too burdened to come to grips with our habits which enrich our [white] beneficiaries".[58]

Far from accepting the poverty that dogs the ghetto, Warith has pushed his
followers to identify and seize all opportunities for social mobility. After a gap of
nearly a decade, by 1984 the Black Muslims have again become interested in
small privately-owned businesses as a road to break out of the cycle of poverty.
However, they are also alert to new openings in the professions within white corporate capitalism and in government. One early 1984 *American Muslim Journal*
item told readers that "there are many opportunities for employment in the legal
profession... Legal assistants are needed in law offices, life insurance companies,
banks, real estate companies, corporate firms and other businesses needing

research on legal matters". "There are openings on the horizon for such high-tech legal skills as computer law".[59] In the same journal issue, eligible readers were encouraged to apply for financial help which the Time Inc. Scholars Programme offered minority students to get through college, and one columnist suggested specific methods for Muslim and other American Blacks who want to become small businessmen.[60]

Thus we see how, in the culturo-political and economic orientation now encouraged by Warith, the Black Muslims have been shedding strident millenarism for an apparent realism. It is tempting to conclude that their initially diffuse protestations, backed up as they were by rhetoric vehemently antagonistic to white overlordship, have become 'institutionalized' into a much more accommodating position. Appearances can be deceptive, however, because not only do the antagonisms lurk below the surface, and can be stirred up afresh in the independent campaigners of the movement, but the new 'pragmatism', even 'internationalism', is probably more apparent than real. Warith is trying to put the lid on a bottle, but it may already have burst open with the factionalizing of Farrakhan, whose grouping is fast achieving parity with Warith's. The weakness in Warith's position is that it stresses an individualist religion, while Farrakhan, even if the Jews have branded him a 'black Hitler', calls more strongly for the building of a national movement. For all Warith's conscious de-ethnicizing and internationalization of the movement, moreover, Farrakhan has amassed burgeoning support which includes immigrant Pakistanis and Arabs. A consistent stream of diplomats and visitors from the Islamic world pass through Farrakhan's Chicago headquarters each year.[61] Yet paradoxically, a key advantage for Farrakhan's group is its very parochialism. Warith's branch of the movement lacks sting, or the flamboyant, gripping, verbally confrontationist leadership Farrakhan has brought to the fore. Conscious of criticisms, Warith sticks to his milder message of "sobering up, stressing principles and practical direction, clear-headedness" and so forth, at the cost of popularity.[62] With him there is no strident evocation of the Devil, whether as white or Jew, and little of the cargoistic, millenarian and retributive rhetoric emanating from the Farrakhan circle. Can either faction's positions, however, Warith's pragmatism and new patriotism, or Farrakhan's special neo- millenarism, so change conditions that they will cease looking like unrealistic dreams of "heaven on earth"?[63] We shall have to wait and see.

Notes

The writer is grateful to Dr Sulayman Nyang of Howard University, USA., to Labee Uqdah of Los Angeles, and to the Interlibrary loan section of the Australian National Library for supplying issues of Black Muslim magazines. Huseyin Elmas of Melbourne, Australia, provided stenographic back-up. Mrs Shirly Muhammad of Chicago supplied texts of Imam Warith's speeches.

1. The two major classic works that analyzed the Black Muslim movement for the period of Elijah Muhammad's leadership are C.E.Lincoln's, *The Black Muslims in America*, Boston, 1961 (cf. also his *Race, Religion and the Continuing American Dilemma*, New York, 1984), and E.U. Essien-Udom, *Black Nationalism: a search for an identity in America*, Chicago, 1962. An upwardly mobile Black American intellectual, Lincoln highlighted with relish the anti-white rage the Muslims voiced in the 1950's and 60's, magnifying the threat they posed to the American system. As a Black Nigerian, Essien-Udom was detached as well as sympathetic, and caught both the pathos and heroism inherent in the Muslim's endeavours within a racist context. Neither Lincoln nor Udom were attuned to orthodox Islam, to which earlier Black Muslim mythology was related by Zafar Ishaq Ansari; cf. his "Aspects of Black Muslim Theology", in *Studia Islamica*, 53 (1981), pp. 137-76. Ansari will shortly publish a whole volume assessing Warith Din Muhammad's transformation of his father's millenarian protest movement into an Arab-like, orthodox Sunni Muslim church. A section is Ansari's sensitive "W.D. Muhammad: the Making of a 'Black Muslim' Leader (1933-1961)", in *American Journal of Islamic Social Sciences*, 2/2 (1985), pp.245-62. In the 1960's and 70's, the processes whereby Black Muslims gradually muted their incendiary denunciations of whites and sought accommodation with mainstream white American society had already caught attention; first by J.H.Laue, "A Contemporary Revitalization Movement in American Race Relations", in *Social Forces*, 42 (1964), pp. 315-25, and M.Parenti, "The Black Muslims: from revolution to institution", in *Social Research*, 31 (1964), pp. 175-94. Cf. also A.R.E. Meier and F.L. Broderick (eds.), *Black Protest Thought in the Twentieth Century*, Indianapolis, 1971; S.E. Ahstrom, *A*

Religious History of the American People, New Haven and London, 1972, pp.1066-70.

2. *New York Times,* 17 June, 1975, cited in D. Pipes, *In the Path of God: Islam and polical Power,* New York, 1983, P. 275.

3. Cf. A. Bontemps and J. Conroy, *Any Place But Here,* New York, 1969 edn., pp.226-9; Malcolm X, *Autobigraphy of Malcolm X,* Harmondsworth 1968 edn, pp. 258-62.

4. *Muhammad Speaks,* 26 Feb., 1965, p. 1.

5. Bontemps and Conroy, *op. cit.*; K. Farid Hassan, "Remembering the Motherplane: reflections on the Nation of Islam", in *Hijrah* (Los Angeles), Fall 1988, pp.14-15.

6. Essien-Udom, *op. cit.,* pp. 194, cf. 164 for the above quotation.

7. *Ibid.,* pp. 164-5 (earlier quotations), p. 169 (last two).

8. Charles 67X, "Meeting of the Minds", in *Muhammad Speaks,* 10 Dec., 1974, p. 2.

9. Cf., e.g., "Visit Muhammad's Temples of Islam, etc.", in *ibid.,* 20 Dec., 1974, p. 23.

10. Essien-Udom, *op. cit.,* pp. 125, 219-20.

11. See P. Goldman, *The Death and Life of Malcolm X,* London, 1974, p. 97.; B. Goodman, *The End of White World Supremacy: Four speeches by Malcolm X,* New York, 1971. p. 8; Malcolm X, *op.cit.,* p. 334.

12. Mary Eloise X, "Two Great Families Unite!" in *Muhammad Speaks,* 14 Feb., 1975, p. 24.

13. Muhammad Ali with R. Durham, *The Greatest: my own story,* St. Albans, 1977 edn., pp. 248-9.

14. See Z.I. Ansari, "W.D. Muhammad, etc.", *loc. cit.,* pp. 255-6.

15. *Ibid.,* p. 260; Malcom X, *op. cit.,* p. 453.

16. Ansari, *loc. cit.,* p. 247. Note Alverda X, "Purification is Divine", in *Muhammad Speaks,* 14 Feb., 1975, p. 3, for the appeal of Wallace's message.

17. *American Muslim Journal,* 8 July 1984, p.15. One highly publicized Interfaith Assemby was arranged by the American Muslim Mission (AMM) Centre at Hurlock.

18. K. Raheem, "Muslims Help Observe MLKs Birthday", in *Ibid.,* 6 Jan. 1984, p.19. This was organized by the Greater Brainerd Area Jaycees in

Chattanooga, on 16 Jan., 1984.

19. I.e., blacks.

20. Raheem, *loc. cit.*

21. Most of the anti-Christian positions taken here can be found in Lincoln, *op.cit.*, pp. 76-80; *Muhammad Speaks,* esp. 13/8 (1973) - 14/25 (1975), cf. also Malcolm X, *op. cit.,*pp.257-8, 298, 320-1

22. W.D. Muhammad, "the Mercy of Allah", in *Radiance* (New Delhi), 3 July, 1977, p.4.

23. "Muslims Take Efforts to Remove Racial Images to Kansas City H.R. Commission", in *American Muslim Journal,* 16 July, 1982, p. 7.

24. Wali Akbar Muhammad, "CRAID Walk in Dallas Climbs to Success", in *ibid.,* 27 Aug., 1982, pp. 5,9; Samuel Ayyub Bilal, "Dallas Hears Three Powerful Talks by Imam Muhammad", in *ibid.,* 10 Sept., 1982, p. 4.

25. "Economist sees Cultural Flaw among Bilalians", in *ibid.,* 13 Jan., 1984. Sowell's book was published in New York in 1983. Cf. Mrs. Sanji Muhammad, "So You Want to Start Your Own Small Business", in *ibid.,* p.11.

26. For the above, see *Ibid.,* 31 Aug., 1984, p.3; Imam W.D. Muhammad, *Religion on the Line: al-Islam, Judaism, Catholicism, Protestantism,* Chicago, 1983, pp. 12-25

27. Imam W.D. Muhammad, "Imam Muhammad Calls us to Goodness and Success!" in *American Muslim Journal,* 6 Jan., 1984, p.1. Sharif's book was published in Chicago in 1983.

28. For coverage of the demonstration, esp. K. Saleem, "Reflections on Camden Muslims' March against Prostitution", in *ibid.,* 20 January 1984, p.10; cf. H. Abdullah, "Ramadan Fuels American Muslims", in *ibid.,* 6 July 1984, pp. 3, 19.

29. D.A. Ali, "Murder of Muslim Ignites Protest", in *ibid.,* 6 April, 1984, p.3 (on the martyrdom); R. Dannin, "Muslims Wage Holy War on Crack", in *Hijrah,* Fall, 1988, pp. 7-10 (on Brooklyn)

30. Imam W.D. Muhammad, "The Dignity of Work: Human Dignity Demands Lawful Employment", in *American Muslim Journal,* 23 July, 1982, pp.1,5.

31. *ibid.,* 30 July, 1982, pp.53,57. Cf.M. Friedman, *Capitalism and Freedom,* Chicago, 1962, pp.133-6.

32. For the background, esp. R.G. Weisbord and A. Stein, "Negro Perceptions of Jews between the World Wars", in *Judaism,* 18 (1969), pp. 428-47; A. Forster and B.R. Epstein, *The New Anti-Semitism,* New York, 1974, pp. 207ff.; Lincoln, *op.cit,* pp 165-9, and note also the vitriole in the magazine *The Moslem World and the USA* (esp., during 1955-7)

33. M. Umrani, "Israel to Get More U.S. Aid", in *American Muslim Journal,* 7 September,1984, p.4. On the terminology in relation to Saudi Arabian recognition of a Zionist state in part of Palestine, W.M. Uqdah, "Saudi's New Ambassador", in *ibid.,* 6th January, 1984, p.4.

34. The *Am. Musl. Jnl.* of 10 August 1984, p.10, for example, advertized panel discussions and lectures on the "Second Annual Commemoration for the Victims of Sabra-Shatila Massacre and Untold Story of Ansar Prison Camp", an occasion organized by the Palestine Human Rights campaign in Chicago in that month. Prominent Arab speakers from the U.S. and overseas addressed the Banquet Dinner and the Palestinian folk singer George Kirmiz performed.

35. "Muhammad Ali Steps In", in *Malay Mail,* 28 November, 1979, p.2.

36. H. el-Amin, "Visit Africa, See its Richness!" in *American Muslim Journal,* 27 Jan., 19874, pp.1,4,18-19.

37. "African Diplomats Feted: CACC Opens Regional Office", in *World Muslim News,* 15 Jan., 1982, p.15.

38. Sabir Kasib Muhammad, "Nigeria Encourages Business with Bilalians", *World Muslim News,* 19 March 1982, p.4). The best pitch for African diplomats to attract Black American businessmen and capital was for them to differentiate Black Americans from their American environment and stress their links and relationship with Black Africa. Instead, Ihonde voiced the sense of many West Africans of how little African and how deeply American Afro-Americans are. He lumped American blacks with American whites. Ihonde's culture-shock at the differentness of America, its insularity and its uncritical Euro-centrism was getting the better of him but he would know the much keener interest Black Americans took in Nigerian art in comparison to white Americans. However, his theme of Americans as decadent drug-addicts who homosexualized red-blooded Nigerian youth was a stereotype definitely applied against Afro-Americans in Nigeria. West African intellectuals have

even vented in their high literature images of American blacks as racial and moral semi-whites, West-corrupted depraved perverts who can be allowed no place in African societies.

As background, we note how the Nigerian Wole Soyinka in his 1965 novel *The Interpreters* gave an acid portrait of a passwhite homosexual Afro-American history lecturer teaching in Nigeria. Golder, the decadent Afro-American pervert in search of an authentic black identity had been too corrupted by the West to be reintegrated into the African world, Soyinka's paradigm ran. See esp. B.B Lindfors, "The Image of the Afro-American in African Literature", *The Literary Criterion* (Mysore) 7/1 (1975), pp. 38-40.

39. C.E. Silberman, *Crisis in Black and White*, New York, 1964, p.151.
40. A.Bontemps and J.Conroy, *op. cit.*, p. 243.
41. Akbar Muhammad, review of Al-Sud Badawi's *Al-Shu'aea al'Sud wa Khasa'isuhu fi al-Shi'r al-'Arabi* (The Black Poets and their Characteristics in Arabic Poetry), Cairo, 1973, in *International Journal of Middle Eastern Studies*, 8 (1977), pp.415-6.
42. Akbar Muhammad, "The Samorian Occupation of Bondoukou: an indigenous view", in *International Journal of African Studies*, 10/2 (1977), pp. 242-58.
43. *Ibid.*, pp. 243, 245.
44. *Ibid.*, p. 249.
45. Akbar Muhammad, "Islamic Struggle in America: the Islamization of America", in *Hijrah*, Oct.-Nov., 1985, p. 10.
46. *Ibid.*, p. 6.
47. D. Walker, "Farrakhan's Black Muslim Nationalism", in G.W. Trompf (ed.), *Islands and Enclaves: nationalisms and separatisms in island and littoral contexts*, NewYork and New Delhi (forthcoming).
48. Goldman, *op.cit.*, pp. 393-4 Lawrence CX and J. Smith, "Farrakhan Warns Blacks 'Stay Vigilant'", in *Muhammad Speaks*, 14 Feb., 1975, p. 7.
49. E.O.Colton, *The Jackson Phenomenon: the man, the power, the message*, New York, 1989, pp 83-6, 203-25; Silberman, *A Certain People: Jews and their lives today*, New York, 1985, pp 339-43 See also James Muhammad, "More Blacks Accept Farrakhan as Leader", in *Final Call*, 27 Jan., 1986, pp. 1, 8.`
50. Jabril Muhammad, "Farrakhan the Traveler: Understanding Jesus: the

Farrakhan, Muhammad Link", in *Final Call,* 30 Sept., 1986, p. 27. *Final Call* is Farrakhan's official organ.

51. Note "Muslims Combat Misconceptions of Al-Islam", in *American Muslim Journal,* 27 April, 1984, pp. 5-23; T. H. El-Amin, "Nightline Keeps Viewers in the Dark", in *ibid.,* 4 May, 1984, p. 21.

52. "Farrakhan's Advice to the Arabs", in *The Muslim World* (Karachi), 8 Dec., 1984, p. 5.

53. "Farrakhan Speaks on London Television", in *Final Call,* 27 Jan., 1986, pp. 17, 23 for quotations and the above positions.

54. Farrakhan was manoeuvring within the sectarian tensions of Ghanaian society. In Ghana he was largely the guest of the smallish group of Muslim Ghanaian academics at the University of Ghana. There must have been signals from them for Farrakhan to deflate at least evangelical fundamentalist Christianity but if so he side-stepped it, striving to help integrate a cohesive black political community that would span the sects.
As for Jerry Rawlings, Farrakhan depicted him as a man who was renewing the vision of Kwame Nkrumah. Nkrumah had been popular among American Black Muslims in the 1960s and had become posthumously popular among educated Ghanaians in the late 1970s and 1980s. Clearly, though, by 1986 Rawlings had become a collaborator with the IMF dealing out tough economic medicine to an increasingly resentful population. See W. Keeling, "Ghana's Strongman Haunted by a Can of Worms", in *Observer* (London), 28 May 1989, p.28.

55. *Dalit Voice,* April 16-30, 1986, cf. also "Untouchable Released", in Final Call, 30 Sept., 1986, pp. 3, 8; and Nate Clay,"Blacks of India: a hidden race, a hidden problem", *ibid,* 27 April, 1986.

56. See esp. Tynetta Muhammad, "The Comer by Night", in *ibid.,* 15 Feb., 1987, p. 36, cf. Jabril Muhammad, "The Warners of God", in *ibid.,* 15 Jan., 1987, p. 25; G. Muhammad, "UFO on Display in Arizona", in *ibid.,* 14 Feb., 1987, p. 1987; "More UFO Sightings in the Midwest", in *ibid.*

57. Wauneta Lone Wolf, "The Mothership on Big Mountain: Presence of Sacred Wheel Indicates 'The Eagle Wants to Land'", in *ibid.,* 30 Sept., 1986, p. 30.

58. Imam W.D. Muhammad, *Religion on the Line, op. cit,* Chicago, 1963, pp. 133-6, and 128-9 for the respective quotations.

59. G. Zarif, "Careers in Law", in *Am.Musl.Jnl.*, 6 Jan., 1984, p.6.
60. Mrs.S. Muhammad, "So You Want to Start your Own Small Business", *loc.cit.*, p.11.
61. See e.g., "Taylor, Deedat Visit Palace", in *Final Call,* 15 Jan., 1987, pp. 12, 24.
62. Thus Warith in *Imam W. Deen Muhammad Speaks from Harlem N.Y.: challenges that face man today,* Chicago, 1985, pp. 146-7. I am grateful to Mrs. Shirley Muhammad of the Clara Muhammad Memorial Education Foundation (Chicago) for supplying me with a copy of this book.
63. One is reminded here that, in its impact and spread of influence, the Black Muslim movement was a successor to the Mission movement under Father Divine (George Baker), and absorbed much of the disillusioned membership of this black sectarian Christian group. Divine's Mission centres provided places of haven for oppressed blacks needing food and support, and, equipped with cafeterias, these centres were called 'heavens'. Father Divine, incidentally, was intensely patriotic. For background, A.H. Fauset, *Black Gods of the Metropolis: Negro cults in the urban north,* Philadelphia, 1944; S. Harris and H. Crittenden, *Father Divine, Holy Husband,* Garden City, 1953, cf. *The New Day,* esp. 36 (1972) - 39 (1975) [Editor]. The last section of the text was written largely by the editor.

Chapter Ten

On Wearing the Victor's Uniforms and Replacing their Churches

Southwest Africa (Namibia) 1920-50

Zedekiah Ngavirue

Background History of Colonialism in South West Africa

During the middle of the nineteenth century the European impact on South West Africa was limited, and the period between 1830 and 1863 was dominated by the great conflict between the hinterland pastoral peoples, the Hereros and the Hottentot Namas, which inevitably drew in the foreign missionaries on one side or the other. The missionaries in the region, who were members of the Lutheran and Pietist Rhenish Missionary Society that began work in 1840, tended to be supportive at a given moment toward any group they considered most oppressed; while the threat of Boer trekkers intruding into the south encouraged the warring groupings to unify themselves against a more serious invasion than actually came from the Cape colony.

In fact, it was neither the British nor Afrikaans colonists to the south who annexed the region, but Germany, which had united under Bismarck and decided upon a course of colonial expansion during the 1880s. As in New Guinea, the Germans began by sponsoring colonial trading companies (such as the *Deutsche Kolonialgesellschaft)*, which secured footholds through Rhenish missionary negotiations. Once appeals to Germany for protection by the trader Adolf Lüderitz suggested the possibility of annexation by that power, an Anglo-German rivalry developed at the metropolitan level, for there were other inter-

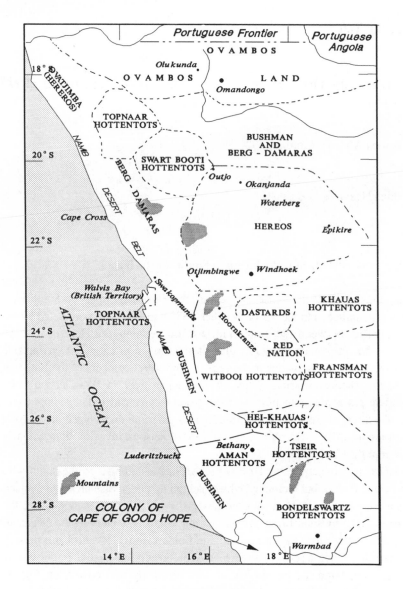

Map 4. South West Africa

ests, those of the British trader R. Lewis, as well as farmers of Dutch extraction to the far south, also present in South West Africa. This was in the context of the Berlin Convention of 1885, in which the European powers 'carved up' Africa for themselves.[1]

Lewis was particularly pleased that the Herero Chief Mahahero actually expelled the German Colonial Company from his territory in 1888, but this drastic action only provided the pretext for a genuine invasion. From the following year to 1908 there was a rapid build-up of German troops, from an initial 21 to about 15,000. The presence of troops at first facilitated the further consolidation of trading concessions, the building of a railway, as well as the founding of the settlement at Windhoek (now Namibia's capital and in the middle of Herero territory). More significantly, however, such further expansion resulted in the Herero and Nama risings in the first decade of this century, rebellions put down through a very large influx of German soldiers. The German strategists had played on the Herero-Nama conflict, and profited by Maharero's death in 1890, when officials and Rhenish missionaries interfered to secure a different successor - Samuel Maharero - instead of the rightful heir. Alienation of land through purchase at absurdly low prices, general ill-treatment and injustice by German officials, as well as stock losses by cattle disease, precipitated a mass African reaction. Samuel Maharero, though now graced withg a German officer's uniform, underwent a *volte face*, and led the first of the "Wars of Resistance" in South West Africa (1904-8).[2]

The threat of German overlordship produced a far greater sense of unity and tenacity of purposes among the African communities.

> For the first time it was revealed how strong was the spirit of freedom and independence which existed among these tribes. These were not weaklings to be won over by purchase or by peaceful policy, as may have been possible in the history of other powers. It was a warrior people not willing to submit without a decisive struggle to our colonizing aspirations that claimed its land and labour force.[3]

Slogans were used to strengthen warrior morale. "To whom does Hereroland belong?" chanted the women behind the battle lines, "It belongs to us!"[4] Legal decrees were announced by Chief Samuel that those peoples not involved in the fight - other tribes such as the Namas, and both the English and the Boers - were not to be touched, that all German men (except for missionaries and a few honest traders) were to be killed, but not their women and children. Samuel even secured a working alliance with the Baster and Nama tribes, and no traitor was known among the Hereros themselves. The men who had learnt to read and write German were ready to intercept messages, and this allowed them to practise effective deception during the fighting.[5]

What began as a tribal rebellion became a full-scale war, with German operations directed from Berlin rather than Windhoek. Disaster befell the Hereros by August 1904, with Chief Samuel fleeing to British territory and hundreds of his people dying in the Omaheke and Kalahari deserts on the way. Only the Rhenish missionaries were able to persuade the German experor to revoke the extermination order by General von Trothe and thus save the Hereros from near genocide.[6] The Nama war which followed lasted longer because the Africans avoided pitched battles, but this only meant that each tribe, less coordinated, was defeated separately, and the brief support offered by the Hereros made little difference. The R.M.S. missionaries were chiefly instrumental in mediating peace treaties and in securing some land for the Namas, and by 1908 the war was over, with enormous reductions to the Herero and Nama populations having been incurred. Their lands virtually all confiscated, their tribal organizations dissolved, and a proscription enforced against owning their own stock, these Africans were reduced to a mere itinerant labour force.[7]

German control of the region continued until 1915. Neither the turbulent period of the Boer War to the south (1899-1901) nor the unification of South Africa (1910) disturbed it. British South African troops occupied South West Africa during the First World War, however, because of its potential military threat to the Commonwealth, and although the region was subsequently divided into two sections (that of the Germans and of the Union), South Africa held the mandate to rule from the League of Nations. Annexation, however, was forestalled, though less through pressure from the Germans (because many of the politically recalcitrant among them were leaving in any case) than through rising African nationalism.

On occupying South West Africa the British promised to redress the grievances of the Africans by providing land for the traditionally pastoral peoples. The occupation authority actually allocated some good land, which seemed to the Hereros to be based on verbal declarations made by the then Governor-General of South Africa, Lord Buxton. Whether or not these promises were ever made, they were certainly not kept.[8] The friendly face of the invaders, then, and their publication of the Blue Book on German cruelties in South West Africa, raised hopes among the local Africans as a whole which were soon to be dashed. The result was a swing back to African tradition. Up to and during the First World War, Christianity had been steadily growing among the Africans. During the War itself, admittedly, Christianity was adopted as a sop by those in German concentration and prisoner-of-war camps, to which the Rhenish missionaries were allowed to provide welfare. But after the War, a distinctly atavistic movement began.

As Lord Hailey puts it of this shift, the Hereros "set themselves to collect cattle, while some of the smaller chiefs began to rekindle the Holy Fires. There was a swing back from mission influences". And this was accompanied by a spontaneous drift of the Africans to traditional centres, the Herero, most noticeably, gravitating toward their traditional centre of Okahandja. This return to the homelands had some precedent in the German period, when Herero or Nama farm workers showed their preference for employment on land in their traditional areas, but in continuing, its possible threat to European control was offset by South Africa's policy to establish nature reserves. Under the Mandate (1920), a Commission was appointed to recommend areas for reservation, the homegoing Hereros thus soon being moved and confined to Oritoto. Segregation was advocated, which included the removal of "black islands" from "essentially European areas", and the prevention of "Kaffir farming" (or the renting of land to Africans). By 1922 the reserves were finalized on inadequate allocations of land, and, along with regulations governing any African's movement from one part of the country to another, they became a major source of discontent.[9]

Minor efforts at resistance to the South African occupation manifested themselves to the north and to the south (among the Kuanyamas and the Bondelswarts respectively), and yet both were quickly suppressed (1917, 1922).[10] Overall, white expectations of a greater native uprising were unfounded, and what characterized the inter-War period was the development of a nationalistic awareness through religion and tradition.

During this period, when both the Germans and South Africans were the chief antagonists, the Hereros and the majority of the Namas concentrated on recovery. Their goal seems to have been merely to wring concessions for land, educational facilities and other basic necessities from those in power. Whatever social activities they engaged in were of the kind that was not considered particularly harmful by the authorities. They were characterized by religiosity, both Christian and atavistic, and tribal revivalism. The way in which "externalized" forms of political expression were substituted for the purely escapist and millenarian modes of adjustment might provide some interesting evidence of a natural healing process.

A common feature of group activity among the Namas and the Hereros after conquest was church attendance. The escape into religion among the dispossessed was so massive that some Germans feared that it might provide a basis for the revival of nationalism. They thought that if people came together in great numbers, sang and prayed in their own language, they would undoubtedly develop a sense of group awareness. Indeed, the various forms of socially internalized activities which proliferated between the two World Wars not only provided an outlet for pent-up political emotions, but also served as one of the series of stepping stones to the post-War resurgence of African nationalism. The development may be observed by following the turns and twists in the path of religiosity and national revivalism.

Emigré Associations: The traces of Garveyism in South West Africa.

Although in the foregoing section it has been suggested that active resistance during the inter-War years was the exception rather than the rule, it is important to point out that the decision of the Africans to adapt themselves to the system was taken gradually and reluctantly. It was in fact forced upon them by circumstances. According to Dr. H. Vedder, who supports the theory that Lord Buxton's unfulfilled promises disillusioned the Africans,[11] the Hereros first resorted to joining the Universal Negro Improvement Association (U.N.I.A.), which they hoped would enable them to realize their aspirations.

The U.N.I.A., which made its first appearance in South West Africa at that critical time when South Africa was changing her earlier face of benevolence, established two branches in the country, one at Windhoek and the other at Lüderitz. There were other organizations in the country during the early 1920s, most of which, according to the government sources were confined to emigrés. These were the International Commercial Workers' Union, a South West African National Congress, the African Peoples Organisation (A.P.O.) and the African National Bond (A.N.B.). The first two were organized by African emigrés, and the latter two by Cape Coloureds, as territorial branches of South African organisations. Like the U.N.I.A. they were based only in Windhoek and Lüderitz, the latter being the chief centre.[12]

The A.P.O. and the A.N..B. were mainly concerned with matters affecting the interests of the Coloureds, and were regarded by the administration as loyal organizations. The difference between them was that the latter allied itself with the National Party of South Africa, while the former sympathized with the South African Party. The roles or the extent of activities of the International Commercial Workers' Union and the South West Africa National Congress in South West Africa are not known. Only the U.N.I.A. seems to have made an impact in the country, although by 1925 it was reported to be on the decline. During its best days in South West Africa, the U.N.I.A. was the only emigré organization which drew a large number of adherents from the local population.[13] According to secondary sources it received individual contributions estimated at £2 per year from many Hereros.[14] The popularity of Garveyism among the Hereros is perhaps borne out by the possession of the name Garvey by quite a few people born in the 1920s.[15]

What was the message of the U.N.I.A. which attracted so many? According to H. Vedder, the people joined the movement because it promised to give "Africa to the Africans". In a letter to the *Allgemeine Zeitung* (9 March 1924), the U.N.I.A.'s chief representative, Fritz H. Headley, who was based at Lüderitz, set out the goals of his movement as follows:

> The objects of the Universal Negro Improvement Association and African Communities League, shall be, to establish a Universal Confraternity among the race: to promote the spirit of pride and love; to reclaim the fallen; to administer to and assist the needy; to assist in civilizing the backward Tribes of Africa; to assist in the development of Independent

Negro Nations and Communities or Agencies in the principal countries
and Cities of the World; for the representation and protection of all
Negroes irrespective of nationality; to promote a conscientious worship
among the natives of Africa; to establish Universities, Colleges,
Academies and Schools for the racial Education and culture of the people;
to conduct a world wide Commercial and Industrial Intercourse for the
good of the people; to work for better conditions in all Negro
Communities".[16]

It is perhaps true that these goals were too broad and too difficult to realize. The
movement, therefore, began to lose its hold on the people. According to government sources, by 1925 the U.N.I.A. was "only kept alive by newspapers received
from the Union and America which contained inflammatory articles".[17] Dr
Vedder's explanation for the decline of the movement is that it made false and
fantastic promises. The people were told that Marcus Garvey would come and
liberate them. "The ships of Garvey were expected with the greatest eagerness.
These failing to arrive, his airship was expected! Again disappointed, it gradually
dawned upon them that they had been deceived".[18]

The letter of the chief representative of U.N.I.A., referred to above, reveals
other factors which worked to undermine the influence of the movement in
South West Africa. Headley's letter which was a reply to an attack on his organization by the *Allgemeine Zeitung* alleged that it was the Germans who misrepre-
sented the aims of the U.N.I.A.: he claimed that the Germans even went to the
Windhoek Location to urge the Africans "to refrain from giving their moral and
financial support" to the U.N.I.A., "as their interest [was] not bound up with the
interest of the Liberian Negro". Headley's answer to this argument was that:

... the Negroes that are domiciled in the Pro- tectorate [S.W.A.], has [*sic*]
as much interest at stake into the Financial and Industrial development of
the Republic of Liberia, as he has at the present time, if any, in the
Windhoek Native Location, for just as those Germans, that are domiciled
in different parts of the Universe, are interested, in the development of the
German Empire, so it must be with all modern thinking Negroes, at Home
and Abroad.

Headly repeated his argument of the relationship between the blacks in the
Windhoek Location and the Republic of Liberia, more than once, declaring that:

All Negroes, are in duty bound to assist, are but just laying the foundations for brighter days, when the Negroes also will be in a positive position to present his quota to the World's Civilization.

He acknowledged that "... all great reform movements has had there [*sic*] ups and downs ...", but concluded his letter with this optimistic view:

> ... happily the new Negro, of to-day, peers through his own glasses, seeing that his very existence and also his Salvation and Destiny lies in his own hands, caring not what the critics may do and say, neither what obstacles are placed in our way, we are prepared to carry on and on ever forward, ever watchful, until our goal has been reached and achieved in the final Emancipation, of this oppressed Race, of ours."

It is doubtful whether the money collected by Headly in the Windhoek and Lüderitz Bay locations ever reached the Republic of Liberia or any Negro academy. On the other hand, it may be correct to argue that his main proposition on the relationship between the man in the Windhoek location and the Republic of Liberia was later vindicated: in 1960 Liberia and Ethiopia sued South Africa at the International Court of Justice on behalf of the people of South West Africa.

Adaptation and Internalized Activities

The decline of the U.N.I.A. in South West Africa was almost matched by the trend among the Africans towards adaptation to the ruling system. The demand for the return of Africa to the Africans was now replaced by petitions to the government for the improvement of the native reserves and for protection under the Union Jack. When the South African prime minister, J.B.M. Hertzog, visited the mandate in 1924, he was presented with the following petition:

> 1. We have no property Reserve. The farms on which we graze our cattle are small and either situated within the European property or in arid as the Epukiro District. Though boreholes may be of assistance yet they are liable to become damaged and we Natives do not understand how to repair such damage. If we had a Reserve of our own we could make our own pits the way we know how. We could cultivate a patch for our crops and be of no nuisance to the Europeans. The Grazing fees we have to pay are heavy. Had we a Reserve these fees would be cancelled. Yet we would

contribute to the Public chest. Natives in the Union we understand pay a Poll Tax. We would submit to like treatment.

2. We believe that under the Union Jack every person is a free individual. As we have heard that a movement is on foot to force Natives to carry a "pass" as it was the Regulation under the German Regime. We beg to say that we have the strongest objection to submit to such a "Pass Law".

3. We have heard it said that natives are lazy. We would respectfully submit that Farms servants are woefully underpaid. Even servants in town bars and those employed by the Government are also underpaid. Let the European Masters pay a fair wage and the natives will not be wanting. Our Sub-Native Commissioner is helpful to us. We are very thankful to him. Perhaps the Honourable the Premier could have the law so amended as to assist underpaid natives to receive more generous treatment.
Your Petitioners will ever pray.

The above petition was read to General Hertzog[19] by John Samuel Aron Mungunda, on behalf of all the Africans. J.S.A. (commonly A.S.) Mungunda, a direct descendant of the Mungunda dynasty of the Hereros, was to pursue this line of accommodation with the authority even as late as the 1960s when the winds of change were blowing all over Africa.[20]

But in 1924 he was not alone in accepting what seemed inevitable. The senior headman (later chief and post-War activist) for the Hereros, Hosea Kutako, was also there; and so was Chief Frederick Maharero.[21] The latter had brought the body of his father, Chief Samuel Maharero, from Botswana for re-burial at Okahandja the previous year; but the government had turned down his people's request that he be officially recognized as their paramount chief. The government had stated that Frederick Maharero and his younger brother Alfred Maharero would be permitted to return to South West Africa, and the former could be appointed as a headman of a native reserve, but not as a paramount chief. According to the Administrator's report for 1923,

... it was explained to the natives that quite apart from any question of policy the reserve system made such a position impossible. The Hereros would be concentrated in various reserves widely separated, and each reserve would be subject to the direct control of the Superintendent or Magistrate as the case may be. If Frederick were appointed paramount chief, his people would naturally look to him for instructions and clashing would be almost inevitable.[22]

Thus in 1924, after the main petition was read, Kutako raised the question of Frederick Maharero's appointment with Hertzog, but apparently to no avail. Frederick Maharero himself simply thanked the government for having allowed him to return his father's body;[23] and subsequently returned to exile in Botswana.

Social scientists have advanced the hypothesis that defeated people often take to "such internalized collective behaviour as religious revivalism" or to an energy-absorbing activity such as dancing.[24] Among the Namas and Hereros the 1920s and 1930s were characterized by the revival of traditional symbols, which were at first purely internalized but gradually assumed externalized features. This phenomenon seems to have started with the burial ceremony of Chief Samuel Maharero at Okahandja on 26 August 1923.

The body of Samuel Maharero who had died in exile in Botswana on 14 March 1923, was brought back to South West Africa and buried with full traditional rites in the family grave where Tjamuaha (his grandfather) and Maharero (his father) were buried, in 1861 and on 7 October 1890 respectively. The occasion drew a large number of people, estimated by the press at 3,000 Hereros and 100 Europeans, who included government representatives. The Administration also attempted to give the occasion an air of a state funeral. The coffin was covered with the Union Jack, and a funeral oration by the Administrator was read by the secretary for South West Africa, C. Courtney-Clerk. The goal of the Administration was, as evidenced by the wreaths laid by Courtney-Clerk, and as can be ascertained from the official report of the occasion, to achieve good will and also to use the occasion for communicating policy. The emphasis of the Administrator's speech was on co-operation between the whites and blacks in developing the country, but "each rendering his help in the form permitted by his present status".[25]

The significance of Samuel Maharero's re-interment at Okahandja was, however, in the revival of the wearing of the red scarves or bands as traditional symbols. On that day, there were 150 men on horseback, a line of 800 men on foot and a band.[26] This was a symbolic resurrection of the Herero army in the eclectic style which it had adopted before the risings of 1904 to 1907. But, above all, the red scarf, or red band around the arm - the symbols of Chief Maharero's people - were to form the basis of a Herero association, the *Otjiserandu* or Red Band Organization. The 26th of August was to become a national day on which the Hereros would make pilgrimage annually to Okahandja to pay homage to the chiefs by repeating the ceremony performed at Chief Samuel Maharero's funeral.[27] It was essentially in order to take care of the arrangements for this occasion that *Otjiserandu* was called into being.

The revival of Samuel Maharero's symbol was soon followed by the revival of other people's symbols, or the adoption of symbols by those peoples who did not have similar means of identity. Among the Namas, the Witbooi clans began to wear white scarves around their hats[28] - the symbol of their traditional "Witkamskap" or White Comb Society. Concerning this symbol, H.H.G. Kreft wrote:

> This white comb or crest was recognised by all as the distinguishing mark of the Witbooi tribe and consisted of a felt hat whereof the bowl, and in the case of the more prominent members of the tribe, the brim and the bowl were covered with a tightly stretched white cloth ending in a knot on top of the cloth projected upwards.[29]

It is not known when and how the white and the red scarves originated as symbols among the Namas and the Hereros. However, the practice of wearing a cloth around the head seems to date back to pre-colonial days; and in photographs or portraits of that time, the cloths worn by the Nama leaders are light and those worn by the Hereros dark.[30] The Namas and the Hereros maintained their loyalty to these symbols during the German colonial period until their traditional societies were dissolved following the risings of 1904 and 1907; but Dr. Bley suggests that the former Governor Theodor Leutwein was not aware of their political significance.[31]

One consequence of the revival of traditional symbols by the Hereros and Namas during the inter-War years was that other groups such as the Damaras and Ovambos (of the police zone) adopted colours of their own, green and blue, respectively. These developments went even further than that. At the time when he was engaged in a conflict with Nikodemus Kavikunua and Kahimemua, the chief of the Mbanderu section of the Hereros, Chief Samuel Maharero's warriors wore red badges.[32] Since that conflict eventually resulted in the execution of both Kavikunua and Kahimemua, it is understandable that the Mbanderus would not have the same feelings as those which the other Hereros have for the red colour.

Hence when this symbol was revived, they adopted green (an overlap with the Damaras) as their colour; the people of the Omaruru chief, Manasse Tjiseseta, who reluctantly accepted Samuel Maharero as paramount, adopted yet another colour, *otjizemba* (black with white dots). By and large, Herero unity was preserved through a compromise arrangement. The 26th of August was to be celebrated by all the Hereros, but not only were the Mbanderus and the Omaruru Hereros to join the parade with their own colours at Okahandja, but homage was to be paid at both the graves of Kahimenua and the Mahareros.

Although the pageantry of colours ruled everywhere, only the Hereros organized an active movement around their symbols. Writing in the 1920s H. Vedder stated:

It is a fact that almost all male Hereros are linked together as members of a great military organization and that everyone knows exactly to what rank he belongs - private, corporal or general![33]

It is true that the movement was para-military in its organization and discipline, but it is not correct to describe it as a military organization. It appears that while it was rooted in Herero tradition the movement's style of organisation was inspired by both the German parades in which some of the Herero elite soldiers once participated[34] and by the ex- servicemen and protective societies discussed above. For example, the motto "Samuel Maharero - God with us", which is inscribed on the flag and the bronze emblem (the latter bears Chief Maharero's head) of *Otjiserandu*, resembles that of the Karibib Ex-servicemen Association, namely, "With God. For the Emperor and Empire" *(Mitt Gott. Für Kaiser u[nd] Reich)*.[35]

Another qualification to Vedder's observation is that the movement has not been confined to men, but has incorporated women and, on the Okahandja Day, even children. The women's section of the movement was for many years led by Mukaahasera Kajata, daughter of the Herero military leader who, together with Samuel Maharero, commanded the Herero troops which beat the German first

Plate 10. A Group of Witbooi Namas with White Scarves and Hats

Plate 11. A Group of Female Members of the *Otjiserandu* in their Uniforms

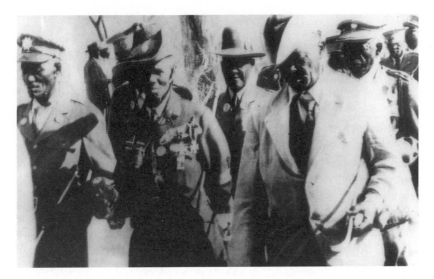

Plate 12. Members of the *Otjiserandu* on Maharero Day: the Old Generation

Plate 13. Marching Members of the *Otjiserandu* on Maharero Day

division at Oviombo on 13 April 1904 (cf. plate 11).]

Adaptation and the Development towards Externalized Activities

At first the activities of Otjiserandu and its sub-sections (called *Otjingrine* and *Otjizemba)* were chiefly energy-absorbing drills, but in the course of time, they extended to mutual aid such as contributions towards funeral costs and assistance to groups or individuals in emergency situations. During the 1930s the movement also began to externalize its energies by asserting itself against established authority. Although the administration was perhaps not cognizant of the psychological significance of this change in the role of Otjiserandu from "internalization" to "externalization", its report of 1939 gives an account which clearly reveals the process.

> It would appear [the Report states] ... that the movement started as a game of make-believe and was intrinsically harmless. As the participants grew older the organization changed its character. An early development - one still stressed - was that it became a sort of mutual aid society, the funds being used for burial purposes. Other developments were that the movement spread so as to be territory-wide, it formed a bloc within the Herero tribe, and in some centres that bloc has been in opposition to constituted authority.[36]

Another tendency of Otjiserandu, which the administration observed during the inter-war period, without necessarily understanding its full implications, was millenarianism. Although this aspect has not been adequately documented, it is evident from the imaginary military titles and government offices held by members of the organization, and their claim the German government recognized their authority.[37] The movement's defiance of authority stemmed partly from this aspect of its character. This is borne out by the fact that the authority rejected was not only that of the government but all authority except that of the movement itself, a known characteristic of millenarian movements (cf. also below).[38] Even the authority of Hosea Kutako, who arose as a great protagonist for African nationalism, came to be questioned by the more millenarist types.

In Aminuis Reserve, the government had to side with this Kutako and deport four leaders of Otjiserandu to another reserve. A militant group of followers (110), who wanted to vacate the reserve in sympathy with their leaders were stopped by a government action - a detachment of 24 police under the command of a Major R. Johnston was dispatched to the area to deal with the Otjiserandu militants.[39] Kutako had himself been connected with the movement years earlier but had withdrawn from it,[40] not so much because of these complicated aspects of the movement but apparently because of the dilemma created by the different colours adopted by the three sections within the Hereros. As a caretaker of the Maherero dynasty he was naturally expected to wear red, a symbol which might have alienated the Mbanderus and made it difficult for him to maintain the cohesion of the Hereros.[41]

While Kutako avoided wearing the symbol of Otjiserandu, he continued his interest in the movement as a whole, playing the role of conciliator between the different sub-sections, and also intervening on its behalf where the European authorities acted unfairly against the organization. For example, when the Okahandja municipality fenced off the Maharero graves thus preventing the pilgrims' access to them, he raised the matter personally with the Administrator, Dr. D.G. Conradie, who consequently instructed the municipality to open a corridor to the graves.[42]

The 1930s were thus characterized by two modes of adjustment. On the one hand, there was the reformist approach, which aimed at securing concessions from the government for a piece of land here and there; educational facilities and better wages. On the other, there was the tendency towards a militant millenarian movement. The reformist approach was the most common and was adopted by almost all the African groups. Since tribal conferences had not yet been instituted,[43] petitions were either raised by deputations to the government, or given at reserve annual conferences, which were sometimes attended by top officials such as the Administrator and the chief Native Commissioner.

Good examples of these methods and the kind of problems raised are Chief Kutako's deputation to the Administrator in 1933 and the Gibeon (Nama reserve) conference of 1934, which dealt, *inter alia,* with reserve conditions and education. Concerning the reserve issue, the Namas asked for government assistance in the construction of a dam, the purchase of a pumping plant, and Kutako complained about the inadequacy and unsuitability of the reserves which had been allocated to the Hereros.[44]

In spite of the fact that one of the petitions was parochial in comparison to the other (even on the other issues not listed here), the issues which they raised were as identical as they were representative of the demands made by the Africans under the circumstances of the inter-War period. The parochialism of the Gibeon petition stemmed partly from the lack of a recognized senior headman who could speak on behalf of all the Namas. Whereas Kutako had been recognized as senior headman of the Hereros on 1 July 1925,[45] the Namas had remained without a government recognized national leader, and the Damaras were to get one only as late as 1954.[46]

The people outside the police zone who did not have the problem of recovery from colonial wars were also reformist. Only Chief Ipumbu of Ukuambi seemed determined to resist, but he was soon banished from his chiefdom. In 1922 the administration reported that the chief was showing "a certain reluctance to submit to the authority of the Resident Commissioner";[47] and the reports of the Finnish Missionary Society for 1927 and 1931 commented that all the chiefs of Ovamboland expect Ipumbu had allowed missionaries to work in their areas.[48] Thus, when Chief Impumbu came into open conflict with the Finnish Mission over a domestic issue in 1932, the government banished him to the Okavango.[49]

It was also during the 1930s that the government began to disarm the Ovambos. In Ukuambi 411 rifles were confiscated during the operation against Ipumbu in 1932, and an additional 279 and 20 rifle barrels a little later. The Ndongas surrendered 2,018 rifles and 231 rifle barrels in 1933; and the Nkolokazis and Eundas 144 rifles.[50] By the end of 1934 a total of 3,021 rifles and 251 loose rifle barrels had been surrendered by the Ovambos.[51]

Millenarian tendencies in reaction to colonial overlordship, however, seem to have been confined to the Herero revivalist movement. This is probably because Herero revivalism was linked with some form of ideology. As already observed, the Herero movement combined traditional ritual and symbols with the symbols and discipline of German militarism. Nama revivalism on the other hand did not go beyond the wearing of the white scarf. The explanation may partly be found in the fact that the Namas, as reported by outside observers, have become generally Christian,[52] and therefore have no traditional religion to revive. Indeed, it was in the movement to establish an independent (or separatist) church from the Rhenish mission that the Namas were to play a leading role.

However, one Witbooi Nama, David Ross alias Aiteb, was drawn into the Herero movement. For some unknown reason, Ross had been awarded the office of *König* (king) of Otjiserandu, and was always to be seen in the Herero procession to the graves. Ross wore a red cloth with white dots around the top of his hat[53] obviously in order to gain acceptance among both the Hereros and the Witboois.

Unaware of the fact that certain "... forms of adjustment may also involve the borrowing of the symbols and the institutional practices of the limiting civilization"[54] for the purpose of turning them against it, the Germans in South West Africa were apparently flattered by the sight of the Hereros in German uniforms and styles. According to the (South African) administration's report for 1939, at first they seemed to be simply amused by what they called *Truppenspieler* (soldier-players) but later, believing that they might influence Otjiserandu, attempted to spread pro-German propaganda in the movement.[55] These allegations made by the administration might not have been taken seriously had the leader of the Deutscher Südwest Bund, Dr. H. Hirsekorn, not shown an interest in the movement.

In his report to the *Auswärtiges Amt* on the meeting of the South West Africa executive committee (i.e. the executive body of the Administration) held at Swakopmund between 10 and 14 January 1939, Dr. Hirsekorn reported, among other things, that the Administrator was planning to introduce a new measure on the procedure of appointing the members of the reserves advisory boards, and according to him, the aim was to man these boards with people who were loyal to the government, and then to exercise influence on the *Truppenspieler*. He pointed out that the Herero headman Hosea Kutako was considered to be particularly reliable by the administration, while the leaders of the *Truppenspieler*, mainly composed of old German native soldiers, were not.[56] Hirsekorn did not commit himself further than that. It appears that according to him, the contrast between Kutako and the leaders of Otjiserandu (or so-called *Truppenspieler*) was obvious.

It is indeed true that while the struggle between the Germans and South Africans over South West Africa was raging, Kutako concerned himself mainly with the welfare of his people, and leaned towards the then Union of South Africa. In 1939 he led a Herero delegation which visited the Transkei Bunga, Lovedale Institute, Fort Hare and Fort Cox. His statement to a session of the Bunga not only condemned German rule but showed clearly that if he were to choose between Germany and the Union of South Africa, he would opt for the latter.[57]

But this position was not peculiar to Kutako. When war broke out in 1939, all the African groups, including the members of the *Truppenspieler* whom the Germans wrongly expected to behave otherwise, joined South Africa and the British empire against Nazi Germany. Many Africans joined the Allied soldiery to stop Nazism, and thus took on the whites' army uniforms in another context, only to return home to face racial and political domination as ever.

After the War, the Otjiserandu passed the role of challenging authority to new nationalistic forces. Its own functions became limited to celebrating the Okahandja Day and serving as a mutual aid society. These are important functions in themselves, and have undoubtedly contributed towards the development of a sense of public spirit among the Hereros. For example, the first petition to the United States on behalf of the Hereros, to be borne by the Rev. Michael Scott, was signed at Okahandja on the eve of Maharero Day.[58]

The movement also changed its style as new modes of expression were adopted. Not only were the German uniforms being replaced by British kilts among the young,[59] which might be simply a matter of fashion and because the Germans lost the war, but as energy was now being taken up by externalized political demonstrations, very little of it could be dissipated in drills and German goose-stepping.

Another feature of the change in the psychological mood of the movement and the people is the abandonment of arbitrary titles and decorations. By 1960 German decorations were to be seen only on a few old people. The couple of iron crosses on *König* Aiteb's breast[60] seemed to be mere relics of that era of adaptation when there were no specific programmes for political change. The people had begun to move away from the purely expressive modes of adjustment towards instrumental ones.

Functionally Specific Organizations and the Resurgence of Nationalism, the Exodus from the Rhenish Mission.

The end of the Second World War ushered in a new era in which the Africans adopted fresh methods of political expression. The expressive techniques of the inter-War period began to recede into the background as functionally specific organizations came into being. The rise of the new organizations was stimulated by a combination of different factors, most of which were local, ranging from the cumulative effect of previous activities to the challenge posed by contemporary problems. External developments were important mainly in providing a suitable climate and lending new organizational techniques. It is, therefore, essential to observe both the tasks for which the post-War organizations were formed and their connections with the past.[61]

Although the year 1946 may be regarded as the landmark between the era of the adaptive and millenarian styles of political expression, on the one hand, and the revival of nationalism on the other, the development towards national political movements was gradual. The first decade of the post-War was characterized by the formation of a few voluntary associations and small *ad hoc* groupings for a variety of purposes. In addition to these associations there were the religious breakaway movements from the Rhenish mission (R.M.S.).

These different organizations not only provided the bridge between the past and the present but were, in a number of respects, the precursors of the political parties. Apart from the theoretical assumption that one organized activity often leads to another, however indirectly,[62] some of the pre-party associations provided the training ground for future political leaders or were themselves transformed into parties. Good examples of this development are *Ozohoze* (Vigilants), which developed into the Chief's Council and later into N.U.D.O., the African Improvement Society, whose members became important adjuncts to the *Ozohoze* and were later absorbed into the chief's council; the South West Africa Student Body and the South West Africa Progressive Association, whose leaders later co-founded the South West African National Union (S.W.A.N.U.), with the chief's Council and the Ovamboland People's Organization (O.P.O.).

While the Hereros engaged in traditional revivalism in the 1930s, the Namas kept faithfully to the mission churches. However, they became increasingly dissatisfied with the subordinate roles to which they were confined by the R.M.S. missionaries. According to the records of the missionaries themselves, the first signs of discontent appeared in 1930 among certain Nama evangelists.[63] But nothing special happened then, as accommodation was the order of the day.

It was the post-War developments which raised the aspirations of the Namas and enabled them to turn their discontent into action against the R.M.S. In July 1946, after some months of agitation, two thirds of the leading Nama evangelists broke away from the R.M.S. They were followed by approximately one third of the membership of the mission. The breakaway movement was led by Zageus Thomas of Keetmanshoop, Petrus Jod of Maltahöhe and Marcus Witbooi of Gibeon, men who were considered by the R.M.S. as the most competent and, until their decision to break away, the most trusted. These men had achieved the rank of chief evangelist which was thus far considered a high position for an African preacher of the mission. They had done so through long years of service, during the period when it was considered normal for Africans to work within the established order. (Jod had, for example, worked for the R.M.S. for 37 years). But things were now changing. These evangelists began to feel that their long years of faithful service had not earned them even the rank of a pastor.[64] Above all, they felt that the time had come for Africans to stand on their own. As they put it: "Man cannot always hide between the cliffs. Man must one day stand up and walk erect."[65]

Just as the Herero petition to the United Nations was precipitated by South Africa's attempt to annex South West Africa, the Nama exodus from the R.M.S. was sparked off by a suggestion from the mission that they be inherited by the Dutch Reformed Church (D.R.C.). At the end of the Second World War, the R.M.S. missionaries, some of whom spent the war years in an internment camp, Andalusia, in South Africa, anticipated repatriation to Germany by the Smuts government. Dr. H. Vedder thus began to inquire from the D.R.C. whether the latter could take over the R.M.S. mission stations, should German missionaries be repatriated. This inquiry leaked out to the press. It was reported in the *Burger* of 31 October 1945, which also commented that the Africans in South West Africa had not reached the stage of running their own church. The Namas were not only opposed to the transfer to the D.R.C., but were provoked by the questioning of African capabilities.[66]

On 12th January 1946 the Namaland Evangelist and Teachers Association issued a manifesto entitled "Agitation against White Associations" which, *inter alia*, responded to the allegation that Africans were incompetent. The manifesto asked that if, after having been under the spiritual tutelage of the R.M.S. for approximately one hundred years, the people were still incapable, weak and almost all pagan, as alleged by the press, how long would they remain so. When would they become capable, strong and Christian? Arguing that the Europeans were morally no better than the Africans, the manifesto then declared that the Namas would henceforth refuse to adhere to associations of the whites, namely the R.M.S. and the D.R.C.[67]

The situation between the issuing of the manifesto in January and the actual break in July was fluid. There were still negotiations going on between the African evangelists and individual missionaries. However, dissatisfied with the missionaries' response to their demands, on 31 May 1946 Zageus Thomas and fourteen others wrote to the superintendent of the R.M.S., F. Rust, stating that their resignation was irrevocable. The decision of the R.M.S. conference held at Keetmanshoop on 26 May 1946, to seek reconciliation at an official level was therefore too late.[68]

The task which faced the Namas on seceding from the R.M.S. was the establishment of a denomination of their own. Although as early as 1943 the Namaland Evangelists and Teachers Association (N.E.T.A.) had, under the leadership of Jod, begun to by-pass the R.M.S. in certain activities,[69] it was not in a position to replace the latter overnight. Since the Namas had resolved not to ally themselves with any white denomination, the practical alternative was to turn to the African Methodist Episcopal Church in South Africa (A.M.E.).[70] The contact between the N.E.T.A. and the A.M.E. was made by Jonas Katjerungu. Katjerungu, a Herero who grew up in Namaland, was one of the first few South West Africans to receive a good secondary education. After his primary education at the Anglican St. Barnabas School in Windhoek, he went to study at Lovedale Institute in South Africa. It was probably there that he came into contact with the Ethiopian movement and the A.M.E. With that kind of background and his special ability at languages - he speaks Herero, Nama, Afrikaans and English with equal facility - Katjerungu provided a suitable link between the N.E.T.A. and the A.M.E. Church in South Africa.

Originally founded in the United States of America as a result of race consciousness among the Negroes which manifested itself in a keen desire for self-government in religious matters, the A.M.E. Church extended its domain to South Africa during the latter years of the nineteenth century when it incorporated the then Ethiopian Church, a South African independent ("separatist") church.[71]

In the early 1930s, that is, previous to the secession of the Namas from the R.M.S., the A.M.E. had established a branch at Lüderitz,[72] but apparently not being able to gain roots in the country, withdrew. The first major appeal of the church, therefore, came in the wake of the post-War revival of African nationalism. Thereafter the church won a great following among the Namas, which included influential people such as Chief Samuel H. Witbooi, and his cousin the Rev. David Witbooi, the latter becoming a minister of the church. Some Damaras and Hereros also began to join the A.M.E. Church. The Herero tendency towards the A.M.E. Church which began in the early 1950s, included leading people such as Festus Kandjou, who was Chief Kutako's right-hand man; B. Karuera (later Rev.) who was to become Kutako's secretary. The A.M.E.'s influence was extended to the Hereros by a South African, the Rev. M.M. Sephula, who had come to South West Africa at the beginning of the 1950s. However, this trend did not last very long since it coincided with a Herero movement to establish a national church, *Oruuano.*

The main aim behind the establishment of Oruuano or Protestant Unity Church was, like that of the Nama secession which preceded it, to have a church without European control. The Herero secession movement was headed by Reinhard Ruzo, a man who has also been in the service of the R.M.S. like his Nama counterparts. Since the break was not based on schismatic differences, Oruuano retained the practices of the parent church in matters of worship.

One of the complaints levelled against the European controlled R.M.S. was that it had neglected education in South West Africa. Even after a century of religious work in the country, i.e. since it gained territorial rights in 1840 (from the London Missionary Society), most of the schools established by this R.M.S., could offer education only up to and including Standard III (about five years education). This and other grievances served to discredit the church. But the actual break seems to have been hastened by the appointment of Dr. H.H.

Vedder, the spiritual leader of the church, to the South African Senate by Dr. D.F. Malan in 1950. This incident, and Dr. Vedder's speeches in the Senate in support of *apartheid*, could not fail to have effects upon the church. According to reports, almost 2,000 people, in Windhoek and its surroundings alone, left the Rhenish mission to join Oruuano. Within a year of its existence, 630 people joined Oruuano in the Waterberg Reserve while many others supported it.[73]

Without prejudging the ethnologist Dr. O. Köhler's assertion that. "The Herero, never very tolerant in matters affecting tribal solidarity, are doubly aware of the implications of divided loyalty in spiritual things",[74] it may be submitted that there has not been any indication of religious intolerance on the part of the Africans. Instead, both the Herero and Nama secessions seem to be typical of the externalized forms of adjustment to which Professor Harold Lasswell refers when he says that, among subjected peoples, "... the precursors of nationalism may appear in the multiplication of native sects in competition with sects and denominations which are foreign controlled". As an example, Professor Lasswell actually quoted developments of this kind in South West Africa.[75]

The development of independent African churches was but the early manifestation of overt nationalism. The churches were by no means suited for the translation of nationalism into political actions. Even the A.M.E. which drew an elite into its leadership has had to pursue a cautious line in order to secure government recognition as a religious body. The church did, however, raise some political issues with the government in its early days. Of particular interest is the 13-point petition which was submitted by David Witbooi to a government representative on 3 September 1948. Among other things, the A.M.E. demanded franchise; the right to purchase land; better wages; and representation in the legislative assembly and the parliament.[76] This programme was too radical for the South West African administration to consider; it appears to have been the last of its kind.

On the whole, the A.M.E. concentrated on consolidating its position as a church and on establishing schools. As in South Africa it became the best organized African church in South West Africa, and consequently managed to draw a following from different ethnic groups.

Having thus been restricted to purely religious matters, what then would be considered to have been the contributions of the independent churches to African nationalism? One of the observations made by Professor Katesa Schlosser, who made a study of the Nama secession, is that the movement boosted the morale of the people.[77] The rise of the morale may be attributed not only to socio-economic advantages such as the high offices acquired by the leaders which were coupled with better salaries, the right to officiate over marriages and the exemption from pass laws; and the facilities for the secondary education of the members provided by the Wilberforce Institute in South Africa; but also the realization of the ideal of autonomy. The latter achievement which figured prominently in the demands made by both Namas and Hereros before secession is particularly relevant to the development of nationalism. The R.M.S. was not only white but also remote. The N.E.T.A. manifesto of January 1946 explicitly demanded the devolution of power to the congregations and their council. Thus, nationalism in this sense was related to the desire for self-government and independence.

The second relationship between nationalism and the religious independence movement is a historical one. Different studies relate the Nama secession to the past attempts of the Oorlam clans to free themselves from white rule, as exemplified by their migration from the Cape and their wars of resistance against the Germans (and also to the nineteenth century expulsion of the R.M.S. by Jonker Afrikaner from Windhoek and by Hendrik Witbooi from Gibeon).[78] It is assumed that this tradition has been handed down through the continuity of leading families such as the Witboois and the Jods, who formed the nucleus of the movement against the R.M.S. in 1946. Marcus Witbooi, who was one of the principal figures in the movement, is a grandson of a well known warrior Chief Hendrik Witbooi; Petrus Jod's father (also Petrus), who was a magistrate at Gibeon during Handrik Witbooi's rule fought in the rising of 1904 to 1907, a fact for which Petrus Jod (junior) was refused entry to a training institute in 1909. He had to work his way up to the position of an evangelist over a number of years.[79]

The theory of historical origins of African nationalism and the exodus movement from the R.M.S. is not confined to the continuity of family and group traditions but extends to the realm of past ideological movements. Thus the ideas preached by the Universal Negro Improvement Association in the 1920s are thought to have had some bearing on the later Herero secession from the R.M.S. It is recalled that in 1922 and 1924 R.M.S. missionaries reported that blacks from America (later also from the Cape) not only got people to swear allegiance to the "Monrovia flag" and to wear pins with black-red-green colours, but incited them against the government and the mission and contemplated the establishment of an independent church under the leadership of the Africans.[80] The South West African religious independence movement may therefore be considered as an heir to both the tradition of resistance and Garveyism. By taking the practical step of linking itself with the A.M.E. Church the movement proved that it was not purely expressive but instrumental as well. While at home it played a significant integrative function, it also paved the way for inter-territorial contacts.

Conclusions; and Aftermath

Reflecting on the Herero Revival Movement and Nama Separatism with a view to gauging the influence of religion on the development of early nationalist sentiment, we notice in them how an appropriation of symbols of power is a common feature. In both cases, however, the symbols derived from the 'old victors', not from the outsiders who had more recently acquired the greatest control over South West Africa's destiny. On the other hand, it was the Germans who had destroyed the territorial integrity of both of these important tribal groupings and had seriously undermined their traditional identity. For the Herero *truppenspieler* groups to parade as they did in old German military uniforms, they had in view 'total' reclamation of what had been lost, the Hereros' 'revivalism' being millenarist in the sense that they expected a future reinvestment of (physical and spiritual) Power to be a people. They were marching, heads held high, and in the stead of their formerly all-powerful overlords, toward the goal of a complete social reinstatement.

This expectation of a reinvestment with power combined religious aspirations with the symbols of European (and therefore superior) warriorhood because the religious and the political were traditionally interdependent. The hopes may have been unrealistic, but they fired the flames of proto-nationalism, and substituted enough for the declining German anti-South African political pressure that annexation from the south was forestalled. What happened, however, was that the Second World War spelt the virtual liquidation of the German section in South West Africa as an independent political group. After South Africa organized a "dubious" referendum (Dec. 1945 - April 1946), with African opinions being gauged through chiefs and headmen, [81] annexation from the south did in fact look imminent. But the deputation of the Smuts government to the United Nations met with disquiet from other nations, particularly India and Denmark. There was just time enough for Chief Kutako, the greatest of the indigenous post-War activists, as well as Chief Frederick Manarero, a refugee in Bechuanaland since the 1904 uprising, to organize petitions to be signed by other Herero and tribal chiefs. Conducted to the United Nations by the missionary Rev. Michael Scott, the petition prevented annexation and produced the solution of South African trusteeship.[82]

The millenarist hopes of Herero revivalism, then, had prevented the repetition of colonialism (at least in the more blatant sense), but were far from actualized in the post-War decades. With the Germans neutralized, the South Africans in South West Africa relapsed into the traditional Afrikaans-English rivalry well known in the south, yet with the two political parties representing each group knowing full well that the competition was really between black and white rather than between themselves. The major concerns of the whites were to secure their own representation in the South African Parliament (by 1950), with the supporters of the National Party also working for an independent and Afrikaner Republic of South Africa (achieved in 1961).[83]

Returning to the Nama and Herero exodus from the Rhenish Mission, one finds the comparable appropriation of power symbolism, but the achievements are to be assessed differently. In Herero revivalism there was a syncretic blend of traditional, Christian and Western military images of power, while with the secession movement from the R.M.S. the activities were much more distinctly Christian. Both movements illustrate the fundamental importance of religion in identity-building and adjustment through socio-political change, and the church secessionism above all reveals the continuing attractiveness of the Christian message. Quite apart from the serious setback to RMS work, the Society's influence was crucial, because the separatism still involved the acceptance of 'the church' as the institution through which Africans could find meaning in a post-tribal situation and a voice for their future.[84]

There is more to be said about post-War missionary activity and the further development of nationalist fronts (especially the Chief-originated South West

African National Union, from 1959, and the more radical, popularly-based South West African People's Organization, from 1969). It was only after the Second World War that the frustrated hopes of the Africans, tending beforehand to be either utopian or accommodationist, were allowed to be vented with much less inhibition. But the struggle for the liberation of South West Africa from South African domination persists, even though independence now approaches.[85]

In this study, to conclude, there is much to ponder as far as international or trans-Oceanic connections are concerned. When the first 21 German soldiers arrived in 1889 to initiate what became the invasion of South West Africa, the German Imperial Navy was virtually non-existent, and they therefore had to sail on an English ship hiding their true intentions.[86] Much later, by 1946, it was a missionary who was chosen by chiefs to represent the indigenous South West African case against annexation to the United Nations in Geneva, a datum reflecting the long-term impact of the German Mission as much as anything else, and thus a discrimination in African attitudes between the worst and best borne by the Europeans. Across the Atlantic in the early 1920s, moreover, had come the message of Garveyism, which allowed 'Africanism' to express in South West Africa both in a millenarist-looking outburst of cultural reinstatement and in separatist Christianity. These expressions of independence, however, came with military symbols and ecclesial institutions which had originated far away. South West Africans themselves only came to cross the seas in substantial numbers during the last great War, returning with a knowledge of more sophisticated African communities, with the new ideas evoked in defeat of Nazism (and thus of use against the rightest *apartheid* order to which they returned), and with a greater awareness of the greater powers to which they might appeal for help - "the Americans, the British, the Russians, the Chinese and the French".[87] Thus far, unfortunately, the hopes that their affairs might be settled by the greater political powers on behalf of the indigenous Africans seem as utopian and millenarist as the dreams of the old *Trüppenspieler* themselves.

Notes

1. For the above, see Z. Ngavirue, 'Political Parties and Interest Groups in South West Africa' (Doctoral dissert., University of Oxford), Oxford, 1971, esp. pp. 56-8, 79-80, 112.
2. Cf. esp. H. Drechsler, *Südwestafrika unter deutscher Koloniealherrschaft,* Berlin, 1966, pp. 55-128; C. von François, *Deutsch-Südwest-Afrika,* Berlin, 1899, esp. pp. 27-59, O. Hintrager, *Südwestafrika in der deutschen Zeit,* Munich, 1955; H. Bley, *Kolonialherrschaft und Sozialstruktur in Deutsch-Südwestafrika, 1894-1914,* Hamburg, 1968, cf. Ngavirue, *op.cit.,* ch.4.
3. One of the comments by the German General Staff (eds.), in *Die Kämpfe der Truppen in Südwestafrika,* Berlin, 1906-7, vo.1, p.3.
4. Quoted in Dreschler, *op.cit.,* p.175.
5. Esp. *ibid.,* pp. 166-7 (decrees); H. Bley, *op.cit.,* pp. 187-8 (alliances, treason); J.K. Krumbach, *Franz Ritter von Epp: ein Leben für Deutschland,* Munich, 1939, p.198 (interceptions).
6. Dreschler, *op.cit.,* pp. 177-84; cf. also G. Frenssen, *Peter Moor's Journey to South West Africa,* London, 1908.
7. See esp. J. Iliffe, "The Herero and Nama Risings: South-West Africa 1904-7", in G. Kibodya (ed.), 'Aspects of South African History' (mimeograph), Dar es Salaam, 1968, pp. 95-111; cf. J.K. Wellington, *South West Africa and its Human Issues,* Oxford, 1967, pp. 208-12; Bley, *op.cit.,* pp. 191-2; etc.
8. On the interpretation of Buxton's promise, Lord Hailey, 'A Survey of Native Affairs in South West Africa' (unpublished typescript, Rhodes House, Oxford), n.p., n.d., p.45; M.J. Olivier, 'Inboorlingbeleid en Administrasie in die Mandaatgebied van Suidwes-Afrika' (Doctoral Dissert., University of Stellenbosch), Stellenbosch, 1961, p.141. For the rest of the above, cf. Ngavirue, *op.cit.,* pp. 216-9, 248.
9. For Hailey's quotation above, Hailey, *op.cit.,* p.45; for the official *apartheid* terminology quoted, Olivier, *op.cit.,* pp. 100-3.
10. See Ngavirue, *op.cit.,* pp. 250-4 for details.
11. H.H.Vedder (with H.L. Kahn and L.Fowce), *The Native Tribes of South West Africa,* London, 1928 (66), pp. 162-3 (hereafter Vedder).
12. See the South West African Administrators' reports for 1924 and1925 (Union

of South Africa Parliamentary Papers: *U.G.* 33, 1925, pp. 25, 27; *U.G.* 26, 1926, p.30).

13. *Ibid.,* 26, 1926, p.30.
14. Vedder, *op.cit.,* p.163.
15. E.g., Kangari Berthold Himumuine (b. 1921), John Garvey Muundjua (1928), Mukaangavi, etc.
16. In Windoek *Advertiser,* 26 July, 1924 (a letter from Headley reproduced from the *Allgemeine Zeitung,* 3 July, 1924).
17. *U.G.* 26, 1926, p.30.
18. Vedder, *op.cit.,* p.163.
19. Petition dated 6 Nov. 1924, Windhoek (reproduced in the *Advertiser,* 8 Nov., 1924).
20. In 1962 he was one of the six members of the advisory board of Katutura Township, Windhoek, who presented the United Nations (Carpio) Commission with a declaration of their loyalty to the South African government, cf. *U.N. Department of Trusteeship and Non-Self-Governing Territories,* s.v. letter 23 Feb., 1966, s.v. Miscellany II.
21. *Advertiser,* 15 Nov., 1924.
22. *U.G.* 21, 1924, p.15.
23. *Advertiser,* 15 Nov., 1924.
24. Thus H. Laswell, *Politics: Who Gets What, When, How,* New York, 1958, pp. 156-7.
25. *Advertiser,* 29 Aug. 1923. For official reports of the occasion, *U.G.* 21, 1924, p.15, cf. Vedder's report in *Berichte,* 1923, pp. 117-122.
26. *Advertiser,* 29 Aug., 1923.
27. O. Levinson, *The Ageless Land,* Cape Town, 1961, p.55.
28. See Plate 10.
29. In the *Journal of the South West African Scientific Society,* 2 (1926-7), p.59.
30. See, e.g., the clothes worn by Jan Booi and three other Oorlams in a portrait in *Berichte,* 5 (1857), p.65, in contrast to those worn by Makarero and Riarua in a photograph of 1876, in N. Mossolow, *Otjikango oder Gross Barmen,* Windhoek, 1968, p.82.
31. H. Bley, *op.cit.,* pp. 82-3.
32. *Ibid.,* p.82.

33. H. Vedder, *op.cit.*, p.163.
34. On the joint German and Herero troop parades before the uprisings (of 1904-8), see Bley, *op.cit.*, p.88.
35. For the medal of the latter, bearing this motto on one side and an eagle on the obverse, see Reich. Kolon. Archiv. (Potsdam), 1739, vol.1, p.124.
36. Report to the League of Nations, *U.G.*, 30, 1940, p.132, para. 747.
37. *Ibid.*, p.132, para. 745.
38. For a list of the various characteristics of such movements, cf., e.g. T. Hodgkin, "Mahdism, Messianism and Marxism in the African Setting" (unpublished paper read at a Seminar in Khartoum), n.p., 1968, p.2.
39. *U.G.*, 30, 1940, p.132, para. 748; p.133, para. 749.
40. *Ibid.*, p.132, para. 748.
41. His *oruzo* being Ombandi, his own dynasty that of Mungunda. For the Herero dynasties, see Ngavirue, *op.cit.*, p.8., and for Kutako's lineage, O. Köhler, *A Study of Gobabis District*, Pretoria, 1959, p.74.
42. Report to the League of Nations, *U.G.*, 16, 1933, pp. 32-3.
43. I.e., the inter-Reserve conference for each ethnic group - the first of this kind being held in 1947, one for the Damaras and the other for the Hereros. The Namas had their first conference as late as 1953, and the Orambos even later. Cf. Olivier, *op.cit.*, pp. 192-3. The Government has so far refused to hold inter-tribal conferences.
44. Reports to the League of Nations for 1933 (*U.G.*, 27, 1934, p.37) and 1934 (*Ibid.*, 26, 1935, p.47) respectively.
45. Köhler, *op.cit.*, p.73.
46. Olivier, *op.cit.*, p.192.
47. Esp. Report of the Administrator, *U.G.*, 21, 1923, p.11.
48. Cf. the Society's *Arberättelse*, for 1927, p.9; 1931, p.5, cf. for 1928 and 1932. According to the 1931 report, the Ngandjera chief was likewise not cooperating with the missionaries.
49. Report to the League of Nations for 1932 (*U.G.*, 16, 1933, pp. 52-7).
50. *Ibid.*, 27, 1934, p.43.
51. *Ibid.*, 26, 1935, p.52.
52. Report of the Odendaal Commission (1962-3) (R.P. No.12, 1964), p.213.
53. See plates 10 and 12.

54. Thus Lasswell again, *op.cit.*, p.159.
55. *U.G.* 30, 1940, pp. 26, 132.
56. Dr Hirsekorn's report dated 27 Jan. 1939, Reich. Kolon. Archiv. Potsdam, No. 1236, pp. 47-8.
57. *U.G.* 30, 1940, pp. 130-1.
58. Cf. M. Scott, *A Time to Speak*, London, 1958, p.225, cf. also p.223.
59. See plate no. 13.
60. See plate no. 12.
61. We owe particularly to T.O. Ranger this insight into the development of African nationalism; cf. esp. his "Connections between 'Primary Resistance' Movements and Modern Mass Nationalism in East and Central Africa", in *Journal of African History*, 9/3-4 (1968), pp. 437-53, 631-41.
62. For this theory of 'cumulative effect', esp. S.M. Lipset, *Political Man*, London, 1963, p.195.
63. K. Schlosser, *Eingeborenenkirchen in Süd und Südwestafrika*, Kiel, 1958, pp. 78, 112.
64. *Ibid.*, pp. 71, 100.
65. *Ibid.*, p.86.
66. *Ibid.*, pp. 97-8.
67. *Ibid.*, pp. 88-9; J. Baumann, *Mission Okumene in Südwestafrika*, Leiden and Cologne, 1965, pp. 59-60.
68. *Ibid.*, p.60; Schlosser, *op.cit.*, p.98.
69. *Ibid.*, p.80.
70. *Ibid.*, p.74.
71. Cf. B. Sundkler, *Bantu Prophets of South Africa*, London, 1961 edn., pp. 40-3.
72. Schlosser, *op.cit.*, p.112.
73. Köhler, *The Otjiwarongo District*, Pretoria, n.d., p.53, cf. *Advertiser*, 3 Oct., 1960.
74. Köhler, *Otjiwarongo*, *op.cit.*, p.68.
75. *Op.cit.*, p.159. His figure of 300, however, is too large for South West Africa; it obviously includes parts of South Africa.
76. Schlosser, *op.cit.*, p.118.
77. *Ibid.*, p.121. Schlosser has made an elaborate investigation of the Nama

secession movement, yet without assessing the personal qualities of the missionaries with whom the Nama bargained.

78. *Ibid.*, pp. 86-7; H. Loth, *Die christliche Mission in Südwestafrika. Zur destruktiven Rolle der Rheinischen Missionsgesellschaft beim Prozess der Staatsbildung in Südwestafrika, 1842-1893 (Studien zur Kolonialgeschichte und Geschichte der nationalen und kolonialen Befreiungsbewegung 9)*, Berlin, 1963, pp. 107-110, 126.

79. Schlosser, *op.cit.*, pp. 76, 82.

80. J. Baumann, *Mission und Ökumene in Südwestafrika. Dargestellt am Lebenswerk von Hermann Heinrich Vedder*, Leiden, 1965, p.124. He referred to three reports: two from the missionary F. Meier, one published in *Berichte*, for 1922, p. 189; another one of 2 Nov. 1922; and the third from another missionary, Pönninghaus, published in *Berichte*, for 1924, p.136.

81. See American Committee on Africa, *South West Africa: United Nations Stepchild*, New York, 1960, p.9.

82. Scott, *op.cit.*, esp. pp. 222-4.

83. Ngavirue, *op.cit*., esp. 240-1.

84. For comparison and background, R. Oliver, *The Missionary Factor in East Africa*, London, 1952.

85. Ngavirue, *op.cit.*, esp. pp. 290, 292, 301f., 305ff.

86. von François, *op.cit.*, pp. 30-33.

87. The nations named by Chief Kutako as those to be consulted before acceptance of South Africa's annexation; quoted in Scott, *op.cit.*, p.222.

Select Bibliography

Adas, Michael
1987   *Prophets of Rebellion: millenarian protest movements against the European colonial order (Studies in Comparative World History)*. Cambridge: Cambridge University Press.

Barkun, Michael
1974   *Disaster and the Millennium..* New Haven and London: Yale University Press.

Burridge, Kenelm
1969   *New Heaven New Earth: a study of millenarian activities.* Oxford: Basil Blackwell.

Christiansen, Palle
1969   *The Melanesian Cargo Cult : Millenarianism as a factor in cultural change.* Copenhagen: Akademisk Forlag.

Desroche, Henri
1969   *Dictionnaire des Messianismes et Millénarismes.* Paris: Presse Universitaire.

Desroche, Henri
1979   *The Sociology of Hope.* Trans. C. Martin-Sperry, London: Routledge and Kegan Paul

Festinger, Leon
1956   *When Prophecy Fails.* Minneapolis: Minnesota University Press.

Gesch, Patrick F.
1985   *Initiative and Initiation (Studia Instituti Anthropos 33).* St. Augustin: Anthropos Institute

Halsell, Grace
1986   *Prophecy and Politics: militant evangelists on the road to nuclear war.* Westport: Lawrence Hill.

Hobsbawm, Erich J.
1971   *Primitive Rebels.* Manchester: Manchester University Press.

Kilani, Mondher
1983   *Les Cultes du cargo mélanesiens: mythe et rationalité en anthropologie.* Lausanne: Den Bas.

Lanternari, Vittorio
1963   *The Religions of the Oppressed : a study of modern messianic cults.* Trans. L. Sergio, New York: The New American Library.

Lawrence, Peter
1964   *Road Belong Cargo: a study of the cargo movement in the southern Madang District, New Guinea.* Manchester: Manchester University Press.

Lewy, Guenter
1974   *Religion and Revolution.* New York : Oxford University Press.

May, Ronald L. (Ed.)
1982   *Micronationalist Movements in Papua New Guinea (Political and Social Change Monographs 1).* Canberra; Australian National University

Mühlmann, Wilhelm (Ed.)
1961   *Chiliasmus und Nativismus: Studien zur Psychologie, Soziologie und historischen Kasuistik der Umsturbewegungen (Studien zur Soziologie der Revolution I).* Berlin: Reimer.

Olson, Theodore
1982   *Millennialism, Utopianism and Progress*. Toronto and
            London: Toronto University Press.

Rotberg, Robert. I and Ali A. Mazrui (ed)
1970   *Protest and Power in Black Africa*. New York: Oxford University
            Press.

Sierksma, Fokke
1960   *Een nieuwe hemel en een niewe aarde*. London: Routledge and
            Kegan Paul.

Steinbauer, Friedrich
1979   *Melanesian Cargo Cults*. Trans. M. Wohwill, Brisbane:
            University of Queensland Press.

Strelan, John G.
1977   *Search for Salvation: studies in the history and theology of cargo
            cults*. Adelaide : Lutheran Publishing House.

Thrupp, Sylvia L. (Ed.)
1970   *Millennial Dreams in Action: studies in revolutionary religious
            movements*. New York: Schocken Books.

Trompf, Garry W. (Editor).
1977   *Prophets of Melanesia : six essays*. Suva: Institute of Papua New
            Guinea Studies and Institute of South Pacific Studies.

Tuveson, Ernest L.
1974   *Redeemer Nation: The Idea of America's Millennial Role*.
            Chicago: the University of Chicago Press.

Wallis, Wilson D.
1918   *Messiahs. Christian and Pagan.* Boston : Badger.

Wilson, Bryan
1973   *Magic and the Millennium: a sociological study of religious movements of protest among tribal and Third-World peoples.* New York : Harper and Row.

Worsley, Peter
1970   *The Trumpet Shall Sound: a study of Cargo Cults in Melanesia.* London : Paladin.

Notes on Contributors

Harold Turner
helped pioneer the study of new religious movements in tribal cultures, and in 1981 founded the world Centre in this field at the Selly Oak Colleges, Birmingham. He has taught at the universities of Sierra Leone, Nigeria and Leicester (where he began the Department of Religion) and at Emory and Aberdeen. His best known works are *African Independent Church* (2 vols.), *From Temple to Meeting House*, and a series of bibliographic volumes on new religious movemernts in primal societies. He remains a Presbyterian minister, but is now in retirement.

Garry Trompf
is currently Associate Professor and Head of the Department of Religious Studies at the University of Sydney, Australia. He was formerly the Professor of History at the University of Papua New Guinea, and has taught at the universities of Melbourne, Oxford, Western Australia, California (at Santa Cruz), at Monash University and the State University of Utrecht. His works include *The Idea of Historical Recurrence in Western Thought* and *Melanesian Religion.*

John Bracht
is a Presbyterian minister in Sydney Australia. A Scotsman, he was converted to Mormonism in his nineteenth year, but left the Mormon Church while studying at Brigham Young University, Hawaii. He successfully completed his Masters degree in Religious Studies at the University of Sydney in 1988, and is now pursuing doctoral studies. He has lectured on Mormonism and new religious movements hundreds of times in Australia.

Gregory Tillett
is currently Lecturer in the School of History, Philosophy and Politics at Macquarie University of Sydney. He completed his doctorate in Religious Studies at the University of Sydney, and is the author of several works on unorthodox religious movements, including *The Elder Brother: a biography of*

C.W. Leadbeater. Between 1985 until 1988 he worked for the New South Wales Anti-Discrimination Board.

Roderic Lacey
is an Australian with his doctoral degree from the University of Wisconbsin. He is currently lecturing at the Institute of Catholic Education at Ballarat, Victoria, and was formerly Senior Lecturer in History at the University of Papua New Guinea. He has co-edited *Documents and Readings in New Guinea History* and *Oral Traditions in Melanesia*, and is well known for his oral historical investigations among the Enga people in the New Guinea highlands between 1971 and 1981.

Patrick Gesch
is an Australian who pursued studies for the Catholic priesthood in Chicago. As a missionary for the Society of the Divine Word, he worked among the Yangoru-Negrie peoples in the Sepik region of New Guinea from 1973 until 1983, but took in some seminary teaching and higher study. Successfully completing doctoral studies at the Department of Religious Studies, University of Sydney, his thesis was published in Germany as *Initiative and Initiation*, the most exhaustive study of a single Melanesian cargo cult ever undertaken. Until recently he has been a co-editor of the journal *Anthropos*, but left Germany for Papua New Guinea again in 1989.

Lamont Lindstrom
is Associate Professor of Anthropology at the University of Tulsa in the United States. After receiving his doctorate from the University of California, Berkeley, he drew on several years fieldwork in Vanuatu to complete various publications on Melanesian linguistics, Pacific War ethnohistory and the politics of knowledge. He edited *Drugs in Western Pacific Societies* and *The Pacific Theater*.

Graham Brookes
is the Secretary for World Mission, Uniting Church in Australia, and is an ordained minister in that church. Between 1974 and 1977 he served as the Secretary of the Commission on Evangelism and Christian Education for the

Protestant Evangelical Church of Timor *(Gereja Masehi Injili di Timor)*,and upon returning to a parish in Australia completed a Masters of Theology thesis on Timorese religious movements with the Melbourne College of Divinity (by 1981).

Karlene Faith
is a Canadian who is Distance Education Coordinator for the School of Criminology at Simon Fraser University, Vancouver. Educated at the Université de Poitiers (France), the Centre for the Study of Intercultural Documentation (Mexico), she took her doctorate at the University of California, Santa Cruz. During pre-doctoral days at the University of California, she undertook important fieldwork in rural Jamaica.

Dennis Walker
received his undergraduate and Masters degrees in Arabic at the University of Melbourne, and is currently engaged in doctoral studies at the same university on comparative nationalism in Muslim societies. While completing this article he was a Lecturer in Middle Eastern Studies (at the University of Melbourne again).

Zedekiah Ngavirue
was originally a social worker in Namibia, who became Chairman of the external wing of SWANU, a well-known indigenous political organization preparing for independence. Taking up studies overseas, he graduated first from Uppsala University, and then with a doctorate from the University of Oxford. He became Senior Lecturer in History while working at the University of Papua New Guinea, but returned to Namibia in 1978 to become SWANU's Vice-President. More recently he became a Director of Rössing Uranium Ltd. (in 1983), and two years later was appointed Chairman.

Index

The Quest for Purity

Dynamics of Puritan Movements

Edited by *W. E. A. van Beek*

1988. 14.8 x 22.8 cm. VIII, 274 pages. With 5 illustrations. Cloth   ISBN 3 11 011382 1

(Religion and Society 26)

This monograph compares 11 societies in which an ideology stressing individual and collective purity is dominant. The implications of such an ideological (theological or political) quest for purity in the realm of social and political organization are explored in individual case studies and integrated in a general model of puritanic movements. In this model, the processes that shape the course and eventual failure of a puritan movement are outlined.

mouton de gruyter

Berlin · New York · Amsterdam

van den Bercken, William

Ideology and Atheism in the Soviet Union

1989. 15.5 x 23 cm. VIII, 191 pages. Cloth.
ISBN 3 11 011406 2

(Religion and Society 28)

This monograph is a study of the character of ideology in modern Soviet society and of the place of atheism in it. It shows that Soviet society is an ideological mono-culture with the state as the highest ideological value system. Atheism is a consequence of the etatistic character of Soviet ideology, because religion represents values which are ultimately incompatible with the state monopoly in the field of ethics and "Weltanschauung".

Soviet ideological atheism differs fundamentally from pragmatical atheism in Western society and from Western science of religion. Soviet atheism has created its own social rites and eductional structures, and is propagated as an integral part of modern world outlook.

The book ends with a survey of the latest developments in Soviet society in the field of religious policy and atheistic propaganda.

mouton de gruyter
Berlin · New York

DATE DUE

OCT 1 '90			

HIGHSMITH   # 45220